MICHELIN

Motoring Atlas France

Contents

PAUL HAMLYN

MICHELIN
touring services

MICHELIN maps and guides

MICHELIN, the world's leading manufacturer of radial tyres, is also a well known name in the field of tourist publications; its annual sales of maps and guides exceed 16m in over 70 countries.

Acting on the belief that motoring would have a great future, the Michelin brothers decided to offer the motorist a touring service, an innovative step at the turn of the century: free or inexpensive publications designed to provide information, assistance and encouragement.

At the wheel, touring, on holiday – these three aspects of travel were met by a simple response – a trio of complementary publications to be used together.

The first of these, the Red Guides, which are published annually, present a selection of hotels and restaurants, with a wide range of prices and facilities. It is, however, probably their award of the stars for good cooking that has established their international reputation; as well as the wealth of essential touring information included in them. There are several guides covering Europe, including the Red Guide to France which alone has sold over 20m copies to date. Readers have such faith in their reliability that the Red Guides are foremost among reference books in this field.

The role of the Michelin Green Guides is to provide tourists with an introduction to the regions of France and other foreign countries. The guides describe the sights, the countryside and picturesque routes; they also contain maps, plans and practical information as well as illustrations and photographs which whet one's appetite for travel. There are over 70 titles covering Europe and North America, which are published in French and other European languages and are revised regularly.

This Motoring Atlas of France is composed of the series of detailed maps originally published in 1910; they have benefited from the evolution of technical processes and have kept up to date with changes in the road network and the needs of the modern motorist. Over the years new symbols have been devised to facilitate the 'reading' of the map.

To improve their service to the customer, Michelin call upon the latest techniques in the compilation and production of their maps and guides. Because of their practical approach, their regular revision and their common concepts, these publications will continue to be an indispensable aid to travel.

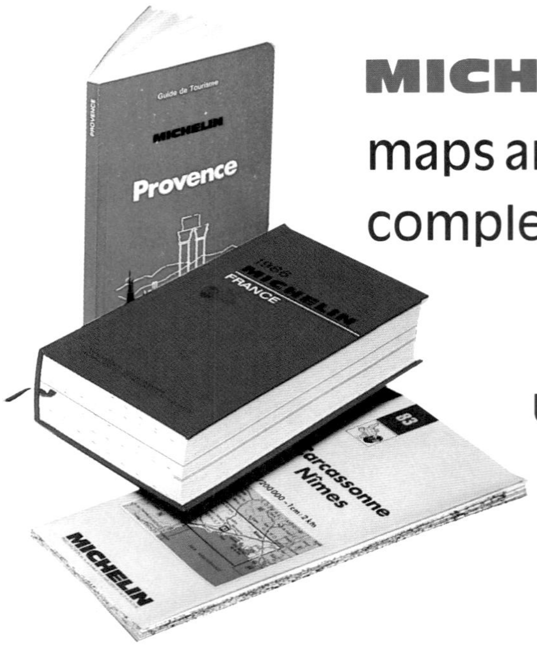

MICHELIN
maps and guides
complement one another:

use them together!

First published 1987 by
The Hamlyn Publishing Group Limited
Bridge House, 69 London Road
Twickenham, Middlesex TW1 3SB

Second impression 1987

ISBN 0 600 55053 2

Printed in Great Britain

Introduction

The first maps

André Michelin published his first guide book in 1900, to provide 'information which will be useful to a motorist travelling in France', and logically this led to the first Michelin road map, in 1907, and then to the first 1:200 000 series which covered the whole of France.

The first edition of this series, published between 1910 and 1913, was the forerunner of the modern series of Michelin sheet maps, still published at the scale decided by André Michelin early in the century. These maps in turn are the basis of this atlas, which, like the first Michelin maps and guides, is a thoroughly practical companion for travellers using the roads of France; it also looks beyond the roads to many of the topographical and man-made features of this varied country.

The roads of France

In European terms France is a large country, and it is still predominantly rural, characterized more by open country and villages or small towns than sprawling urban areas – outside Paris, only the conurbations of Lyon and Marseille have populations of more than a million. It is thus a country where the road network has traditionally been important, and it has become steadily more important through the last three decades.

There are more than 1.5 million kilometres (930 000 miles) of roads. The network includes over 6500 km (over 4000 miles) of motorways, some 800 000 km (almost 500 000 miles) of main roads, and around 700 000 km (around 435 000 miles) of minor roads. The main roads are either 'N' roads, which are regarded as part of the international or national routes network, or 'D' roads which are inter-regional; these are the red and yellow roads on the maps. Other roads are shown in white on the maps.

Many of the trunk roads, most logically those which do not duplicate motorway routes, have been uprated. Often superbly aligned, sometimes still lined with the poplar trees that were once traditional, these can make for enjoyable driving and overall journey speeds very near to the governing legal speed limit. From a driver's point of view the motorways are less interesting, but they do provide straightforward routes between main centres. Most are *autoroutes à péage*, or toll roads. The charge per kilometre varies from motorway to motorway and the toll payments on a long journey can be high. Different rates apply to coaches, goods and utility vehicles, cars towing caravans or trailers, motorcycles, and so on.

Overall, congestion is not a feature of motoring in France, though city rush hours are best avoided. The routes out of Paris or back into the capital can be very congested at weekends or holiday periods, while the almost perpetual congestion on the *périphérique* has become notorious. This ring road does, however, offer quick and easily understood routes from one side of the capital to another, or between suburban districts, and it links the motorways radiating out to the provinces. At peak holiday periods routes through Lyon can be very crowded but are difficult to avoid. Other traffic trouble spots are predictable – for example, parts of the south coast during the summer, or routes to winter sports resorts early in the year.

Using this atlas

The Michelin maps in this atlas provide the best possible guidance for drivers in France, from route pre-planning to on-the-spot selection to avoid a delay. Each spread of two pages in this atlas covers an area of approximately 79 by 114 kilometres (49 by 71 miles), displaying a sizeable area of country. Through routes are obvious and the painstaking work of the cartographers also ensures that the detail of road widths can be seen in advance. Diversions can be devised quickly, perhaps using the yellow or white minor roads.

The yellow roads are often used in signposted alternative routes, with signs frequently directing drivers to good 'D' roads; these can be particularly useful in avoiding built-up areas and often provide good, less congested long-distance routes. This system uses green signs which incorporate the word *Bis* since the routes are known as *Itinéraires Bis* in France.

Many of the 'D' roads are keys to intrinsic delights and the map symbols guide tourists to sites ranging from historic buildings to viewpoints. Many of the places picked out on the maps also merit entries in the renowned Michelin Green Guides, which cover regions of France with detailed descriptions of places of interest and suggestions for tours; the outline maps can be used in conjunction with this atlas. Picturesque roads are distinguished on the maps with green borders.

General rules

- Driving in France is straightforward, with regulations and road signs generally similar to those in most West European countries. The basic rule is drive on the right, overtake on the left.
- Visitors should carry a full driving licence, vehicle registration document and evidence of insurance cover.
- Hazard warning lights or a red warning triangle must be carried, and used in a case of breakdown or accident. A spare set of light bulbs should be carried on a vehicle. Cars and commercial vehicles should have an external mirror on the left-hand side.
- Seat belts must be worn by the driver and front-seat passenger; children under ten may not travel in a front seat unless the car is a two-seater. Motor cyclists and pillion passengers must wear crash helmets.
- Full or dipped headlights must be used in poor visibility and at night and motor cyclists must use dipped headlights at all times, except when full beam is called for. Side lights should be used only as parking lights. Yellow-tinted headlights are preferred but are not compulsory for tourist vehicles.
- Overtaking must not be attempted where a 'no overtaking' sign (a red vehicle and a black vehicle side by side) is displayed, where the manoeuvre would entail crossing an unbroken line on the road, or at the brow of a hill even if the road is not marked.
- Studded tyres may be used between November 15 and March 15, on light vehicles (up to 3500 kg), which are then subject to a 90 kmh/56 mph speed limit.
- Speeding or drink-driving offences are subject to on-the-spot fines, payable in cash, while a drink-driving offence may also result in the vehicle being immobilized on the spot.
- An accident causing injury must be reported to the police or gendarmerie. After an accident causing damage but not injury a Notice of Motoring Accident should be completed and signed by both parties.

Full information on motoring in France is available from French Government Tourist Offices or motoring organizations such as the Automobile Association or the Royal Automobile Club.

Speed limits

Urban areas: 60 kmh/37 mph

Single carriageway roads: 90 kmh/56 mph (**on wet roads:** 80 kmh/50 mph)

Dual carriageway roads: 110 kmh/68 mph (**on wet roads:** 100 kmh/62 mph)

Motorways: 130 kmh/80 mph (**on wet roads:** 110 kmh/68 mph)
A *minimum* speed limit of 80 kmh/50 mph applies to the overtaking lane of motorways in daylight and good weather.

These limits apply to motor cycles over 81cc; light motor cycles (51–80cc) are subject to a 75 kmh/47 mph limit.

Local variations are indicated on speed limit road signs. The *rappel* sign indicates a continuing restriction.

Priority

The system giving priority to traffic entering a road from the right now applies in built-up areas only, and then not in every case; main roads outside built-up areas have priority. Visual confirmation of a 'priority' road is displayed in yellow and black signs; the same sign with a diagonal cancel stripe clearly indicates the end of a 'priority' stretch. Stop signs must be observed as such, with drivers bringing their vehicles to a standstill. In roundabouts with the approach sign illustrated drivers must give way to vehicles already on the roundabout.

More broadly, topography can be read off the maps, with hill shading, for example, fleshing out the bare bones of a named mountain pass or throwing into relief the sweep of one of the superb French river valleys which have provided routes for travellers since prehistoric times.

The maps are also related very directly to the Michelin Red Guide; places, not simply towns but villages and isolated hamlets, that merit entries in the Guide are underlined in red on the maps, while red frames pick out the towns with street plans included in the Guide.

This atlas has been planned as an end in itself, and as part of the Michelin tourist library, where it complements the series of well-established maps and guides. It does not take the place of the yellow sheet maps, which slip conveniently into a pocket or handbag with the local Green Guide, but, in combination, this atlas, the guides and the sheet maps are invaluable to travellers in France.

Route planning

Scale 1:2 600 000 1cm:26km approx 41 miles:1 inch

Motorway or equivalent	The blue rectangles outline the coverage of each page in the 1:200 000 maps sequence which starts on page 2. The blue numbers are map pages.
Major road	
Secondary through route	
N 4 Motorway or road number	
17 Intermediate distances in kilometres	
Regional prefecture	
Prefecture	
Other principal town	

Road signs

The background colours of direction signs are appropriate to categories of roads:

blue - motorways
green - main roads
white - local roads

The *Itinéraire Bis* road signs are used to indicate less congested alternative routes.

Yellow signs with black lettering are used for temporary routes, especially diversions (*déviations*).

Traffic information

Centre de Renseignements Autoroutes (9-12h, 14-18h)
Monday-Friday (1) 47 05 90 01
CNIR (0-24h) (1) 48 94 33 33 Minitel 36 15 (Code Route)

Centres Régionaux d'Information et de Coordination Routière

Bordeaux	56 96 33 33	Metz	87 63 33 33
Créteil	(1) 48 99 33 33	Rennes	99 32 33 33
Lille	20 47 33 33	Rosny-s/Bois	(1) 48 99 33 33
Lyon	78 54 33 33		
Marseille	91 78 78 78		

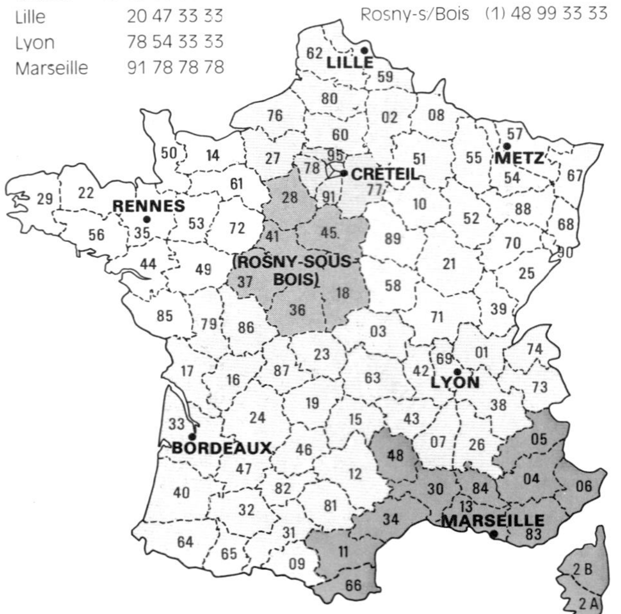

21 Number of *département*

Départements

01	Ain	32	Gers	64	Pyrénées-Atlantiques
02	Aisne	33	Gironde	65	Hautes-Pyrénées
03	Allier	34	Hérault	66	Pyrénées-Orientales
04	Alpes-de-Haute-Provence	35	Ille-et-Vilaine	67	Bas-Rhin
05	Hautes Alpes	36	Indre	68	Haut-Rhin
06	Alpes Maritimes	37	Indre-et-Loire	69	Rhône
07	Ardèche	38	Isère	70	Haute-Saône
08	Ardennes	39	Jura	71	Saône-et-Loire
09	Ariège	40	Landes	72	Sarthe
10	Aube	41	Loir-et-Cher	73	Savoie
11	Aude	42	Loire	74	Haute-Savoie
12	Aveyron	43	Haute-Loire	75	Paris
13	Bouches-du-Rhône	44	Loire-Atlantique	76	Seine-Maritime
14	Calvados	45	Loiret	77	Seine-et-Marne
15	Cantal	46	Lot	78	Yvelines
16	Charente	47	Lot-et-Garonne	79	Deux-Sèvres
17	Charente-Maritime	48	Lozère	80	Somme
18	Cher	49	Maine-et-Loire	81	Tarn
19	Corrèze	50	Manche	82	Tarn-et-Garonne
2A	Corse-du-Sud	51	Marne	83	Var
2B	Haute-Corse	52	Haute-Marne	84	Vaucluse
21	Côte-d'Or	53	Mayenne	85	Vendée
22	Côtes-du-Nord	54	Meurthe-et-Moselle	86	Vienne
23	Creuse	55	Meuse	87	Haute-Vienne
24	Dordogne	56	Morbihan	88	Vosges
25	Doubs	57	Moselle	89	Yonne
26	Drôme	58	Nièvre	90	Territoire-de-Belfort
27	Eure	59	Nord	91	Essonne
28	Eure-et-Loir	60	Oise	92	Hauts-de-Seine
29	Finistère	61	Orne	93	Seine-St-Denis
30	Gard	62	Pas-de-Calais	94	Val-de-Marne
31	Haute-Garonne	63	Puy-de-Dôme	95	Val-d'Oise

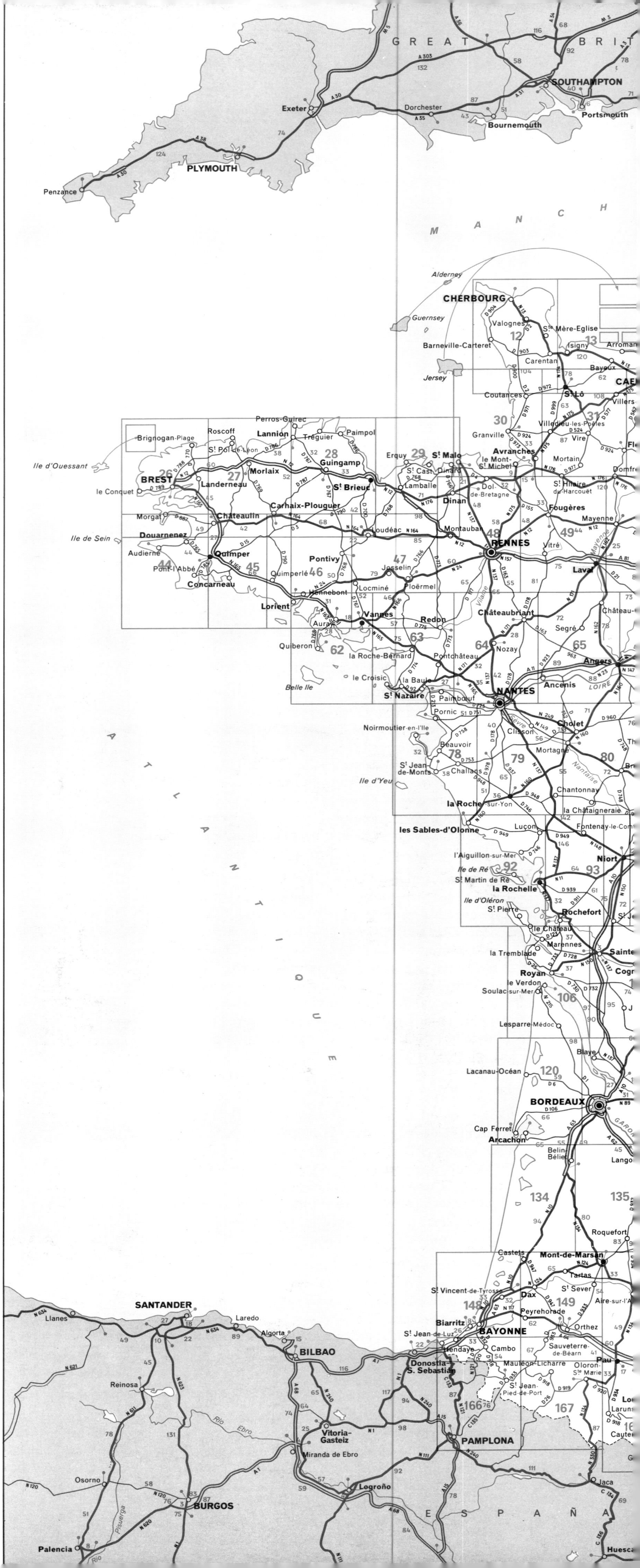

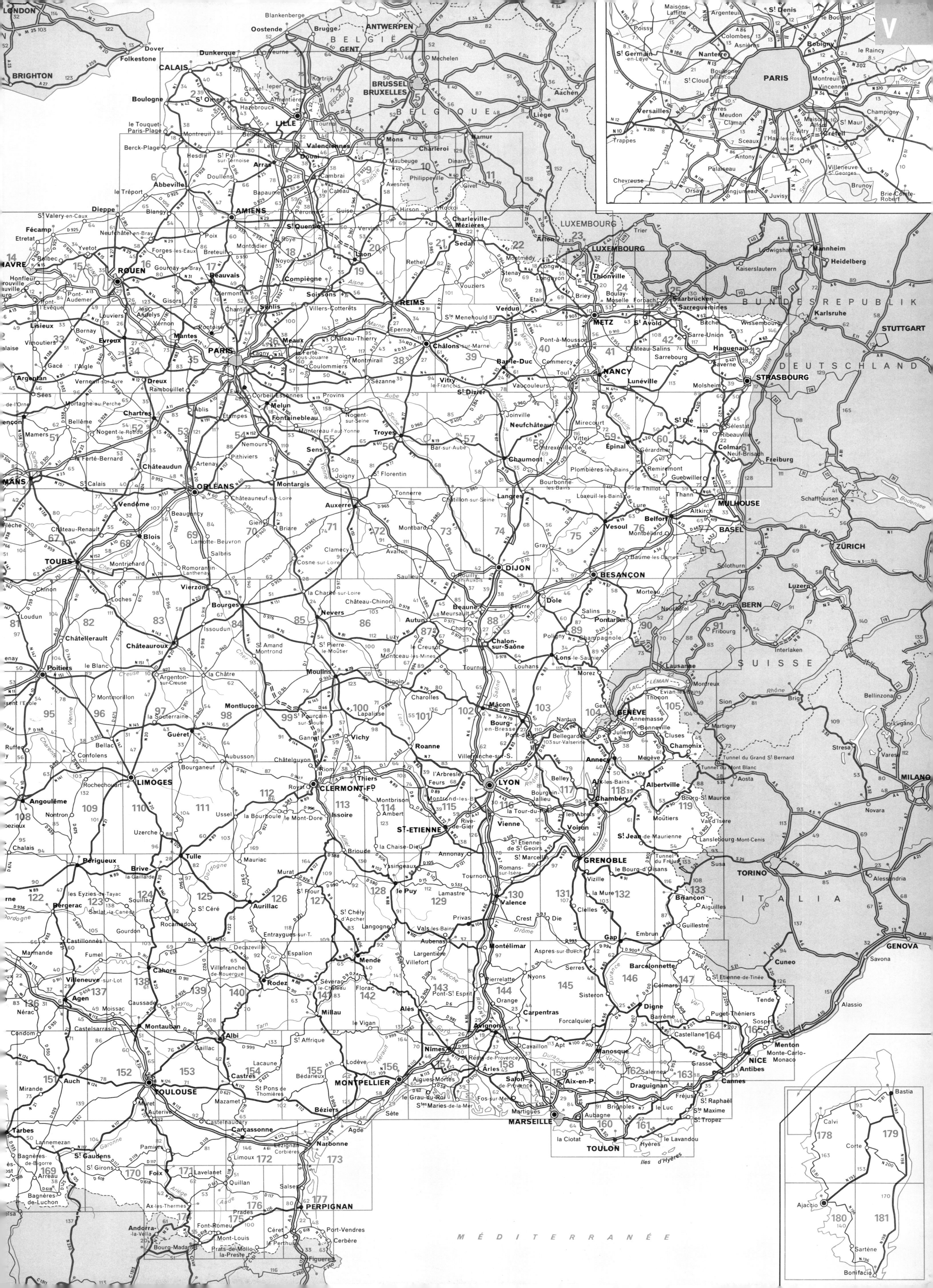
V
LONDON
BRIGHTON
Dover
Folkestone
Oostende
Brugge
ANTWERPEN
BELGIË
GENT
BRUSSEL
BRUXELLES
BELGIQUE
Liège
Aachen
Namur
Charleroi
Mons
Dunkerque
CALAIS
Boulogne
St Omer
LILLE
Valenciennes
Douai
Arras
Cambrai
Abbeville
AMIENS
Dieppe
St Quentin
Laon
Charleville-Mézières
Sedan
LUXEMBOURG
Trier
Mannheim
Heidelberg
Kaiserslautern
Saarbrücken
BUNDESREPUBLIK
DEUTSCHLAND
Karlsruhe
STUTTGART
Le Havre
ROUEN
Beauvais
Compiègne
Soissons
REIMS
Verdun
METZ
Thionville
Evreux
Mantes
PARIS
Meaux
Châlons-sur-Marne
Bar-le-Duc
NANCY
Lunéville
Sarrebourg
Haguenau
STRASBOURG
Chartres
Dreux
Melun
Fontainebleau
Troyes
St Dizier
Chaumont
Épinal
St Dié
Colmar
Freiburg
Le Mans
Châteaudun
ORLÉANS
Montargis
Sens
Auxerre
Langres
Vesoul
Belfort
MULHOUSE
BASEL
ZÜRICH
Tours
Blois
Vierzon
Bourges
Nevers
DIJON
BESANÇON
BERN
Luzern
Poitiers
Châteauroux
Moulins
Chalon-sur-Saône
Lons-le-Saunier
Lausanne
SUISSE
Montluçon
Vichy
Mâcon
Bourg-en-Bresse
GENÈVE
Annecy
Chamonix
LIMOGES
CLERMONT-Fd
LYON
Chambéry
Angoulême
St-ETIENNE
Vienne
GRENOBLE
Périgueux
Brive
Tulle
Le Puy
Valence
TORINO
ITALIA
MILANO
Bergerac
Aurillac
Cahors
Rodez
Mende
Montélimar
Gap
Cuneo
GENOVA
Agen
Montauban
Albi
Millau
Alès
Avignon
Digne
NICE
Monte-Carlo
Monaco
Auch
TOULOUSE
Castres
MONTPELLIER
Nîmes
Arles
Aix-en-P.
Cannes
Antibes
Tarbes
Carcassonne
Béziers
Narbonne
MARSEILLE
TOULON
Foix
PERPIGNAN
Andorra-la-Vella
MÉDITERRANÉE
Bastia
Ajaccio
Bonifacio

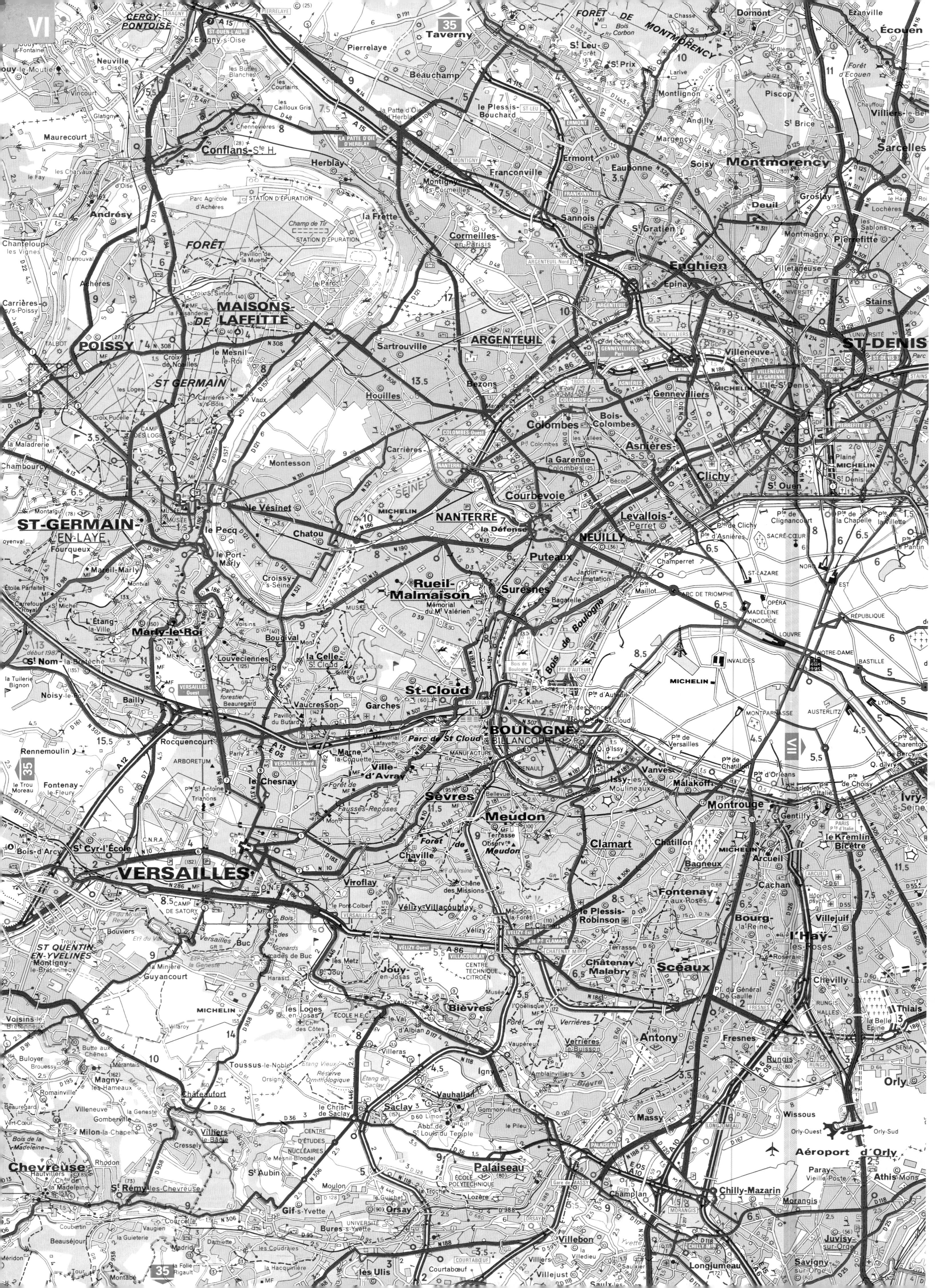
VI
CERGY PONTOISE
Taverny
35
FORÊT DE MONTMORENCY
Écouen
Conflans-Ste H.
Herblay
Franconville
Ermont
Eaubonne
Montmorency
Sarcelles
Andrésy
Cormeilles-en-Parisis
Sannois
Enghien
Epinay
Achères
MAISONS-LAFFITTE
ARGENTEUIL
ST-DENIS
POISSY
Sartrouville
Villeneuve-la-Garenne
ST GERMAIN
Houilles
Bezons
Gennevilliers
Colombes
Bois-Colombes
Asnières
Clichy
Montesson
Courbevoie
Levallois-Perret
St Ouen
ST-GERMAIN-EN-LAYE
le Vésinet
Chatou
NANTERRE
la Défense
NEUILLY
Puteaux
Rueil-Malmaison
Suresnes
Marly-le-Roi
Bougival
Louveciennes
Bois de Boulogne
St-Cloud
Garches
Vaucresson
BOULOGNE BILLANCOURT
Rocquencourt
Parc de St Cloud
Ville-d'Avray
le Chesnay
Sèvres
Meudon
Issy-les-Moulineaux
Vanves
Malakoff
Montrouge
Ivry
Clamart
Chaville
Viroflay
VERSAILLES
St Cyr-l'École
Vélizy-Villacoublay
Le Kremlin-Bicêtre
Bagneux
Fontenay-aux-Roses
Bourg-la-Reine
L'Haÿ-les-Roses
Villejuif
ST QUENTIN-EN-YVELINES
Guyancourt
Buc
Jouy-en-Josas
Châtenay-Malabry
Sceaux
Bièvres
Antony
Thiais
Rungis
Orly
Saclay
Vauhallan
Massy
Aéroport d'Orly
Chevreuse
Palaiseau
Chilly-Mazarin
Orsay
Gif-s-Yvette
Villebon
Longjumeau
Juvisy-sur-Orge
Les Ulis
Savigny-sur-Orge
VII

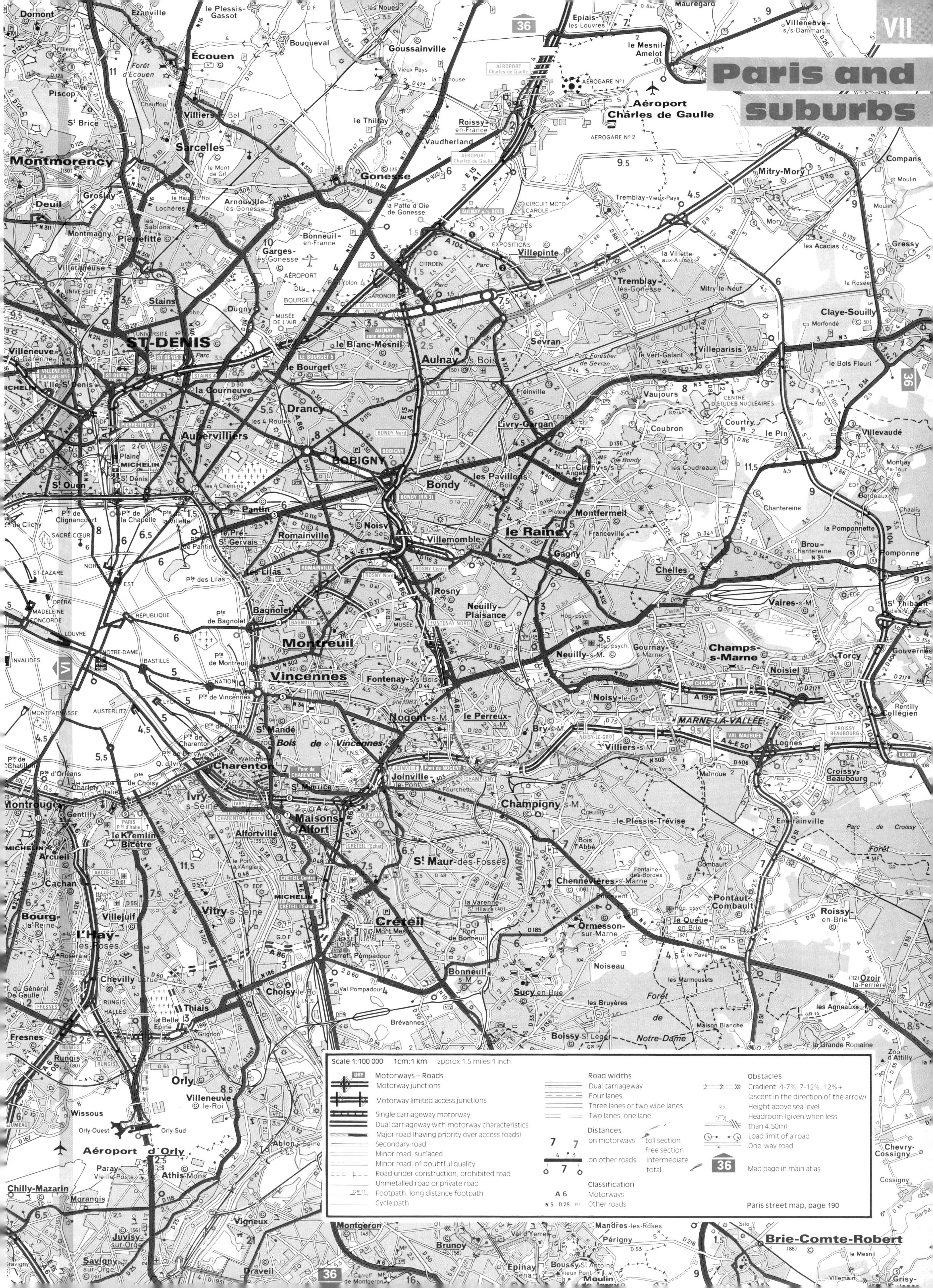
Paris and suburbs
Scale 1:100 000 1cm:1 km approx 1.5 miles:1 inch
Motorways – Roads
Motorway junctions
Motorway limited access junctions
Single carriageway motorway
Dual carriageway with motorway characteristics
Major road (having priority over access roads)
Secondary road
Minor road, surfaced
Minor road, of doubtful quality
Road under construction, prohibited road
Unmetalled road or private road
Footpath, long distance footpath
Cycle path
Road widths
Dual carriageway
Four lanes
Three lanes or two wide lanes
Two lanes, one lane
Distances
on motorways
toll section
free section
on other roads
intermediate
total
Classification
A 6
Motorways
N 5 D 28
Other roads
Obstacles
Gradient: 4-7%, 7-12%, 12%+
(ascent in the direction of the arrow)
Height above sea level
Headroom (given when less than 4.50m)
Load limit of a road
One-way road
36
Map page in main atlas
Paris street map, page 190
Aéroport Charles de Gaulle
Aéroport d'Orly
ST-DENIS
Montmorency
Sarcelles
Écouen
Gonesse
Aulnay-s/s-Bois
Le Bourget
BOBIGNY
Bondy
Montreuil
Vincennes
Charenton
Créteil
Champigny-s-M.
MARNE-LA-VALLÉE
Chelles
Torcy
Orly
Brie-Comte-Robert

Distances and journey times

Distances between principal towns

Distances are shown in kilometres and are calculated from centres and along the best roads from a motoring point of view, not necessarily following the shortest routes. To obtain a round figure conversion from kilometres to miles multiply the kilometre figure by 5 and divide by 8; for a more precise conversion, multiply by 0.6214.

Example: Boulogne-sur-Mer to Marseille 1023 Km

	Agen	Amiens	Angers	Bayonne	Besançon	Bordeaux	Boulogne-sur-Mer	Bourges	Brest	Brive-la-Gaillarde	Caen	Calais	Chambéry	Châteauroux	Cherbourg	Clermont-Ferrand	Dijon	Dunkerque	Genève	Grenoble	Le Havre	Lille	Limoges	Lyon	Le Mans	Marseille	Metz	Montpellier	Mulhouse	Nancy	Nantes	Nice	Nîmes	Orléans	Paris	Pau	Perpignan	Poitiers	Reims	Rennes	La Rochelle	Rouen	St-Étienne	Strasbourg	Toulon	Toulouse	Tours	Troyes	Valence
Amiens	793
Angers	462	440
Bayonne	209	917	528
Besançon	678	559	617	887
Bordeaux	140	725	336	183	695
Boulogne-sur-Mer	894	123	467	1018	611	826
Bourges	430	384	256	592	347	400	485
Brest	747	610	379	813	956	621	674	631
Brive-la-Gaillarde	169	633	346	377	509	194	734	284	687
Caen	646	237	218	770	642	578	301	363	373	528
Calais	937	155	584	1061	605	869	34	528	715	777	342
Chambéry	677	686	636	839	266	661	787	380	1083	467	769	830
Châteauroux	363	413	200	525	408	333	514	67	579	217	344	557	420
Cherbourg	753	356	287	819	761	627	420	484	392	633	119	461	888	459
Clermont-Ferrand	346	534	410	555	337	371	635	194	751	177	544	678	290	188	665
Dijon	623	459	517	832	103	640	560	246	855	457	542	603	271	348	661	282
Dunkerque	936	144	583	1060	604	868	78	527	718	776	345	43	829	556	464	677	602
Genève	769	684	637	931	177	693	785	381	1080	499	767	828	89	438	886	322	199	827
Grenoble	652	711	642	814	287	656	812	386	1107	462	794	855	55	426	913	285	295	854	144
Le Havre	717	179	316	841	605	649	243	390	480	639	107	284	732	419	226	580	505	287	730	757
Lille	864	115	511	988	532	796	115	455	813	704	342	112	757	484	461	605	530	73	755	782	285
Limoges	237	542	255	412	471	220	643	193	596	91	437	686	468	126	542	178	416	685	486	463	548	613
Lyon	523	607	538	812	248	548	708	282	1003	354	690	751	98	322	809	177	191	750	156	104	653	678	355
Le Mans	495	349	94	619	562	427	373	229	402	377	151	413	689	193	266	381	462	492	687	714	222	420	286	610
Marseille	520	922	845	682	564	648	1023	589	1319	511	1005	1066	342	634	1124	457	507	1065	434	282	968	993	635	315	925
Metz	887	345	617	1094	256	902	476	448	919	718	567	470	534	590	686	545	263	469	423	559	530	397	680	455	526	770
Montpellier	356	905	687	518	547	484	1006	572	1091	341	988	1049	325	548	1107	364	490	1048	417	300	951	976	432	298	718	168	753
Mulhouse	805	527	744	1014	136	822	658	473	1082	636	769	652	383	534	888	463	230	651	294	438	732	579	598	375	689	690	242	673
Nancy	836	362	582	1031	198	839	493	396	884	667	540	487	483	455	659	494	212	486	365	508	503	414	629	404	490	719	56	702	184
Nantes	451	529	89	517	706	325	556	345	296	393	283	673	725	279	302	452	606	672	726	737	379	600	302	627	183	959	706	795	833	671
Nice	675	1077	1000	837	719	803	1178	744	1474	666	1160	1221	388	789	1279	612	662	1220	477	334	1123	1148	790	470	1080	187	925	323	845	874	1114
Nîmes	404	856	740	566	498	532	957	523	1139	394	939	1000	276	516	1058	391	441	999	368	251	902	927	485	249	859	125	704	52	624	653	843	280
Orléans	525	276	214	649	397	457	377	106	545	357	255	420	524	137	376	289	297	419	522	549	282	347	266	445	137	760	402	743	524	382	303	915	694
Paris	647	148	294	771	413	579	244	238	596	486	240	292	540	266	359	388	312	291	537	564	203	219	395	460	202	776	331	759	539	304	383	931	710	130
Pau	157	916	527	108	956	191	1017	555	812	334	769	1060	734	488	818	511	899	1059	826	709	840	987	362	707	618	577	1093	413	1082	1030	516	732	461	648	770
Perpignan	320	1053	770	482	695	448	1154	655	1055	422	971	1197	473	639	1061	465	638	1196	565	448	1099	1124	513	446	820	316	901	152	821	850	759	471	200	779	907	377
Poitiers	313	480	136	439	615	247	581	187	477	210	333	624	564	120	423	274	515	623	555	559	404	551	119	430	182	731	657	551	742	594	178	886	604	212	334	438	638
Reims	782	156	429	906	323	714	288	329	731	621	379	282	555	401	498	489	284	281	469	579	342	209	530	475	337	791	188	774	370	205	518	946	725	265	142	905	922	469
Rennes	558	414	119	624	708	432	478	383	244	465	176	518	835	347	195	535	607	522	832	859	283	565	374	755	154	1071	671	902	834	636	107	1226	1005	297	348	623	866	255	483
La Rochelle	313	614	186	379	749	187	715	323	442	291	396	758	700	256	448	410	649	757	691	695	483	685	223	566	261	822	791	657	876	728	146	977	705	346	468	378	621	136	603	253
Rouen	690	113	289	814	541	622	177	326	497	575	124	218	668	355	248	516	441	221	666	693	87	218	484	589	195	904	419	887	668	439	378	1059	838	218	139	813	1035	377	230	300	511
St-Étienne	461	659	533	701	300	517	760	277	897	323	742	803	144	323	861	146	243	802	213	139	705	730	324	59	506	308	507	291	427	456	598	463	242	383	512	577	439	420	527	660	556	641
Strasbourg	910	502	775	1119	242	927	634	579	1077	741	725	628	493	640	844	569	335	627	404	548	688	555	703	480	683	796	163	779	113	148	864	951	730	559	488	1188	927	815	346	829	949	576	532
Toulon	581	983	906	743	625	709	1084	650	1380	572	1066	1127	403	695	1185	518	568	1126	495	335	1029	1054	696	376	986	64	831	229	751	780	1020	153	186	821	837	638	377	792	852	1132	883	965	369	857
Toulouse	116	851	566	298	783	244	952	502	851	218	767	995	561	435	857	395	726	994	653	536	839	922	309	534	616	404	989	240	909	938	555	559	288	575	704	182	204	434	839	662	417	793	527	1015	465
Tours	413	380	109	537	515	345	481	147	484	295	233	524	527	111	348	299	415	523	528	533	304	451	204	429	82	736	557	636	642	494	198	891	670	112	234	536	738	100	369	236	234	277	424	715	797	534
Troyes	646	275	431	842	236	650	425	221	733	500	399	419	427	280	518	328	152	418	351	451	362	346	409	347	340	663	233	646	320	184	520	818	597	187	162	841	794	405	122	485	539	298	399	332	724	718	305
Valence	551	706	629	713	348	679	807	373	1103	419	789	850	124	418	908	241	291	849	217	99	752	777	419	99	709	216	554	199	474	503	693	371	150	544	560	608	347	515	575	855	651	688	92	580	277	435	520	447
Valenciennes	853	108	500	977	475	785	164	444	802	692	345	161	746	472	464	594	435	122	621	770	287	50	601	666	408	982	299	965	529	343	589	1137	916	336	207	976	1113	540	151	554	674	221	718	456	1043	910	440	289	766

Journey times between principal towns

The times are shown in hours and minutes and are calculated for an average car taking into account normal driving conditions and excluding any stops.

Example: Boulogne-sur-Mer to Marseille 11.01

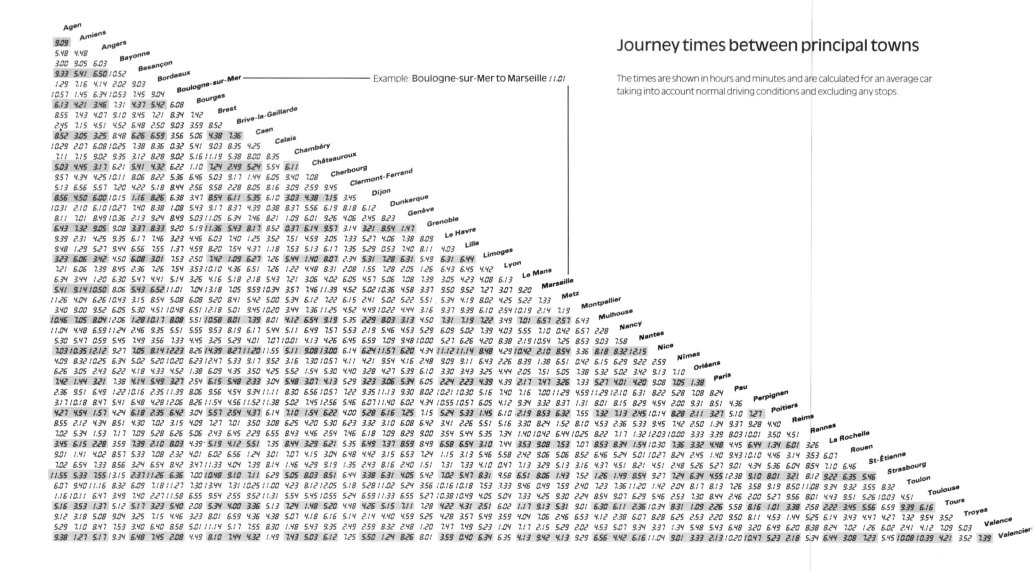

	Agen	Amiens	Angers	Bayonne	Besançon	Bordeaux	Boulogne-sur-Mer	Bourges	Brest	Brive-la-Gaillarde	Caen	Calais	Chambéry	Châteauroux	Cherbourg	Clermont-Ferrand	Dijon	Dunkerque	Genève	Grenoble	Le Havre	Lille	Limoges	Lyon	Le Mans	Marseille	Metz	Montpellier	Mulhouse	Nancy	Nantes	Nice	Nîmes	Orléans	Paris	Pau	Perpignan	Poitiers	Reims	Rennes	La Rochelle	Rouen	St-Étienne	Strasbourg	Toulon	Toulouse	Tours	Troyes	Valence
Amiens	9.09
Angers	5.48	4.48
Bayonne	3.00	9.05	6.03
Besançon	9.33	5.41	6.50	10.52
Bordeaux	1.29	7.16	4.14	2.02	9.03
Boulogne-sur-Mer	10.57	1.45	6.34	10.53	7.45	9.04
Bourges	6.13	4.21	3.46	7.31	4.37	5.42	6.08
Brest	8.55	7.43	4.07	9.10	9.45	7.21	8.34	7.42
Brive-la-Gaillarde	2.45	7.15	4.51	4.52	6.48	2.50	9.03	3.59	8.52
Caen	8.52	3.05	3.25	8.48	6.26	6.59	3.56	5.06	4.38	7.36
Calais	10.29	2.07	6.08	10.25	7.38	8.36	0.32	5.41	9.03	8.35	4.25
Chambéry	7.11	7.15	9.02	9.35	3.12	8.28	9.02	5.16	11.19	5.38	8.00	8.35
Châteauroux	5.03	4.45	3.17	6.21	5.41	4.32	6.22	1.10	7.24	2.49	5.24	5.54	6.11
Cherbourg	9.57	4.34	4.25	10.11	8.06	8.22	5.36	6.46	5.03	9.17	1.44	6.05	9.40	7.08
Clermont-Ferrand	5.13	6.56	5.57	7.20	4.22	5.18	8.44	2.56	9.58	2.28	8.05	8.16	3.09	2.59	9.45
Dijon	8.56	4.50	6.00	10.15	1.16	8.26	6.38	3.47	8.54	6.11	5.35	6.10	3.03	4.38	7.15	3.45
Dunkerque	10.31	2.10	6.10	10.27	7.40	8.38	1.08	5.43	9.17	8.37	4.39	0.38	8.37	5.56	6.19	8.18	6.12
Genève	8.11	7.01	8.49	10.36	2.13	9.24	8.49	5.03	11.05	6.34	7.46	8.21	1.09	6.01	9.26	4.06	2.45	8.23
Grenoble	6.43	7.32	9.05	9.08	3.37	8.33	9.20	5.19	11.36	5.43	8.17	8.52	0.37	6.14	9.57	3.14	3.21	8.54	1.47
Le Havre	9.39	2.31	4.25	9.35	6.17	7.46	3.23	4.46	6.03	7.40	1.25	3.52	7.51	4.59	3.05	7.33	5.27	4.06	7.38	8.09
Lille	9.48	1.29	5.27	9.44	6.56	7.55	1.37	4.59	8.20	7.54	4.37	1.18	7.53	5.13	6.17	7.35	5.29	0.53	7.40	8.11	4.03
Limoges	3.23	6.06	3.42	4.50	6.08	3.01	7.53	2.50	7.42	1.09	6.27	7.26	5.44	1.40	8.07	2.34	5.31	7.28	6.31	5.49	6.31	6.44
Lyon	7.21	6.06	7.39	8.45	2.36	7.26	7.54	3.53	10.10	4.36	6.51	7.26	1.22	4.48	8.31	2.08	1.55	7.28	2.05	1.26	6.43	6.45	4.42
Le Mans	6.34	3.44	1.20	6.30	5.47	4.41	5.14	3.26	4.16	5.18	2.18	5.43	7.21	3.06	4.02	6.05	4.57	5.06	7.08	7.39	3.05	4.23	4.08	6.13
Marseille	5.41	9.14	10.50	8.06	5.43	6.52	11.01	7.04	13.18	7.05	9.59	10.34	3.57	7.46	11.39	4.52	5.02	10.36	4.58	3.37	9.50	9.52	7.27	3.07	9.20
Metz	11.26	4.04	6.26	10.43	3.15	8.54	5.08	6.08	9.20	8.41	5.42	5.00	5.34	6.12	7.22	6.15	2.41	5.02	5.22	5.51	5.34	4.19	8.02	4.25	5.22	7.33
Montpellier	3.40	9.00	9.52	6.05	5.30	4.51	10.48	6.51	12.18	5.01	9.45	10.20	3.44	7.36	11.25	4.52	4.49	10.22	4.44	3.16	9.37	9.39	6.10	2.54	10.19	2.14	7.19
Mulhouse	10.46	7.05	8.04	12.06	1.28	10.17	8.08	5.51	10.58	8.01	7.39	8.01	4.12	6.54	9.19	5.35	2.29	8.03	3.13	4.50	7.31	7.19	7.22	3.49	7.01	6.57	2.57	6.43
Nancy	11.04	4.48	6.59	11.24	2.46	9.35	5.51	5.55	9.53	8.19	6.17	5.44	5.11	6.49	7.57	5.53	2.19	5.46	4.53	5.29	6.09	5.02	7.39	4.03	5.55	7.10	0.42	6.57	2.28
Nantes	5.30	5.47	0.59	5.45	7.49	3.56	7.33	4.45	3.25	5.29	4.01	7.07	10.01	4.13	4.26	6.45	6.59	7.09	9.48	10.00	5.27	6.26	4.20	8.38	2.19	10.54	7.25	8.53	9.03	7.58
Nice	7.03	10.35	12.12	9.27	7.05	8.14	12.23	8.26	14.39	8.27	11.20	11.55	5.11	9.08	13.00	6.14	6.24	11.57	6.20	4.34	11.12	11.14	8.48	4.29	10.42	2.10	8.54	3.36	8.18	8.32	12.15
Nîmes	4.09	8.32	10.25	6.34	5.02	5.20	10.20	6.23	12.47	5.33	9.17	9.52	3.16	7.30	10.57	4.11	4.21	9.54	4.16	2.48	9.09	9.11	6.43	2.26	8.39	1.38	6.51	0.42	6.15	6.29	9.22	2.59
Orléans	6.26	3.05	2.43	6.22	4.18	4.33	4.52	1.38	6.09	4.35	3.50	4.25	5.52	1.54	5.30	4.40	3.28	4.27	5.39	6.10	3.30	3.43	3.25	4.44	2.05	7.51	5.05	7.38	5.32	5.02	3.42	9.13	7.10
Paris	7.42	1.44	3.21	7.38	4.14	5.49	3.27	2.54	6.15	5.48	2.33	3.04	5.48	3.07	4.13	5.29	3.23	3.06	5.34	6.05	2.24	2.23	4.39	4.39	2.17	7.47	3.26	7.33	5.27	4.01	4.20	9.08	7.05	1.38
Pau	2.36	9.51	6.49	1.22	10.16	2.35	11.39	8.06	9.56	4.54	9.34	11.11	8.30	6.56	10.57	7.22	9.35	11.13	9.30	8.02	10.21	10.30	5.16	7.40	7.16	7.00	11.29	4.59	11.29	12.10	6.31	8.22	5.28	7.08	8.24
Perpignan	3.17	10.18	8.47	5.41	6.48	4.28	12.06	8.26	11.54	4.56	11.52	11.38	5.02	7.45	12.56	5.46	6.07	11.40	6.02	4.34	10.55	10.57	6.05	4.12	9.34	3.32	8.37	1.31	8.01	8.15	8.29	4.54	2.00	9.31	8.51	4.36
Poitiers	4.27	4.54	1.57	4.24	6.18	2.35	6.42	3.04	5.57	2.54	4.37	6.14	7.10	1.54	6.22	4.00	5.28	6.16	7.25	7.15	5.24	5.33	1.45	6.10	2.19	8.53	6.32	7.55	7.32	7.13	2.45	10.14	8.28	2.11	3.27	5.10	7.27
Reims	8.55	2.12	4.34	8.51	4.30	7.02	3.15	4.09	7.27	7.01	3.50	3.08	6.25	4.20	5.30	6.23	3.32	3.10	6.08	6.42	3.41	2.26	5.51	5.16	3.30	8.24	1.52	8.10	4.53	2.36	5.33	9.45	7.42	2.50	1.34	9.37	9.28	4.40
Rennes	7.02	5.34	1.53	7.17	7.09	5.28	6.26	5.06	2.43	6.45	2.29	6.55	8.43	4.46	2.54	7.46	6.18	7.09	8.29	9.00	3.54	5.44	5.35	7.34	1.40	10.42	6.44	10.25	8.22	7.17	1.32	12.03	10.00	3.33	3.39	8.03	10.01	3.50	4.51
La Rochelle	3.45	6.15	2.28	3.59	7.39	2.10	8.03	4.39	5.19	4.12	5.51	7.35	8.44	3.29	6.21	5.35	6.49	7.37	8.59	8.49	6.58	6.54	3.10	7.44	3.53	9.08	7.53	7.07	8.53	8.34	1.54	10.30	7.36	3.32	4.48	4.45	6.44	1.34	6.01	3.26
Rouen	9.01	1.41	4.02	8.57	5.33	7.08	2.32	4.01	6.02	6.56	1.24	3.01	7.07	4.15	3.04	6.48	4.42	3.15	6.53	7.24	1.15	3.13	5.46	5.58	2.42	9.06	5.06	8.52	6.46	5.24	5.01	10.27	8.24	2.45	1.40	9.43	10.10	4.46	3.14	3.53	6.07
St-Étienne	7.02	6.54	7.33	8.56	3.24	6.54	8.42	3.47	11.33	4.04	7.39	8.14	1.46	4.29	9.19	1.35	2.43	8.16	2.40	1.51	7.31	7.33	4.10	0.47	7.13	3.29	5.13	3.16	4.37	4.51	8.21	4.51	2.48	5.26	5.27	9.01	4.34	5.36	6.04	8.54	7.10	6.46
Strasbourg	11.55	5.33	7.55	13.15	2.37	11.26	6.36	7.00	10.48	9.10	7.11	6.29	5.05	8.03	8.51	6.44	3.38	6.31	4.05	5.42	7.02	5.47	8.31	4.58	6.51	8.06	1.43	7.52	1.26	1.49	8.54	9.27	7.24	6.34	4.55	12.38	9.10	8.01	3.21	8.12	9.22	6.35	5.46
Toulon	6.07	9.40	11.16	8.32	6.09	7.18	11.27	7.30	13.44	7.31	10.25	11.00	4.23	8.12	12.05	5.18	5.28	11.02	5.24	3.56	10.16	10.18	7.53	3.33	9.46	0.49	7.59	2.40	7.23	7.36	11.20	1.42	2.04	8.17	8.13	7.26	3.58	9.19	8.50	11.08	9.34	9.32	3.55	8.32
Toulouse	1.16	10.11	6.47	3.49	7.40	2.27	11.58	6.55	9.54	2.55	9.52	11.31	5.54	5.45	10.55	5.24	6.59	11.33	6.55	5.27	10.38	10.49	4.05	5.04	7.33	4.25	9.30	2.24	8.54	9.07	6.29	5.46	2.53	7.30	8.44	2.46	2.00	5.27	9.56	8.01	4.43	9.51	5.26	10.03	4.51
Tours	5.16	3.53	1.37	5.12	5.17	3.23	5.40	2.08	5.34	4.00	3.36	5.13	7.24	1.48	5.20	4.48	4.26	5.15	7.11	7.28	4.22	4.31	2.51	6.02	1.17	9.13	5.31	9.01	6.30	6.11	2.36	10.34	8.31	1.09	2.26	5.58	8.16	1.01	3.38	2.58	2.22	3.45	5.56	6.59	9.39	6.16
Troyes	9.12	3.18	5.08	9.04	3.25	7.15	4.46	3.23	8.01	6.59	4.36	4.38	5.07	4.18	6.16	5.14	2.14	4.40	4.59	5.25	4.28	3.57	5.49	3.59	4.04	7.06	2.46	6.53	4.12	2.38	6.07	8.28	6.25	2.53	2.20	9.50	8.11	4.53	1.44	5.25	6.14	3.43	4.47	4.27	7.32	9.54	3.52
Valence	5.29	7.10	8.47	7.53	3.40	6.40	8.58	5.01	11.14	5.17	7.55	8.30	1.48	5.43	9.35	2.49	2.59	8.32	2.48	1.20	7.47	7.49	5.23	1.04	7.17	2.15	5.29	2.02	4.53	5.07	9.34	3.37	1.34	5.48	5.43	6.48	3.20	6.49	6.20	8.38	8.24	7.02	1.26	6.02	2.41	4.12	7.09	5.03
Valenciennes	9.38	1.27	5.17	9.34	6.48	7.45	2.08	4.49	8.10	7.44	4.32	1.49	7.43	5.03	6.12	7.25	5.50	1.24	8.26	8.01	3.59	0.40	6.34	6.35	4.13	9.42	4.13	9.29	6.56	4.42	6.16	11.04	9.01	3.33	2.13	10.20	10.47	5.23	2.18	5.34	6.44	3.08	7.23	5.45	10.08	10.39	4.21	3.52	7.39

Verklaring van tekens
Zeichenerklärung
Légende
Key

Autobahnen – Straßen		Wegen
Autobahn: getrennte Fahrbahnen		Autosnelweg: met gescheiden rijbanen
Autobahn: nur eine Fahrbahn		Autosnelweg: met één rijbaan
zweibahnige Straße, autobahnähnlich		Weg met gescheiden rijbanen van het type autosnelweg
Numerierte Anschlußstellen: uneingeschränkt	1	Aansluiting met nummer: volledig (in alle richtingen)
Numerierte Anschlußstellen: eingeschränkt	2 7 10	Aansluiting met nummer: gedeeltelijk
Hauptverkehrsstraße mit Vorfahrtsberechtigung		Hoofdweg
Straße 2. Ordnung		Secundaire verbindingsweg
Nebenstraße befestigt		Andere weg: verhard
unbefestigt oder in schlechtem Zustand		Andere weg: onverhard of slecht berijdbaar
Radweg		Fietspad
Wirtschaftsweg, Pfad		Bedrijfsweg of karrespoor; voetpad
Autobahn/Straße, im Bau befindlich		In aanleg: autosnelweg; andere weg
Datum der Verkehrsfreigabe	12-1988	Vermoedelijke datum van openstelling

Straßenbreite		Breedte
Getrennte Fahrbahnen		Gescheiden rijbanen
4 Fahrspuren, 3 Fahrspuren		4 rijstroken; 3 rijstroken
2 breite Fahrspuren, 2 Fahrspuren		2 brede rijstroken; 2 rijstroken
1 Fahrspur, 1 sehr schmale Fahrspur		1 rijstrook; 1 smalle rijstrook

Entfernungen (in km)		Afstanden
Gesamtentfernung	15 17	Totale afstanden
Autobahnen, Mautstrecke, mautfreie Strecke		Autosnelwegen: tolweg; tolvrij
Teilentfernung	7 8 12 5	Tussenstanden
Gesamtentfernung	11	Totale afstanden
übriges Straßennetz		Andere wegen
Teilentfernung	6 5	Tussenstanden

Verkehrshindernisse		Hindernissen
Steigung, Gefälle: 5 – 9%, 9 –13%, 13% u.m. (Steigung in Pfeilrichtung)		Hellingen, afdalingen 5-9%; 9-13%; +13% (pijlen in de richting van de helling)
Paß mit Höhenangabe (in m über N.N.)	1250	Bergpas en hoogte boven de zeespiegel
Schwierige oder gefährliche Strecke		Moeilijk of gevaarlijk traject
Bahnübergänge, schienengleich; Unter-, Überführung		Spoorwegovergangen: gelijkvloers, overheen, onderdoor
Zulässige Gesamthöhe (angegeben wenn unter 4,50 m)		Vrije hoogte (aangegeven onder 4,50 m)
Autofähre (im Roten Michelin-Führer - Telefonnummern der wichtigsten Fährunternehmen)	B	Auto-veerpont (tel.nr. in Rode Michelingids van Frankrijk)
Personenfähre		Pont voor voetgangers en fietsers
Höchstbelastung einer Brücke, einer Fähre (angegeben wenn unter 19 t)	6	Maximumdraagvermogen van een brug, van een veerpont (aangegeven onder 19t)
Zugbrücke oder Drehbrücke		Ophaalbrug, beweegbare brug of draaibrug
Beschränkung des zulässigen Gesamtgewichts		Maximumdraagvermogen van een hoofd- of secundaire weg
Einbahnstraße		Weg met eenrichtingsverkeer
Schmale Straße: Überholen schwierig oder unmöglich, Nebenstraße mit Gewichtsbeschränkung		Smalle weg (passeren moeilijk of onmogelijk), kleine weg met beperkt draagvermogen
Straße mit eingeschränkter Befahrbarkeit		Beperkt toegankelijke weg
Gesperrte Straße		Verboden weg

Unterkünfte		Plaatsen en verblijf
Gekennzeichnete Orte sind in den Michelin-Führern aufgeführt		*Het onderstaande verwijst naar diverse Michelingidsen*
Rote Umgrenzung: Stadtpläne im Roten Michelin-Führer		Rood-omlijnde plaats: stadsplattegrond in de Rode Michelingids van Frankrijk
Rot unterstrichen: Im Roten Michelin-Führer aufgeführter Ort	St Jean	Rood onderstreepte plaatsnaam: plaats die vermeld is in de Rode Michelingids van Frankrijk
Im Michelin-Führer "Camping Caravaning France" gelistete Campingplätze		Kampeerterrein dat vermeld is in de Michelingids "Camping Caravaning France"
Abgelegenes Hotel oder Restaurant		Afgelegen hotel of restaurant
Campingplatz		Kampeerterrein

Sehenswürdigkeiten		Bezienswaardigheden
Orte in den Grünen Michelin-Reiseführern aufgeführt		*De meeste bezienswaardigheden zijn beschreven in de Groene Michelingidsen*
Orientierungstafel, Rundblick, Aussichtspunkt		Oriëntatietafel met panorama, uitzichtpunt
Landschaftlich schöne Strecke, Kirchliches Gebäude		Schilderachtig traject, kerk of kapel
Schloß, Burg, Ruine, Megalith, Leuchtturm		Kasteel; ruïne; hunebed of dolmen; vuurtoren
Windmühle, Höhle, sonstige Sehenswürdigkeit		Windmolen; grot; andere bezienswaardigheid

Sport- und Freizeiteinrichtungen		Sport, Recreatie
Stadion, Golfplatz, Pferderennbahn		Stadion, golfbaan, renbaan
Reitanlage, Strandbad, Schwimmbad		Manege; zwemgelegenheid; zwembad
Jachthafen, Segelflugplatz, Freizeitpark		Zeilsport; zweefvliegen; recreatiepark
Seilbahn, Sessellift, Schutzhütte		Kabelspoor of stoeltjeslift; berghut
Fernwanderweg	GR	Lange-afstands-wandelpad

Sonstige Symbole		Andere tekens
Bahnlinie mit Bahnhof, Straßenbahn		Spoorweg met station; tramweg
Landeplatz im Gebirge, Flugplatz, Flughafen		Landingsbaan in de bergen; vliegveld; luchthaven
Funk-, Fernsehturm		Telecommunicatietoren of -mast
Notrufsäule		Telefoon voor noodgevallen
Staatsgrenze		Rijksgrens
Zollstation		Douanekantoor
Erdöl- oder Erdgasquelle, Steinbruch, Bergwerk		Olie- of gasput; steengroeve; mijn
Materialtransportbahn, Fabrik, Staudamm		Kabelvrachtvervoer; fabriek; stuwdam
Leuchtturm, Windmühle, Wasserturm		Vuurtoren; windmolen; watertoren
Krankenhaus, Kirche oder Kapelle		Verpleeginrichting; kerk of kapel
Friedhof, Bildstock, Schloß, Burg, Festung, Ruine		Begraafplaats; kruisheuvel; kasteel; fort; ruïne
Denkmal, Höhle, Forsthaus	Mon! MF	Monument; grot; boswachtershuis
Wald oder Gehölz, Staatsforst		Bos; domaniaal woud
Verwaltungssitz:		Hoofdplaats van:
Präfektur (Departement)	P	Département (Prefectuur)
Unterpräfektur (Bezirk)	SP	Arrondissement (Onderprefectuur)
Kanton (Kreis)	©	Canton

Maßstab 1:200 000
1cm entspricht 2 km

Schaal 1:200 000
1cm op de kaart = 2km in het terrein

0 1 2 3 4 5km

Motorways – Roads		Autoroutes – Routes
Motorway: dual carriageway		Autoroute: à chaussées séparées
Motorway: single carriageway		Autoroute: à une seule chaussée
Dual carriageway with motorway characteristics		Double chaussée de type autoroutier (sans carrefour à niveau)
Numbered junctions: complete	1	Échangeur numéroté: complet
Numbered junctions: limited	2 7 10	Échangeurs numérotés: partiels
Major road (having priority)		Route principale (en France classée à grande circulation)
Secondary road network		Itinéraire régional ou de dégagement
Other road: surfaced		Route: revêtue
Unsurfaced or of doubtful quality		Non revêtue ou de mauvaise viabilité
Cycle track		Piste cyclable
Service road or cart track, footpath		Chemin d'exploitation, sentier
Motorway, road under construction		Autoroute, route en construction
Scheduled opening date	12-1988	Date prévue de mise en service

Road width		Largeur des routes
Dual carriageway		Chaussées séparées
Four lanes, three lanes		Quatre voies, trois voies
Two wide lanes, two lanes		Deux voies larges, deux voies
One lane, one narrow lane		Une voie, une voie étroite

Distances in kilometres		Distances
Total	15 17	Sur autoroute: totalisées
Motorway toll section, free section		Sur section à péage, sur section libre
Intermediate	7 8 12 5	Sur autoroute: partielles
Total	11	Sur route: totalisées
On other roads		
Intermediate	6 5	Sur route: partielles

Obstacles		Obstacles
Gradient: 5-9%, 9-13%, 13%+ (ascent in the direction of the arrow)		Pente: 5–9%, 9–13%, 13% et plus (flèches dans le sens de la montée)
Pass and height in metres above sea level	1250	Col et sa cote d'altitude
Difficult or dangerous stretch of road		Parcours difficile ou dangereux
Level crossing, railway under, over road		Passages: à niveau, supérieur, inférieur
Headroom (given when less than 4.50 m)		Hauteur limitée (ind. au-dessous de 4,50 m)
Car ferry (Michelin Red Guide France gives the phone numbers of main ferries)	B	Bac passant les autos (le Guide Michelin France donne le numéro de téléphone)
Ferry (pedestrians and cycles only)		Bac pour piétons et cycles
Load limit of a bridge, of a car ferry (given when less than 19 tonnes)	6	Limite de charge d'un pont, d'un bac (indiquée au-dessous de 19 t)
Drawbridge or swing bridge		Pont mobile
Load limit of a major or secondary road		Limite de charge d'une route
One-way road		Route à sens unique
Narrow road: passing difficult or impossible, local road with load limit		Une voie étroite: croisement difficile, impossible; route communale à charge limitée
Road subject to restrictions		Route réglementée
Prohibited road		Route interdite

Accommodation		Hébergement
The information below corresponds with places selected in the Michelin Guides		*Indications limitées aux ressources sélectionnées dans les Guides Michelin*
Red frame: town plans in the Michelin Red Guide France		Schémas encadrés: plans traités dans les Guides "Hôtels et Restaurants"
Red underlining: town or place mentioned in the Michelin Red Guide France	St Jean	Noms soulignés: localités ou sites figurant dans ces mêmes guides
Camp sites listed in the Michelin Camping Caravanning Guide		Localités ou sites retenus dans le Guide "Camping-Caravaning"
Secluded hotel or restaurant		Hôtel, restaurant isolé
Location of camping site		Terrain de camping

Tourist information		Eléments touristiques
Most of these sites are described in the Michelin Green Guides		*Les Guides Verts Michelin décrivent la plupart de ces curiosités*
Viewing table, panorama, viewpoint		Table d'orientation, panorama, point de vue
Scenic route, ecclesiastical building		Parcours pittoresque, édifice religieux
Chateau, ruins, megalith, lighthouse		Château, ruines, mégalithe, phare
Windmill, cave, other place of interest		Moulin à vent, grotte, autre curiosité

Sports and recreation facilities		Sports – Loisirs
Stadium, golf course, race course		Stade, golf, hippodrome
Equestrian centre, swimming place, pool		Centre équestre, baignade, piscine
Sailing, gliding, country park		Voile, vol à voile, parc de loisirs
Cable car, chair lift, mountain hut		Téléphérique, télésiège, refuge de montagne
Long distance footpath	GR	Sentier de grande randonnée

Other features		Equipements – Environnement
Railway, station, tramway		Voie ferrée, station, tramway
Mountain airfield, airfield, airport		Altiport, aérodrome, aéroport
Telecommunications tower or mast		Tour ou pylône de télécommunications
Emergency telephone		Borne d'appel d'urgence
National boundary		Frontière
Customs post		Bureau de douane
Oil or gas well, quarry, mine		Pétrole ou gaz naturel, carrière, mine
Overhead conveyor, factory, dam		Transporteur aérien, usine, barrage
Lighthouse, windmill, water tower		Phare, moulin à vent, château d'eau
Hospital or hospice, church or chapel		Hôpital ou hospice, église ou chapelle
Cemetery, cross, chateau, fort, ruins		Cimetière, calvaire, château, fort, ruines
Statue or building, cave, forester's lodge	Mon! MF	Monument, grotte, maison forestière
Forest or wood, state forest		Forêt ou bois, forêt domaniale
Seat of local government:		Chef-lieu de:
Prefecture	P	Département
Sub-prefecture	SP	Arrondissement
Canton	©	Canton

Scale 1:200 000
1cm:2km approx 3 miles:1 inch

Échelle 1/200 000
1cm: 2km

0 1 2 3 4 5km

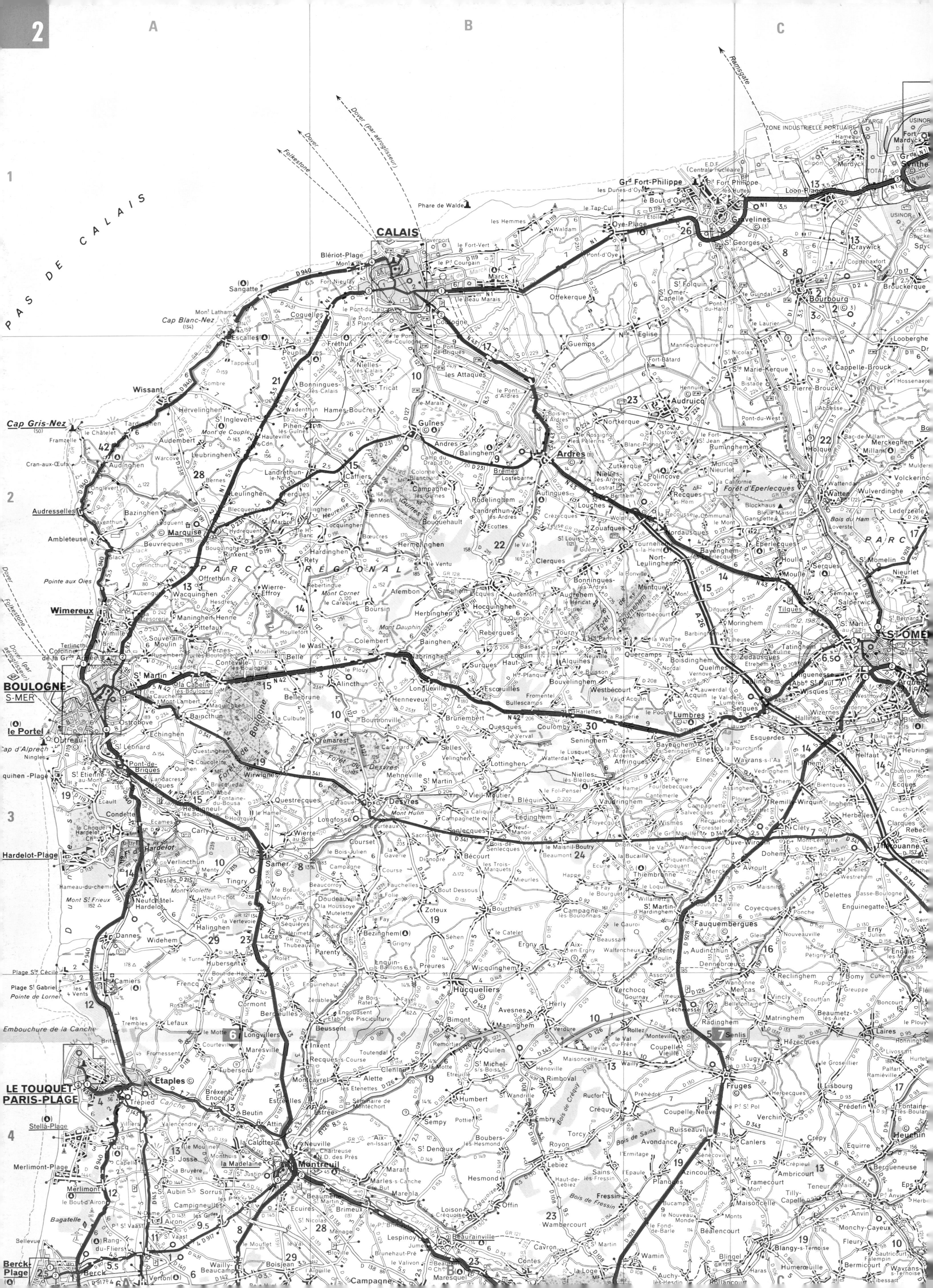
A
B
C
1
2
3
4
PAS DE CALAIS
Dover (par aéroglisseur)
Dover
Folkestone
Ramsgate
CALAIS
Phare de Walde
Blériot-Plage
Sangatte
Cap Blanc-Nez
Coquelles
Fréthun
Coulogne
Marck
Gravelines
Grd Fort-Philippe
Oye-Plage
Loon-Plage
Mardyck
Fort Mardyck
Grde Synthe
Bourbourg
Craywick
Brouckerque
ZONE INDUSTRIELLE PORTUAIRE
Wissant
Cap Gris-Nez
Audinghen
Audresselles
Ambleteuse
Marquise
Guînes
Ardres
Audruicq
Nortkerque
Les Attaques
St Folquin
St Omer-Capelle
Guemps
Hames-Boucres
Pihen-lès-Guînes
Landrethun-le-Nord
Caffiers
Fiennes
Hardinghen
Rety
PARC
RÉGIONAL
Wimereux
Wimille
BOULOGNE-S-MER
le Portel
Outreau
Cap d'Alprech
St Martin
St Léonard
Pont-de-Briques
Forêt de Boulogne
Forêt de Guînes
Forêt de Desvres
Forêt d'Eperlecques
Desvres
Samer
Hardelot-Plage
Condette
Neufchâtel-Hardelot
Dannes
Camiers
Embouchure de la Canche
Etaples
LE TOUQUET-PARIS-PLAGE
Stella-Plage
Merlimont-Plage
Merlimont
Berck-Plage
Berck
Montreuil
Beaurainville
Hucqueliers
Fauquembergues
Fruges
Lumbres
ST OMER
Arques
Watten
Eperlecques
Thérouanne
Heuchin
Lisbourg
Blangy-s-Ternoise
Wambercourt
Campagne

DUNKERQUE
De Panne
Bray-Dunes
Veurne
(Furnes)
Diksmuide
(Dixmude)
Malo-les-Bains
Rosendaël
St Pol
Synthe
Coudekerque-Branche
Ghyvelde
Hondschoote
Bergues
Alveringem
Houthulst
Staden
Hooglede
Kortemark
Langemark
Poperinge
Ieper
Zonnebeke
Moorslede
Wormhout
Esquelbecq
Bambecque
Herzeele
Steenvoorde
Cassel
Kemmel
Mesen
Wervik
Menen
Comines
Bailleul
Hazebrouck
Armentières
Houplines
Nieppe
Steenwerck
Merville
Estaires
Aire
Isbergues
Lillers
Béthune
LILLE
Lomme
Lambersart
Roubaix
La Madeleine
Haubourdin
Seclin
Auchel
Bruay en-Artois
Noeux-les-Mines
Bully
Lens
Liévin
Carvin
Hénin-Beaumont
Houdain
Vermelles
La Bassée
Forêt de Nieppe
Forêt de Phalempin
A 25
A 26
A 21
A 19

Torhout
Aalter
GENT
(GAND)
Lichtervelde
Wingene
Ruiselede
Tielt
Pittem
Deinze
St-Martens-Latem
Ardooie
Roeselare
(Roulers)
Meulebeke
Nazareth
Rumbeke
Ingelmunster
Izegem
Oostrozebeke
Zulte
Kruishoutem
Moorslede
Lendelede
Waregem
Ledegem
Oudenaarde
(Audenarde)
KORTRIJK (COURTRAI)
Wevelgem
Zwevegem
Menen
(Menin)
Wervik
Halluin
Kluisbergen
Avelgem
Comines
Mouscron
Ronse
(Renaix)
Tourcoing
ROUBAIX
Wattrelos
Marcq
LILLE
Villeneuve-d'Ascq
TOURNAI
DOORNIK
Haubourdin
Leuze-en-Hainaut
Seclin
Orchies
Péruwelz
St Amand-les-Eaux
Condé-s-l'Escaut
Beloeil
Bernissart
Marchiennes
Bruay

5
BRUSSEL
BRUXELLES
MECHELEN
(MALINES)
Aalst
(Alost)
Dendermonde
(Termonde)
Vilvoorde
(Vilvorde)
Zaventem
Ninove
Geraardsbergen
Grammont
Halle
(Hal)
Waterloo
Nivelles
(Nijvel)
Soignies
(Zinnik)
Braine-le-Comte
La Louvière
MONS
(BERGEN)
CHARLEROI
Binche
Ath (Aat)
Lessines
(Lessen)
Enghien
(Edingen)
Tubize
(Tubeke)
Wetteren
Zottegem
Willebroek
Tervuren
Forêt de Soignes
Zoniënwoud
Chièvres
Jurbise
Seneffe
Gosselies

A
B
1
2
3
4
Embouchure de la Canche
LE TOUQUET-PARIS-PLAGE
Etaples
Trépied
Canche
Stella-Plage
Cucq
Merlimont-Plage
Merlimont
le Bout-d'Airon
Bagatelle
Rang-du-Fliers
Berck-Plage
Berck
Verton
Waben
Groffliers
Baie d'Authie
Conchil-le-Temple
Fort-Mahon-Plage
Vieux-Fort-Mahon
Quend-Plage-les-Pins
Monchaux
Quend
Colline-Beaumont
Vieux-Quend
Villers-s-Authie
Vron
St Quentin-en-Tourmont
Domaine du Marquenterre
Parc Ornithologique
Rue
Baie de Somme
Favières
le Crotoy
le Hourdel
Cayeux-s-Mer
Brighton
St Valery-s-Somme
Cap Hornu
Noyelles-s-Mer
Lanchères
Pendé
Brutelles
Saigneville
Onival
Ault
Woignarue
Friville-Escarbotin
Mers-les-Bains
le Tréport
Calvaire des Terrasses
Eu
Mesnil-Val
Criel-Plage
Mont Jolibois
Criel-s-Mer
Tocqueville-s-Eu
Biville-s-Mer
E.D.F. Centrale nucléaire (en constr on)
St Martin-Plage
Berneval-le-Gd
Belleville-s-Mer
Bracquemont
Puys
Neuville
Envermeu
Forêt d'Arques
Arques-la-Bataille
St Nicolas-d'Aliermont
Gamaches
Blangy-s-Bresle
Haute Forêt d'Eu
Triage d'Eu
Oisemont
Abbeville
Monts de Caubert
Moyenneville
Hallencourt
Nouvion
Forêt de Crécy
Forest-Montiers
Rue
Montreuil
Campagne-lès-Hesdin
Abbe de Valloires
Argoules
Nempont-St Firmin
la Madelaine
St Josse
Beussent
Inxent
Recques-s-Course
Longvilliers
Brexent-Enocq
Estréelles
Attin
Neuville
la Calotterie
Beaumerie-St Martin
Ecuires
Airon-St Vaast
Wailly-Beaucamp
Boisjean
Sorrus
Campigneulles-les-Pts
Tigny-Noyelle
Machy
Cambron
Mareuil
Huppy
Limeux
Senarpont
Foucaucourt-lors-Nesle
Nesle-Normandeuse
Bazinval
Melleville
Sept-Meules
Avesnes-en-Val
Grandcourt
Londinières
Bailly-en-Rivière
St Ouen-s/s-Bailly
Douvrend
Dampierre-St Nicolas
St Jacques-d'Aliermont
N. D. d'Aliermont
Wanchy-Capval
Campneuseville
Réalcamp
Fouarmont
Aumale
Villers-Campsart
Liomer
Hornoy
Brocourt
Beaucamps-le-Vx
Le Quesne
St Aubin-Rivière
Inval-Boiron
Andainville
Epaumesnil
Lignières-en-Vimeu
Villeroy
Cannessières
Fontaine-le-Sec
Vergies
Wiry-au-Mont
Woirel
Forceville-en-Vimeu
Citerne
Hocquincourt
Frucourt
Doudelainville
Bailleul
Béhen
Huchenneville
Bray-lès-Mareuil
Feuquières-en-Vimeu
Fressenneville
Woincourt
Chépy
Aigneville
Valines
Nibas
Franleu
Quesnoy
Ochancourt
Bourseville
Tully
Allenay
Vaudricourt
Hautebut
Arrest
Boismont
Pinchefalise
Estrébœuf
Tilloy
Mons-Boubert
Port-le-Grand
Bray
Sailly-Flibeaucourt
Buigny-St Maclou
Hautvillers-Ouville
Lamotte-Buleux
Gd Laviers
Mautort
Yonval
Bienfay
Miannay
Lambercourt
Acheux-en-Vimeu
Tœufles
Ercourt
Tours-en-Vimeu
Grébault-Mesnil
Vismes
Maisnières
Frettemeule
Martainneville
St Maxent
Fresnes-Tilloloy
Biencourt
Cerisy-Buleux
Framicourt
Rambures
Neslette
Bouttencourt
Bouillancourt-en-Séry
Monthières
Dargnies
Embreville
Beauchamps
Incheville
Ponts-et-Marais
Longroy
Millebosc
Guerville
Baromesnil
Monchy-s-Eu
Cuverville-s-Yères
Touffreville-s-Eu
St Remy
Assigny
Brunville
Canehan
Guilmécourt
St Martin-en-Campagne
Greny
Auquemesnil
Derchigny
Glicourt
Tourville-la-Chapelle
Intraville
Gouchaupré
Sauchay
Grèges
Ancourt
Bellengreville
Martin-Eglise
Vassonville
Penly
Flocques
Etalondes
Baie d'Authie
Canal de la Somme
Somme
Authie
Maye
Grde Dune
N 1
N 28
N 39
D 940
D 925
D 1015
D 938
D 32
17

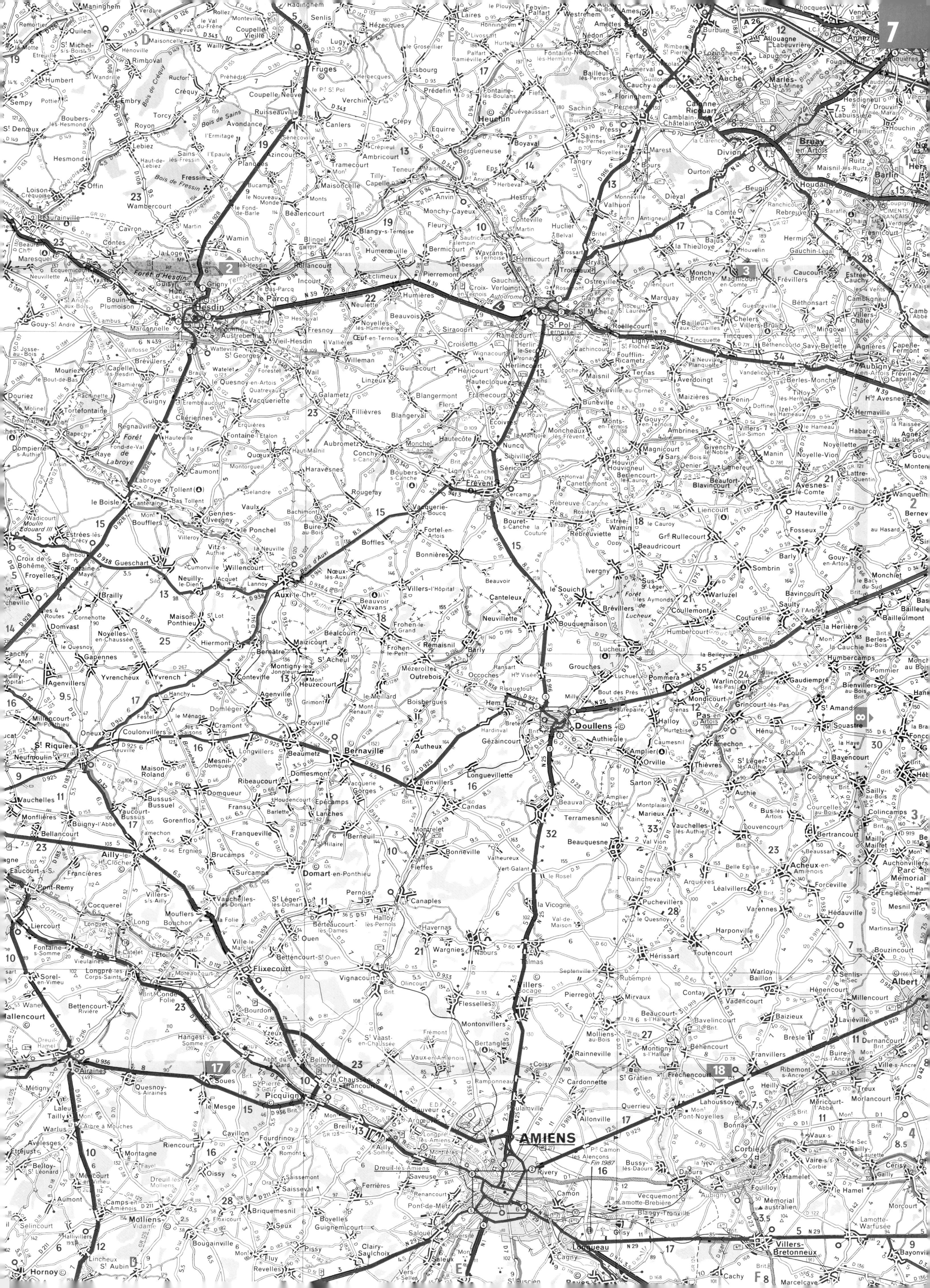
Fruges
Hesdin
Forêt d'Hesdin
Heuchin
Auchel
Bruay en Artois
Barlin
Houdain
St Pol
Frévent
Auxi-le-Château
Doullens
St Riquier
Ailly-le-Haut-Clocher
Pont-Remy
Airaines
Picquigny
Flixecourt
AMIENS
Albert
Corbie
Villers-Bretonneux
Longueau
Bernaville
Domart-en-Ponthieu
Beauquesne
Acheux-en-Amiénois
Pas-en-Artois
Avesnes-le-Comte
Aubigny-en-Artois
Molliens-Vidame
Hornoy
Beaurainville
Crécy
Somme
N 1
N 25
N 29
N 39
D 916
D 925
D 928
D 938
A 26

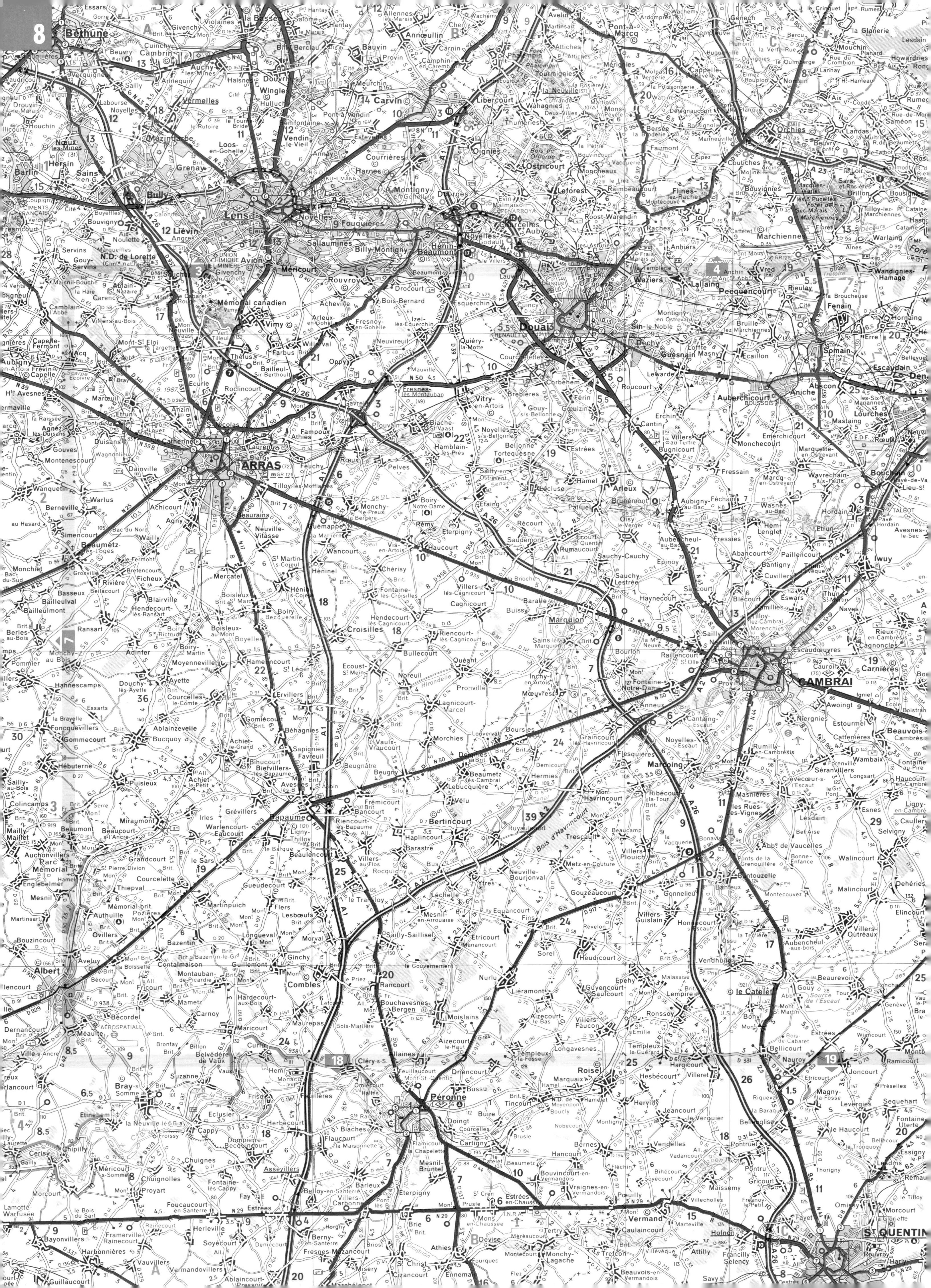
Béthune
Lens
Liévin
Carvin
Douai
Arras
Cambrai
Bapaume
Albert
Péronne
St Quentin
Orchies
Marchiennes
Hénin-Beaumont
Vimy
Mémorial canadien
N.D. de Lorette
Somain
Aniche
Bouchain
Arleux
Marquion
Croisilles
Beaumetz-lès-Loges
Avesnes-le-Comte
Bertincourt
Marcoing
Le Catelet
Roisel
Combles
Bray-sur-Somme
Vermand
Caulaincourt
Bois d'Havrincourt
Sensée
Somme
Escaut

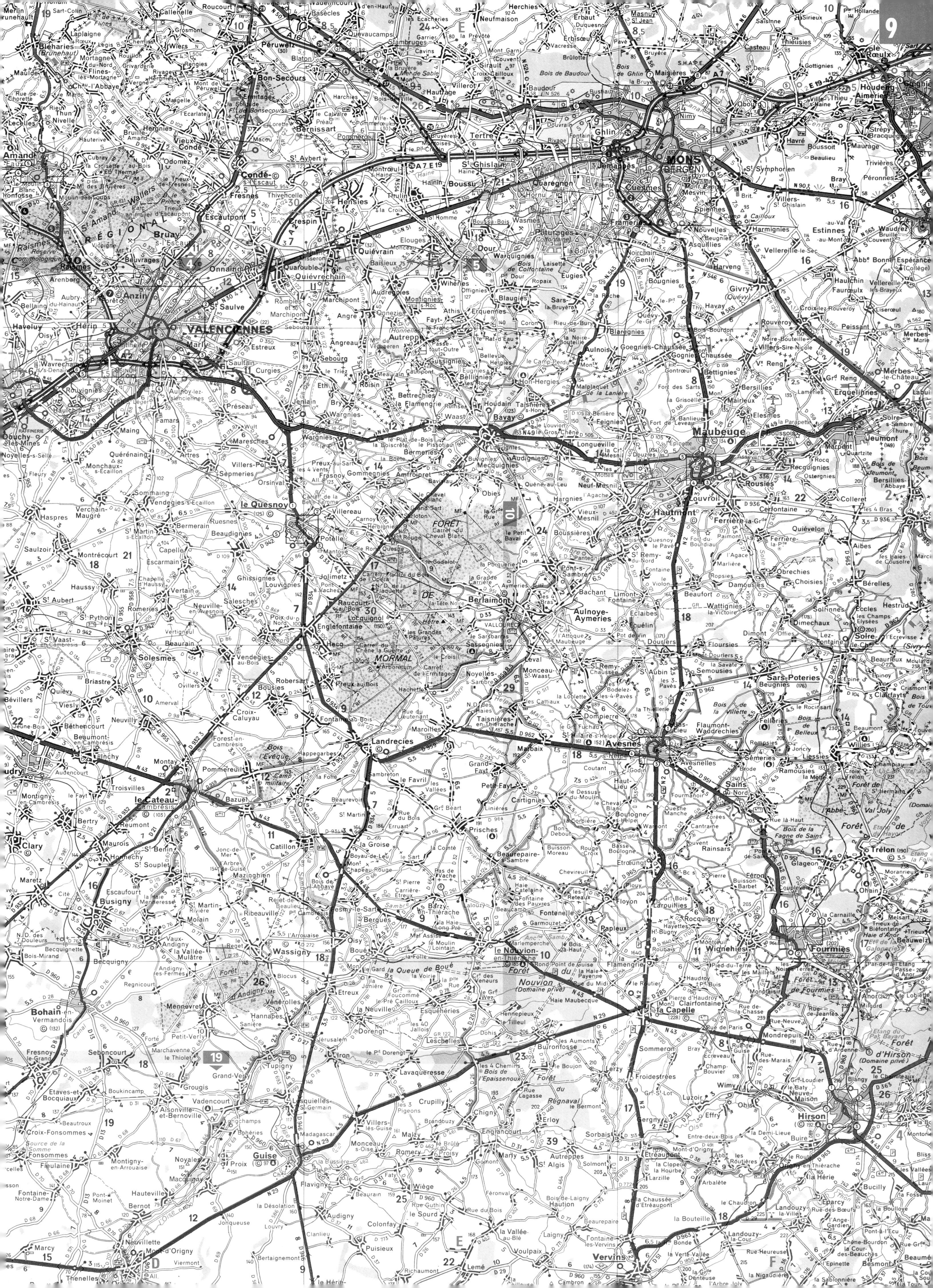
VALENCIENNES
MONS (BERGEN)
Maubeuge
Avesnes
Le Quesnoy
Bavay
Landrecies
Le Cateau-Cambrésis
Guise
Vervins
Hirson
Fourmies
Le Nouvion-en-Thiérache
La Capelle
Condé
Anzin
Péruwelz
Quiévrain
Dour
Solesmes
Caudry
Bohain-en-Vermandois
Wassigny
Sains-du-Nord
Trélon
Jeumont
Hautmont
Berlaimont
Aulnoye-Aymeries
Erquelinnes
Binche
FORÊT DE MORMAL
Forêt du Nouvion
Forêt d'Hirson
Forêt de Fourmies
Forêt d'Andigny
Bois l'Évêque
PARC NATUREL RÉGIONAL

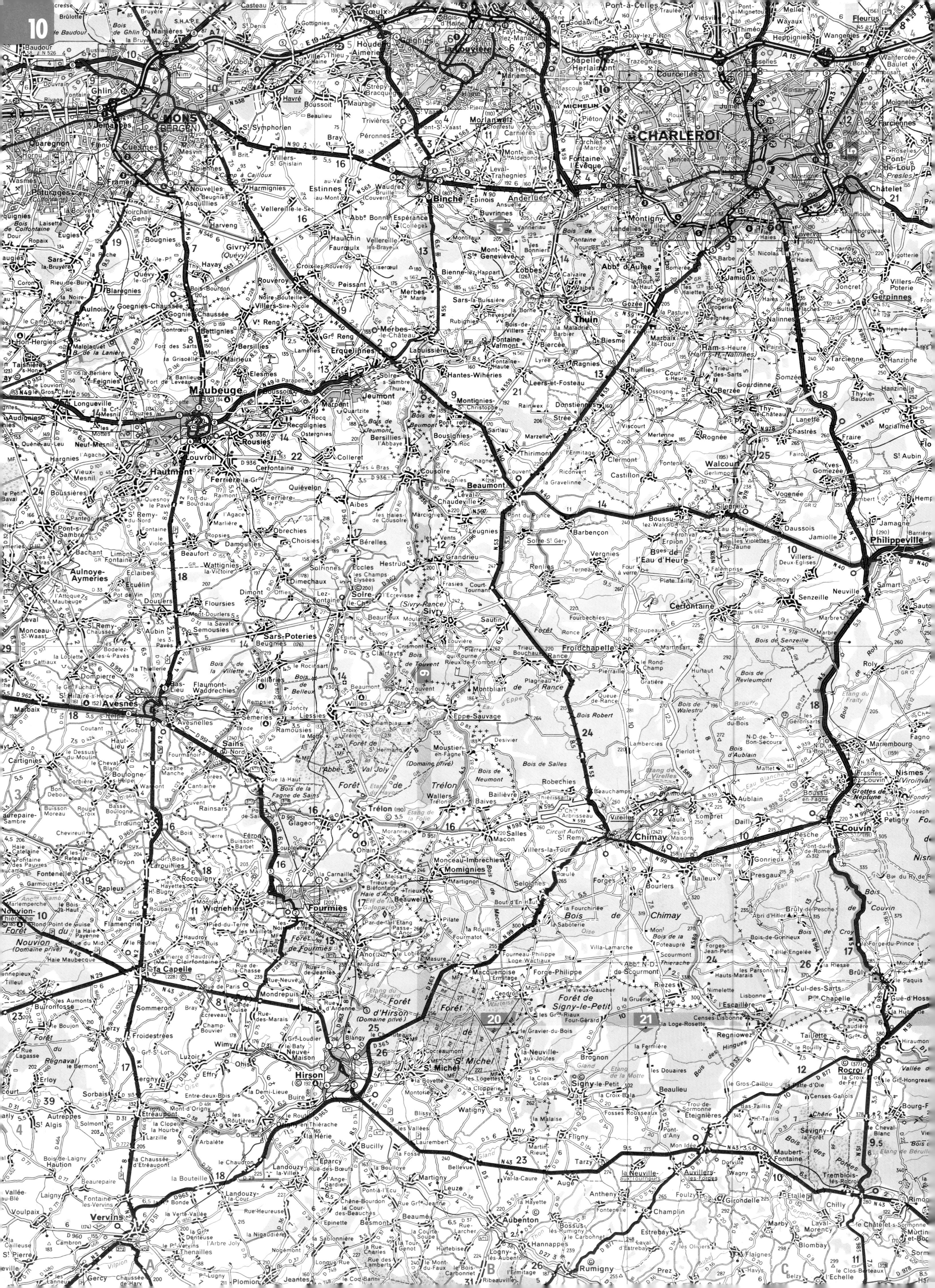
MONS (BERGEN)
CHARLEROI
la Louvière
Binche
Maubeuge
Hautmont
Beaumont
Philippeville
Avesnes
Chimay
Couvin
Fourmies
Hirson
la Capelle
Vervins
Rocroi
Aubenton
Walcourt
Thuin
Sivry
Trélon
Sains-du-Nord
Signy-le-Petit
Froidchapelle
Momignies
Jeumont
Erquelinnes
Fleurus
Châtelet
Anderlues
Morlanwelz
Courcelles
Gerpinnes
Cerfontaine
Mariembourg
Nismes
Forêt de Trélon
Forêt de Signy-le-Petit
Forêt de St Michel
Bois de Chimay
St Michel
Maubert-Fontaine
Auvillers-les-Forges
Rumigny
Etréaupont
Nouvion-en-Thiérache
Aulnoye-Aymeries
Pont-s-Sambre
Bavai

Namur
(Namen)
Andenne
Sclayn
Jambes
Erpent
Malonne
Floreffe
Wépion
Fosses-la-Ville
Profondeville
Annevoie-Rouillon
Lustin
Godinne
Yvoir
Anhée
Maredsous
Mettet
Dinant
Bouvignes
Anseremme
Hastière
Celles
Ciney
Assesse
Gesves
Ohey
Havelange
Hamois
Emptinne
Spontin
Leignon
Marche-en-Famenne
Rochefort
Han-s-Lesse
Grotte de Han
Wellin
Beauraing
Givet
Fumay
Haybes
Revin
Monthermé
Château-Regnault
Bogny-s-Meuse
Nouzonville
Bouillon
Paliseul
Libin
Tellin
Nassogne
Houyet
Gedinne
Bièvre
Vresse
Daverdisse
Florennes
Agimont
Doische
Vireux-Wallerand
Aubrives
Charnois
Bertrix
Herbeumont
Baillonville
Modave
Marchin
Maffe
Tellin
Wavreille
Ochamps
Forêt de Luchy
Forêt d'Hargnies-Laurier
Forêt de Château-Regnault
Bois de St Remacle
Lesse et Lomme
Meuse
21
22

A
B
C
1
2
3
4
Cap de la Hague
Raz Blanchard
Goury
Auderville
Baie d'Ecalgrain
Nez de Jobourg
Omonville-la-Rogue
Beaumont
Vauville
Anse de Vauville
Biville
Pointe de Nacqueville
Pointe de Querqueville
Grande Rade
CHERBOURG
Equeurdreville-Hainneville
Octeville
Tourlaville
Cap Lévy
Fermanville
Raz du Cap Lévy
Basses du Sen
Basses du Renier
St Pierre-Eglise
Raz de Barfleur
Pointe de Barfleur
Gatteville-le-Phare
Barfleur
Montfarville
Réville
Quettehou
St Vaast-la-Hougue
Ile de Tatihou
Valognes
Bricquebec
Les Pieux
Flamanville
Cap de Flamanville
Pointe du Rozel
Le Rozel
Quinéville
Montebourg
Ste Mère-Eglise
Carteret
Cap de Carteret
Barneville-Carteret
Portbail
St Sauveur-le-Vicomte
Carentan
La Haye-du-Puits
Lessay
Créances
Pirou
Périers
St Sauveur-Lendelin
Marigny
Guernsey (Saint Peter Port)
Jersey (Gorey)
Service saisonnier
30
31

D E F

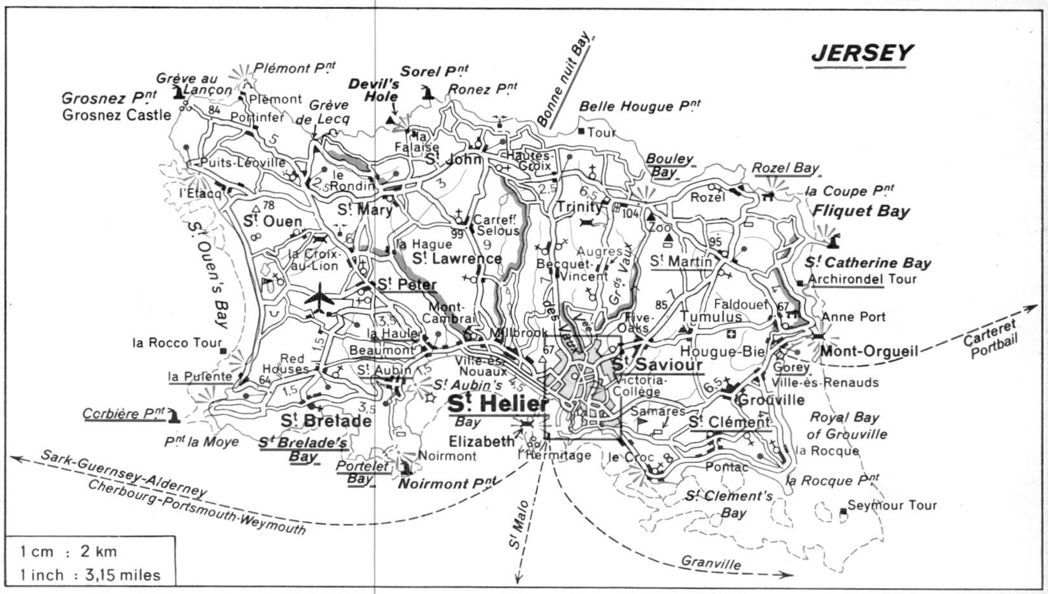
JERSEY
Grosnez Pnt
Grosnez Castle
Plémont Pnt
Devil's Hole
Sorel Pnt
Ronez Pnt
Bonne nuit Bay
Belle Hougue Pnt
Bouley Bay
Rozel Bay
la Coupe Pnt
Fliquet Bay
St Ouen
St Mary
St John
Trinity
St Lawrence
St Martin
St Catherine Bay
Archirondel Tour
St Peter
St Ouen's Bay
Anne Port
Mont-Orgueil
Gorey
St Saviour
St Helier
St Brelade
St Brelade's Bay
Corbière Pnt
la Rocco Tour
Elizabeth
Noirmont Pnt
Portelet Bay
St Clément
Grouville
Royal Bay of Grouville
la Rocque
la Rocque Pnt
St Clement's Bay
Seymour Tour
Sark-Guernsey-Alderney
Cherbourg-Portsmouth-Weymouth
St Malo
Granville
Carteret Portbail
1 cm : 2 km
1 inch : 3,15 miles

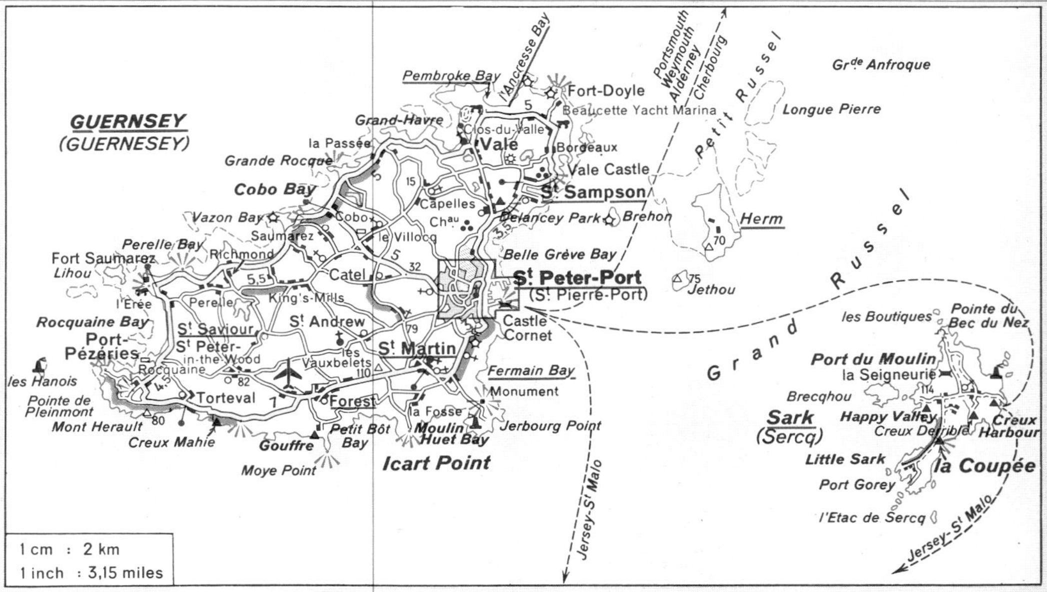
GUERNSEY
(GUERNESEY)
Pembroke Bay
l'Ancresse Bay
Fort-Doyle
Beaucette Yacht Marina
Grand-Havre
Vale
la Passée
Grande Rocque
Cobo Bay
Vale Castle
St Sampson
Vazon Bay
Delancey Park
Brehon
Herm
Fort Saumarez
Lihou
Perelle Bay
Richmond
Catel
Belle Grève Bay
St Peter-Port
(St Pierre-Port)
Jethou
Rocquaine Bay
Port-Pézéries
St Saviour
St Peter-in-the-Wood
St Andrew
St Martin
Castle Cornet
les Hanois
Pointe de Pleinmont
Mont Herault
Torteval
Forest
Fermain Bay
Monument
Creux Mahie
Gouffre
Petit Bôt Bay
Moulin Huet Bay
Jerbourg Point
Icart Point
Moye Point
Jersey-St Malo
Gr de Anfroque
Longue Pierre
Petit Russel
Grand Russel
Portsmouth Weymouth Alderney Cherbourg
les Boutiques
Pointe du Bec du Nez
Port du Moulin
la Seigneurie
Brecqhou
Sark
(Sercq)
Happy Valley
Creux Derrible
Creux Harbour
Little Sark
la Coupée
Port Gorey
l'Etac de Sercq
Jersey-St Malo
1 cm : 2 km
1 inch : 3,15 miles

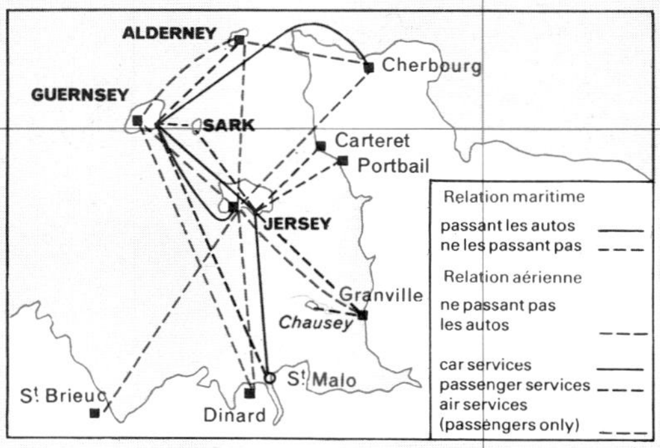
ALDERNEY
GUERNSEY
SARK
JERSEY
Cherbourg
Carteret
Portbail
Granville
Chausey
St Brieuc
Dinard
St Malo
Relation maritime
passant les autos
ne les passant pas
Relation aérienne
ne passant pas les autos
car services
passenger services
air services (passengers only)

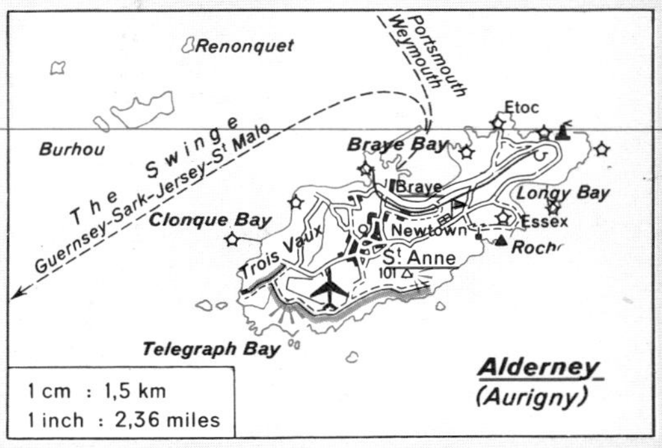
Renonquet
Portsmouth Weymouth
Etoc
Burhou
The Swinge
Guernsey-Sark-Jersey-St Malo
Braye Bay
Braye
Longy Bay
Clonque Bay
Newtown
Essex
Trois Vaux
St Anne
Telegraph Bay
1 cm : 1,5 km
1 inch : 2,36 miles
Alderney
(Aurigny)

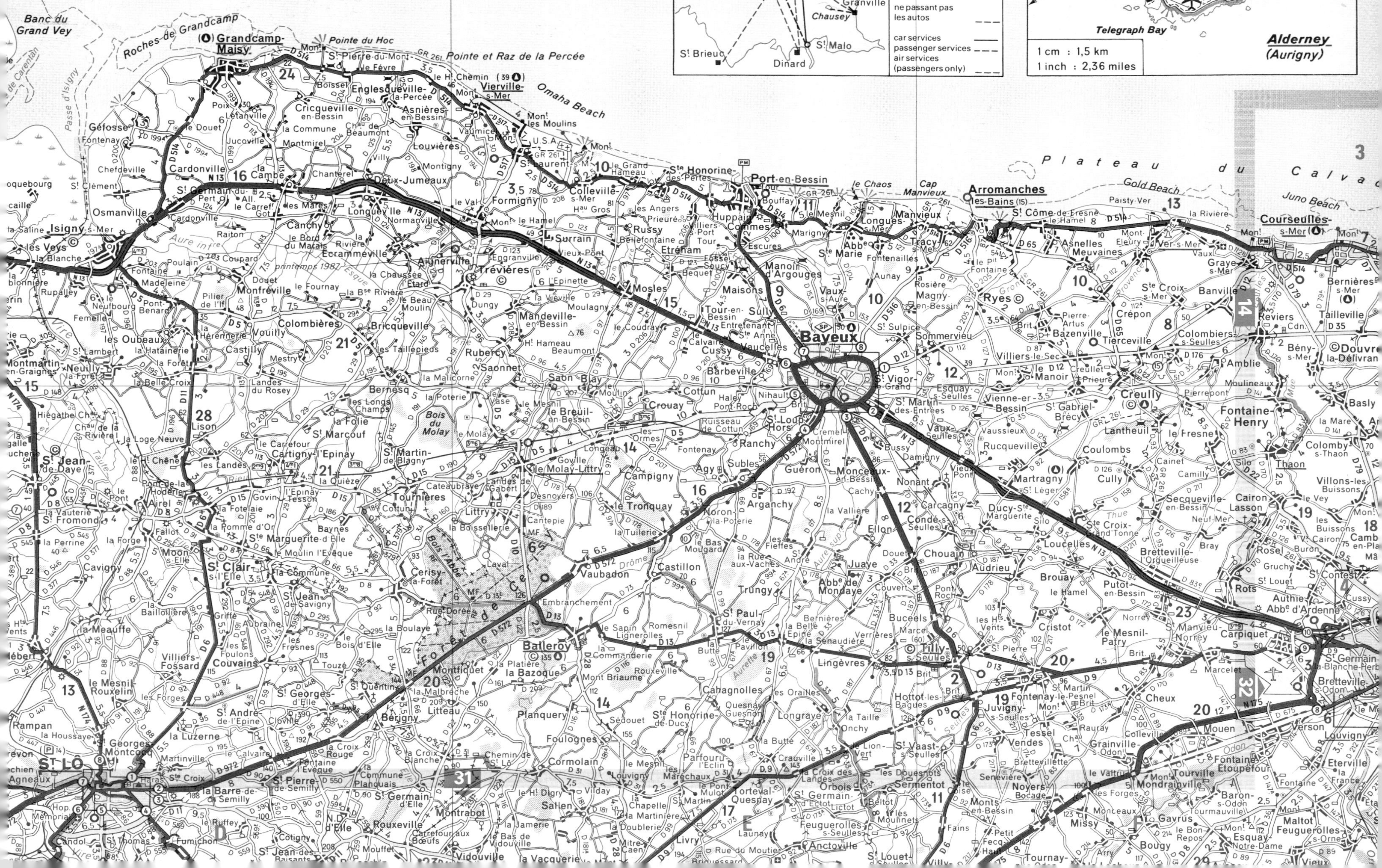
Iles St Marcouf
Banc du Grand Vey
Roches de Grandcamp
Grandcamp-Maisy
Pointe du Hoc
Pointe et Raz de la Percée
Omaha Beach
Vierville-s-Mer
St Pierre-du-Mont
Englesqueville-la-Percée
Cricqueville-en-Bessin
Asnières-en-Bessin
Louvières
Isigny-s-Mer
Osmanville
Cardonville
la Cambe
Deux-Jumeaux
St Laurent
Colleville-s-Mer
Ste Honorine-des-Pertes
Port-en-Bessin
Plateau du Calvados
Arromanches-les-Bains
Gold Beach
Juno Beach
Courseulles-s-Mer
Longues
Manvieux
Tracy
Ryes
Bayeux
Trévières
Formigny
Mosles
Etréham
Sully
Vaux
Vaucelles
St Vigor-le-Grand
Creully
Crépon
Banville
Reviers
Colombiers-s-Seulles
Fontaine-Henry
Thaon
Tilly-s-Seulles
Balleroy
Forêt de Cerisy
Cerisy-la-Forêt
St Clair-s-l'Elle
Couvains
Lison
Montfréville
Colombières
St Jean-de-Daye
Airel
Moon-s-Elle
St Lô
Torigni-s-Vire
Caumont
Juvigny
Villers-Bocage
Noyers-Bocage
Carpiquet
Bretteville
Rots
Audrieu
Brouay
Cristot
Fontenay-le-Pesnel
Castillon
Juaye
Le Molay-Littry
Littry
Vaubadon
Noron-la-Poterie
Subles
Agy
Ranchy
St Martin-de-Blagny
Tournières
Cartigny-l'Epinay
Bernesq
Rubercy
Saonnet
Mandeville-en-Bessin
Aignerville
Planquery
Montfiquet
Cormolain
Sallen
St Germain-d'Elle
Ste Marguerite-d'Elle
Berigny
St Pierre-de-Semilly
la Barre-de-Semilly
Villiers-Fossard
Rampan
St Georges-Montcocq
la Luzerne
Cavigny
Pont-Hébert
Lingèvres
Hottot-les-Bagues
Longraye
Livry
St Vaast-s-Seulles
Tessel
Vendes
Mondrainville
Tourville
Fontaine-Etoupefour
Eterville
Louvigny
Verson
Mouen
Cheux
Le Mesnil-Patry
Putot-en-Bessin
Secqueville-en-Bessin
Cairon
Lasson
Villons-les-Buissons
Douvres-la-Délivrande
Basly
Colomby-s-Thaon
Anguerny
Bény-s-Mer
Tailleville
Bernières-s-Mer
Amblie
Lantheuil
Coulombs
Martragny
Ducy-Ste Marguerite
Loucelles
Bretteville-l'Orgueilleuse
Sommervieu
Magny-en-Bessin
Villiers-le-Sec
Esquay-s-Seulles
Vienne-en-Bessin
Nonant
Condé-s-Seulles
Ellon
Chouain
Arganchy
Monceaux-en-Bessin
Cussy
Barbeville
Cottun
Crouay
Tour-en-Bessin
Maisons
Manoir d'Argouges
Blay
Campigny
le Tronquay
Trungy
St Paul-du-Vernay
Juaye-Mondaye
Buceels
Chemin
Pointe du Hoc
Grandcamp

A
B
C
1
2
3
Etretat
Falaise d'Aval
Falaise d'Amont
la Manneporte
Aiguille de Belval
Valleuse du Curé
Cap d'Antifer
Port pétrolier du
Havre-Antifer
St Jouin
Heuqueville
Cauville
Octeville
Montivilliers
Harfleur
Gonfreville
Cap de la Hève
Ste Adresse
Southampton
Rosslare
Portsmouth
Cork
Service saisonnier
LE HAVRE
Honfleur
Côte de Grâce
Villerville
Trouville
DEAUVILLE
Bénerville-s-Mer
Blonville-s-Mer
Villers-s-Mer
Falaise des Vaches Noires
Houlgate
Cabourg
Dives-s-Mer
Merville-Franceville-Plage
Ouistreham
Riva-Bella
Sword Beach
Juno Beach
Rade de Caen
Calvados
Courseulles-s-Mer
St Aubin-s-Mer
Langrune-s-Mer
Luc-s-Mer
Lion-s-Mer
Douvres-la-Délivrande
Pont-l'Evêque
Portsmouth
13
32
33

D
E
F
Fécamp
Yport
St Valery-en-Caux
Veules-les-Roses
Veulettes-s-Mer
Varengeville
Offranville
Cany-Barville
Valmont
Goderville
Fauville-en-Caux
Doudeville
Yerville
Bacqueville-en-Caux
Yvetot
Bolbec
Lillebonne
Caudebec-en-Caux
St Wandrille
Barentin
Pavilly
Duclair
Jumièges
Tancarville
Pont de Tancarville
Quillebeuf
Pont-Audemer
Beuzeville
Bourg-Achard
Routot
Montfort-s-Risle
Bourgtheroulde-Inf.
Elbeuf
Cormeilles
Forêt de Brotonne
Parc Régional de Brotonne
Marais Vernier
Seine

DIEPPE
ROUEN
Neufchâtel-en-Bray
Forges-les-Eaux
Londinières
Envermeu
Arques
Offranville
Varengeville
Tôtes
Bellencombre
St Saëns
Buchy
Blangy
Aumale
Clères
Montville
Darnétal
Boos
Lyons-la-Forêt
Fleury-s-Andelle
Étrépagny
Elbeuf
Pont-de-l'Arche
Pavilly
Maromme
Sotteville
Bacqueville-en-Caux
Longueville
Auffay
Forêt d'Eawy
Forêt de Lyons
Forêt d'Eu
Forêt d'Arques
Forêt du Hellet
Forêt de Bray
Argueil
Gournay
Sommery
Bosc-le-Hard
Isneauville
Quincampoix
Belleville-s-Mer
Berneval-le-Gd
Grèges
Martin-Église
Bailly-en-Rivière
Mesnières-en-Bray
Bully
Aubermesnil
Blainville-Crevon
Ry
Elbeuf-s-Andelle
Bois-Guillaume
Mont-St Aignan
Déville
Le Houlme
Malaunay
Grand Quevilly
Petit Quevilly
Canteleu
St Étienne du Rouvray
Oissel
Grand Couronne
Orival
Caudebec
St Aubin
Léry
Poses
Amfreville-s-les-Monts
Côte des 2 Amants
Écouis
Charleval
Fleury-la-Forêt
Lorleau
Rosay
Abbaye de Mortemer
Abbaye de Fontaine-Guérard
Pont-St-Pierre
Romilly
Alizay
Vascoeuil
Perriers
Saumont
Ménerval
Haute Forêt d'Eu
Basse Forêt d'Eu
Forêt de Bacqueville
Forêt de Longboel
Forêt de Roumare
Forêt Verte
Forêt de la Londe
Phare d'Ailly
Pourville
Puys
N. Dame Bon-Secours
Hautot-s-Mer
Manoir d'Ango

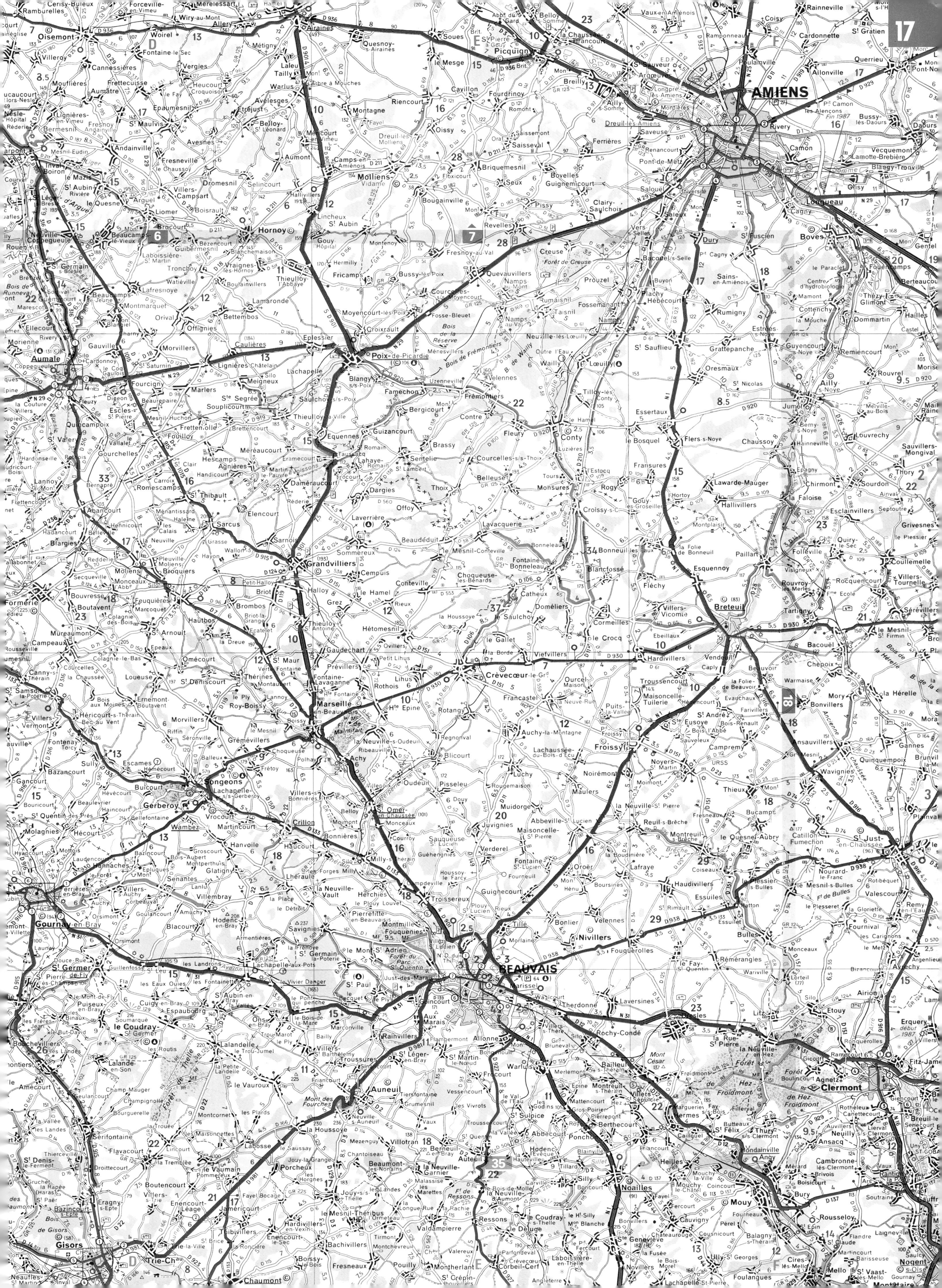

17
AMIENS
Oisemont
Airaines
Picquigny
Poix-de-Picardie
Aumale
Hornoy
Conty
Grandvilliers
Breteuil
Crèvecœur-le-Gd
Marseille-en-Beauvaisis
Songeons
Gerberoy
Froissy
St Just-en-Chaussée
Formerie
Gournay-en-Bray
BEAUVAIS
Auneuil
Noailles
Mouy
Clermont
Gisors
Chaumont
Nogent
Le Coudray-St Germer
Milly-s-Thérain
Boves

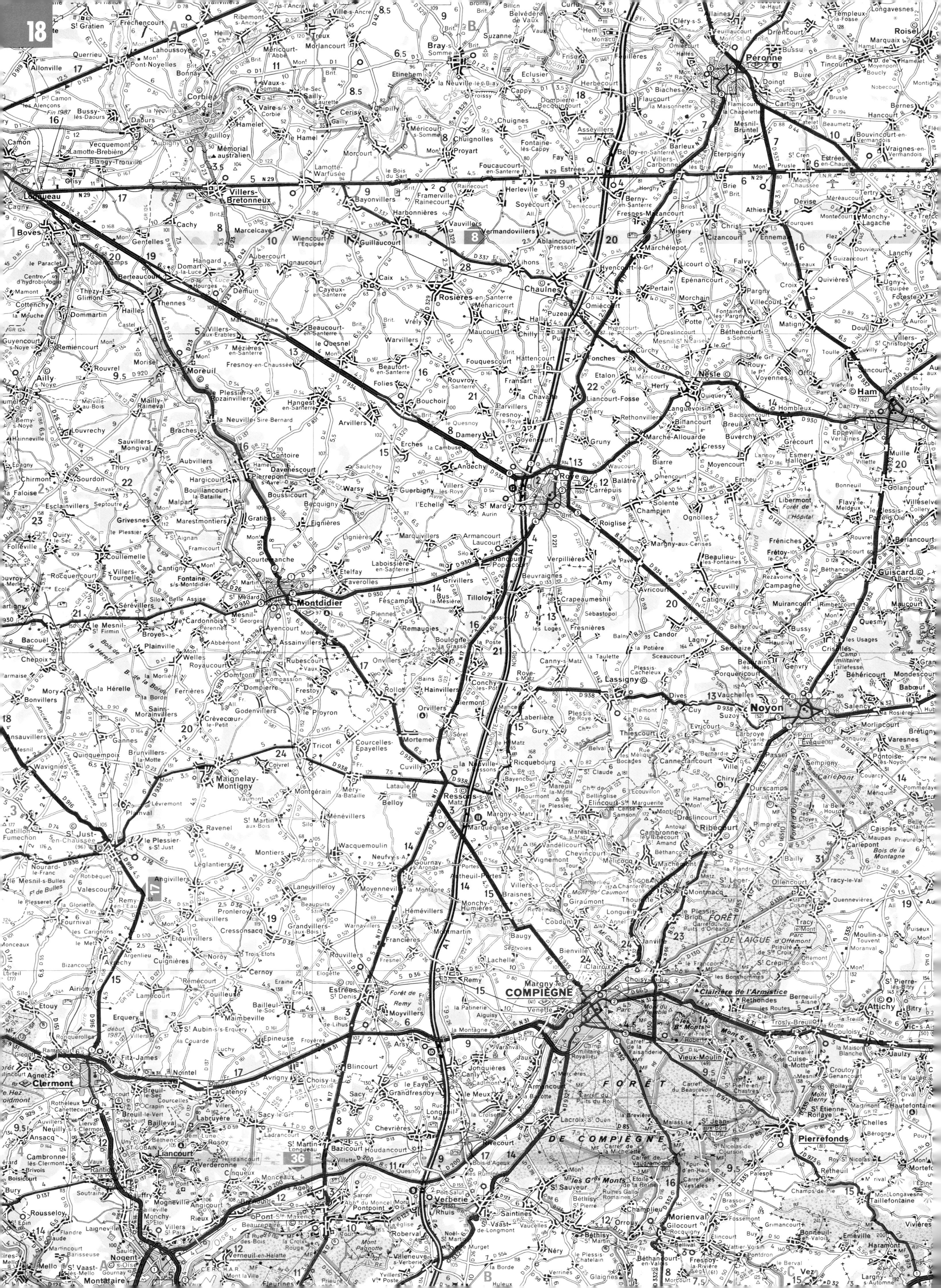
Péronne
Bray-s-Somme
Corbie
Villers-Bretonneux
Longueau
Boves
Moreuil
Ailly-s-Noye
Rosières-en-Santerre
Chaulnes
Nesle
Ham
Roye
Montdidier
Lassigny
Noyon
Guiscard
Maignelay-Montigny
St Just-en-Chaussée
Ressons-s-Matz
Estrées-St Denis
COMPIÈGNE
Clermont
Liancourt
Pont-Ste Maxence
Verberie
Pierrefonds
Attichy
Nogent-s-Oise
Montataire
FORÊT DE COMPIÈGNE
FORÊT DE LAIGUE
Clairière de l'Armistice
Mémorial australien
Vieux-Moulin
Ribecourt
Crèvecœur-le-Petit
Tricot
Cuvilly
Conchy-les-Pots
Breteuil
Fitz-James
Bailleul-le-Soc
Sacy-le-Gd
Margny-les-Compiègne
Choisy-au-Bac
Thourotte
Morienval
Béthisy-St Pierre
Saintines
Rhuis
Senlis
Vic-s-Aisne
Bussy
Croix
Hombleux
Athies
Estrées-en-Chaussée
Foucaucourt-en-Santerre
Albert

St QUENTIN
Gauchy
Guise
Ribemont
Moy
la Fère
Tergnier
Chauny
St Gobain
LAON
Crécy-s-Serre
Marle
Sains
Coucy
Anizy-le-Chau
Vailly-s-Aisne
SOISSONS
Braine
Fismes
Craonne
Longpont
Sissonne
St Quentin Sud-Laon: ouverture prévue été 1987
Forêt de St Gobain
Forêt de Samoussy
Basse Forêt de Coucy
Forêt de Pinon
Camp militaire
Mont Fendu
Chemin des Dames
A 26
N 2
N 29
N 31
N 32
N 44

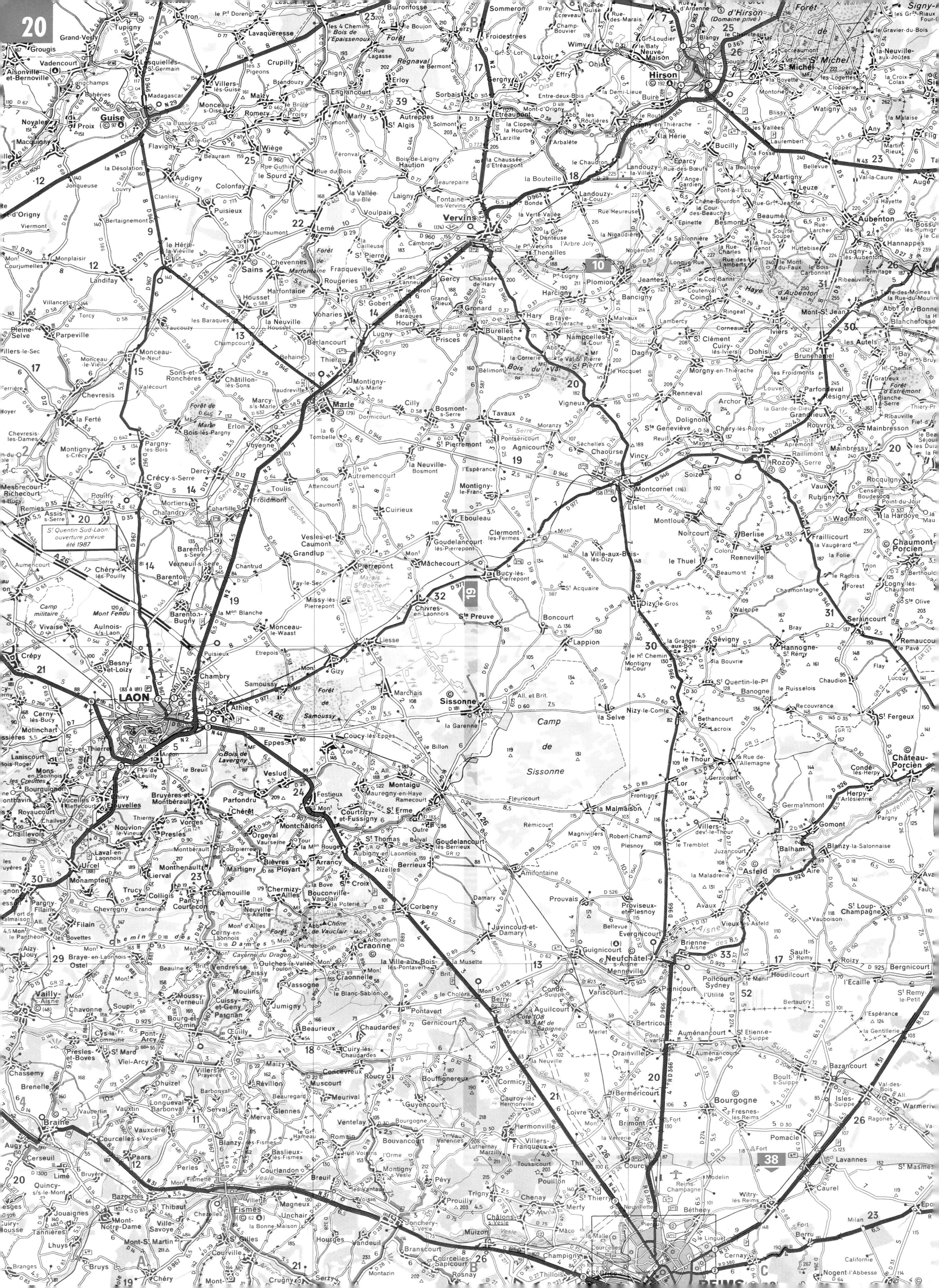
Guise
Hirson
Vervins
Marle
Laon
Sissonne
Camp de Sissonne
Crécy-s-Serre
Montcornet
Rozoy-s-Serre
Aubenton
Chaumont-Porcien
Château-Porcien
Neufchâtel-s-Aisne
Asfeld
Craonne
Corbeny
Berry-au-Bac
Fismes
Braine
Vailly-s-Aisne
Bazancourt
Reims
Forêt de Samoussy
Forêt de Marfontaine
Forêt du Regnaval
Forêt de St Michel
St Michel
Sains
Liesse
Chivres-en-Laonnois
St Quentin Sud-Laon: ouverture prévue été 1987
Camp militaire
Mont Fendu

Revin
Rocroi
Monthermé
Château-Regnault
Bogny-s-Meuse
Nouzonville
CHARLEVILLE-MÉZIÈRES
Villers-Semeuse
Sedan
Bazeilles
Douzy
Flize
Donchery
Signy-l'Abbaye
Novion-Porcien
Poix-Terron
Omont
Raucourt-et-Flaba
Rethel
Attigny
Tourteron
le Chesne
Vouziers
Buzancy
Grandpré
Juniville
Machault
Monthois
Bétheniville
Renwez
Rimogne
Maubert-Fontaine
Auvillers-les-Forges
Liart
Chémery
Stonne
Forêt de Signy
Forêt d'Élan
Forêt du Mont Dieu
Forêt de la Croix-aux-Bois
Forêt de Sedan
Bois de Vendresse
Aisne
Meuse
Sommepy

Libramont-Chevigny
Ochamps
Paliseul
Naomé
Carlsbourg
Nollevaux
Bertrix
Herbeumont
Forêt d'Herbeumont
Bouillon
Corbion
Poupehan
Rochehaut
Frahan
Alle
Sensenruth
Noirefontaine
les Hayons
Cugnon
Auby
Forêt de Luchy
Recogne
St Pierre
Neufchâteau
Léglise
Mellier
Forêt de Neufchâteau
Forêt de Rulles
Habay-la-Vieille
Rulles
Straimont
Suxy
Forêt de Chiny
Chiny
Ste Cécile
Muno
Fontenoille
Florenville
Chassepierre
Jamoigne
Tintigny
Etalle
St Vincent
Bellefontaine
Buzenol
St Léger
Meix-devt Virton
Virton
Ethe
Latour
Rouvroy
Harnoncourt
Torgny
Gérouville
Abbe d'Orval
Forêt d'Orval
Villers-devt-Orval
Margny
Williers
Tremblois-lès-Carignan
Carignan
Blagny
Linay
Pure
Messincourt
Douzy
Bazeilles
Sedan
Givonne
Floing
Illy
Fleigneux
Forêt de Sedan
Réserve de Chasse du Dos-de-Loup
Francheval
Pouru-St Remy
Mouzon
Raucourt-et-Flaba
Villers-devt-Mouzon
Autrecourt
Mairy
Amblimont
Euilly
Vaux-lès-Mouzon
Moulins-St Hubert
Malandry
la Ferté-s-Chiers
Margut
Signy-Montlibert
Sapogne-s-Marche
Avioth
Thonne-le-Thil
Thonnelle
Montmédy
Velosnes
Bazeilles-s-Othain
Marville
Iré-le-Sec
Juvigny-s-Loison
Stenay
Inor
Martincourt-s-Meuse
Beaumont-en-Argonne
Létanne
Yoncq
Stonne
la Besace
Forêt de Jaunay
Forêt de Dieulet
Beaufort-en-Argonne
Mouzay
Forêt de Wœvre
Louppy-s-Loison
Remoiville
Jametz
Delut
Dombras
Damvillers
Ecurey-en-Verdunois
Brandeville
Murvaux
Dun-s-Meuse
Doulcon
Liny-devt-Dun
Sivry-s-Meuse
Consenvoye
Dannevoux
Brieulles-s-Meuse
Cunel
Romagne-s-Montfaucon
Montfaucon
Nantillois
Cierges-s-Montfaucon
Gesnes-en-Argonne
Sommerance
Fléville
Cornay
Apremont
Buzancy
Nouart
Beauclair
Halles-s-les-Côtes
Sassey-s-Meuse
Bayonville
Rémonville
Landres
Bantheville
St Juvin
Grandpré
Champigneulle
Varennes-en-Argonne
Montblainville
Véry
Cheppy
Béthincourt
Malancourt
Forêt de Montfaucon
Forges-s-Meuse
Regnéville-s-Meuse
Samogneux
Brabant-s-Meuse
Champneuville
Louvemont
Forêt de Verdun
Bois des Caures
Ville-devt-Chaumont
Azannes-et-Soumazannes
Gremilly
Ornes
Mogeville
Maucourt-s-Orne
Spincourt
Billy-s/s-Mangiennes
Mangiennes
Pillon
Longuyon
Arrancy-s-Crusne
Sorbey
Rouvrois-s-Othain
Duzey
St Laurent-s-Othain
Villers-le-Rond
Colmey
Charency
Allondrelle
Tellancourt
Virton
Mussy-la-Ville
Habay-la-Neuve
Vaux-s-Sure
Fauvillers
Witry
Hollange
Chaumont

LUXEMBOURG
LUXEMBURGISCHER
NATURPARK
SUISSE
LUXEMBOURGEOISE
Diekirch
Ettelbruck
Echternach
Mersch
Arlon
(Aarlen)
Longwy
Esch-s-A.
Differdange
Pétange
Bascharage
Dudelange
Bettembourg
Mondorf-les-Bains
Remich
Grevenmacher
Wormeldange
Junglinster
Larochette
Redange
Steinfort
Capellen
Hesperange
Rumelange
Thionville
Hayange
Florange
Uckange
Richemont
Hagondange
Rombas
Moyeuvre
Briey
Audun-le-Tiche
Villerupt
Cattenom
Sierck-les-Bains
Perl
Metzervisse
Algrange
Fontoy
Knutange
Maizières-lès-Metz
Homécourt
Auboué
Amnéville
Rosselange
Clouange
Mont-St Martin
Herserange
Athus
Aubange
Messancy
Attert
Beckerich
Saeul
Useldange
Vichten
Bissen
Nommern
Heffingen
Consdorf
Berdorf
Beaufort
Waldbillig
Fischbach
Lintgen
Lorentzweiler
Steinsel
Walferdange
Kopstal
Niederanven
Sandweiler
Schuttrange
Contern
Strassen
Mamer
Garnich
Dippach
Leudelange
Roeser
Frisange
Schifflange
Kayl
Ottange
Entrange
Hettange-Grande
Yutz
Kédange-s-Canner
Ebersviller
Luttange
Chailly-lès-Ennery
Ennery
Vigy
Buding
Distroff
Kuntzig
Guénange
Bertrange
Tucquegnieux
Landres
Piennes
Mercy-le-Bas
Audun-le-Roman
Crusnes
Errouville
Aumetz
Tressange
Havange
Angevillers
Fillières
Bazailles
Ville-au-Montois
Serrouville
Joudreville
Boulígny
Dommary
Pierrepont
Longuyon
Baslieux
Laix
Cons-la-Grandville
Tiercelet
Hussigny-Godbrange
Rehon
Mexy
Saulnes
Halanzy
Musson
Châtillon
Rachecourt
Habergy
Toernich
Sesselich
Waltzing
Heinsch
Bonnert
Tontelange
Nothomb
Perlé
Tintange
Boulaide
Bigonville
Rambrouch
Folschette
Grosbous
Mertzig
Feulen
Wahl
Heiderscheid
Esch-sur-Sûre
Erpeldange
Schieren
Colmar-Berg
Reisdorf
Wallendorf
Bollendorf
Bettendorf
Medernach
Ermsdorf
Müllerthal
Rodenbourg
Betzdorf
Flaxweiler
Machtum
Manternach
Biwer
Mensdorf
Oberdonven
Lenningen
Greiveldange
Stadtbredimus
Dalheim
Bous
Waldbredimus
Burmerange
Wellenstein
Remerschen
Schengen
Oberperl
Apach
Kirsch-lès-Sierck
Montenach
Kemplich
Klang
Dalstein
Monneren
Veckring
Inglange
Valmestroff
Elzange
Manom
Terville
Guentrange
Nilvange
Ranguevaux
Moyeuvre-Petite
Vitry-s-Orne
Malancourt
Pierrevillers
Marange-Silvange
Montois-la-Mgne
Fleury
Flévy
Trémery
Malroy
Bettelainville
Burtoncourt
Aboncourt
Rurange-lès-Thionville
Metzeresche
Koenigsmacker
Kerling-lès-Sierck
Oudrenne
Hunting
Malling
Rettel
Contz-les-Bains
Beyren-lès-Sierck
Puttelange-lès-Thionville
Rodemack
Roussy-le-Village
Zoufftgen
Volmerange-les-Mines
Kanfen
Escherange
Rochonvillers
Boulange
Bassompierre
Beuvillers
Lommerange
Trieux
Avril
Mance
Anoux
Lantéfontaine
Lubey
Gondrecourt
Affléville
Norroy-le-Sec
Mairy-Mainville
Mont-Bonvillers
Murville
Anderny
Preutin
Malavillers
Sancy
Bazonville
Mercy-le-Haut
Joppécourt
Fléville
Ozerailles
Les Baroches
Génaville
Valleroy
Moutiers
Jœuf
Mouaville
Rouvres-en-Woëvre
Xivry-Circourt
Ollières
Domprix
Avillers
Haucourt-la-Rigole
Domremy-la-Canne
Baroncourt
Eton
Beuveille
Doncourt-lès-Longuyon
Villers-la-Montagne
Haucourt-Moulaine
Morfontaine
Bréhain-la-Ville
Ville-Houdlémont
Cutry
Ugny
Chenières
Boismont
Mainbottel
St Supplet
40
41
24

LUXEMBOURG
Hespérange
Bettembourg
Esch-s-A.
Dudelange
Audun-le-Tiche
Rumelange
Mondorf-les-Bains
Remich
Perl
Sierck-les-Bains
Saarburg
Mettlach
Cattenom
Thionville
Hayange
Florange
Uckange
Metzervisse
Bouzonville
Briey
Moyeuvre Grande
Rosselange
Hagondange
Maizières-lès-Metz
Homécourt
Boulay-Moselle
Woippy
METZ
Montigny
Ars-s-M.
Gorze
Chambley
Pont-à-Mousson
Thiaucourt-Regniéville
Rémilly
Pange
Vigy
Courcelles-Chaussy
Faulquemont
Créhange
Dieuze
Delme
Solgne
Verny
Nomeny
Louvigny
A31
E25
A4
N3
N43
A8
23
40
41

SAARBRÜCKEN
SAARLOUIS
HOMBURG
Sarreguemines
St. Wendel
Neunkirchen
St. Ingbert
Völklingen
Dillingen
Merzig
Lebach
Tholey
Ottweiler
Sulzbach
Dudweiler
Püttlingen
Heusweiler
Quierschied
Riegelsberg
Wadgassen
Überherrn
Forbach
Stiring-Wendel
Grossrosseln
Pte Rosselle
Freyming-Merlebach
Carling
L'Hôpital
St Avold
Blieskastel
Kirkel
Bexbach
Kusel
Wadern
Weiskirchen
Schmelz
Beckingen
Wallerfangen
Kleinblittersdorf
Grosbliederstroff
Sarralbe
Sarre-Union
Puttelange-aux-Lacs
Rohrbach-lès-Bitche
Grostenquin
Morhange
Gersheim
Mandelbachtal
Waldmohr
Sankt Ingbert
SCHWARZWALD
Forêt du Warndt
A 1
A 6
A 8
A 4
A 620
A 62

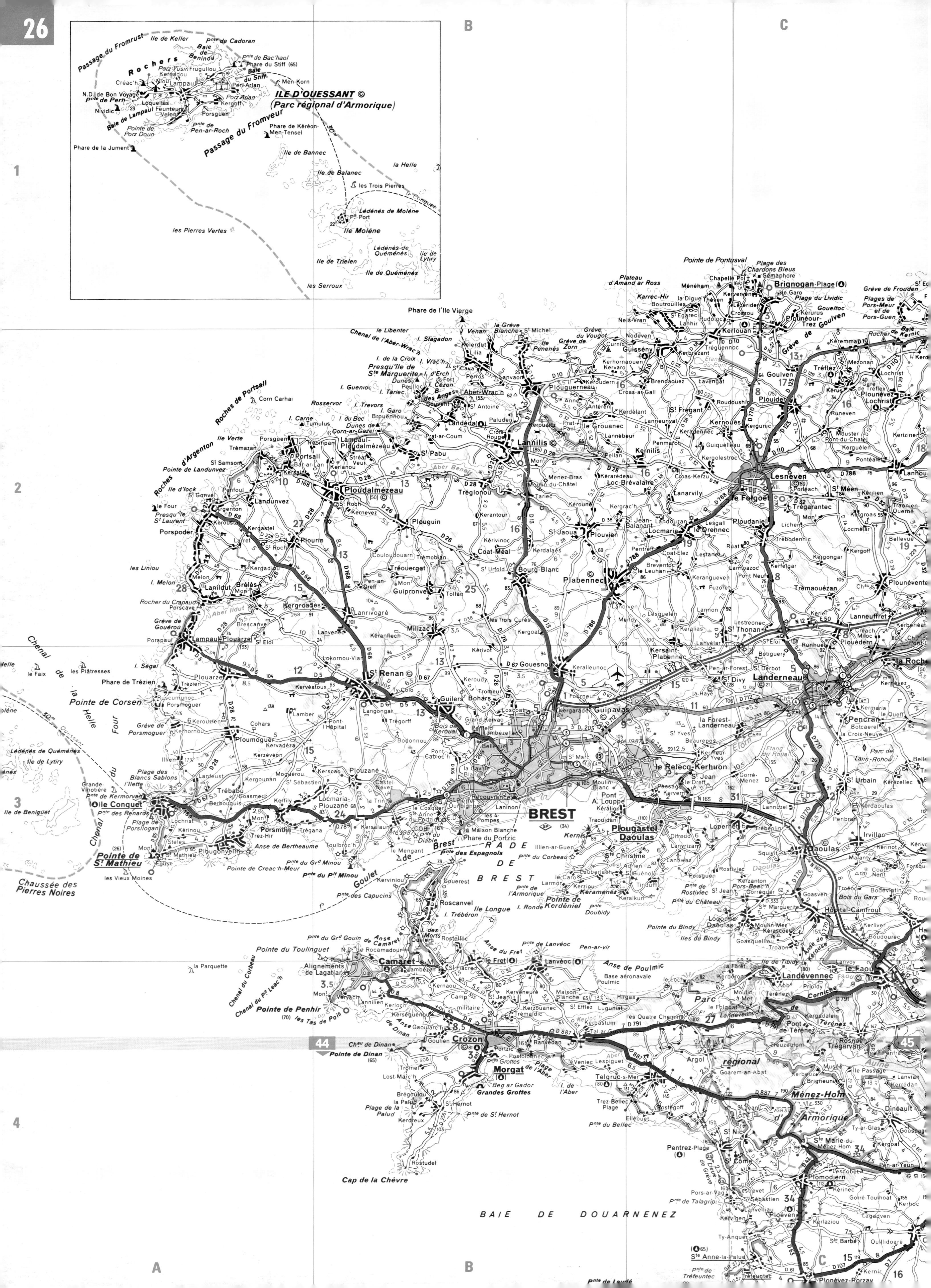
ILE D'OUESSANT ©
(Parc régional d'Armorique)
Passage du Fromrust
Passage du Fromveur
Ile de Keller
Baie de Beninou
Rochers
Lampaul
Baie de Lampaul
Pointe de Porz Doun
Phare de la Jument
Phare de Kéréon Men-Tensel
Ile de Bannec
Ile de Balanec
les Trois Pierres
Ledénès de Molène
Ile Molène
Ile de Trielen
Ile de Quéménès
les Serroux
les Pierres Vertes
la Helle
Phare de l'Ile Vierge
Chenal de l'Aber-Wrac'h
Presqu'île de Ste Marguerite
l'Aber-Wrac'h
Landéda
Lannilis ©
Plouguerneau
Guissény
Kerlouan
Brignogan-Plage
Pointe de Pontusval
Plounéour-Trez
Goulven
Plouider
Lesneven
le Folgoet
Roches de Portsall
Portsall
Ploudalmézeau
Roches d'Argenton
Argenton
Landunvez
Porspoder
Ploudalmézeau
Plourin
Plouguin
Tréglonou
Coat-Méal
Bourg-Blanc
Plabennec
Plouvien
Ploudaniel
Lanildut
Brélès
Lanrivoaré
Milizac
Guipronvel
Lampaul-Plouarzel
Plouarzel
St Renan ©
Gouesnou
Kersaint-Plabennec
Landerneau
Guipavas
Guilers
Bohars
Ploumoguer
Plouzané
Locmaria-Plouzané
le Conquet
Plougonvelin
Pointe de St Mathieu
Ile de Beniguet
Chenal du Four
Chenal de la Helle
Pointe de Corsen
Chaussée des Pierres Noires
BREST
le Relecq-Kerhuon
Plougastel Daoulas
Daoulas
Dirinon
Hôpital-Camfrout
RADE DE BREST
Goulet de Brest
Pte des Espagnols
Roscanvel
Ile Longue
Pointe de Kerdéniel
Anse de Camaret
Camaret
Lanvéoc
Anse de Poulmic
Landévennec
le Faou
Pointe du Toulinguet
Pointe de Penhir
Alignements de Lagatjar
Crozon
Morgat
Pointe de Dinan
Cap de la Chèvre
Telgruc-s-Mer
Argol
Parc régional d'Armorique
Ménez-Hom
Ste Marie-du-Ménez-Hom
Plomodiern
Ploéven
Ste Anne-la-Palud
Plonévez-Porzay
BAIE DE DOUARNENEZ
A
B
C
1
2
3
4
44
45

D
E
F
Ile Plate
Ile de Malban
Ile de Bono
Ile aux Moines
les Sept Iles
(Réserve naturelle)
Trégastel-Plage
Ploumanac'h
Ile Grande
Trégastel
Pleumeur Bodou
Trébeurden
Lannion
Pointe de Séhar
Baie de Lannion
Locquirec
St Michel-en-Grève
Lieue de Grève
Plestin-les-Grèves
Lanmeur
Plouégat-Guérand
Plouaret
Le Vieux-Marché
Plounérin
Plounévez-Moëdec
Loguivy-Plougras
Plougras
Guerlesquin
Botsorhel
Plougonven
Plouigneau
Morlaix
Baie de Morlaix
Pointe de Primel
Primel-Trégastel
Plougasnou
St Jean-du-Doigt
Carantec
Tumulus de Barnenez
Taulé
Henvic
Locquénolé
Ile de Batz
Roscoff
St Pol-de-Léon
Ile de Sieck
Santec
Kérouzéré
Cléder
Plouescat
Sibiril
Plougoulm
Plouénan
Mespaul
Plouzévédé
Berven
Kerjean
Plouvorn
Lambader
Plougourvest
Landivisiau
Lampaul-Guimiliau
Guimiliau
St Thégonnec
Pleyber-Christ
Plourin-lès-Morlaix
Ploudiry
Sizun
Commana
Roc Trévezel
Plounéour-Ménez
Le Cloître-St-Thégonnec
Scrignac
Berrien
Huelgoat
Locmaria-Berrien
Poullaouen
Brennilis
La Feuillée
St Herbot
Loqueffret
Lannédern
Brasparts
Lopérec
Pont-de-Buis-lès-Quimerch
St Ségal
Port-Launay
Pleyben
Lothey
Gouézec
Châteauneuf-du-Faou
Plonévez-du-Faou
Landeleau
Collorec
Plouyé
Carhaix-Plouguer
Cléden-Poher
Plounévézel
Kergloff
Callac
Maël-Carhaix
Plévin
Paule
Glomel
Motreff
Spézet
St Goazec
Roc de Toullaëron
Forêt de Beffou
Forêt du Cranou
Forêt de Fréau
Montagne St Michel
Signal de Toussaines
PARC NATUREL RÉGIONAL D'ARMORIQUE
N12-E50
N164
D786
D785
D764
D769
Plymouth
Cork

A
B
C
Perros-Guirec
Ploumanach
Trégastel
Trévou-Tréguignec
Port-Blanc
Penvénan
Tréguier
Lézardrieux
Paimpol
Pointe de l'Arcouest
Ile de Bréhat
Pleubian
Lannion
La Roche-Derrien
Pontrieux
Plouha
St Quay-Portrieux
Binic
Etables-s-Mer
Bégard
Pédernec
Guingamp
Belle-Isle-en-Terre
Plouaret
Lanvollon
Châtelaudren
Plouagat
Pordic
St Brieuc
Bourbriac
Callac
Quintin
Corlay
Uzel
Plœuc-s-Lié
Rostrenen
Gouarec
Mûr-de-Bretagne
Plouguenast
Maël-Carhaix
Forêt de Lorge
Gorges du Corong
Gorges de Toul Goulic
Lac de Guerlédan

D
E
F
1
2
3
4
Petit Léjon
Cap Fréhel
Fort la Latte
Rohinet
Rohein
Cap d'Erquy
DE SAINT-BRIEUC
Plateau des Jaunes
Erquy
Sables-d'Or-les-Pins
Pléhérel-Plage
Plurien
Pléboulle
Matignon
Baie de la Frénaye
St Cast-le-Guildo
Pointe de St Cast
Ile Agot
St Lunaire
DINARD
St Briac-s-Mer
Lancieux
St Jacut-de-la-Mer
Ploubalay
Ile de Cézembre
St MALO
Paramé
Rothéneuf
Pointe de la Varde
Jersey-Sark
Guernsey-Alderney
Portsmouth
le Val-André
Pléneuf-Val-André
Pointe de Pléneuf
Dahouët
St Alban
Planguenoual
Hénanbihen
Ruca
Pléven
St Pôtan
Pluduno
Créhen
Plancoët
Corseul
Languenan
Pleslin
Plouër-s-Rance
Pleurtuit
Trémereuc
Quévert
DINAN
Lanvallay
Yffiniac
Hillion
Morieux
Les Ponts-Neufs
Coëtmieux
Andel
Lamballe
Maroué
Noyal
Landéhen
Pommeret
Quessoy
Meslin
Plestan
Quintenic
Landébia
Forêt de la Hunaudaie
Chau de la Hunaudaie
Plédéliac
St Rieul
Tramain
Jugon-les-Lacs
Dolo
Plénée-Jugon
Plorec
Bourseul
Pléan-le-Petit
Pélan
Landes de Pélan
Trébédan
Languédias
Mégrit
Trédias
Yvignac
Brusvily
Vildé-Guingalan
Aucaleuc
St Carné
Calorguen
Trévron
Evran
St André-des-Eaux
St Juvat
Tréfumel
Le Quiou
Plouasne
Guenroc
Guitté
Caulnes
Quédillac
Médréac
St Pern
Plumaudan
Broons
Sévignac
Rouillac
Eréac
Lanrelas
Mérillac
Langourla
Trémeur
Abbé de Boquen
Forêt de Boquen
Collinée
St Gouéno
St Jacut-du-Mené
Plessala
Langast
Moncontour
Trédaniel
Plémy
Trébry
St Glen
Penguily
Bréhand
St Trimoël
Le Gouray
St Vran
Forêt de la Hardouinais
LANDES DU MENÉ
Plumaugat
St Jouan-de-l'Isle
St Launeuc
Loudéac
St Méen
Landujan
St M'Hervon
Bobital
St Samson
Plélan-le-Petit
Plesder
Tressaint
St Solen
St Hélen
Le Hinglé
Les Champs Géraux
Coëtquen

A
B
1
2
3
4
Lessay
Périers
Coutances
Granville
Avranches
LE MONT ST MICHEL
Cancale
ST MALO
Paramé
St Servan-s-Mer
Rothéneuf
Iles Chausey
Grande Ile
Grd Romont
le Pignon
Jersey (St Helier)
B A I E
D U   M O N T   S A I N T   M I C H E L
Pointe du Grouin
Ile des Landes (Réserve naturelle)
Pointe du Meinga
Pointe du Roc
Banc de Tombelaine
Tombelaine
Bec d'Andaine
Roches du Sac de Pirou
Sénéquet
Pointe d'Agon
Coutainville
Blainville-s-Mer
Pirou
Créances
Gouville-s-Mer
Agon
Heugueville
Tourville-s-Sienne
St Malo-de-la-Lande
Gratot
Brainville
Regnéville-s-Mer
Montmartin-s-Mer
Hauteville
Annoville
Lingreville
Muneville-s-Mer
Bricqueville-s-Mer
Bréhal
Cérences
Lengronne
Gavray
Coudeville
Bréville-s-Mer
Donville-les-Bains
Hudimesnil
St Pair
Jullouville
Carolles
St Jean-le-Thomas
Champeaux
Pointe de Champeaux
Sartilly
la Haye-Pesnel
Genêts
Marcey
Pontaubault
Ducey
St Sauveur-Lendelin
Le Vivier-s-Mer
Cherrueix
Châteauneuf-d'Ille-et-Vilaine
12
29
48
49

Bayeux
St Lô
Balleroy
Caumont-l'Eventé
Villers-Bocage
Aunay-s-Odon
Le Bény-Bocage
Vire
Villedieu-les-Poêles
Percy
Tessy-s-Vire
Torigni-s-Vire
Canisy
Marigny
Hambye
St Sever-Calvados
Condé-s-Noireau
Tinchebray
Flers
Sourdeval
Mortain
Brécey
St Pois
Isigny-le-Buat
Barenton
St Clair-s-l'Elle
Cerisy-la-Forêt
Forêt de Cerisy
Littry
Le Molay-Littry
Tilly-s-Seulles
St Jean-de-Daye
Cerisy-la-Salle
Forêt de St Sever
Forêt de Mortain
Forêt de Halouze
Roches de Ham
Mont Robin
Mont Pinçon
Juvigny-le-Tertre
Vassy
Montchamp
PARC
RÉGIONAL
NORMANDIE
MAINE

Houlgate
Cabourg
Ouistreham
Dives-s-Mer
Merville-Franceville-Plage
Hérouville-St Clair
CAEN
Mondeville
Troarn
Dozulé
Cambremer
Mézidon-Canon
Bourguébus
Bretteville-s-Laize
Thury-Harcourt
St Pierre-s-Dives
Livarot
Falaise
Pont-d'Ouilly
Clécy
Morteaux-Coulibœuf
Trun
Flers
Putanges-Pont-Écrepin
Argentan
Écouché
Messei
Briouze
Rânes
Château d'O
Mortrée
Forêt de Cinglais
Forêt de Gouffern
Brèche au Diable
Roche d'Oëtre
Mont Ormel
Creully
Douvres-la-Délivrande
Fontaine-Henry
Evrecy
Aunay-s-Odon
Condé-s-Noireau
Athis-de-l'Orne
Vimoutiers

LISIEUX
Cormeilles
Blangy-le-Château
Thiberville
Bernay
Orbec
Broglie
Brionne
Montfort-s-Risle
Beaumont-le-Roger
Le Neubourg
Bourgtheroulde
Vimoutiers
Gacé
Montreuil-l'Argillé
la Ferté-Frênel
Rugles
l'Aigle
Breteuil
Conches
Beaumesnil
le Merlerault
Moulins-la-Marche
Courtomer
Lieurey
Le Bec-Hellouin
Forêt de Beaumont
Forêt de Conches
Forêt de Breteuil
Forêt de St Evroult
Forêt de l'Aigle
Forêt de Chaumont
Bois de Broglie
Fl de la Trappe
14
15
34
51
52

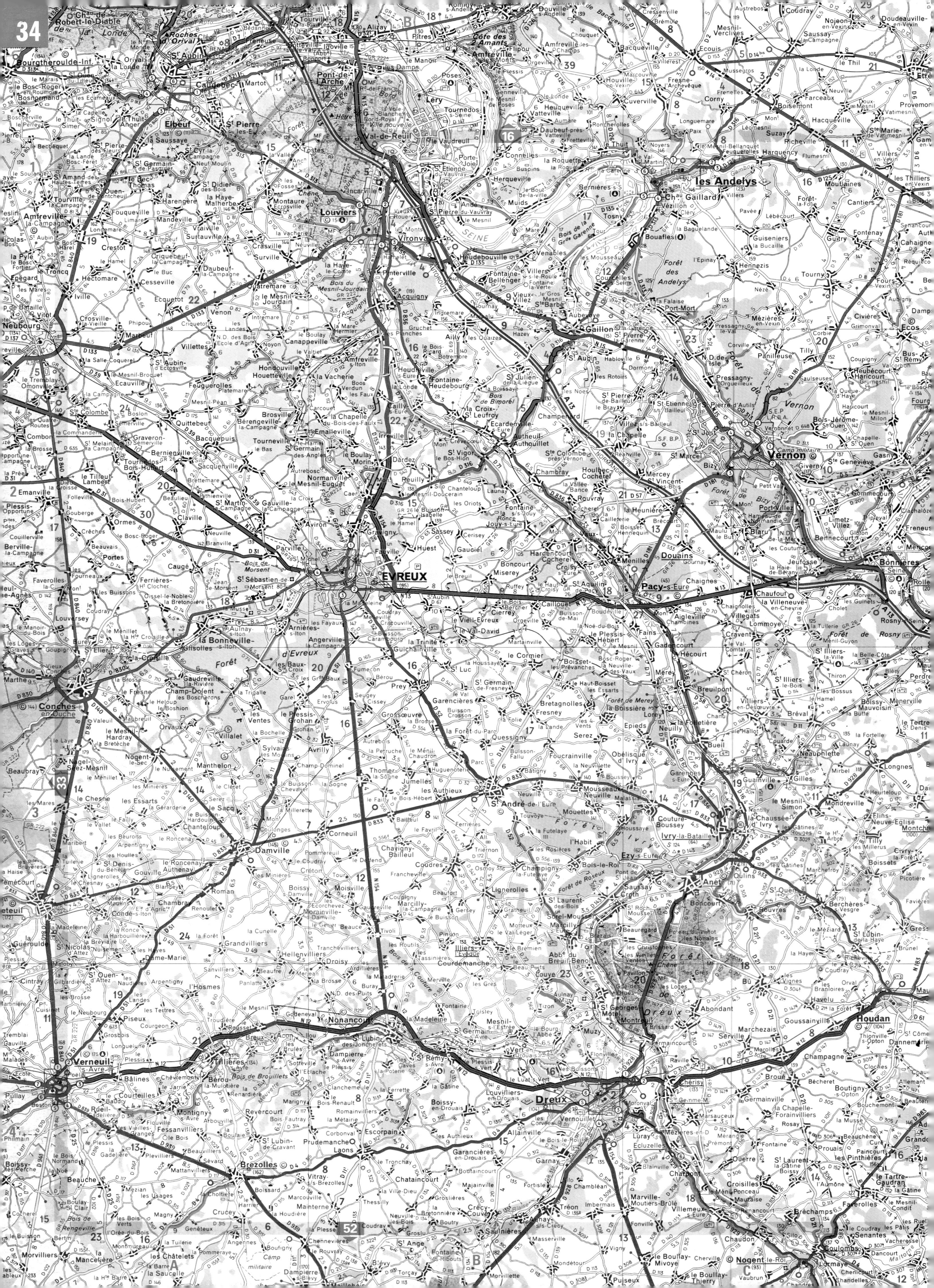

Bourgtheroulde-Inf.
Elbeuf
St Pierre-lès-Elbeuf
Caudebec
St Aubin
Pont-de-l'Arche
Alizay
Pîtres
Val-de-Reuil
Le Vaudreuil
Louviers
Vironvay
Léry
Poses
Amfreville-sous-les-Monts
Les Andelys
Château Gaillard
Forêt des Andelys
Gaillon
Acquigny
Heudebouville
Vernon
Giverny
Forêt de Bizy
Bonnières
Pacy-s-Eure
Douains
Ménilles
Évreux
Forêt d'Évreux
Conches-en-Ouche
Le Neubourg
Amfreville-la-Campagne
la Bonneville-s-Iton
Gravigny
Damville
St André-de-l'Eure
Forêt de Merey
Ivry-la-Bataille
Ezy-s-Eure
Anet
Forêt de Dreux
Dreux
Nonancourt
Tillières
Verneuil-s-Avre
Brezolles
Houdan
Nogent-le-Roi
Breteuil
SEINE
NORMANDIE
AUTOROUTE
Seine
Eure
A13
N13
N12
N15
N154
Côte des 2 Amants
Camp militaire

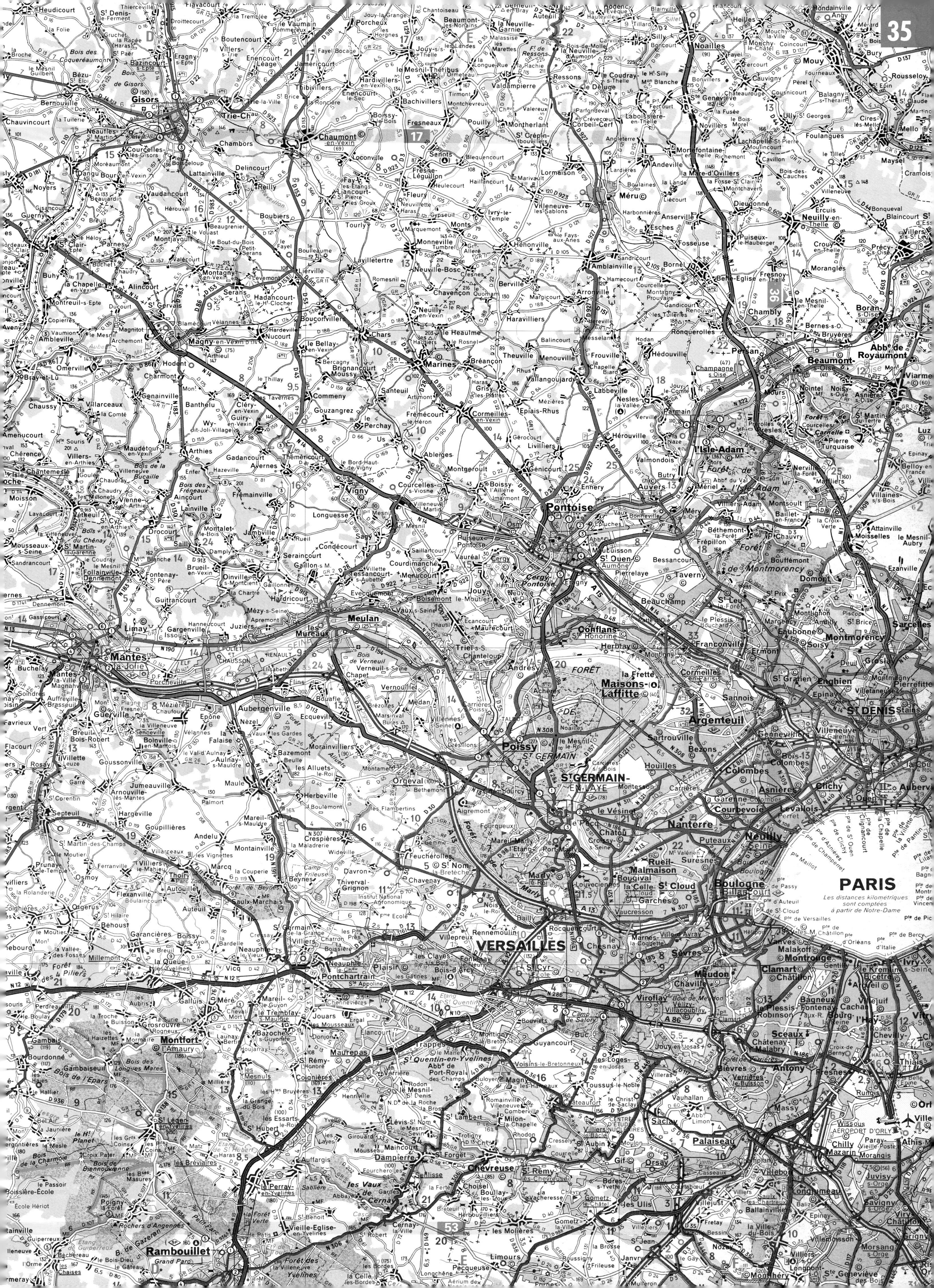
PARIS
Les distances kilométriques sont comptées à partir de Notre-Dame
VERSAILLES
St DENIS
Pontoise
Cergy Pontoise
Gisors
Chaumont en-Vexin
Magny-en-Vexin
Marines
Méru
Beaumont-s-Oise
l'Isle-Adam
Meulan
Mantes-la-Jolie
Poissy
St GERMAIN-EN-LAYE
Argenteuil
Nanterre
Rueil-Malmaison
Boulogne
Neuilly
Montmorency
Enghien
Maisons-Laffitte
Conflans-Ste-Honorine
Rambouillet
Montfort-l'Amaury
Chevreuse
Orsay
Palaiseau
Massy
Antony
Sceaux
Meudon
Clamart
Montrouge
Viroflay
Sèvres
St Cloud
Maurepas
St Quentin-en-Yvelines
Trappes
Dampierre
Limours
Longjumeau
Juvisy
Chambly
Neuilly-en-Thelle
Noailles
Mouy
Persan
Abbe de Royaumont
Forêt de Montmorency
Forêt de l'Isle-Adam
Forêt de Marly
Forêt de Rambouillet
Forêt des Yvelines
Les Vaux de Cernay
Aéroport d'Orly
17
36
53

A
B
C
SENLIS
Chantilly
Forêt de Chantilly
Creil
Nogent-s-Oise
Montataire
Liancourt
Verberie
Pont Ste Maxence
Crépy-en-Valois
Nanteuil-le-Haudouin
Ermenonville
Abbe de Chaalis
Betz
Luzarches
Beaumont-s-Oise
Abbe de Royaumont
Viarmes
Dammartin-en-Goële
Roissy
AEROPORT CHARLES DE GAULLE
MEAUX
Mitry-Mory
Claye-Souilly
Sarcelles
Montmorency
Enghien
St DENIS
Aubervilliers
Bobigny
Drancy
Aulnay-s/s-Bois
Sevran
Villepinte
Le Raincy
Chelles
Lagny
Montreuil
Vincennes
Nogent-s-M
Joinville
Champigny
St Maur
Créteil
Maisons-Alfort
Ivry
Vitry-s-Seine
Orly
AEROPORT D'ORLY
Choisy-le-Roi
Villeneuve-St Georges
Montgeron
Brunoy
Juvisy-s-Orge
Savigny-s-Orge
Draveil
Forêt de Sénart
Brie-Comte-Robert
Tournan-en-Brie
Fontenay-Trésigny
Rozay-en-Brie
Coulommiers
Crécy-la-Chapelle
Forêt de Crécy
Forêt d'Armainvilliers
Lizy-s-Ourcq
Trilport
Quincy-Voisins
Esbly
PARIS
Les distances kilométriques sont comptées à partir de Notre-Dame
N 2
N 3
N 4
N 17
N 19
N 324
N 330
N 34
N 36
A 1
A 4
18
35
54

Villers-Cotterêts
Longpont
la Ferté-Milon
Neuilly-St Front
Oulchy-le-Château
Fère-en-Tardenois
Fismes
Bazoches
Château-Thierry
Dormans
Condé-en-Brie
Charly
la Ferté-s/s-Jouarre
Jouarre
Montmirail
Rebais
Coulommiers
la Ferté-Gaucher
Esternay
Sézanne
Villiers-St Georges
Montfaucon
Viels-Maisons
Orbais
Châtillon-s-Marne
Forêt du Gault
Forêt de la Traconne
Forêt de Vassy
Forêt de Fère
Forêt de Nesles
Forêt de Ris
Bois de Condé
Bois Belleau
AUTOROUTE
A4
N3
N4
N34
38
19
55

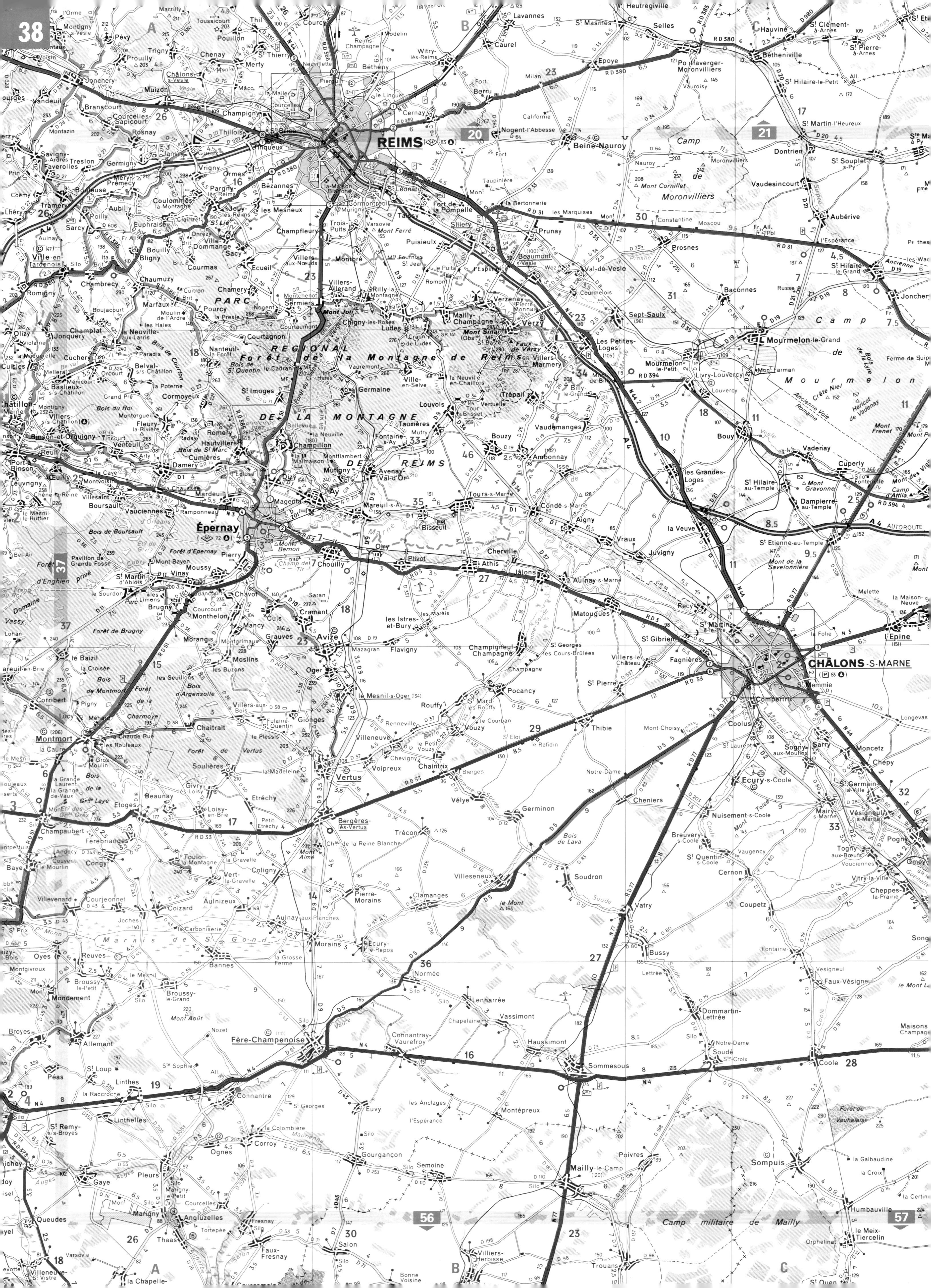
REIMS
Épernay
CHÂLONS-S-MARNE
PARC REGIONAL
Forêt de la Montagne de Reims
DE LA MONTAGNE DE REIMS
Camp de Moronvilliers
Camp de Mourmelon
Camp militaire de Mailly
Mourmelon-le-Grand
Mourmelon-le-Petit
Fère-Champenoise
Sommesous
Mailly-le-Camp
Vertus
Avize
Ay
Verzy
Sillery
Bouzy
Ambonnay
Tours-s-Marne
Condé-s-Marne
Jâlons
Montmort
Sézanne
Champaubert
Pogny
Vitry-la-Ville
Coole
Sompuis
Connantre
Bergères-lès-Vertus
Ecury-s-Coole
Cormontreuil
Tinqueux
Fismes
Pontfaverger-Moronvilliers
Bétheniville
Beine-Nauroy
Sept-Saulx
Suippes
L'Epine
Forêt de Vauhalaise
A4 AUTOROUTE
N 4
N 44
N 3
N 31
N 51
N 77
20
21
37
56
57

Sommepy-Tahure
Camp militaire de Suippes
Somme-Suippe
Suippes
Cernay-en-Dormois
Ville-s-Tourbe
Binarville
Apremont
Varennes-en-Argonne
Montfaucon
Forêt de Montfaucon
Forêt de Hesse
Bois de la Gruerie
Vienne-le-Château
Les Islettes
Clermont-en-Argonne
Ste Menehould
Valmy
Auve
Forêt de Beaulieu
Triaucourt-en-Argonne
Givry-en-Argonne
Vaubécourt
Possesse
Revigny-s-Ornain
BAR-LE-DUC
Sermaize-les-Bains
Heiltz-le-Maurupt
Vitry-le-François
Thiéblemont-Farémont
Forêt de Trois-Fontaines
St Dizier
Ancerville
Stainville
Ligny-en-Barrois
St Remy-en-Bouzemont
Larzicourt
Hallignicourt
Fains-les-Sources
Savonnières-devant-Bar
Vavincourt
Seigneulles
Chaumont-s-Aire
Ippécourt
Souilly
Nixéville
Blercourt
Dombasle-en-Argonne
Récicourt
Avocourt
Esnes-en-Argonne
Malancourt
Le Mort-Homme
Cote 304
Chattancourt
Forges-s-Meuse
Septsarges
Gercourt
Nantillois
Cierges-s-Montfaucon
Fléville
Exermont
Cornay
Châtel-Chéhéry
Grandham
Vaux-lès-Mouron
Liry
Marvaux
Manre
Aure
Gratreuil
Fontaine-en-Dormois
Massiges
Minaucourt-le-Mesnil-lès-Hurlus
Virginy
Wargemoulin-Hurlus
Laval-s-Tourbe
St Jean-s-Tourbe
Hans
Somme-Bionne
Somme-Tourbe
Courtémont
Dommartin-s-Hans
Maffrécourt
Chaudefontaine
Moiremont
Florent-en-Argonne
Le Claon
Le Neufour
Aubréville
Neuvilly-en-Argonne
Boureuilles
Vauquois
Cheppy
La Chalade
Futeau
Passavant-en-Argonne
Beaulieu-en-Argonne
Brizeaux
Waly
Foucaucourt-s-Thabas
Nubécourt
Evres
Beauzée-s-Aire
Les Charmontois
Belval-en-Argonne
Sommeilles
Laheycourt
Villotte-devt-Louppy
Louppy-le-Château
Nettancourt
Brabant-le-Roi
Rancourt-s-Ornain
Contrisson
Andernay
Mognéville
Couvonges
Beurey-s-Saulx
Robert-Espagne
Trémont-s-Saulx
Combles-en-Barrois
Brillon-en-Barrois
Saudrupt
Haironville
Sommelonne
Chancenay
Bettancourt-la-Ferrée
Cheminon
Maurupt
Pargny-s-Saulx
Etrepy
Bignicourt-s-Saulx
Blesme
Scrupt
Dompremy
Favresse
Reims-la-Brûlée
Marolles
Luxémont
Frignicourt
Blacy
Couvrot
Loisy-s-Marne
Soulanges
Ablancourt
Aulnay-l'Aître
Lisse-en-Champagne
Bassuet
Vanault-les-Dames
Vernancourt
Charmont
Bussy-le-Repos
Contault
St Mard-s-le-Mont
Noirlieu
Somme-Yèvre
Dommartin-Varimont
Epense
La Neuville-aux-Bois
Le Vieil-Dampierre
Sivry-Ante
Dampierre-le-Château
Herpont
Tilloy-et-Bellay
St Remy-s-Bussy
La Croix-en-Champagne
Somme-Vesle
Poix
Moivre
Coupéville
St Jean-s-Moivre
Dampierre-s-Moivre
Francheville
Le Fresne
Vanault-le-Châtel
Changy
Outrepont
Merlaut
Plichancourt
Brusson
Matignicourt
Orconte
Cloyes-s-Marne
Norrois
Blaise-s-s-Arzillières
Arzillières-Neuville
Moncetz-l'Abbaye
Isle-s-Marne
Hauteville
Ambrières
Arrigny
Eclaron
Moëslains
Valcourt
Marnaval
Chamouilley
Cousances-les-Forges
Aulnois-en-Perthois
Rupt-aux-Nonains
Bazincourt-s-Saulx
Lavincourt
Nant-le-Grand
Behonne
Naives-devant-Bar
Resson
Longeville-en-Barrois
Tannois
Rembercourt-aux-Pots
Erize-la-Petite
Les Marats
Condé-en-Barrois
Rosnes
Pretz
Sommaisne
Amblaincourt
Rignaucourt
Courcelles-s-Aire
Rarécourt
Froidos
Lavoye
Autrécourt-s-Aire
Fleury-s-Aire
St André-en-Barrois
Julvécourt
Vadelaincourt
Les Souhesmes
Ville-sur-Cousances
Jubécourt
Brocourt-en-Argonne
Brabant-en-Argonne
Parois
Jouy-en-Argonne
Montzéville
Béthelainville
Fromeréville-les-Vallons
Sivry-la-Perche
Rampont

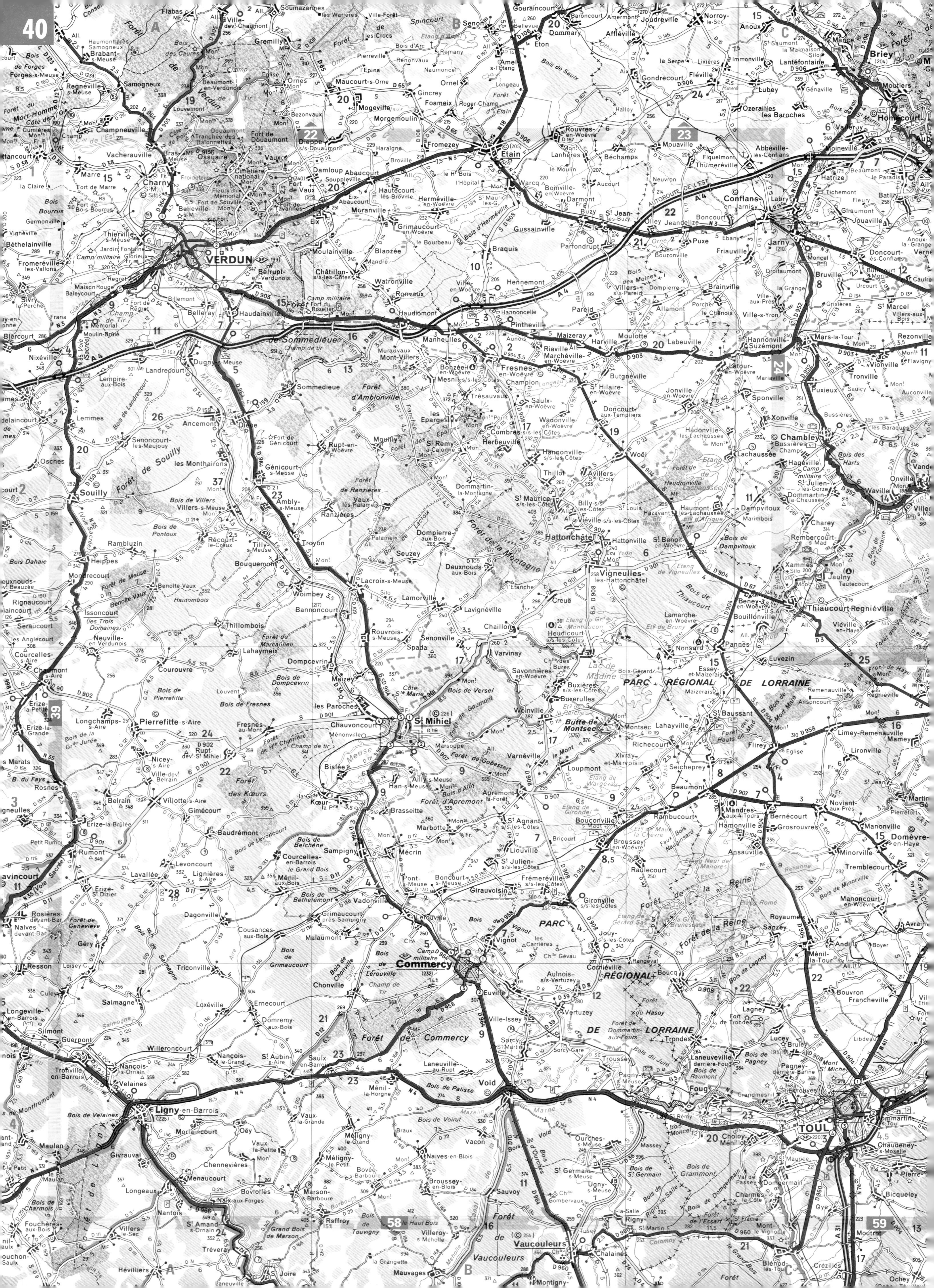
VERDUN
Etain
Briey
Homécourt
Conflans-en-Jarnisy
Jarny
Charny
Souilly
Dieue
Fresnes-en-Woëvre
Vigneulles-lès-Hattonchâtel
Thiaucourt-Regniéville
Chambley
St Mihiel
Pierrefitte-s-Aire
Commercy
PARC RÉGIONAL DE LORRAINE
Forêt de Commercy
Ligny-en-Barrois
Void
Vaucouleurs
TOUL
Forêt de la Reine
Forêt de Sommedieue
Forêt de Souilly
Forêt de la Montagne
Butte de Montsec
Sampigny
Lérouville
Foug
Gondreville
Dommartin-lès-Toul
Vignot
Euville
AUTOROUTE DE L'EST
A 4
N 3
N 4
22
23
24
39
58
59

METZ
NANCY
Pont-à-Mousson
Château-Salins
Lunéville
St Avold
Boulay-Moselle
Creutzwald
Faulquemont
Morhange
Delme
Nomeny
Verny
Woippy
Hagondange
Amnéville
Maizières
Rombas
Rosselange
Montigny
Pange
Vigy
Carling
l'Hôpital
Dieulouard
Pompey
Frouard
Liverdun
Champigneulles
Maxéville
Malzéville
Essey
Tomblaine
Laxou
Villers
Vandœuvre
Jarville
St Nicolas-de-Port
Dombasle-s-Meurthe
Varangéville
Neuves-Maisons
Vic-s-Seille
Moyenvic
Parc régional de Lorraine
Forêt de Parroy
Forêt de Vitrimont
Forêt d'Amance
Bois de Faulx
Forêt de Champenoux
Moselle
24
42
59
60

SAARBRÜCKEN
Forbach
Stiring-Wendel
Freyming-Merlebach
Sarreguemines
Bitche
Puttelange-aux-Lacs
Sarralbe
Sarre-Union
Drulingen
la Petite-Pierre
Phalsbourg
Lutzelbourg
Saverne
Dieuze
Sarrebourg
Mittersheim
Fénétrange
Marmoutier
Dabo
Wangenbourg
Abreschviller
Réchicourt-le-Château
Blâmont
Cirey-s-Vezouze
Oberhaslach
Parc Régional de Lorraine
Forêt de Fénétrange
60
61
41
25

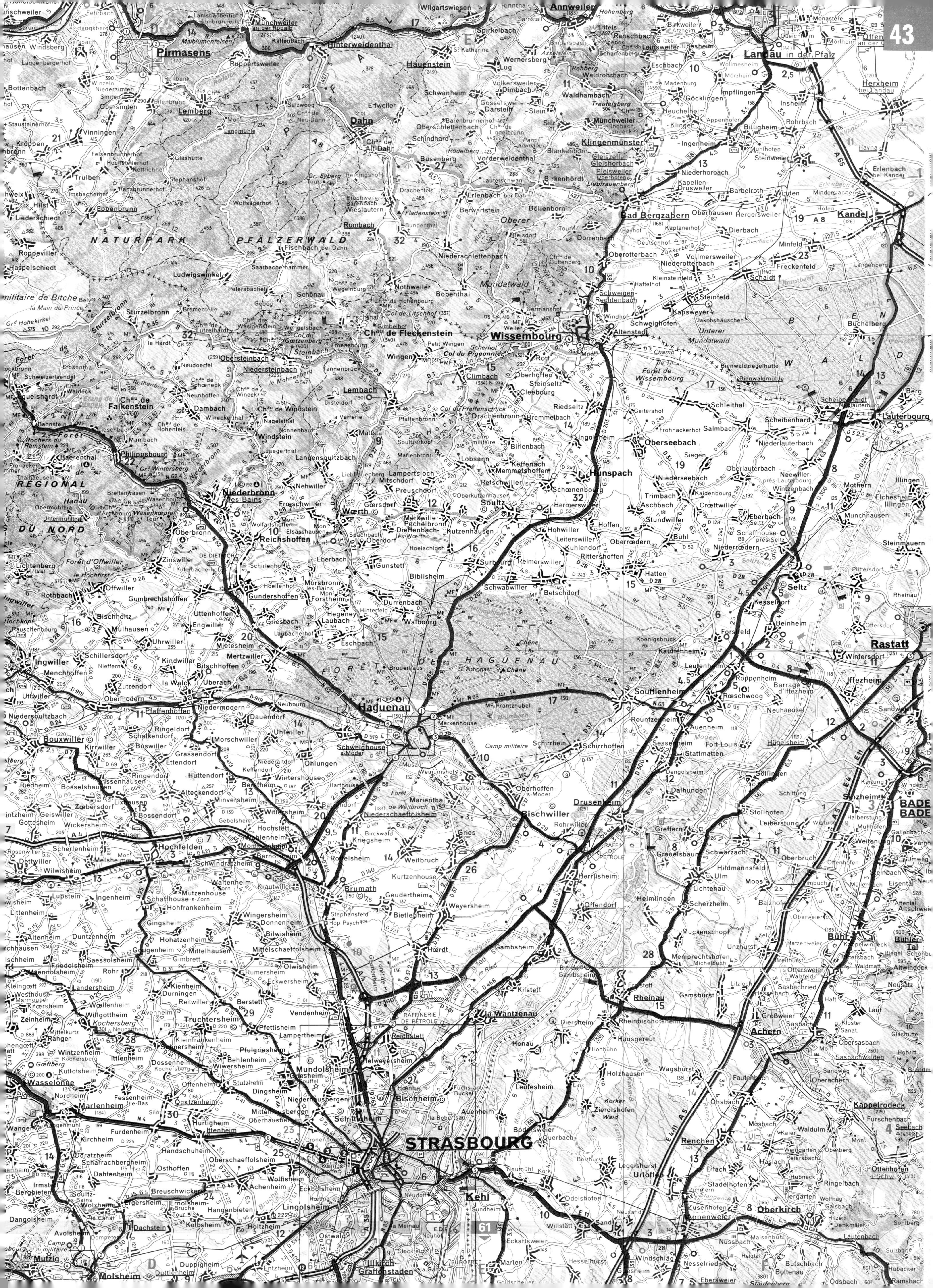
Pirmasens
Annweiler
Landau in der Pfalz
Hinterweidenthal
Hauenstein
Dahn
Lemberg
Eppenbrunn
NATURPARK
PFÄLZERWALD
Bad Bergzabern
Kandel
Klingenmünster
Herxheim
Wissembourg
Lembach
Niederbronn-les-Bains
Reichshoffen
Wœrth
Soultz-sous-Forêts
Hunspach
Lauterbourg
Seltz
Rastatt
Philippsbourg
Bitche
RÉGIONAL
DU NORD
Ingwiller
Bouxwiller
Pfaffenhoffen
Haguenau
FORÊT DE HAGUENAU
Soufflenheim
Drusenheim
Bischwiller
Brumath
Hochfelden
Wasselonne
Marlenheim
Mutzig
Molsheim
STRASBOURG
Kehl
Illkirch-Graffenstaden
La Wantzenau
Rheinau
Achern
Bühl
Kappelrodeck
Renchen
Oberkirch
Appenweier
Sinzheim
Baden-Baden

A
B
C
1
2
3
4
26
Crozon
Morgat
Pointe de Dinan
Chau de Dinan
Beg ar Gador
Grandes Grottes
Plage de la Palud
Pte de St Hernot
Rostudel
Cap de la Chèvre
Telgruc-s-Mer
Trez-Bellec Plage
Pte du Bellec
Argol
Ménez-Hom
Armorique
Ste Marie-du-Ménez-Hom
Pentrez-Plage
St Nic
St Côme
Plomodiern
Pte de Talagrip
Ploéven
Ste Anne-la-Palud
Plonévez-Porzay
BAIE DE DOUARNENEZ
Pointe du Millier
Pte de la Jument
Pte de Leydé
Douarnenez
Tréboul
Locronan
Kerlaz
Plogonnec
Le Juch
Pointe de Beuzec
Pte de Luguénés
Réserve du Cap Sizun
Pte de Brézellec
Pte de Penharn
Pte de Castelmeur
Pointe du Van
Tévennec
Ile de Sein
Nerroth
Raz de Sein
Pointe du Raz
Baie des Trépassés
Phare de la Vieille
Sémapnore
Port de Bestrée
Pte de Feunteunod
Pont des Chats
Cléden-Cap-Sizun
Goulien
Plogoff
Beuzec-Cap-Sizun
Poullan-s-Mer
N.D. de Kérinec
Pont-Croix
Confort Meilars
Mahalon
Primelin
St Tugen
Esquibien
Audierne
Plouhinec
Pte de Lervily
Plage de Kersiny
Plage de Mesperleuc
Pte de Souc'h
Pouldergat
Guengat
Guiler-s-Goyen
Landudec
la Trinité
Plozévet
Ploneis
Poul-ar-Marquis
QUIMPER
Plogastel-St Germain
Pluguffan
Penhors
Pouldreuzic
Peumerit
Plovan
Chlle de Languidou
Tréogat
Plonéour-Lanvern
Tréméoc
Tréguennec
St Jean-Trolimon
N.D. de Tréminou
Pont-l'Abbé
Combrit
Etang de Kergalan
Etang de St Vio
N.D. de Tronoën (Calvaire)
Pte de la Torche
Plage de Pors-Carn
St Guénolé
Rochers
N.D. de la Joie
Phare d'Eckmühl
Pointe de Penmarch
Penmarch
Kérity
Plomeur
Plobannalec
Guilvinec
Lechiagat
Lesconil
Treffiagat
Loctudy
Ile-Tudy
Plage du Teven
Pte de St Oual
BAIE D'AUDIERNE

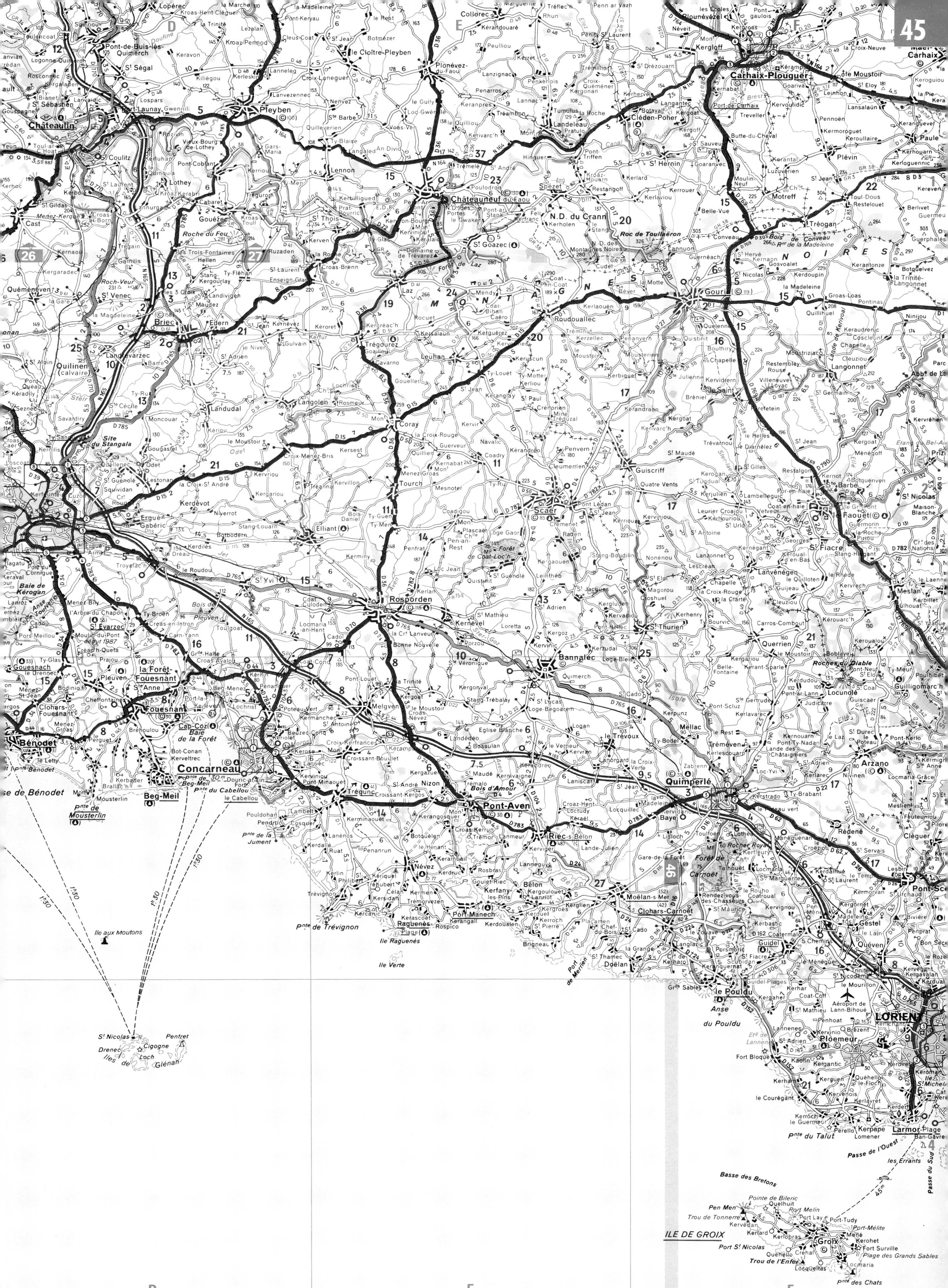
Châteaulin
Pleyben
Pont-de-Buis-lès-Quimerch
Carhaix-Plouguer
Châteauneuf-du-Faou
Landeleau
Cléden-Poher
Spézet
Gourin
Briec
Edern
Coray
Rosporden
Elliant
Scaër
Bannalec
Quimperlé
Le Faouët
Guiscriff
Tourch
Melgven
Concarneau
Fouesnant
la Forêt-Fouesnant
Bénodet
Beg-Meil
Trégunc
Pont-Aven
Nizon
Névez
Riec-s-Belon
Moëlan-s-Mer
Clohars-Carnoët
le Pouldu
Guidel
Quéven
Lorient
Ploemeur
Larmor-Plage
Port-Manech
Raguenès-Plage
Baie de la Forêt
Baie de Kérogan
Anse de Bénodet
Pte de Mousterlin
Pte de Trévignon
Ile aux Moutons
Ile Raguenès
Ile Verte
Iles de Glénan
St Nicolas
Penfret
Cigogne
Drenec
Loch
Ile de Groix
Groix
Port St Nicolas
Pen Men
Pointe de Biléric
Port Tudy
Pte des Chats
Passe de l'Ouest
Passe du Sud
Basse des Bretons
Anse du Pouldu
Forêt de Carnoët
Roche du Feu
Site du Stangala
Forêt de Laz
Roc de Toullaëron
N.D. du Crann
Arzano
Cléguer
Pont-Scorff
Meslan
Querrien
St Thurien
Mellac
Locunolé
Baye
Kernével
Ergué-Gabéric
Langolen
Trégourez
Leuhan
Laz
Lennon
Plonévez-du-Faou
Collorec
Motreff
Tréogan
Plévin
Paule
Langonnet
Roudouallec
Le Saint
St Goazec
Landrévarzec
Landudal
Quilinen (calvaire)
Gouesnach
Clohars-Fouesnant
Pleuven
St Evarzec
St Yvi
Cap-Coz
Kerlaz
26
27
46
D
E
F

Carhaix-Plouguer
Maël-Carhaix
Rostrenen
Plouguernével
Gouarec
Corlay
Mur-de-Bretagne
Gourin
Le Faouët
Plouray
Guémené-s-Scorff
Cléguérec
Pontivy
Kernascléden
Quimperlé
Arzano
Plouay
Pont-Scorff
Hennebont
Lanester
LORIENT
Ploemeur
Port-Louis
Larmor-Plage
Riantec
Baud
Pluvigner
Auray
Ste Anne-d'Auray
Belz
Etel
Erdeven
Landévant
Le Pouldu
Guidel
Bubry
Quistinic
Languidic
Camors
ILE DE GROIX
Groix
NOIRES
Forêt de Quénécan
Forêt de Camors
Forêt de Lanvaux
Lac de Guerlédan

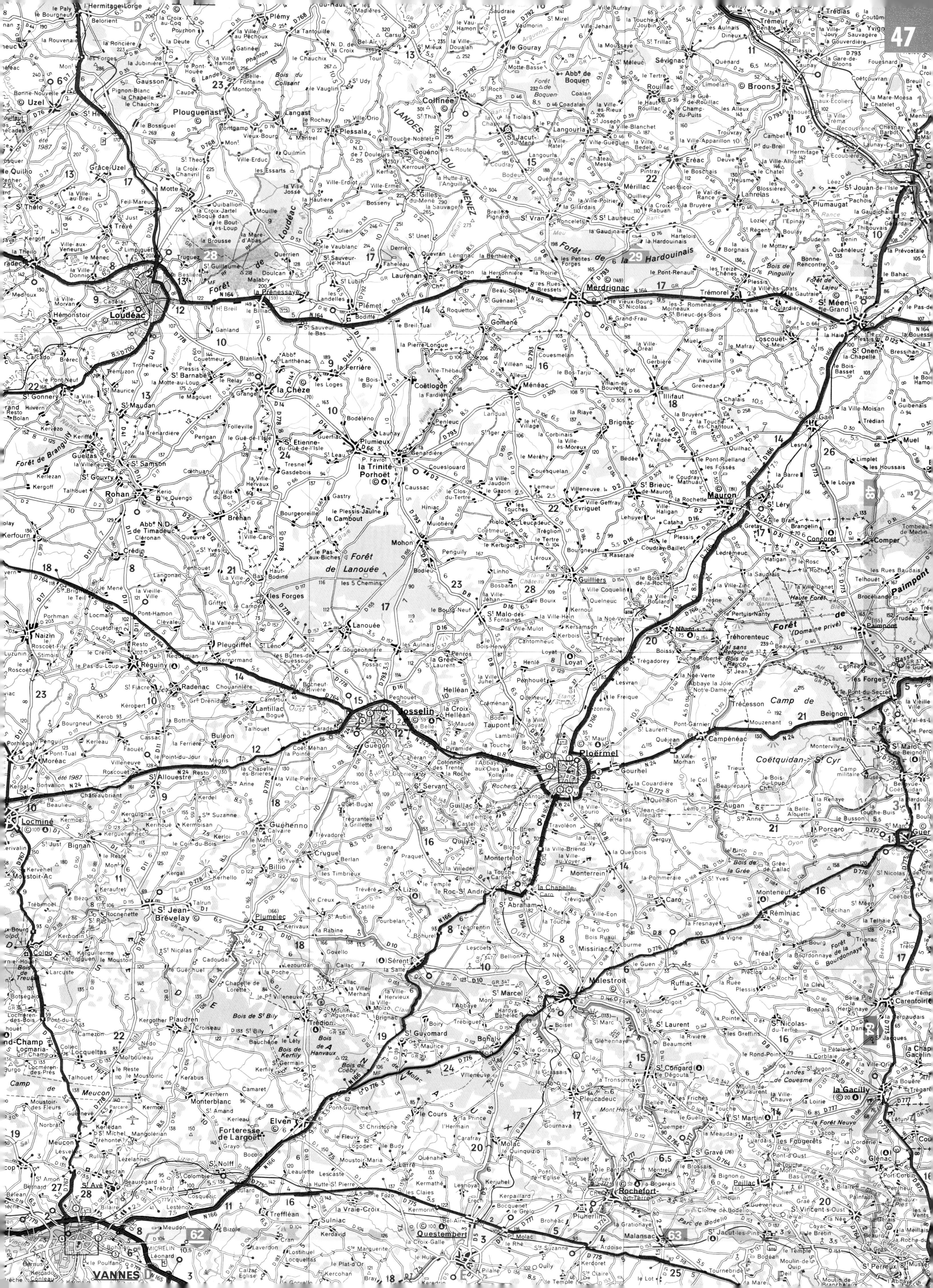
Uzel
Loudéac
Plouguenast
Plémy
Collinée
Merdrignac
Broons
St Méen-le-Grand
Plémet
La Chèze
Rohan
la Trinité Porhoët
Mauron
Ménéac
Guilliers
Josselin
Ploërmel
Locminé
Moréac
St Jean-Brévelay
Plumelec
Sérent
Malestroit
Elven
Questembert
Rochefort-en-Terre
La Gacilly
Vannes
Forêt de Loudéac
Forêt de la Hardouinais
Forêt de Lanouée
Forêt de Paimpont
Camp de Coëtquidan - St Cyr
Landes du Méné
Mauron
Paimpont
Guer
Carentoir
Tréhorenteuc
Campénéac
Allaire
Malansac
Pleucadeuc
St Martin
Réminiac
Caro
Augan

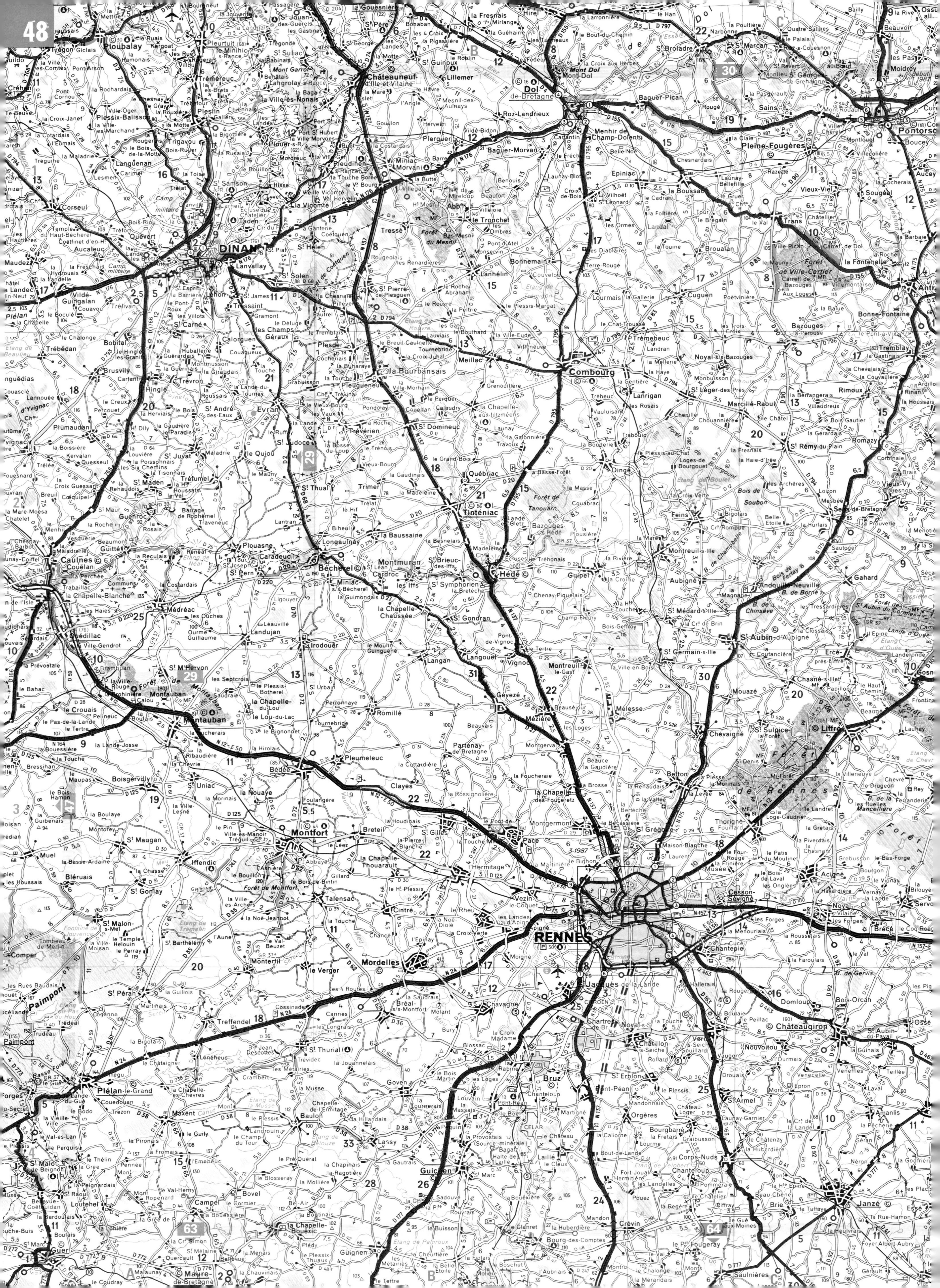
Dinan
Ploubalay
Pleurtuit
Châteauneuf-d'Ille-et-Vilaine
Dol de-Bretagne
Mont Dol
Pontorson
St Broladre
Pleine-Fougères
Plesder
Combourg
Tinténiac
Hédé
Bécherel
Caulnes
Montauban
Bédée
Montfort
Pacé
Rennes
Cesson-Sévigné
Chantepie
Liffré
St Aubin-d'Aubigné
Sens-de-Bretagne
Vezin-le-Coquet
Mordelles
Bruz
Châteaugiron
Janzé
Guichen
Plélan-le-Grand
Paimpont
Guer
Maure-de-Bretagne
Evran
Jugon
Corseul
Lanvallay
Tressé
Pleugueneuc
Médréac
Irodouër
Romillé
Gévezé
Melesse
Betton
Noyal-s-Vilaine
Chavagne
St Jacques-de-la-Lande
Chartres-de-Bretagne
Châtillon-s-Seiche
Crévin
Bourg-des-Comptes
Guignen

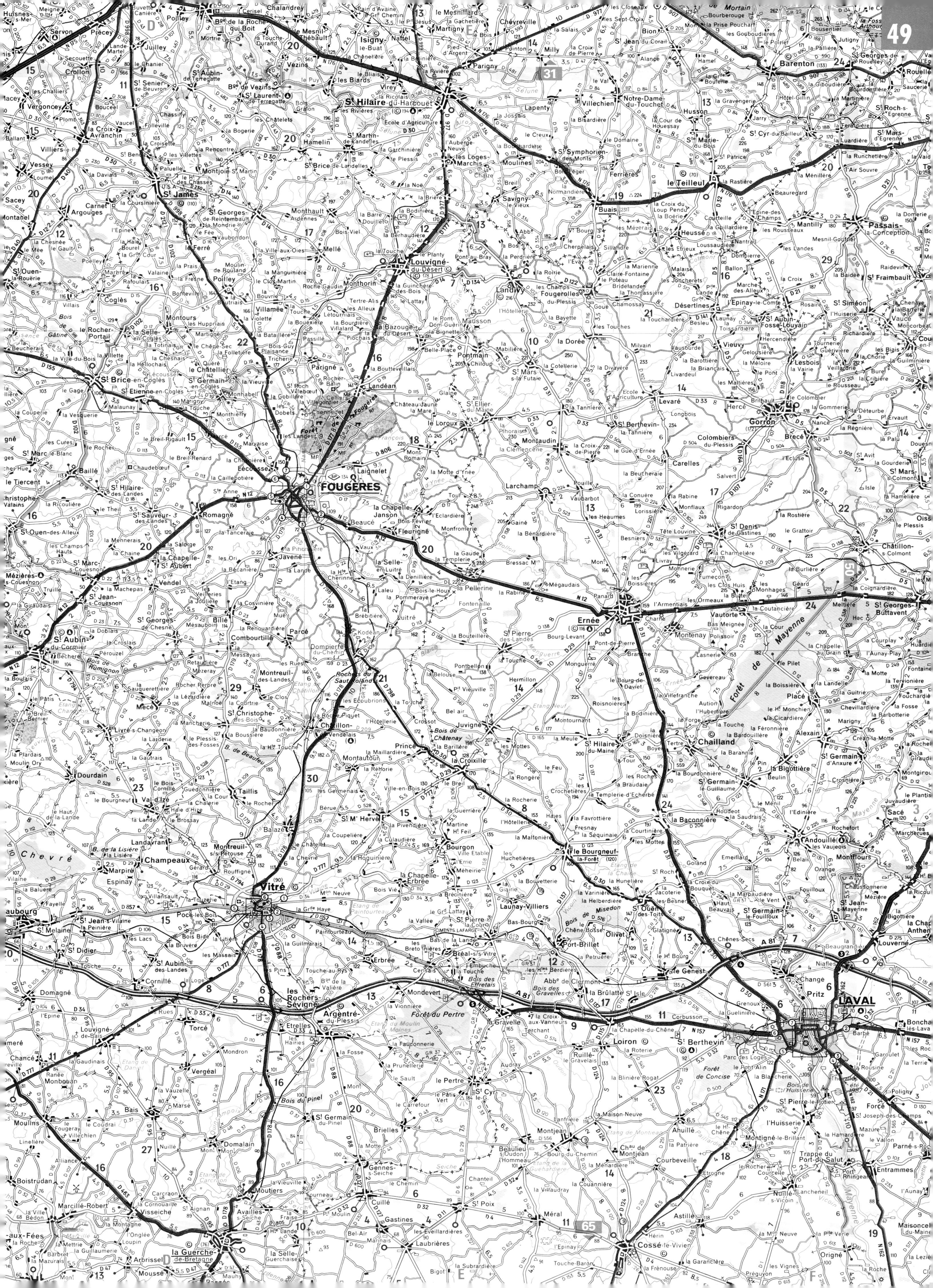
FOUGÈRES
Vitré
LAVAL
Ernée
Louvigné-du-Désert
St James
St Hilaire-du-Harcouët
Gorron
Landivy
le Teilleul
Barenton
Passais-la-Conception
St Brice-en-Coglès
Chailland
Andouillé
Montaudin
le Bourgneuf-la-Forêt
Loiron
St Berthevin
Argentré-du-Plessis
la Guerche-de-Bretagne
Cossé-le-Vivien
Châtillon-en-Vendelais
St Aubin-du-Cormier
Coglès
Isigny-le-Buat
Forêt de Mayenne
Forêt du Pertre
Forêt de Concise

NORMANDIE
MAINE
Domfront
la Ferté-Macé
BAGNOLES-DE-L'ORNE
Juvigny-s-Andaine
Tessé-la-Madeleine
Couterne
Carrouges
Passais-la-Conception
St Fraimbault
Ceaucé
Lassay
Pré-en-Pail
Mont des Avaloirs
Javron
Ambrières-le-Grand
Couptrain
le Horps
Villaines-la-Juhel
Mayenne
Martigné-s-Mayenne
Montsûrs
Evron
Bais
Ste Suzanne
Sillé-le-Guillaume
LAVAL
Argentré
St Denis-d'Orques
Brûlon
Loué
Meslay-du-Maine
Saulges
PARC RÉGIONAL
Forêt de la Grande Charnie
Mont Rochard
Mont Souprat
Multonne
Alpes Mancelles
St Léonard-des-Bois
Forêt de Sillé
Butte de Montaigu
Mont du Saule
Grotte de Rochefort
Grotte à Margot
Forêt des Andaines
Fresnay

Sées
Courtomer
Moulins-la-Marche
Mortagne-au-Perche
Forêt du Perche
Tourouvre
ALENÇON
Forêt d'Écouves
Forêt de Perseigne
Forêt de Bellême
Bellême
Mamers
le Mêle-s-Sarthe
Pervenchères
Noce
Bonnétable
la Ferté-Bernard
Beaumont-s-Sarthe
Ballon
Marolles-les-Braults
Tuffé
Connerré
Montfort-le-Rotrou
LE MANS
Bouloire
Forêt de Vibraye
Le Theil
Saint-Paterne
Fresnaye-s-Chédouet
Courgeon
Bazoches-s-Hoëne
Marchemaisons
Savigné-l'Évêque
Changé
MAINE

Nogent-le-Rotrou
Châteaudun
Châteauneuf-en-Thymerais
la Loupe
Senonches
Illiers-Combray
Brou
Cloyes-s-le-Loir
Mondoubleau
Montmirail
Vibraye
Authon-du-Perche
Thiron
Courville-s-Eure
la Ferté-Vidame
Longny-au-Perche
Rémalard
Bonneval
Forêt de Senonches
Forêt de la Ferté-Vidame
Forêt de Champrond
Forêt de Montmirail
Forêt de Bois Ruffin
Forêt de Vibraye
34
51
68
A
B
C
1
2
3
4

Rambouillet
Nogent-le-Roi
Maintenon
Épernon
Gallardon
Chartres
Ablis
Auneau
Dourdan
Étampes
Limours
St Arnoult-en-Y.
Voves
Angerville
Méréville
Toury
Janville
Orgères-en-Beauce
Artenay
Patay
Neuville-aux-Bois
Chevilly
Loury
Outarville
Pithiviers
Étréchy
Forêt de Rambouillet
A 10
A 11
N 10
N 20
N 154
35
54
69

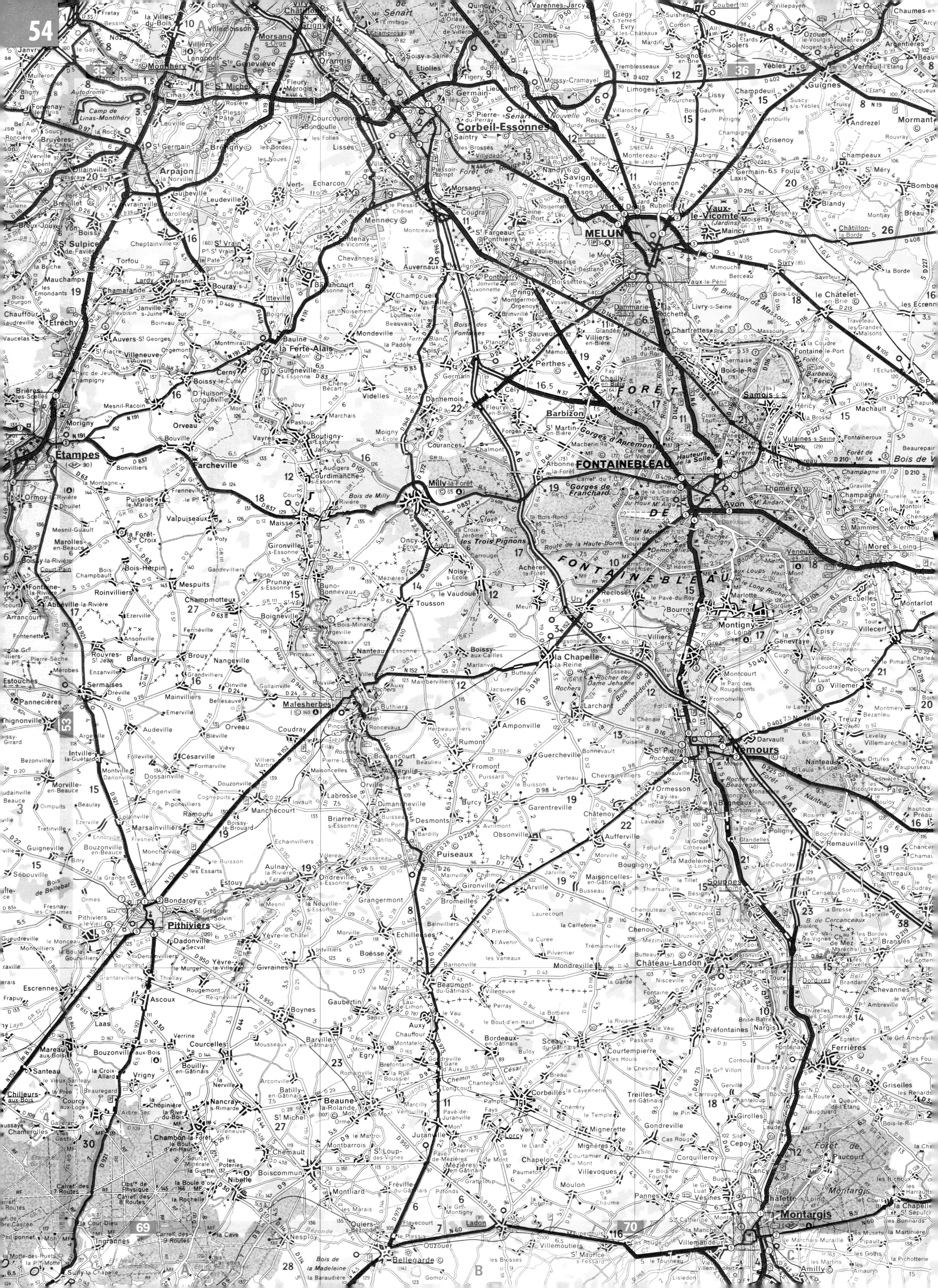

35
36
53
69
70
Montlhéry
Arpajon
Corbeil-Essonnes
Évry
Melun
Vaux-le-Vicomte
Étampes
Étréchy
Mennecy
Milly-la-Forêt
Barbizon
Fontainebleau
Forêt de Fontainebleau
Gorges d'Apremont
Gorges de Franchard
Avon
Moret-s-Loing
Nemours
La Chapelle-la-Reine
Malesherbes
Pithiviers
Puiseaux
Château-Landon
Souppes
Beaune-la-Rolande
Bellegarde
Montargis
Forêt de Montargis
Ferrières
Dordives
Nangeville
Boutigny-s-Essonne
La Ferté-Alais
Perthes
Samois-s-S.
Thomery
Champagne-s-Seine

Provins
Nangis
Nogent-s-Seine
Sens
Villeneuve-s-Yonne
Joigny
Courtenay
Montereau-Faut-Yonne
Pont-s-Yonne
Bray-s-Seine
Donnemarie-Dontilly
Villiers-St Georges
Villenauxe-la-Grande
Sergines
Chéroy
Cerisiers
Villeneuve-l'Archevêque
St Julien-du-Sault
Brienon-s-Armançon
AUTOROUTE DU SOLEIL
36
37
56
71
72

37
38
55
72
73
TROYES
Romilly-s-Seine
Méry-s-Seine
Arcis-s-Aube
Anglure
Estissac
Aix-en-Othe
Bouilly
Chaource
Ervy-le-Châtel
St Florentin
Lusigny-s-Barse
Piney
Ramerupt
Marcilly-le-Hayer
Villemaur-s-Vanne
Chatres
Plancy-l'Abbaye
Nogent-s-Aube
Camp militaire de
Forêt d'Aumont
Forêt de Rumilly
Forêt de Cussangy
Forêt de Chamoy
Bois des Brosses
Bois de Bucey
Bois des Fays
Forêt des Rajeuses
Bois de Margouvernes
Barbonne-Fayel
Fontaine-Denis-Nuisy
Villenauxe
St Just
Sauvage
Crancey
Maizières-la-Gde-Paroisse
Mesgrigny
St Mesmin
Savières
Payns
St Lyé
Barberey-St Sulpice
La Chapelle-St Luc
Ste Savine
St André-les-Vergers
Les Noës
St Julien-les-Villas
St Parres-aux-Tertres
Pont-Ste Marie
Creney
Voué
Aubeterre
Feuges
Villacerf
Mergey
St Benoît-s-Seine
Vailly
Fontvannes
Torvilliers
St Germain
Rosières
Bréviandes
Buchères
Verrières
Isle-Aumont
Moussey
St Thibault
Clérey
Fresnoy-le-Château
Laines-aux-Bois
St Pouange
Souligny
Roncenay
Villery
Machy
Javernant
Cresantignes
Jeugny
Auxon
Chamoy
Montigny-les-Monts
Davrey
Lantages
Vougrey
Praslin
Chesley
Vanlay
Turgy
Cussangy
Lagesse
Maisons-lès-Chaource
Avirey
Bagneux-la-Fosse
Balnot-la-Grange
Bernon
Prusy
Vallières
Neuvy-Sautour
Chailley
Soumaintrain
Courtaoult
Chessy-les-Prés
Germigny
Vergigny
Flogny
Dosches
Laubressel
Thennelières
Courteranges
Montiéramey
Mesnil-Sellières
Rouilly-Sacey
Bouy-Luxembourg
Onjon
Longsols
Charmont-s-Barbuise
Montsuzain
Les Grandes-Chapelles
Rilly-Ste Syre
Premierfait
Droupt-St Basle
Droupt-Ste Marie
Vallant-St Georges
Orvilliers-St Julien
Ossey-les-Trois-Maisons
Fontaine-les-Grès
Echemines
Prunay-Belleville
Villeloup
Dierrey-St Pierre
Dierrey-St Julien
Faux-Villecerf
Mesnil-St Loup
Pâlis
Planty
St Benoist-s-Vanne
Vulaines
Rigny-le-Ferron
Bérulle
Cérilly
Fournaudin
St Mards-en-Othe
Nogent-en-Othe
Maraye-en-Othe
Eaux-Puiseaux
Vosnon
Sormery
Villemoiron-en-Othe
Paisy-Cosdon
Neuville-s-Vanne
Bucey-en-Othe
Prugny
Vauchassis
Chennegy
Bercenay-en-Othe
Sommeval
Champfleury
Salon
Herbisse
Allibaudières
Villiers-Herbisse
Trouans
Dosnon
Grandville
Lhuitre
Torcy
Villette-s-Aube
Pouan-les-Vallées
Champigny-s-Aube
Viâpres-le-Petit
Rhèges
Bessy
Charny-le-Bachot
Boulages
Longueville-s-Aube
Etrelles-s-Aube
Bagneux
St Oulph
Clesles
Granges-s-Aube
Marsangis
St Saturnin
Courcemain
Faux-Fresnay
Queudes
Bethon
Potangis
Esclavolles-Lurey
Marcilly-s-Seine
Conflans-s-Seine
Saron-s-Aube
Baudement
Pars-les-Romilly
Gélannes
St Hilaire-s/s-Romilly
St Loup-de-Buffigny
St Martin-de-Bossenay
La Fosse
Rigny-la-Nonneuse
Marigny-le-Châtel
Avon-la-Pèze
St Flavy
St Lupien
Nozay
St Etienne-s/s-Barbuise
St Remy-s/s-Barbuise
Mesnil-la-Comtesse
Vinets
Isle-Aubigny
St Nabord-s-Aube
Vaupoisson
Ortillon
Chaudrey
Morembert
Coclois
Mesnil-Lettre
Avant-lès-Ramerupt
Vericourt
Montaulin
Rouilly-St Loup
Ruvigny
Courgerennes
Vaudes
Chappes
Fouchères
Rumilly-lès-Vaudes
Virey-s-Bar
Jully-s-Sarce
Villiers-s/s-Praslin
Arrelles
Pargues
Ville noyenne
Montceaux-lès-Vaudes
Villy-le-Maréchal
Villy-le-Bois
Longeville
Cormost
Les Loges-Margueron
Metz-Robert
Les Bordes-Aumont
St Phal
Fays
Montfey
Coursan-en-Othe
Racines
Lasson
Turny
Venizy
Champlost
Mercy
Vachy
Prunelles
Bellechaume
Boeurs-en-Othe
Villeneuve-au-Chemin
Les Croûtes
Beugnon

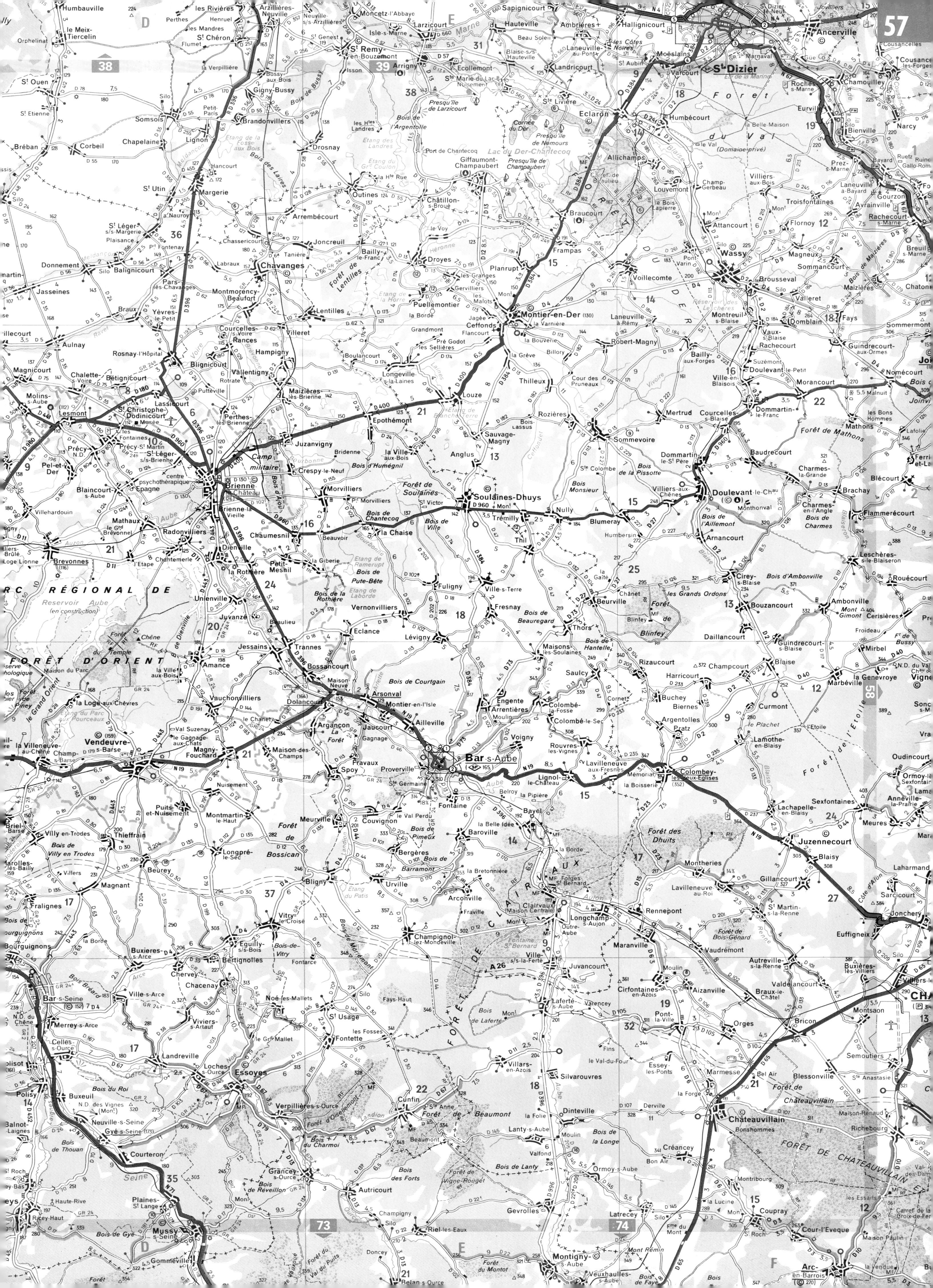
38
39
58
73
74
St Dizier
Ancerville
Chamouilley
Eclaron
Humbécourt
Allichamps
Louvemont
Wassy
Brousseval
Montier-en-Der
Lac du Der-Chantecoq
Giffaumont-Champaubert
Forêt du Der
Droyes
Puellemontier
Chavanges
Joncreuil
Arrembécourt
Outines
Margerie
Somsois
Brandonvillers
Humbauville
St Remy-en-Bouzemont
Larzicourt
Hauteville
Sapignicourt
Eurville
Bienville
Lentilles
Rosnay-l'Hôpital
Brienne-le-Château
Lesmont
Précy-St Martin
St Léger-s-Brienne
Epagne
Radonvilliers
Dienville
La Rothière
Unienville
Juvanzé
Amance
Vendeuvre-s-Barse
Magny-Fouchard
Dolancourt
Arsonval
Jaucourt
Bar-s-Aube
Proverville
Fontaine
Baroville
Bayel
Lignol-le-Château
Colombey-les-Deux-Eglises
Juzennecourt
Blaisy
Soulaines-Dhuys
Morvilliers
Chaumesnil
Ville-s-Terre
Fresnay
Thors
Beurville
Cirey-s-Blaise
Doulevant-le-Château
Dommartin-le-Franc
Sommevoire
Louze
Maizières-lès-Brienne
Juzanvigny
Epothémont
Anglus
Fuligny
Vernonvilliers
Eclance
Lévigny
Trannes
Bossancourt
Forêt de Soulaines
Forêt de Lentilles
Forêt d'Orient
Parc Régional de la Forêt d'Orient
Forêt de Clairvaux
Clairvaux
Ville-s-la-Ferté
Longchamp-s-Aujon
Maranville
Juvancourt
Laferté-s-Aube
Cirfontaines-en-Azois
Rennepont
Bricon
Orges
Châteauvillain
Forêt de Châteauvillain
Essoyes
Loches-s-Ource
Landreville
Bar-s-Seine
Polisy
Mussy-s-Seine
Gyé-s-Seine
Courteron
Neuville-s-Seine
Buxeuil
Verpillières-s-Ource
Cunfin
Forêt de Beaumont
Autricourt
Grancey-s-Ource
Riel-les-Eaux
Gevrolles
Montigny-s-Aube
Dinteville
Lanty-s-Aube
Silvarouvres
Villars-en-Azois
Fontette
St Usage
Noé-les-Mallets
Ville-s-Arce
Chervey
Bertignolles
Eguilly-s-Bais
Vitry-le-Croisé
Champignol-lez-Mondeville
Urville
Bligny
Bergères
Couvignon
Meurville
Spoy
Magnant
Beurey
Longpré-le-Sec
Thieffrain
Villy-en-Trodes
Puits-et-Nuisement
Montmartin-le-Haut
Cour-l'Evêque
Coupray
Arc-en-Barrois
Marbéville
Blécourt
Flammerécourt
Ambonville
Bouzancourt
Rizaucourt
Saulcy
Maisons-lès-Soulaines
Fays
Doulevant-le-Petit
Morancourt
Nomécourt
Vaux-s-Blaise
Montreuil-s-Blaise
Voillecomte
Courcelles-s-Blaise
Mertrud
Ville-en-Blaisois
Forêt de Mathons
Forêt du Val
Forêt de l'Etoile
Reservoir Aube

Vaucouleurs
Forêt de Vaucouleurs
Joinville
Chevillon
Gondrecourt-le-Château
Domremy-la-Pucelle
Coussey
Neufchâteau
Liffol-le-Grand
Andelot
Vignory
Bologne
Bourmont
Clefmont
CHAUMONT
Nogent-en-Bassigny
Montigny-le-Roi
Forêt de Montiers
Forêt du Vau
Forêt du Pavillon
Forêt de la Crête
Forêt d'Ageville
Forêt de Corgebin
Forêt de la Garenne
Forêt de Clefmont
Forêt du Jarney
Forêt de Mureau
Forêt de Morimond
Saudron
Bure
Houdelaincourt
Abainville
Poissons
Doulaincourt
Froncles
Reynel
St Blin
Manois
Chalvraines
Humberville
Prez-s/s-Lafauche
Lafauche
Grand
Epizon
Germay
Échenay
Biesles
Foulain
Luzy-s-Marne
Verbiesles
Is-en-Bassigny
Meuse
Marne
Rognon
39
40
57
74
75

Lunéville
Forêt de Vitrimont
Pont-St Vincent
Richardménil
Flavigny-s-Moselle
Maizières
Ochey
Colombey-les-Belles
Bulligny
Allain
Bagneux
Crépey
Germiny
Houdelmont
Pierreville
Pulligny
Ceintrey
Crévéchamps
Tonnoy
Damelevières
Blainville-s-l'Eau
Saffais
Haussonville
Romain
Méhoncourt
Gerbéviller
Vézelise
Tantonville
Haroué
Bayon
Vitrey
Ogéviller
Sion
Saxon-Sion
Vaudémont
Signal de Vaudémont
Forcelles-s-Gugney
Diarville
Houséville
Xirocourt
Gripport
Charmes
Forêt de Charmes
Chamagne
Bainville-aux-Miroirs
Vandeléville
Tramont-Lassus
Gémonville
Pulney
Gugney
Aroffe
Soncourt
Aouze
Removille
Pleuvezain
Courcelles
Bouzanville
Boulaincourt
Xaronval
Vomécourt-s-Madon
Florémont
Essegney
Langley
Moriville
Portieux
Vincey
Châtel-s-Moselle
Rehaincourt
Saint-Amond
Mirecourt
Mazirot
Poussay
Juvaincourt
Ramecourt
Domvallier
Biécourt
Totainville
Oëlleville
Repel
Dommartin-s-Vraine
Houécourt
Ménil-en-Xaintois
Dombasle-en-Xaintois
Rapey
Gugney-aux-Aulx
Madegney
Regney
Nomexy
Vaxoncourt
Pallegney
Zincourt
Badménil-aux-Bois
Villers
Jorxey
Ahéville
Vroville
Vaubexy
Derbamont
Bazegney
Girmont
Thaon-les-Vosges
Dignonville
Mattaincourt
Thiraucourt
Remicourt
Offroicourt
Hymont
Velotte
Racécourt
Circourt
Bouxières-aux-Bois
Oncourt
Mazeley
Gigney
Fomerey
Dompaire
Madonne-et-Lamerey
Bocquegney
Hennecourt
Uxegney
Domèvre-s-Avière
Darnieulles
Golbey
Épinal
Chantraine
Chaumousey
Sanchey
Les Forges
Deyvillers
Longchamp
Jeuxey
Dogneville
Estrennes
Bazoilles-et-Ménil
Valleroy-aux-Saules
Maroncourt
Hagécourt
Madecourt
Rozerotte
Domèvre-s/s-Montfort
Girovillers-s/s-Montfort
Parey-s/s-Montfort
Domjulien
They-s/s-Montfort
Remoncourt
Rancourt
Heucheloup
Bainville-aux-Saules
Begnécourt
Gelvécourt
Damas-et-Bettegney
Gorhey
Adompt
Légéville-et-Bonfays
Les Ableuvenettes
Ville-s-Illon
Dommartin-aux-Bois
Girancourt
Vittel
Contrexéville
Bulgnéville
Norroy
Mandres-s-Vair
Haréville
Valleroy-le-Sec
Valfroicourt
Xirocourt
Frénois
Esley
Pont-lès-Bonfays
Sans-Vallois
Les Vallois
Dommartin-lès-Vallois
Lerrain
Pierrefitte
Harol
Thuillières
Lignéville
Monthureux-le-Sec
St Baslemont
Senonges
Jésonville
Dombasle-devant-Darney
Escles
Dombrot-le-Sec
Provenchères-lès-Darney
Relanges
Bonvillet
Darney
Forêt Domaniale de Darney
Belrupt
Viviers-le-Gras
Gignéville
Marey
Martigny-les-Bains
Serocourt
Belmont-lès-Darney
Nonville
Attigny
Morizécourt
Hennezel
Grandrupt-de-Bains
Harsault
Bleurville
Tignécourt
Monthureux-s-Saône
Claudon
Gruey-lès-Surance
Hautmougey
Bains-les-Bains
Xertigny
Bois du Haumont
Isches
St Julien
Fouchécourt
Godoncourt
Fignéville
Regnévelle
Martinvelle
Pont-du-Bois
Selles
Ambiévillers
Montmotier
Fontenoy-le-Château
Trémonzey
Passavant-la-Rochère
Bousseraucourt
Ameuvelle
Fresnes-s-Apance
Châtillon-s-Saône
Vougécourt
Vauvillers
Fontenois-la-Ville
Betoncourt-St Pancras
Dampvalley
Ailleviller-et-Lyaumont
Plombières-les-Bains
Le Val-d'Ajol
Bellefontaine
Hadol
Dounoux
Arches
Uriménil
Uzemain
Charmois-l'Orgueilleux
Vioménil
Dinozé
Remiremont

Blâmont
Cirey-s-Vezouze
Baccarat
Badonviller
Raon-l'Etape
Senones
Moyenmoutier
Rambervillers
St Dié
Brouvelieures
Bruyères
Corcieux
Fraize
Gérardmer
Remiremont
Plombières-les-Bains
Bussang
Munster
Schirmeck
Saales
Provenchères
Donon
Col du Donon
Col du Bonhomme
Col de la Schlucht
Hohneck
Grand Ballon
Col de Saales
Col de Ste Marie
Lapoutroie
Orbey
Soultzeren
Muhlbach
Wasserbourg
Lautenbach
Guebwiller
Murbach
Ventron
Cornimont
La Bresse
Saulxures-s-Moselotte
Rupt-s-Moselle
Vagney
Le Tholy
Granges-s-Vologne
Xonrupt-Longemer
Docelles
Eloyes
Arches
Epinal
Forêt de Mondon
Forêt de Champ
Forêt de Rambervillers
Forêt de Glonville
St Clément
Lunéville
Thiaville
Celles-s-Plaine
Anould
Plainfaing
Clefcy
St Léonard
Saulcy-s-Meurthe
Ste Marie-aux-Mines
Wisembach
Taintrux
Etival-Clairefontaine
Ménil
St Maurice-s-Mortagne
Deyvillers
Jeuxey
Vaudéville
Longchamp
Padoux
Girecourt-s-Durbion
Dompierre
Grandvillers
Fontenay
Aydoilles
Docelles
Jussarupt
Laveline-du-Houx
Faucompierre
Tendon
Le Syndicat
St Amé
Julienrupt
Sapois
Rochesson
Thiéfosse
Ferdrupt
Le Ménil
Kruth
Oderen
Fellering
Le Markstein
Rimbach
Sondernach
Metzeral
Mittlach
Petit Ballon
Lautenbachzell
Grand Ventron
Petit Drumont
Grand Drumont

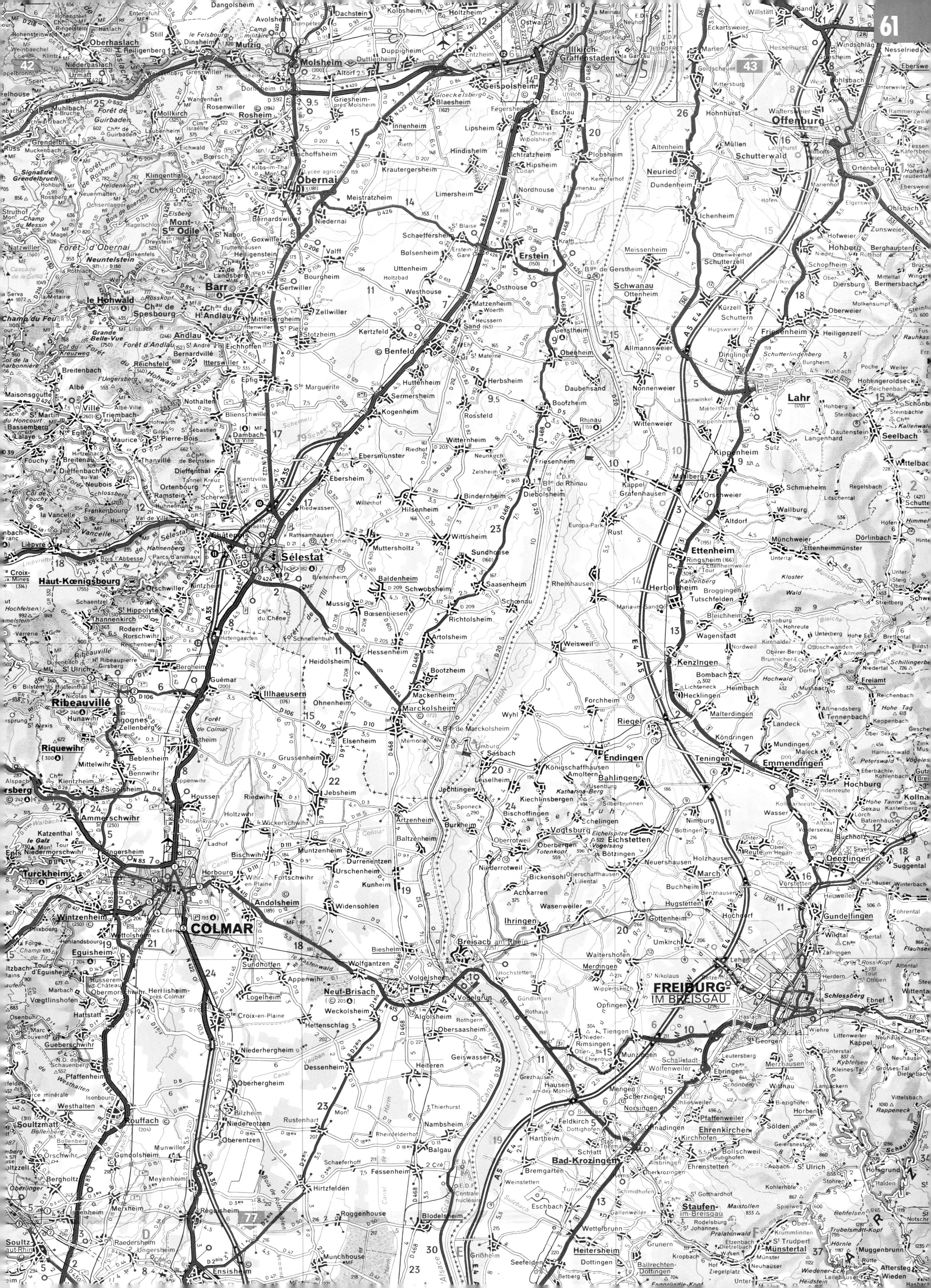
42
43
77
Molsheim
Mutzig
Dachstein
Illkirch-Graffenstaden
Geispolsheim
Rosheim
Obernai
Mont-Ste Odile
Barr
le Hohwald
Andlau
Dambach-la-Ville
Erstein
Benfeld
Sélestat
Châtenois
Haut-Kœnigsbourg
Ribeauvillé
Riquewihr
Kaysersberg
Ammerschwihr
Turckheim
Wintzenheim
COLMAR
Eguisheim
Rouffach
Soultzmatt
Ensisheim
Neuf-Brisach
Marckolsheim
Breisach am Rhein
FREIBURG IM BREISGAU
Bad-Krozingen
Staufen-im-Breisgau
Heitersheim
Müllheim
Emmendingen
Denzlingen
Kenzingen
Herbolzheim
Ettenheim
Lahr
Offenburg
Kehl
Seelbach
Endingen
Riegel
Ihringen
Vogtsburg
Gundelfingen
Schauinsland
Münstertal
RHIN
Canal du Rhône au Rhin

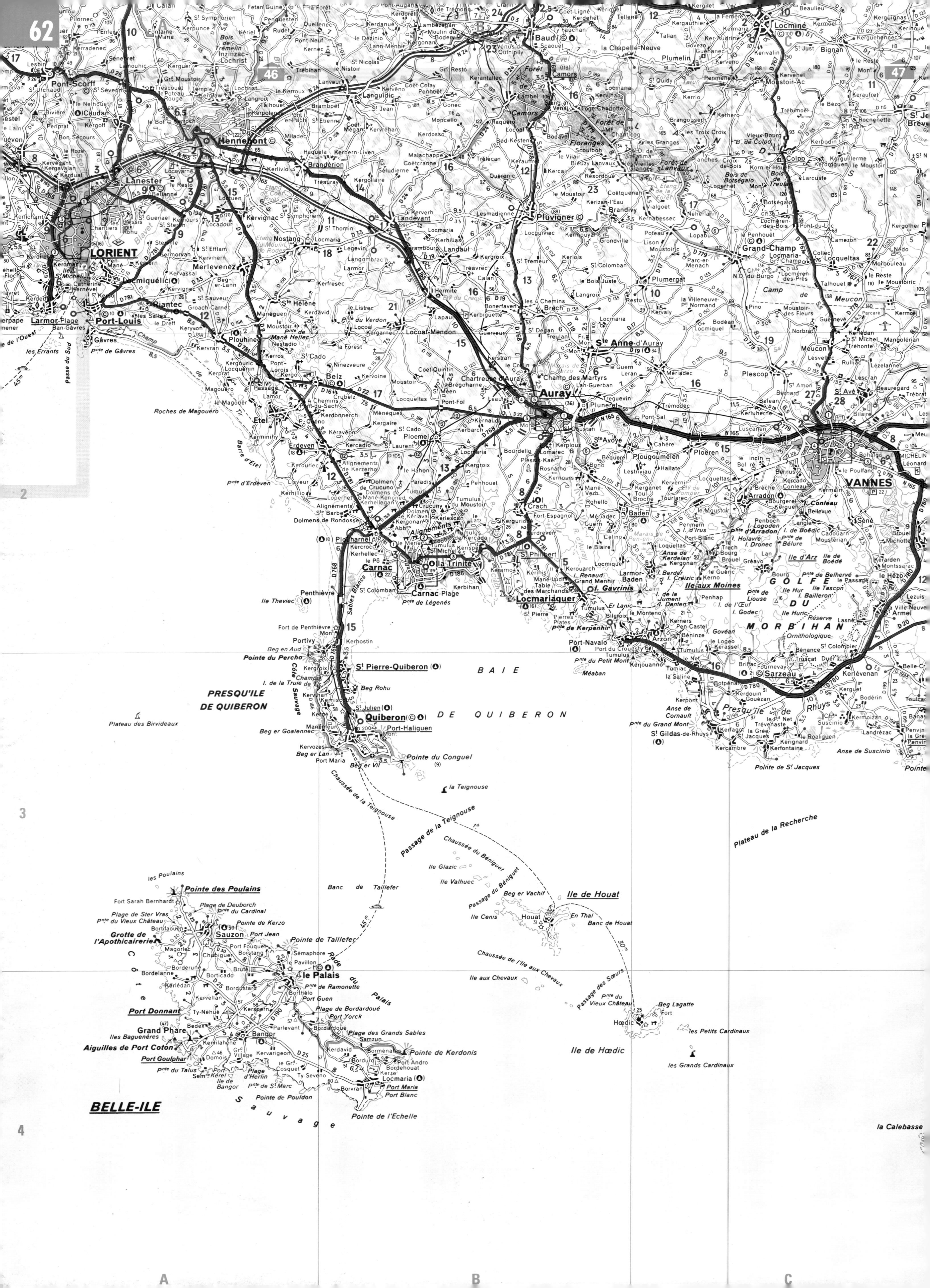

LORIENT
Lanester
Hennebont
Pont-Scorff
Port-Louis
Larmor-Plage
Locmiquélic
Riantec
Merlevenez
Kervignac
Nostang
Landévant
Plouhinec
Etel
Belz
Erdeven
Plouharnel
Carnac
Carnac-Plage
la Trinité
Locmariaquer
Auray
Pluvigner
Ste Anne-d'Auray
Brech
Crach
Baud
Camors
Locminé
Grand-Champ
Plumergat
Plougoumelen
Ploeren
Arradon
Baden
VANNES
St Avé
Séné
Arzon
Sarzeau
St Gildas-de-Rhuys
Port-Navalo
Presqu'île de Rhuys
GOLFE DU MORBIHAN
Ile aux Moines
Ile d'Arz
I. Gavrinis
Penthièvre
Portivy
St Pierre-Quiberon
Quiberon
Port-Haliguen
PRESQU'ILE DE QUIBERON
Côte Sauvage
BAIE DE QUIBERON
Pointe du Conguel
la Teignouse
Passage de la Teignouse
Chaussée de la Teignouse
Plateau des Birvideaux
Plateau de la Recherche
Ile de Houat
Ile de Hœdic
Ile aux Chevaux
les Grands Cardinaux
les Petits Cardinaux
BELLE-ILE
le Palais
Sauzon
Bangor
Locmaria
Pointe des Poulains
Grotte de l'Apothicairerie
Port Donnant
Grand Phare
Aiguilles de Port Coton
Port Goulphar
Pointe de Kerdonis
Pointe de l'Echelle
Rade du Palais
Côte Sauvage
la Calebasse
A
B
C
2
3
4
46
47

Guéhenno
Plumelec
Elven
Forteresse de Largoët
St Nolff
Theix
Surzur
Questembert
Malestroit
Sérent
St Marcel
Rochefort-en-Terre
Pluherlin
Malansac
Guer
Carentoir
La Gacilly
St Congard
Pleucadeuc
Redon
St Nicolas-de-Redon
Allaire
Peillac
Bains-s-Oust
Renac
Muzillac
Péaule
Noyal-Muzillac
Billiers
Damgan
Ambon
La Roche-Bernard
Nivillac
Marzan
Arzal
Camoël
Pénestin
Férel
Herbignac
Missillac
Pontchâteau
St Gildas-des-Bois
Guenrouet
Savenay
Campbon
Donges
Montoir-de-Bretagne
Trignac
St Nazaire
St Brevin-les-Pins
Paimbœuf
Corsept
Pornichet
La Baule
le Pouliguen
Batz-s-Mer
le Croisic
Guérande
La Turballe
Piriac-s-Mer
Mesquer
Assérac
St Lyphard
St Joachim
Grande Brière
Parc Régional de Brière
Forêt de la Roche Bernard
Forêt de la Bourdonnaye
Landes de Cojoux
Rade du Croisic
Pointe du Croisic
Pointe de Chémoulin
Côte Sauvage
Chenal du Nord
Ile Dumet
Pointe de Pen-Lan
Pointe du Castelli
Loire
Vilaine
Oust
N 165
N 166
N 171
D 775
D 776
D 773
D 774
47
48
64
78

Bain-de-Bretagne
Châteaubriant
Guémené-Penfao
Grand-Fougeray
Derval
Nozay
Blain
Savenay
Nort-s-Erdre
Carquefou
Orvault
Rougé
Retiers
Martigné-Ferchaud
Moisdon-la-Rivière
La Meilleraye-de-Bretagne
Riaillé
Pipriac
Messac
Renac
Redon
Plessé
Le Gâvre
Forêt du Gâvre
Saffré
Joué-s-Erdre
Ligné
Couffé
Champtoceaux
Mauves
Sucé-s-Erdre
La Chapelle-s-Erdre
Héric
St Etienne-de-Montluc
Le Temple-de-Bretagne
Cordemais
Vigneux-de-Bretagne
Treillières
Sion-les-Mines
St Vincent-des-Landes
Issé
Treffieux
Marsac-s-Don
Conquereuil
Lusanger
Sulpice-des-Landes
Forêt de Teillay
Forêt de Domnaiche
Forêt du Theil
Forêt de Javardan
Forêt de Vioreau
Forêt de la Groulaie
Teillay
Ercé-en-Lamée
Le Sel-de-Bretagne
Poligné
Pancé
Pléchâtel
Crévin
Bourg-des-Comptes
Guignen
Lohéac
Maure-de-Bretagne
Campbon
Bouvron
Fay-de-Bretagne
Malville
Vay
Puceul
Abbaretz
Petit-Mars
Les Touches
Teillé
Mouzeil
Soudan
Erbray
Louisfert
Ruffigné
Sainte-Colombe
Coësmes
Thourie
Sulvache
Fercé
Noyal-s-Bruz
La Roche-aux-Fées
Le Theil-de-Bretagne
Saulnières
Avessac
Massérac
Fégréac
Langon
Brain-s-Vilaine
Quilly
Bouée
Lavau-s-Loire
Frossay
Thouaré
Sautron
NANTES

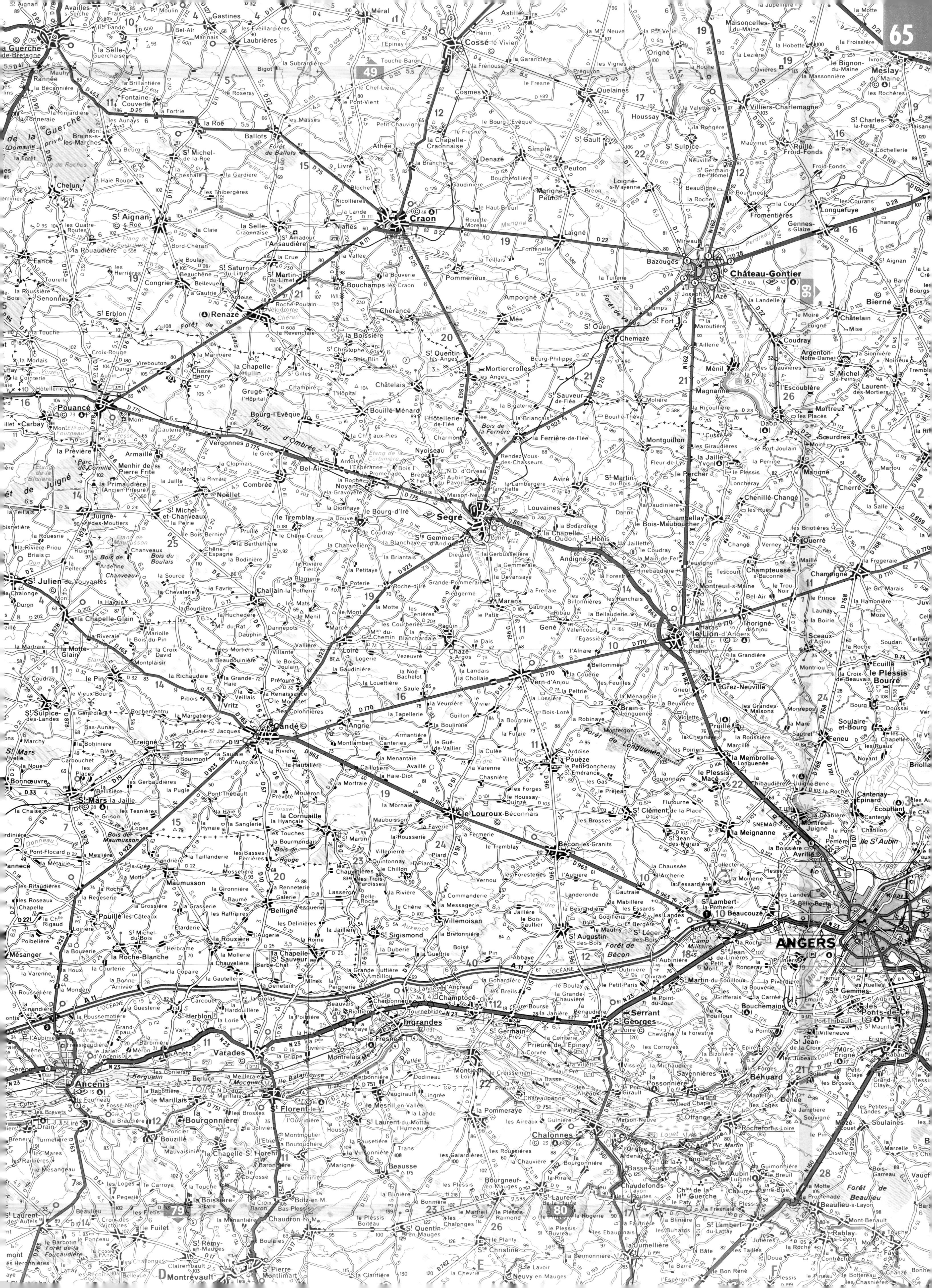
La Guerche-de-Bretagne
Cossé-le-Vivien
Craon
Château-Gontier
Meslay-du-Maine
Renazé
Pouancé
Segré
Le Lion-d'Angers
Candé
Le Louroux-Béconnais
Bécon-les-Granits
Angers
Ancenis
Varades
Ingrandes
Champtocé
St Georges-s-Loire
Chalonnes
Les Ponts-de-Cé
St Florent-le-V.
Montrevault
Beaulieu-s-Layon
Forêt de Longuenée
Forêt d'Ombrée
Forêt de Ballots
Forêt de Bécon
A 11 L'OCÉANE
LOIRE
49
79
80
99

Sablé-s-Sarthe
Solesmes
Brûlon
Meslay-du-Maine
Grez-en-Bouère
Bouessay
Malicorne-s-Sarthe
la Suze-s-Sarthe
la Flèche
Durtal
Châteauneuf-s-Sarthe
Tiercé
Seiches-s-le-Loir
Baugé
Longué
Beaufort-en-Vallée
ANGERS
Trélazé
les Ponts-de-Cé
Brissac-Quincé
les Rosiers
Gennes
Saumur
Vernantes
Précigné
Morannes
Daumeray
Bazouges-s-le-Loir
Jarzé
Corzé
Mazé
Sarrigné
A 11: Durtal-Angers
Ouv. prévue: 7-1987
Forêt de Chandelais
Forêt de Monnaie
Forêt de Pontménard
Forêt de Pincé
Landes du Bailleul
Chambiers
Grand Bois de Jarzé
Bois de Brissac
Forêt de Beaulieu
Loire
Sarthe
Loir

LE MANS
Allonnes
Arnage
Mulsanne
Ruaudin
Parigné-l'Evêque
Challes
Volnay
Surfonds
Bouloire
Maisoncelles
Ecorpain
Montaillé
St Calais
Conflans-s-Anille
Marolles-lès-St Calais
Teloché
Laigné-en-Belin
St Gervais-en-Belin
Moncé-en-Belin
St Mars-d'Outillé
Brette-les-Pins
Guécélard
Ecommoy
Marigné-Laillé
le Grand-Lucé
Pruillé-l'Eguillé
St Vincent-du-Lorouer
Tresson
Evaillé
Ste Cérotte
St Gervais-de-Vic
Savigny-s-Braye
Cogners
la Chapelle-Huon
Bessé-s-Braye
Vancé
St Georges-de-la-Couée
Courdemanche
St Pierre-du-Lorouer
Forêt de Bercé
Jupilles
Château-l'Hermitage
Pontvallain
Mayet
Requeil
Bénéhart
Lavenay
la Chapelle-Gaugain
Poncé-s-le-Loir
Ruillé-s-Loir
Couture-s-Loir
Sougé
Troo
St Jacques-des-Guérets
Thoiré-s-Dinan
Beaumont-Pied-de-Bœuf
Verneil-le-Chétif
Chahaignes
la Chartre-s-le-Loir
Lhomme
Marçon
Sarcé
Flée
Luceau
Château-du-Loir
Vouvray-s-Loir
Aubigné-Racan
Coulongé
Montabon
Nogent-s-Loir
Dissay-s/s-Courcillon
Villebourg
Beaumont-s-Dême
Epeigné-s-Dême
Bueil-en-Touraine
Chemillé-s-Dême
Vaas
la Bruère-s-Loir
St Aubin-le-Dépeint
St Christophe-s-le-Nais
St Paterne-Racan
Neuvy-le-Roi
Louestault
Marray
la Ferrière
Montrouveau
St Laurent-en-Gâtines
Château-Renault
Chenu
Brèches
Villiers-au-Bouin
Couesmes
Château-la-Vallière
Marcilly
Braye-s-Maulne
la Roche-Racan
Neuillé-Pont-Pierre
Beaumont-la-Ronce
Nouzilly
Crotelles
Monnaie
Souvigné
Sonzay
Semblançay
Rouziers-de-Touraine
St Antoine-du-Rocher
Cerelles
Charentilly
Chanceaux
Mettray
N.D. d'Oé
Parçay-Meslay
Rochecorbon
Vouvray
St Cyr
St Pierre
Montlouis-s-Loire
TOURS
St Avertin
Joué
Ballan-Miré
Chambray
Veretz
Larçay
Fondettes
Luynes
St Etienne-de-Chigny
Savonnières
Villandry
Langeais
Cinq-Mars
Mazières-de-Touraine
Cléré-les-Pins
Ambillou
Hommes
Savigné-s-Lathan
Rillé
Channay-s-Lathan
Courcelles-de-Touraine
Avrillé-les-Ponceaux
St Symphorien-les-Ponceaux
Continvoir
Gizeux
Parçay-les-Pins
Lublé
St Laurent-de-Lin
St Michel-s-Loire
Lignières
Vallères
Druye
Pernay
Forêt de Château-la-Vallière
Bois de Tivoli
Bois de Crémille
Landes de St Martin
Forêt de Beaumont
Bois de Gâtines
Forêt de Rochecotte
Bois de la Duporterie

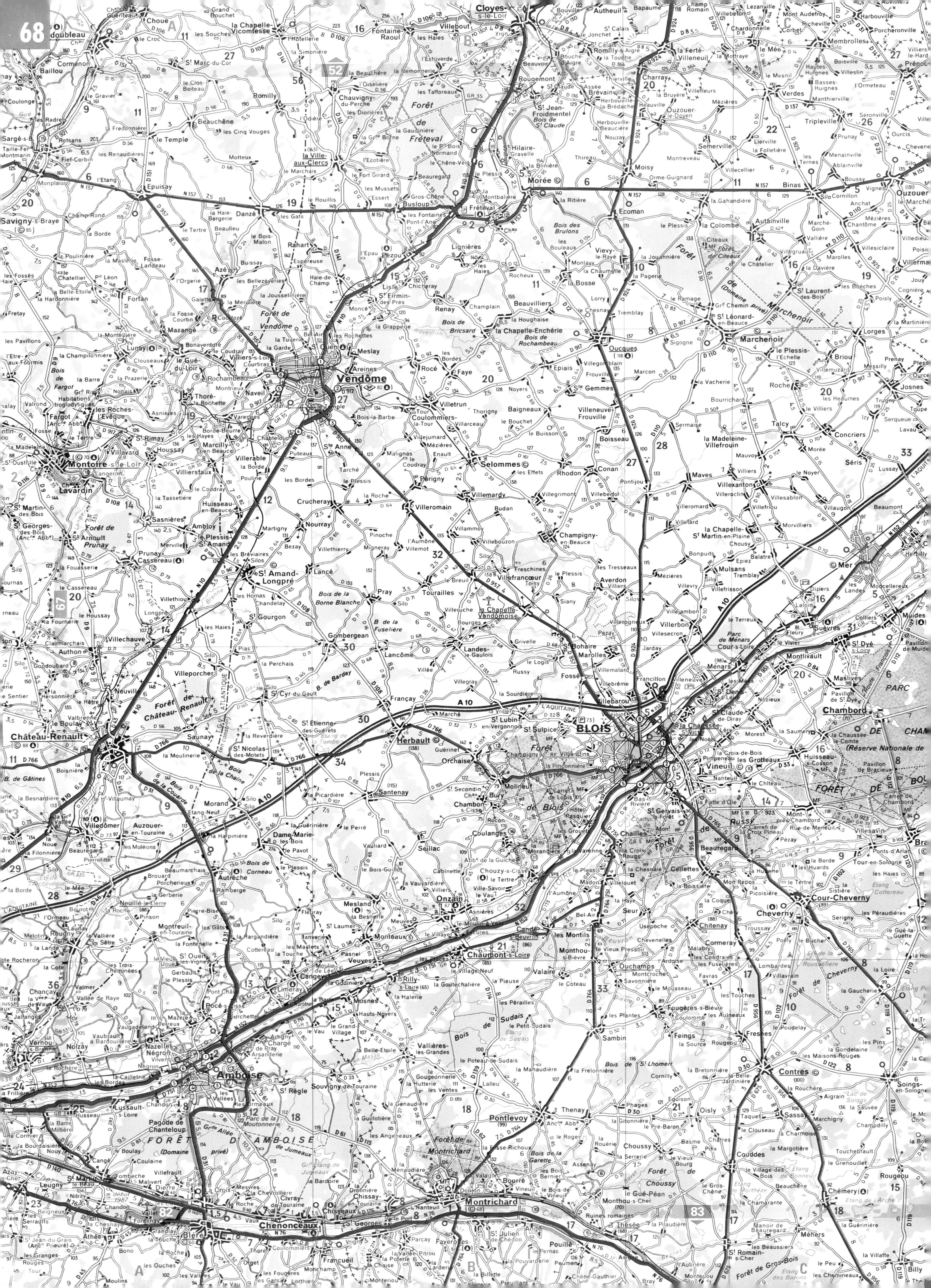
Cloyes-s-le-Loir
Vendôme
Montoire-s-le-Loir
Lavardin
Château-Renault
Blois
Amboise
Chenonceaux
Montrichard
Pontlevoy
Chaumont-s-Loire
Onzain
Herbault
Selommes
Oucques
Marchenoir
Mer
Chambord
Cour-Cheverny
Cheverny
Contres
Bléré
Morée
Fréteval
Saint-Amand-Longpré
Forêt de Fréteval
Forêt de Vendôme
Forêt de Château-Renault
Forêt de Blois
Forêt de Russy
Forêt d'Amboise
Forêt de Marchenoir
Forêt de Montrichard
Forêt de Choussy
Bois de Sudais
Parc de Chambord
A 10
L'AQUITAINE
N 10
N 152
N 157
N 76

ORLÉANS
Beaugency
Meung-s-Loire
Cléry-St André
Olivet
Fleury-les-Aubrais
St Jean-de-Braye
St Jean-de-la-Ruelle
Jargeau
Châteauneuf-s-Loire
St Benoît-s-Loire
Sully-la-Chapelle
Loury
Ingrannes
Tigy
Vienne-en-Val
La Ferté-St Aubin
Ligny-le-Ribault
Marcilly-en-Villette
Ménestreau-en-Villette
Sennely
Vannes-s-Cosson
Isdes
Vouzon
Souvigny-en-Sologne
Lamotte-Beuvron
Chaon
Chaumont-s-Tharonne
Yvoy-le-Marron
Villeny
La Marolle-en-Sologne
Dhuizon
Neung-s-Beuvron
La Ferté-Beauharnais
Nouan-le-Fuzelier
Brinon-s-Sauldre
Clémont
St Viâtre
Pierrefitte-s-Sauldre
Vernou-en-Sologne
Courmemin
Marcilly-en-Gault
Millançay
Veilleins
Souesmes
Ménétréol-s-Sauldre
Salbris
Selles-St Denis
La Ferté-Imbault
Romorantin-Lanthenay
Villeherviers
Nançay
Neuvy-s-Barangeon
FORÊT D'ORLÉANS
Forêt de Lamotte Beuvron
Forêt de Bruadan
Forêt de Chaon
LOIRE
53
70
83
84

Montargis
Amilly
Bellegarde
Ladon
Quiers-s-Bezonde
Ouzouer
Villemandeur
Nesploy
Ingrannes
Seichebrières
Sully-la-Chapelle
Combreux
Vitry-aux-Loges
Sury-aux-Bois
Châtenoy
Lorris
Vieilles-Maisons-s-Joudry
Noyers
Thimory
Oussoy-en-Gâtinais
Chevillon-s-Huillard
Vimory
Chailly-en-Gâtinais
Presnoy
Auvilliers-en-Gâtinais
Beauchamps-s-Huillard
Châteauneuf-s-Loire
St Martin d'Abbat
Germigny-des-Prés
St Aignan-des-Gués
Bray
Bouzy-la-Forêt
St Benoît-s-Loire
Sigloy
Tigy
Neuvy-en-Sullias
Bonnée
Les Bordes
FORÊT D'ORLÉANS
Ouzouer-s-Loire
Dampierre-en-Burly
Sully-s-Loire
St Père-s-Loire
St Aignan-le-Jaillard
Vannes-s-Cosson
Vigiain
Lion-en-Sullias
St Florent
St Gondon
Gien
Nevoy
Poilly-lez-Gien
Langesse
Montereau
Varennes-Changy
Nogent-s-Vernisson
Les Bézards
Boismorand
Les Choux
Châtillon-Coligny
Montcresson
Solterre
Pressigny-les-Pins
Conflans-s-Loing
Ouzouer-s-Trézée
La Bussière
Briare
St Brisson-s-Loire
Autry-le-Châtel
Châtillon-s-Loire
Ousson-s-Loire
Bonny-s-Loire
Beaulieu
Isdes
Villemurlin
Cerdon
Coullons
Souvigny-en-Sologne
Clémont
Brinon-s-Sauldre
Argent-s-Sauldre
Blancafort
Cernoy-en-Berry
Pierrefitte-ès-Bois
Santranges
Belleville-s-Loire
Aubigny-s-Nère
Ste Montaine
Concressault
Barlieu
Oizon
Dampierre-en-Crot
Vailly-s-Sauldre
Sury-ès-Bois
Léré
Souesmes
Ménétréol-s-Sauldre
Ennordres
La Verrerie
Villegenon
Thou
Assigny
Subligny
Savigny-en-Sancerre
Boulleret
Presly
Jars
Le Noyer
La Chapelle-d'Angillon
Ivoy-le-Pré
Menetou-Râtel
Sury-en-Vaux
Nançay
Neuvy-s-Barangeon
Méry-ès-Bois
Sens-Beaujeu
Sancerre
St Satur
Bannay
54
84
85

Joigny
Auxerre
Toucy
St Fargeau
Bléneau
Charny
Aillant-s-Tholon
Seignelay
Migennes
Châteaurenard
St Sauveur-en-Puisaye
Courson-les-Carrières
Coulanges-la-Vineuse
Coulanges-s-Yonne
Clamecy
Varzy
Donzy
Cosne-s-Loire
St Amand-en-Puisaye
Entrains-s-Nohain
Tannay
Chevannes
Mézilles
Champignelles
Lavau
Arquian
Bouhy
Druyes-les-Belles-Fontaines
Forêt de Frétoy
Forêt de Donzy
Forêt des Courgeonneries
Forêt des Dames
Forêt de Dracy
Autoroute du Soleil
55
72
85
86

AUXERRE
Migennes
Cheny
Charmoy
Seignelay
Pontigny
Ligny-le-Châtel
Chablis
Flogny-la-Chapelle
Tonnerre
Tanlay
St Florentin
Chéu
Vergigny
Monéteau
Venoy
Chichée
Noyers
Vermenton
Cravant
Coulanges-la-Vineuse
Courson-les-Carrières
Mailly-le-Château
Châtel-Censoir
Voutenay-s-Cure
Vézelay
Avallon
L'Isle-s-Serein
Guillon
Montréal
Clamecy
Coulanges-s-Yonne
Tannay
Quarré-les-Tombes
St Père
Lormes
Forêt de Frétoy
Forêt de Pontigny
A6
N6
N151
N77
N65
56
71
86
87

56
57
74
87
Mussy-s-Seine
Riel-les-Eaux
Montigny-s-Aube
Balnot-la-Grange
Bragelogne
Beauvoir-s-Sarce
Gommeville
Charrey-s-Seine
Belan-s-Ource
Forêt des Brosses
Noiron-s-Seine
Villers-Patras
Thoires
Veuxhaulles-s-Aube
Boudreville
Dancevoir
Channes
Molesmes
Forêt de Charme-Boulerain
Obtrée
Chaumont-le-Bois
Brion-s-Ource
Bissey-la-Côte
Courban
Arthonnay
Pothières
Villedieu
Mosson
Forêt de l'Hôpital
Vix
Mont Lassois
Massingy
Louesme
Lignerolles
Forêt de Maulnes
Vertault
Vannaire
Étrochey
Poinçon-lès-Larrey
Larrey
Bouix
Montliot
Crépan
Prusly-s-Ource
Les Goulles
La Chaume
Channay
Marcenay
Ste Colombe-s-Seine
Villotte-s-Ource
Forêt de la Chaume
Nicey
Griselles
Cérilly
Châtillon-s-Seine
Maisey-le-Duc
Lucey
Gurgy-la-Ville
Cruzy-le-Châtel
Laignes
Bissey-la-Pierre
Vanvey
Villiers-le-Duc
Voulaines-les-Templiers
Leuglay
Faverolles-lès-Lucey
Forêt de Gland
Gland
Buncey
Gigny
Balot
Ampilly-le-Sec
Chamesson
Forêt de Chamesson
Forêt de Châtillon
Recey-s-Ource
Menesble
Sennevoy
Fontaines-les-Sèches
Massoult
Nesle
Nod-s-Seine
St Germain-le-Rocheux
Essarois
Stigny
Coulmier-le-Sec
Aisey-s-Seine
Rochefort
Bure-les-Templiers
Terrefondrée
Planay
Puits
Chemin-d'Aisey
Busseaut
Montmoyen
Verdonnet
Savoisy
Ravières
Forêt du Grand Jailly
Semond
Beaulieu
Nuits
Asnières-en-Montagne
Étais
Mauvilly
St Marc-s-Seine
St Broing-les-Moines
Cry
Arrans
Magny-Lambert
Villaines-en-Duesmois
Bellenod-s-Seine
Meulson
Moitron
Perrigny-s-Armançon
Rochefort
Beaunotte
Aignay-le-Duc
Minot
Aisy-s-Armançon
Rougemont
Quemigny-s-Seine
Fontaines-en-Duesmois
Duesme
Étalante
Buffon
Anc^ne Abb^e de Fontenay
Forêt de Millon
Jours-lès-Baigneux
Marmagne
Montbard
Chaume-lès-Baigneux
Salives
Quincerot
Fresnes
Lucenay-le-Duc
Échalot
Quincy-le-Vicomte
Nogent-lès-Montbard
St Germain-lès-Senailly
Baigneux-les-Juifs
Poiseul-la-Grange
Senailly
Montigny-Montfort
Eringes
Seigny
Bussy-le-Grand
Poiseul-la-Ville
Athie
Viserny
Champ-d'Oiseau
Grignon
Les Laumes
Ménétreux-le-Pitois
Bussy-Rabutin
Darcey
Léry
Villaines-les-Prévôtes
Venarey-les-Laumes
Alise-Ste Reine
Flavigny-s-Ozerain
Frôlois
Lamargelle
Corpoyer-la-Chapelle
Chanceaux
Bard-lès-Époisses
Genay
Millery
Villars-et-Villenotte
Gissey-s-s-Flavigny
Pellerey
Corrombles
St Germain-Source-Seine
Thenissey
Hauteroche
Poncey-s-l'Ignon
Torcy-et-Pouligny
Semur-en-Auxois
Magny-la-Ville
Blessey
Vic-de-Chassenay
Pont-et-Massène
Chassey
La Roche-Vanneau
Boux-s-s-Salmaise
Vaux Saules
Francheville
Courcelles-lès-Semur
Jailly-les-Moulins
Salmaise
Champagny
Arnay-s-s-Vitteaux
St Seine-l'Abbaye
Villeneuve-s-Charigny
Villeberny
Verrey-s-s-Salmaise
Blaisy
Charigny
Dampierre-en-Montagne
Charencey
Villy-en-Auxois
St Martin-du-Mont
Montigny-St Barthélemy
Bierre-lès-Semur
Montigny-s-Armançon
Brianny
Posanges
Marcilly-lès-Vitteaux
Massingy-lès-Vitteaux
Champrenault
Turcey
Trouhaut
Précy-s-Thil
Dompierre-en-Morvan
Vitteaux
Vesvres
Chevannay
St Hélier
Prenois
La Roche-en-Brenil
Marcigny-s-Thil
St Thibault
Boussey
Saffres
Blaisy-Haut
Pasques
Lacour-d'Arcenay
Nan-s-s-Thil
Normier
Beurizot
Uncey-le-Franc
Marcellois
Baulme-la-Roche
Lantenay
Molphey
Montlay-en-Auxois
Fontangy
Charny
Soussey-s-Brionne
Grosbois-en-Montagne
Savigny
Mâlain
Ancey
Velars-s-Ouche
La Motte-Ternant
Thorey-s-s-Charny
Gissey-le-Vieil
Martrois
St Anthot
Vielmoulin
Sombernon
Fleurey-s-Ouche
Pralon
Missery
Eguilly
Aubigny-lès-Sombernon
Remilly-en-Montagne
Pont-de-Pany
Saulieu
Blancey
Bellenot-s-s-Pouilly
Civry-en-Montagne
Mont-St Jean
Montoillot
Agey
Ste Marie-s-Ouche
Forêt de Pasques
Sources de la Seine
Forêt de Jugny
Forêt de Miltot
Centre d'Études Nucléaires

Montigny-s-Aube
Arc-en-Barrois
Cour-l'Evêque
Bugnières
Faverolles
Rolampont
Tronchoy
Dampierre
Leffonds
Marac
Lannes
Charmoilles
Dancevoir
Boudreville
Aubepierre-s-Aube
Ternat
Ormancey
Beauchemin
Humes
Jorquenay
Changey
Neuilly-l'Évêque
Bannes
Lignerolles
Forêt d'Arc
Giey-s-Aujon
Courcelles-s-Aujon
St Loup-s-Aujon
Vauxbons
Mardor
St Ciergues
Peigney
Langres
Louesme
les Goulles
la Chaume
Rochetaillée
Voisines
Perrancey
Chatenay-Mâcheron
Corlée
St Maurice
St Vallier-s-Marne
Rouvres-s-Aube
Arbot
Gurgy-la-Ville
Lucey
Aulnoy-s-Aube
Vitry-en-Montagne
Courcelles-en-Montagne
Vieux-Moulins
Noidant-le-Rocheux
Balesmes-s-Marne
Faverolles-lès-Lucey
Gurgy-le-Château
Leuglay
Voulaines-les-Templiers
Bay-s-Aube
Chameroy
Perrogney
Buxerolles
Rouelles
Chambain
Germaines
Auberive
Pierrefontaines
Brennes
Bourg
Flagey
Noidant-Chatenoy
Chalindrey
Recey-s-Ource
Menesble
Colmier-le-Haut
Colmier-le-Bas
Aprey
Orcevaux
Verseilles-le-Haut
Longeau
Percey-le-Pautel
Violot
Heuilley-Cotton
Essarois
Chaugey
Villars-Montroyer
Praslay
St Georges
Aujeurres
Villiers-lès-Aprey
Baissey
Prangey
Villegusien
Heuilley-le-Grand
Bure-les-Templiers
Terrefondrée
Montmoyen
Villars-Santenoge
Vivey
Leuchey
St Michel
Chassigny
St Broingt-le-Bois
Beaulieu
Musseau
Vaillant
St Broingt-les-Fosses
Courcelles-Val-d'Esnoms
Poinson-lès-Grancey
Poinsenot
Lamargelle-aux-Bois
Esnoms-au-Val
Prauthoy
Dommarien
St Broing-les-Moines
Beneuvre
Mouilleron
Vesvres-s/s-Chalancey
Moitron
Villemervry
Chalancey
Chatoillenot
Montsaugeon
Choilley
Aignay-le-Duc
Minot
Bussières
Neuvelle-lès-Grancey
Grancey-le-Château
Villemoron
Rivière-les-Fosses
Vaux-s-Aubigny
Dardenay
Isômes
Etalante
Fraignot
Courlon
Cussey-les-Forges
Vernois-lès-Vesvres
Cusey
Percey-sous-Montormentier
Salives
Echalot
Barjon
Avot
Forêt de Cussey
Bousenois
Occey
Percey-le-Grand
Orain
Marey-s-Tille
Foncegrive
Selongey
Sacquenay
Le Meix
Avelanges
Poiseul-la-Grange
Poiseul-lès-Saulx
Villey-s-Tille
Orville
Chazeuil
Chaume-et-Courchamp
Léry
Courtivron
Saulx-le-Duc
Luxerois
Crécey-s-Tille
Véronnes
Lamargelle
Tarsul
Diénay
Is-s-Tille
Echevannes
Fontaine-Française
Frénois
Moloy
Marcilly-s-Tille
Til-Châtel
Chanceaux
Pellerey
Poncey-s-l'Ignon
Villecomte
Lux
Bourberain
Fontenelle
Vernot
Gemeaux
Bèze
Dampierre-et-Flée
Vaux-Saules
Francheville
Chaignay
Champagny
Saussy
Marsannay-le-Bois
Pichanges
Spoy
Epagny
Blagny-s-Vingeanne
St Seine-l'Abbaye
Savigny-le-Sec
Flacey
Vièvigne
Oisilly
Val-Suzon
Etaules
Messigny-et-Vantoux
Norges-la-Ville
Clénay
Brognon
Beire-le-Châtel
Tanay
Mirebeau
Renève
Trouhaut
Darois
Bretigny
St Julien
Arceau
Magny-St Médard
Bèzouotte
Jancigny
Asnières-lès-Dijon
Bellefond
Savolles
Charmes
Cuiserey
Pasques
Prenois
Ahuy
Ruffey-lès-Echirey
Orgeux
Arcelot
St Sauveur
Hauteville-lès-Dijon
Fontaine-lès-Dijon
Varois
Arc-s-Tille
Belleneuve
Montmançon
Lantenay
Plombières-lès-Dijon
Talant
DIJON
Couternon
Binges
Trochères
Drambon
Maxilly-s-Saône
Ancey
Velars-s-Ouche
Quetigny
Remilly-s-Tille
Etevaux
St Léger
Savigny-s/s-Mâlain
Mâlain
Prâlon
Fleurey-s-Ouche
Chevigny
Bressey-s-Tille
Cirey-lès-Pontailler
Vonges
Sombernon
Chenôve
Longvic
Neuilly
Chambeire
Tellecey
Izier
Cessey-s-Tille

Bourbonne-les-Bains
Fresnes-s-Apance
Châtillon-s-Saône
Jonvelle
Ameuvelle
Vauvillers
Vougécourt
Fontenois-la-Ville
Dampvalley-lès-Pancras
Mailleroncourt-St Pancras
Laneuvelle
Vicq
Andilly-en-Bassigny
Lavernoy
Varennes-s-Amance
Genrupt
Montcharvot
Melay
Bourbévelle
Corre
Ranzevelle
Girefontaine
Celles-en-Bassigny
Marcilly-en-Bassigny
Plesnoy
Troischamps
Chézeaux
Forêt de Marcilly
Voisey
Blondefontaine
Ormoy
Polaincourt-et-Clairefontaine
Anjeux
Jasney
Champigny-s/s-Varennes
Arbigny-s/s-Varennes
Neuvelle-lès-Voisey
Barges
Betaucourt
Saponcourt
Anchenoncourt-et-Chazel
Magny-lès-Jussey
Raincourt
Cendrecourt
Hortes
Bize
Laferté-s-Amance
Guyonvelle
Cemboing
Vernois-s-Mance
Rosières-s-Mance
Jussey
Tartécourt
Senoncourt
St Remy
Rosoy-s-Amance
Maizières-s-Amance
Betoncourt-s-Mance
Pisseloup
St Marcel
Venisey
Contréglise
Bassigny
Chaudenay
Rougeux
Montesson
Charmoy
Vitrey-s-Mance
Noroy-lès-Jussey
Montureux-lès-Baulay
Buffignecourt
Menoux
Cubry-lès-Faverney
Bourguignon-lès-Conflans
Corgirnon
Pierrefaites
Ouge
Chauvirey-le-Châtel
Montigny-lès-Cherlieu
Gevigney
Amance
Baulay
Fouchécourt
Faverney
Mersuay
Equevilley
Les Loges
Fayl-Billot
Chauvirey-le-Vieil
La Quarte
Bougey
Augicourt
Aboncourt
Port d'Atelier-Amance
Breurey-lès-Faverney
Broncourt
Preigney
Cintrey
Oigney
Lambrey
Purgerot
Fleurey-lès-Faverney
Poinson-lès-Fayl
Pressigny
La Rochelle
Melin
Semmadon
Arbecey
Chargey-lès-Port
Conflandey
Amoncourt
Bussières-lès-Belmont
Charmes-St Valbert
Molay
Malvillers
Provenchère
Villers-s-Port
Belmont
Genevrières
Voncourt
Savigny
Gourgeon
Lavigney
Combeaufontaine
Chaux-lès-Port
Port-s-Saône
Saulles
Valleroy
Bourguignon-lès-Morey
Farincourt
Morey
St Julien
Tornay
Gilley
Betoncourt-les-Ménétriers
Cornot
La Neuvelle-lès-Scey
Bougnon
Auxon
Grattery
Vauchoux
Scey-s-Saône-et-St Albin
Frettes
Suaucourt
Villers-Vaudey
Confracourt
Ferrières-lès-Scey
Charmoille
Pusey
Argillières
Fleurey-lès-Lavoncourt
Vauconcourt
Rupt-s-Saône
Chemilly
Montigny-lès-Vesoul
Coulevon
Vesoul
Pierrecourt
Fouvent-le-Haut
St Andoche
Francourt
Chantes
Chassey-lès-Scey
Pontcey
Vaivre
Frotey
Montarlot-lès-Champlitte
Renaucourt
Lavoncourt
Mont-St Léger
Grandecourt
Ovanches
Bucey-lès-Traves
Noidans-lès-Vesoul
Larret
Volon
Theuley
Fédry
Traves
Boursières
Navenne
Quincey
Champlitte
Champlitte-la-Ville
Courtesoult
Roche-et-Raucourt
Brotte-lès-Ray
Tincey
Vanne
Cubry-lès-Soing
Aroz
Clans
Velle-le-Châtel
Margilley
Vaite
Membrey
Recologne
Ray-s-Saône
Ferrières-lès-Ray
Charentenay
Soing
Vy-le-Ferroux
Raze
Baignes
Andelarre
Andelarrot
La Demie
Neuvelle-lès-Champlitte
Mont-le-Franois
Achey
Delain
Denèvre
Noidans-le-Ferroux
Rosey
Vallerois-Lorioz
Framont
Montot
Dampierre-s-Salon
Seveux
Vellexon
Fresne-St Mamès
Velleguindry
Vellefaux
Savoyeux
Vezet
Le Pont-de-Planches
Neuvelle-lès-la-Charité
Mailley
Echenoz-le-Sec
Ecuelle
Autet
Mercey-s-Saône
Greucourt
Lieffrans
Le Magnoray
Filain
Vars
Oyrières
Quitteur
Motey-s-Saône
St Gand
La Vernotte
Les Bâties
Grandvelle-et-le-Perrenot
Fahy-lès-Autrey
Auvet-et-la-Chapelotte
Vereux
Beaujeu
Bourguignon-lès-la-Charité
Maizières
Pennesières
Authoison
Montureux
Chargey-lès-Gray
Autrey-lès-Gray
St Vallier
Ste Reine
Vereux
La Chapelle-St Quillain
Fretigney
Recologne-lès-Rioz
Fondremand
Hyet
Roche-s-Linotte
Villers-Pater
Bouhans
Rigny
Igny
Vellemoz
Etrelles
Vaux-le-Moncelot
Frasne-le-Château
Quenoche
Ruhans
Aubertans
Nantilly
Arc-lès-Gray
Gray
Angirey
Villers-Bouton
Trésilley
Les Fontenis
La Malachère
Poyans
Ancier
St Broing
Sauvigney-lès-Gray
Citey
Vantoux
Vellefrey
Vellemoz
Rioz
Beaumotte-lès-Montbozon
Gray-la-Ville
Battrans
St Loup
Velesmes
Bucey-lès-Gy
Vellecleire
Oiselay-et-Grachaux
Cordonnet
Montarlot-lès-Rioz
Traitiéfontaine
Blarians
Velet
Mantoche
Echevanne
Forêt des Hauts-Bois
Gy
Bonnevent-Velloreille
Neuvelle-lès-Cromary
Cirey
Vandelans
Esmoulins
Champvans
Cresancey
Villefrancon
Velloreille-lès-Choye
Choye
Boult
Sorans
Apremont
Le Tremblois
Noiron
Champtonnay
Autoreille
Montboillon
Chaux
Cromary
Thurey-le-Mont
Germigney
Arsans
Cugney
Charcenne
Gezier-et-Fontenelay
Etuz
Boulot
Bussières
Voray-s-l'Ognon
Perrouse
Moncey
Chaudefontaine
Montseugny
Vadans
Lieucourt
Vénère
Bonboillon
Tromarey
Avrigney
Courcuire
Chambornay-lès-Pin
Cussey-s-l'Ognon
Geneuille
Chevroz
Buthiers
Vieilley
Champoux
Marchaux
Valay
Chevigney
La Grande Résie
Aubigney
Chancey
Hugier
Cult
Beaumotte-lès-Pin
Pin
Emagny
Sauvagney
Vregille
Moncley
Auxon-dessus
Devecey
Châtillon-le-Duc
Tallenay
Bonnay
Amagney
Broye
La Résie-St Martin
Motey-Besuche
Brussey
Chevigney-s-l'Ognon
Auxon-dessous
Miserey-Salines
Forêt de Chailluz
Braillans
Novillars
Vaire-Arcier
Sauvigney-lès-Pesmes
Chaumercenne
Montagney
Marnay
Ruffey-le-Château
Chaucenne
Thise
Roche-lez-Beaupré
Cléry
Pesmes
Bay
Sornay
Chenevrey
Chazoy
Recologne
Noironte
Pouilley-les-Vignes
Pirey
Ecole
Chalèze
Vielverge
Mutigney
Burgille
Cordiron
Audeux
Franey
Chalezeule
Courchapon
Placey
58
59
89
90

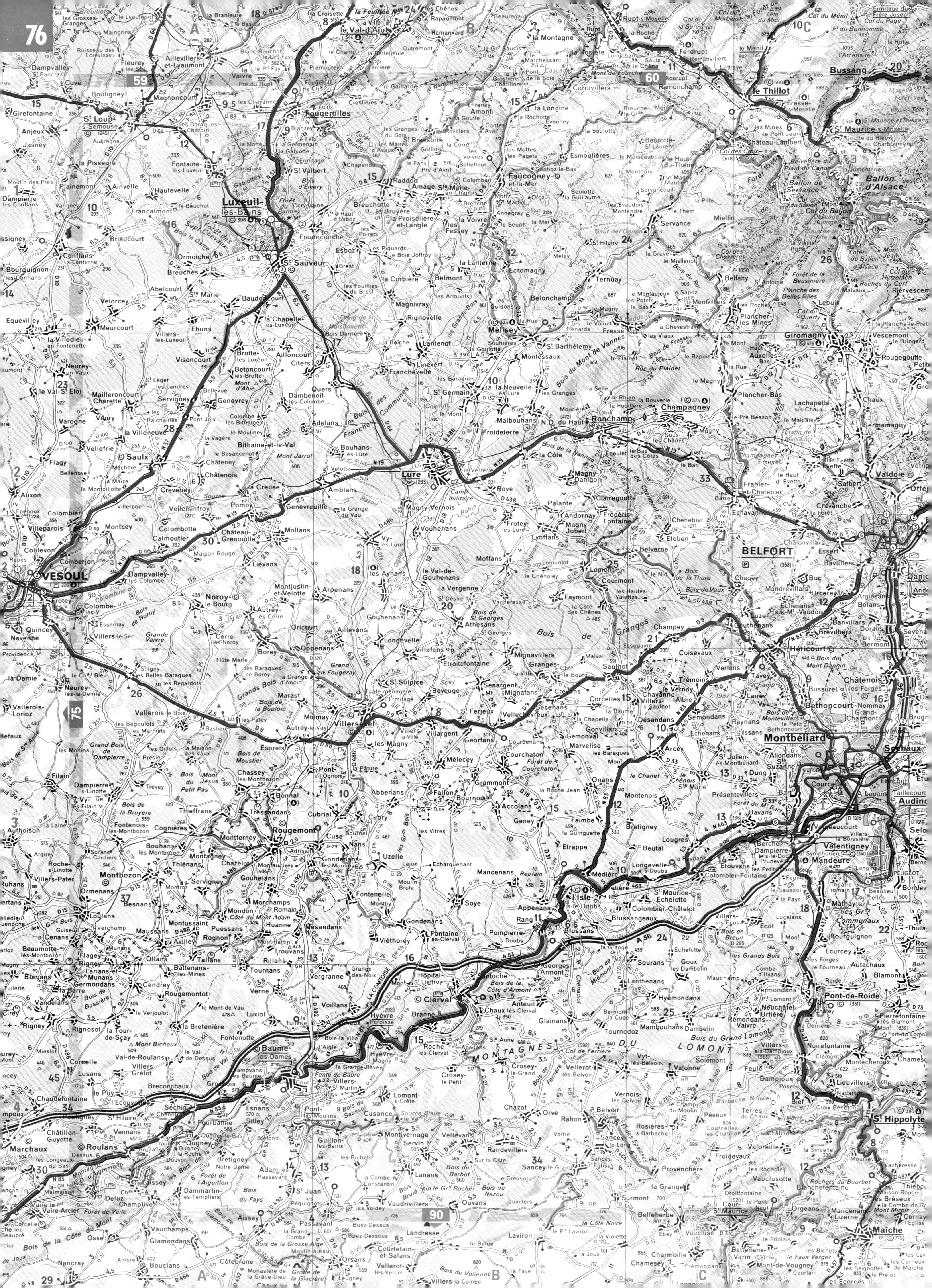
Luxeuil-les-Bains
St Loup s-Semouse
Fougerolles
le Val-d'Ajol
Faucogney-et-la-Mer
le Thillot
Bussang
Ballon d'Alsace
Giromagny
Mélisey
Ronchamp
Champagney
Lure
Vesoul
BELFORT
Héricourt
Montbéliard
Sochaux
Audincourt
Valentigney
Mandeure
Villersexel
Rougemont
Montbozon
l'Isle-s-le-Doubs
Clerval
Baume-les-Dames
Roulans
Pont-de-Roide
St Hippolyte
Maîche
Saulx
Noroy-le-Bourg
Valdoie
Giromagny
MONTAGNES DU LOMONT
59
60
75
90

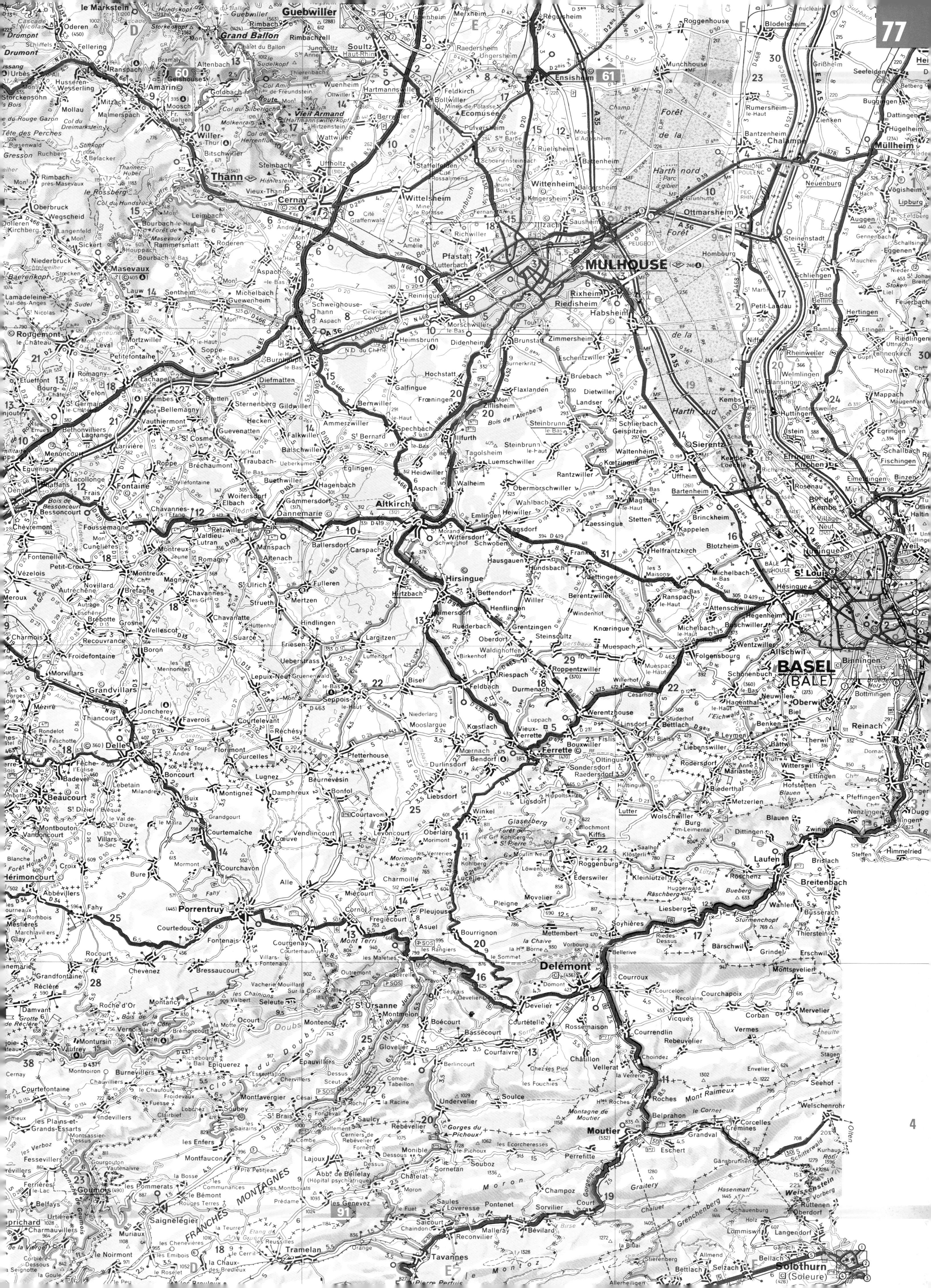

Guebwiller
Grand Ballon
Soultz Haut-Rhin
Ensisheim
Thann
Cernay
Wittelsheim
Masevaux
MULHOUSE
Rixheim
Riedisheim
Habsheim
Illzach
Pfastatt
Lutterbach
Müllheim
Neuenburg
Ottmarsheim
Chalampé
Sierentz
St Louis
Huningue
Weil
BASEL (BÂLE)
Binningen
Altkirch
Dannemarie
Hirsingue
Ferrette
Delle
Beaucourt
Hérimoncourt
Porrentruy
Delémont
St Ursanne
Moutier
Laufen
Breitenbach
Reinach
Solothurn (Soleure)
Tavannes
Tramelan
Saignelégier
Goumois
Rougemont-le-Château
Fontaine
Grandvillars
Bessoncourt
Lachapelle
Seppois
Oberwil
Bevilard
Reconvilier
FRANCHES MONTAGNES
Forêt de la Harth nord
Harth sud
Rhin

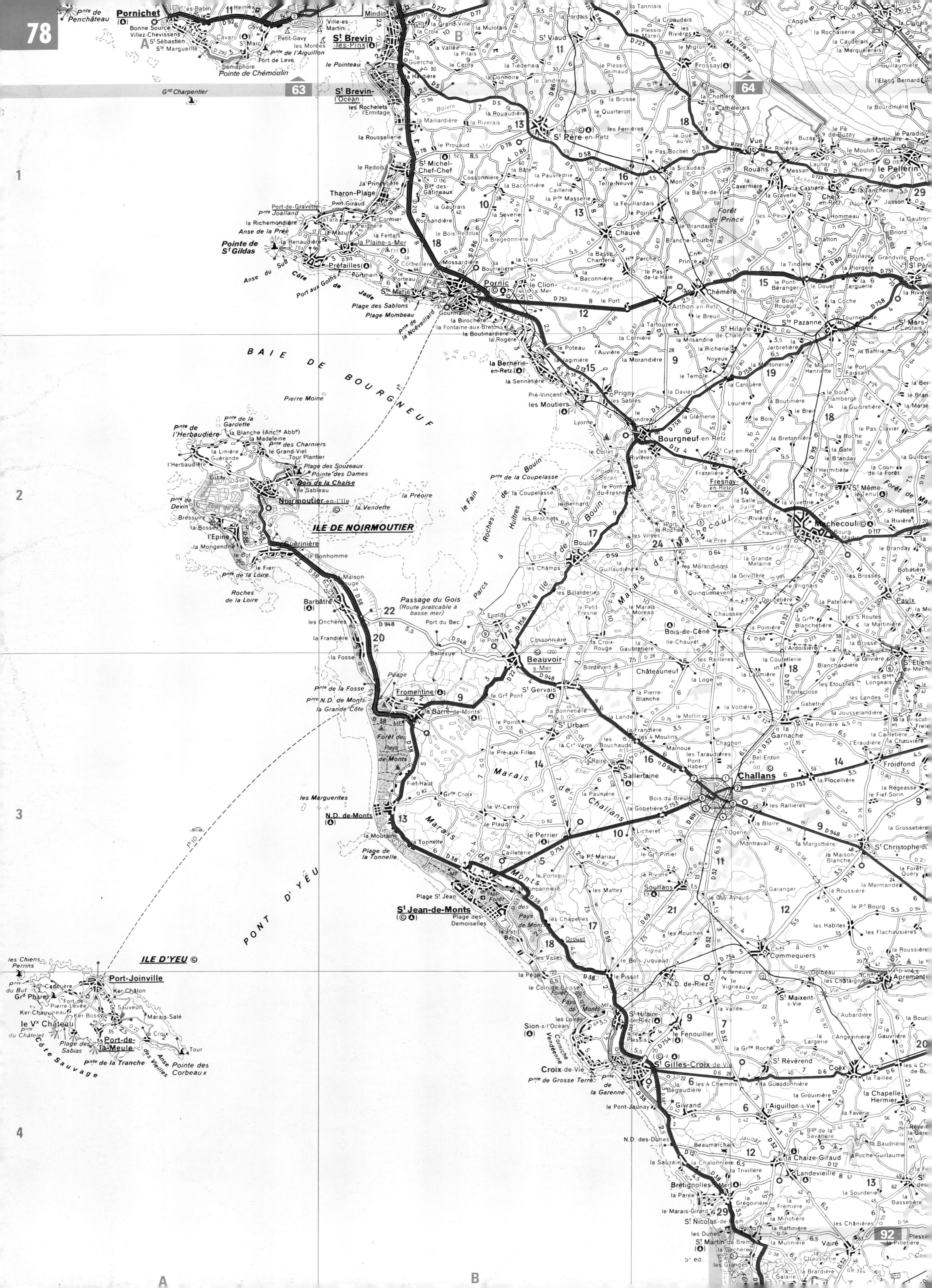
Pornichet
Pte de Penchâteau
St Sébastien
Ste Marguerite
Pointe de Chémoulin
Grd Charpentier
63
64
St Brevin-les-Pins
St Brevin-l'Océan
Mindin
St Michel-Chef-Chef
Tharon-Plage
Pointe de St Gildas
Préfailles
Ste Marie
Pornic
St Père-en-Retz
Frossay
Vue
Rouans
Le Pellerin
Chauvé
Chéméré
Arthon-en-Retz
St Hilaire-de-Chaleons
Ste Pazanne
la Bernerie-en-Retz
Les Moutiers
Prigny
Bourgneuf-en-Retz
Fresnay-en-Retz
Machecoul
BAIE DE BOURGNEUF
Pierre Moine
Pte de l'Herbaudière
l'Herbaudière
Bois de la Chaise
Noirmoutier-en-l'Ile
ILE DE NOIRMOUTIER
l'Epine
la Guérinière
Pte de la Loire
Roches de la Loire
Barbâtre
Passage du Gois (Route praticable à basse mer)
Port du Bec
Bouin
Beauvoir-s-Mer
Bois-de-Céné
Paulx
Fromentine
la Barre-de-Monts
Forêt des Pays de Monts
St Gervais
St Urbain
Châteauneuf
Sallertaine
Challans
Froidfond
Marais de Challans
N.D.-de-Monts
St Jean-de-Monts
Soullans
St Christophe-du-Ligneron
Commequiers
Apremont
PONT D'YEU
ILE D'YEU
Port-Joinville
le Vx Château
Port-de-la-Meule
Côte Sauvage
Sion-s-l'Océan
St Hilaire-de-Riez
St Gilles-Croix-de-Vie
Croix-de-Vie
Le Fenouiller
St Maixent-s-Vie
St Révérend
Coëx
Givrand
l'Aiguillon-s-Vie
la Chapelle-Hermier
la Chaize-Giraud
Landevieille
Bretignolles-s-Mer
St Nicolas-de-Brem
St Martin-de-Brem
Vairé
92
A
B
C
1
2
3
4

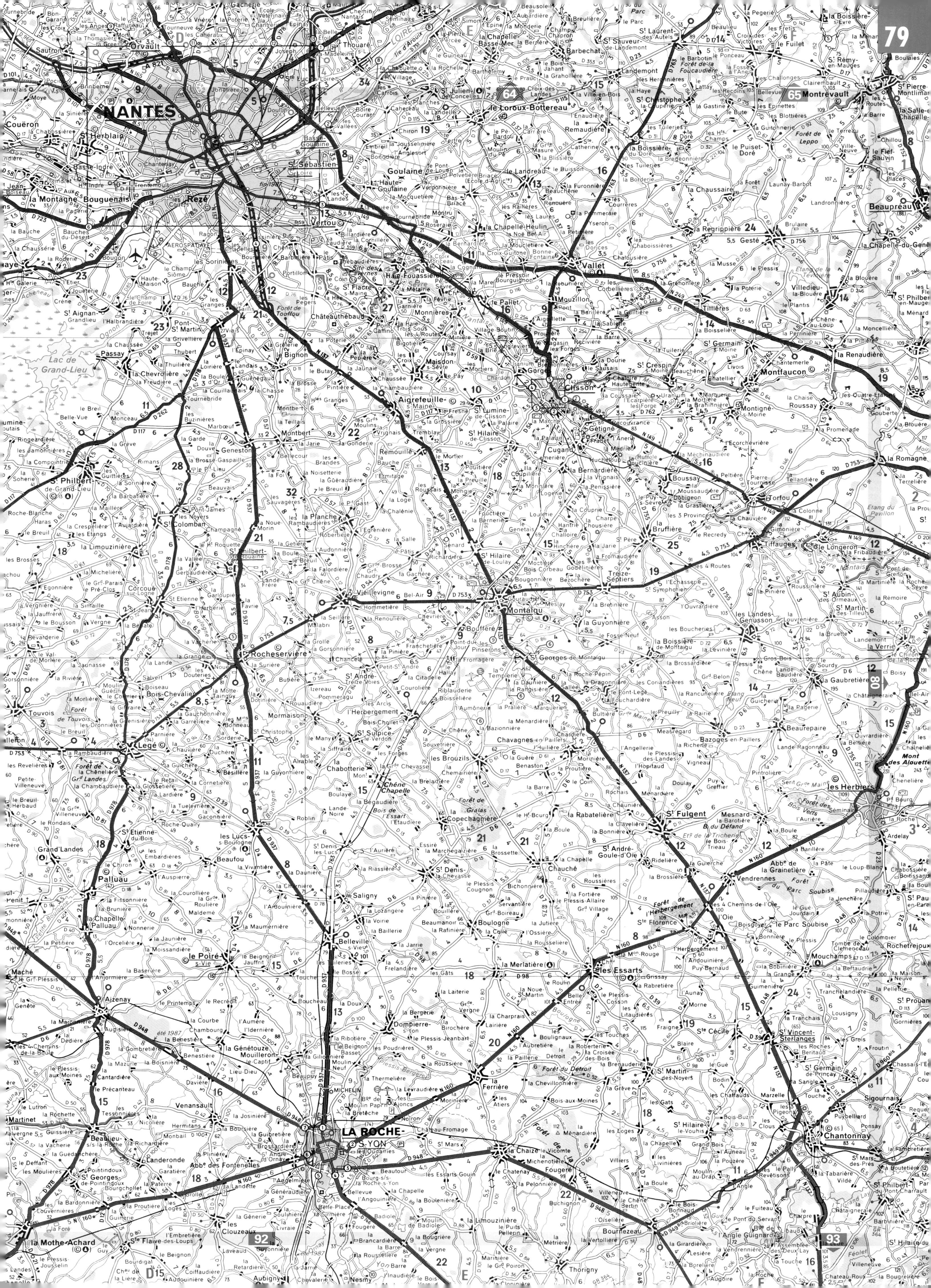

NANTES
Orvault
Sautron
Couëron
St Herblain
Basse-Indre
Indre
la Montagne
Bouguenais
Rezé
Vertou
St Sébastien
Basse-Goulaine
Haute-Goulaine
Carquefou
Thouaré
St Julien-de-Concelles
le Loroux-Bottereau
la Chapelle-Basse-Mer
Barbechat
Landemont
St Laurent-des-Autels
St Sauveur-de-Landemont
St Christophe-la-Couperie
Montrevault
la Boissière-sur-Evre
St Pierre-Montlimart
la Salle-et-Chapelle
Beaupréau
le Fief-Sauvin
Villedieu-la-Blouère
la Chapelle-du-Genêt
la Regrippière
Gesté
Vallet
Mouzillon
le Pallet
Tillières
St Germain-s-Moine
St Crespin-s-Moine
Montfaucon
Cholet
Clisson
Gétigné
Gorges
Maisdon-s-Sèvre
Aigrefeuille-s-Maine
St Lumine-de-Clisson
St Hilaire-de-Clisson
Montbert
Geneston
Remouillé
Château-Thébaud
la Haie-Fouassière
St Fiacre-s-Maine
Monnières
Haute-Goulaine
Pont-St Martin
St Aignan-Grandlieu
le Bignon
Passay
la Chevrolière
Lac de Grand-Lieu
St Philbert-de-Grand-Lieu
St Colomban
St Philbert-de-Bouaine
Corcoué-sur-Logne
Vieillevigne
Montaigu
Boufféré
Rocheservière
Bois-Chevalier
Touvois
Legé
la Bernardière
Boussay
Torfou
Tiffauges
la Bruffière
Treize-Septiers
St Symphorien
la Boissière-de-Montaigu
les Landes-Genusson
St Aubin-des-Ormeaux
St Martin-des-Tilleuls
la Verrie
la Gaubretière
les Herbiers
Mont des Alouettes
Beaurepaire
Bazoges-en-Paillers
Chavagnes-en-Paillers
St Fulgent
St André-Goule-d'Oie
Chauché
les Brouzils
St Sulpice-le-Verdon
l'Herbergement
Mormaison
St André-Treize-Voies
la Chabotterie
Copechagnière
St Denis-la-Chevasse
les Lucs-s-Boulogne
Beaufou
Palluau
St Etienne-du-Bois
Grand'Landes
la Chapelle-Palluau
Saligny
Belleville-s-Vie
le Poiré-s-Vie
Boulogne
la Merlatière
les Essarts
Vendrennes
Mouchamps
St Vincent-Sterlanges
Ste Cécile
Dompierre-s-Yon
Aizenay
la Génétouze
Mouilleron-le-Captif
Venansault
Ferrière
la Chaize-le-Vicomte
Fougeré
St Martin-des-Noyers
St Hilaire-le-Vouhis
Chantonnay
Sigournais
St Germain-de-Prinçay
St Philbert-du-Pont-Charrault
Bournezeau
Thorigny
LA ROCHE-S-YON
Landeronde
Beaulieu-s/s-la-Roche
St Georges-de-Pointindoux
la Mothe-Achard
les Clouzeaux
Ste Flaive-des-Loups
Nesmy
Aubigny
Chaillé-s-Ormeaux
Rochetrejoux
St Prouant
Forêt de Touvois
Forêt de la Chênelière
Forêt de Gralas
Forêt du Détroit
Forêt de l'Herbergement
Forêt de Leppo
Forêt du Parc Soubise
64
65
80
92
93

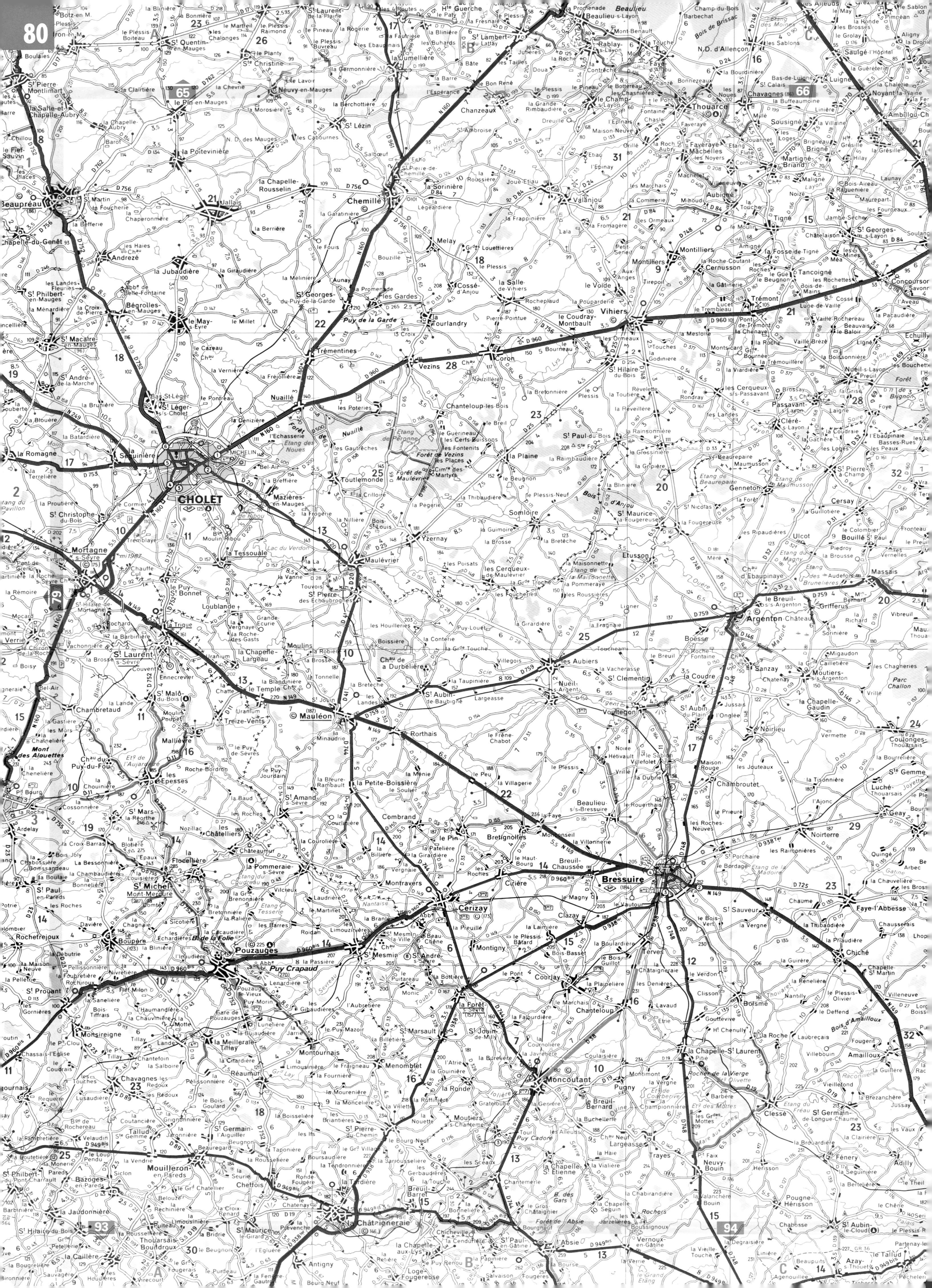
Beaupréau
Chemillé
Cholet
Mortagne s-Sèvre
Maulévrier
Mauléon
Vihiers
Coron
Vezins
Nuaillé
Trémentines
Jallais
Thouarcé
Argenton Château
Bressuire
Cerizay
Pouzauges
Moncoutant
la Châtaigneraie
Chanteloup
les Aubiers
St Michel-Mont-Mercure
les Epesses
Chavagnes
Mouilleron-en-Pareds
Tigné
Montilliers
Cersay
Massais
Faye-l'Abbesse
Chiché
Clessé
Vernoux-en-Gâtine
l'Absie
St Laurent-s-Sèvre
la Tessoualle
Yzernay
Somloire
Etusson
Nueil-s-Argent
Voultegon
Courlay
Breuil-Chaussée
St Sauveur
Boismé
Amailloux
Faye-d'Anjou
Rablay-s-Layon
Beaulieu-s-Layon
le Champ-s-Layon
Valanjou
Melay
Aubigné
Passavant-s-Layon
Cléré-s-Layon
Nueil-s-Layon
St Pierre-Montlimart
St Quentin-en-Mauges
le Pin-en-Mauges
la Poitevinière
Andrezé
le May-s-Èvre
St Macaire-en-Mauges
St Léger-s-Cholet
Mazières-en-Mauges
Toutlemonde
St Christophe-du-Bois
la Séguinière
la Romagne
Puy du Fou
Réaumur
Montournais
Menomblet
St Pierre-du-Chemin
Breuil-Barret
St Paul-en-Gâtine
Largeasse
Trayes
Neuvy-Bouin
Pugny
St Germain-de-Longue-Chaume
Adilly
St Aubin-le-Cloud
Azay-s-Thouet
Le Tallud
Forêt de Vezins
Forêt de Chanteloup
Bois d'Anjou
Bois d'Amailloux
Forêt de l'Absie
Puy Crapaud
Bois de la Folie

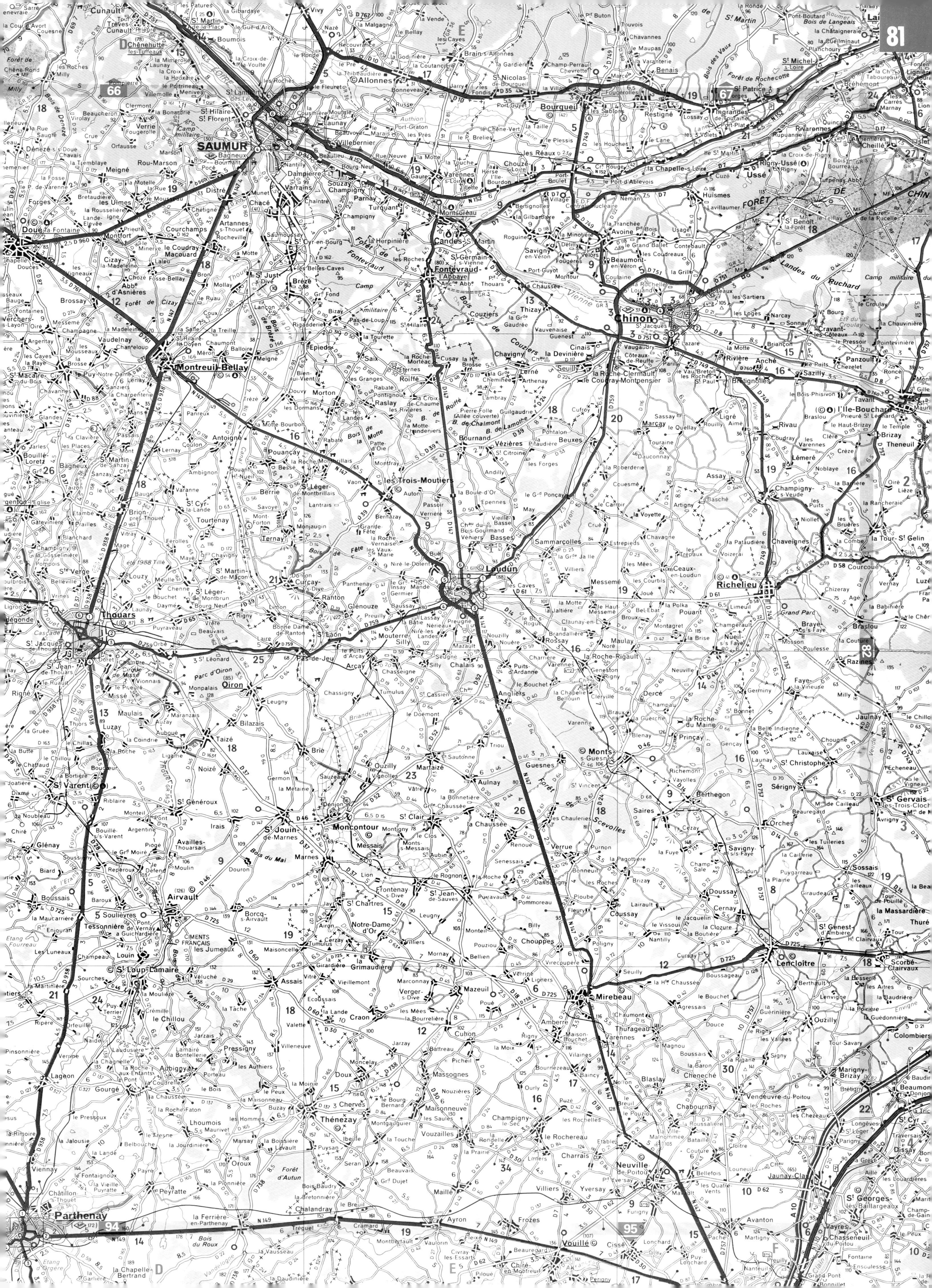
SAUMUR
Chênehutte-les-Tuffeaux
Allonnes
Bourgueil
Benais
Brain-s-Allonnes
St Nicolas-de-Bourgueil
Restigné
Ingrandes-de-Touraine
St Patrice
St Michel-s-Loire
Forêt de Rochecotte
Bagneux
Distré
Doué-la-Fontaine
Montfort
Artannes-s-Thouet
Chacé
Varrains
Dampierre
Souzay-Champigny
Parnay
Turquant
Montsoreau
Candes-St Martin
Fontevraud-l'Abbaye
Forêt de Fontevraud
Avoine
Savigny-en-Véron
Beaumont-en-Véron
Chinon
Ussé
Rigny-Ussé
Huismes
Forêt de Chinon
Landes du Ruchard
Camp militaire
Brézé
St Just-s-Dive
Montreuil-Bellay
Épieds
Couziers
Bois de Couziers
Thizay
Cinais
La Devinière
Seuilly
La Roche-Clermault
Le Coudray-Montpensier
Rivière
Anché
Sazilly
Panzoult
L'Ile-Bouchard
Marçay
Ligré
Brizay
Theneuil
Les Trois-Moutiers
Morton
Raslay
Roiffé
Bournand
Vézières
Beuxes
Ternay
Curçay-s-Dive
Loudun
Richelieu
Champigny-s-Veude
Chaveignes
La Tour-St Gelin
Thouars
St Jacques
St Jean-de-Thouars
Oiron
Parc d'Oiron
Moutiers
Pas-de-Jeu
Arçay
Chalais
Angliers
La Roche-Rigault
Faye-la-Vineuse
St Varent
Luzay
Taizé
Moncontour
St Jouin-de-Marnes
Marnes
Aulnay
Monts-s-Guesnes
Guesnes
Forêt de Scevolles
Berthegon
Sérigny
St Gervais-les-Trois-Clochers
Orches
Sossais
Airvault
Glénay
Boussais
St Loup-Lamairé
Assais
Craon
Cuhon
Mirebeau
Lencloître
Scorbé-Clairvaux
Thurageau
Varennes
Ouzilly
Marigny-Brizay
Vendeuvre-du-Poitou
Chabournay
Thénezay
Doux
Massognes
Champigny-le-Sec
Le Rochereau
Neuville-de-Poitou
Jaunay-Clan
Dissay
Ayron
Parthenay
Vouillé
Cissé
Chasseneuil-du-Poitou
St Georges-lès-Baillargeaux
Beaumont
St Cyr
66
67
82
94
95

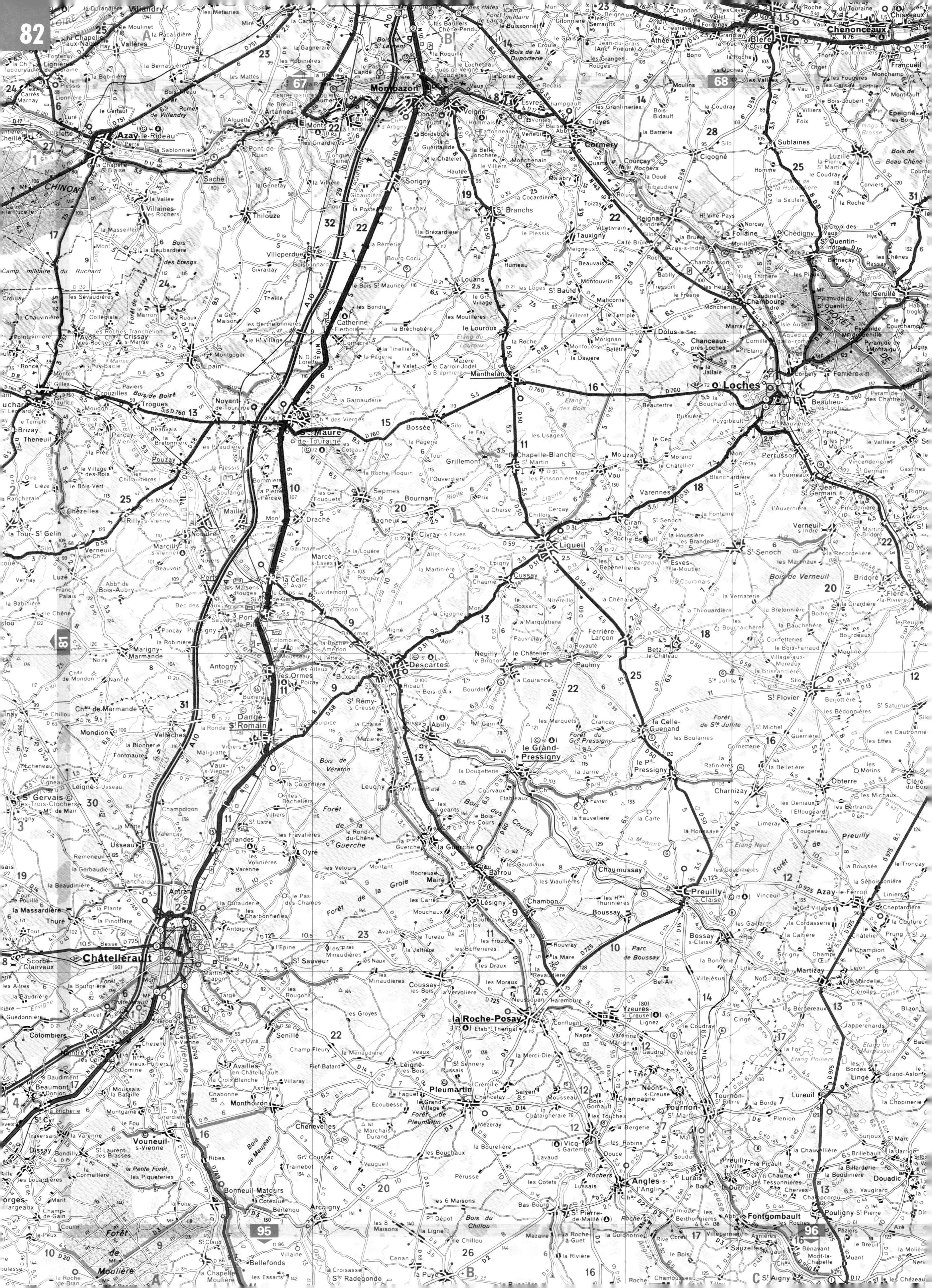
Villandry
Azay-le-Rideau
Chinon
Montbazon
Veigné
Esves
Truyes
Cormery
Sorigny
Bléré
Chenonceaux
Francueil
Saché
Thilouze
Villeperdue
Louans
Ste Catherine-de-Fierbois
St Branchs
Tauxigny
Reignac-s-Indre
Azay-s-Indre
Chédigny
St Quentin-s-Indrois
Genillé
Chambourg-s-Indre
Dolus-le-Sec
Chanceaux-près-Loches
Loches
Beaulieu-lès-Loches
Manthelan
Neuil
Crissay-s-Manse
Avon-les-Roches
St Epain
Noyant-de-Touraine
Trogues
Crouzilles
Ste Maure-de-Touraine
Bossée
Grillemont
la Chapelle-Blanche-St Martin
Mouzay
Vou
Varennes
Perrusson
St Jean-St Germain
Pouzay
Sepmes
Bournan
Draché
Maillé
Nouâtre
Marcilly-s-Vienne
Ligueil
St Senoch
Verneuil-s-Indre
Cussay
Port-de-Piles
Descartes
Neuilly-le-Brignon
Paulmy
Betz-le-Château
Ferrière-Larçon
Marigny-Marmande
Antogny
les Ormes
Abilly
Dangé-St Romain
le Grand-Pressigny
la Celle-Guenand
le Pt-Pressigny
Charnizay
Obterre
Vellèches
Leugny
Leigné-s-Usseau
St Gervais-les-Trois-Clochers
Usseau
Ingrandes
Oyré
la Guerche
Barrou
Chaumussay
Preuilly-s-Claise
Azay-le-Ferron
Mairé
Lésigny
Bossay-s-Claise
Châtellerault
St Sauveur
Coussay-les-Bois
Martizay
la Roche-Posay
Yzeures-s-Creuse
Senillé
Leigné-les-Bois
Pleumartin
Néons-s-Creuse
Tournon-St Pierre
Tournon-St Martin
Lureuil
Lingé
Vouneuil-s-Vienne
Monthoiron
Chenevelles
Vicq-s-Gartempe
Angles-s-l'Anglin
Preuilly-la-Ville
Douadic
Bonneuil-Matours
Archigny
Fontgombault
Pouligny-St Pierre
la Puye
Forêt de Moulière
Cenon-s-Vienne
Naintré
Beaumont
Dissay
St Cyr
Colombiers
Scorbé-Clairvaux
Thuré
Availles-en-Châtellerault
67
68
81
95
96

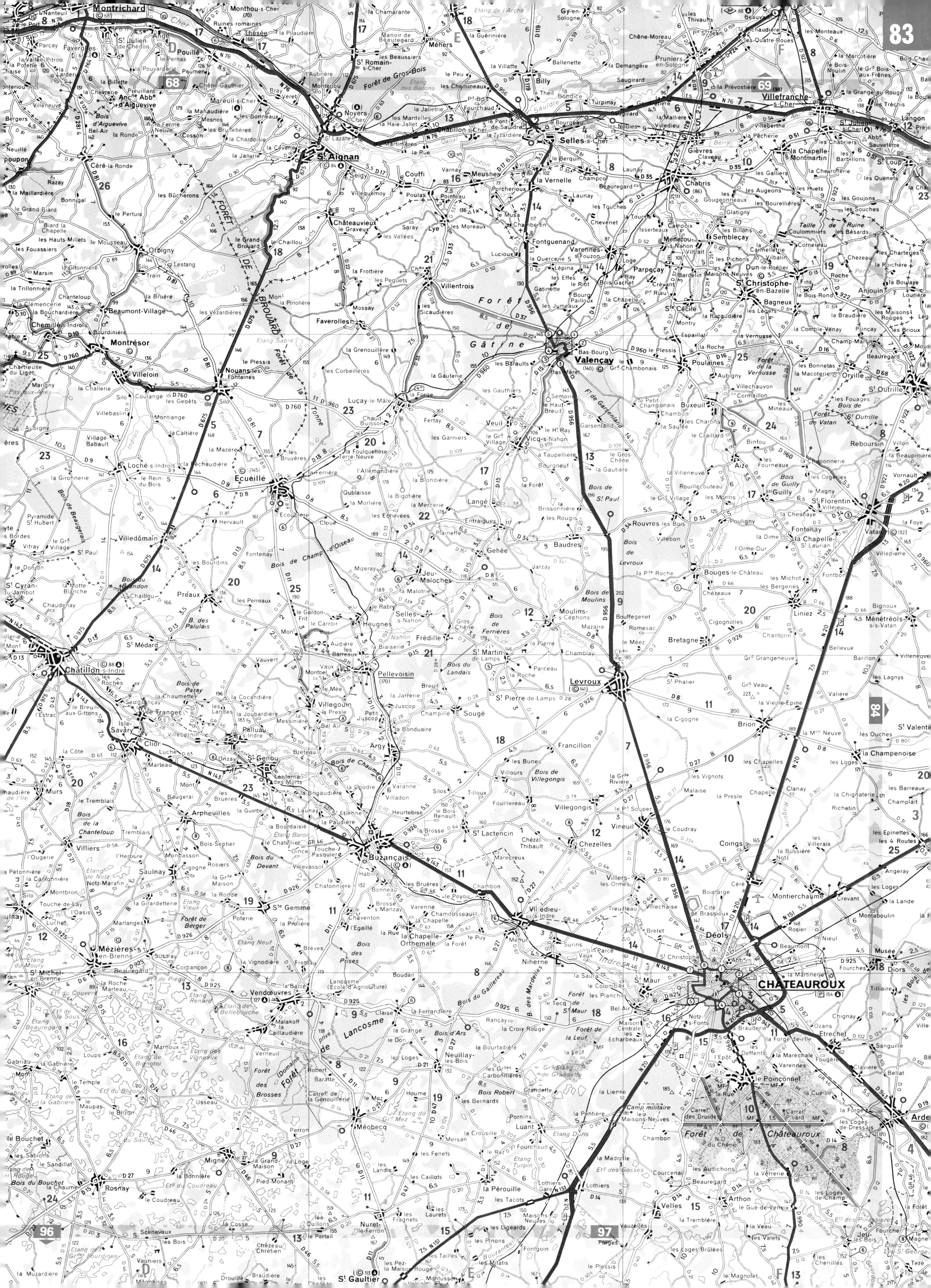
Montrichard
St Aignan
Selles-s-Cher
Villefranche-s-Cher
Chabris
Valençay
Montrésor
Nouans-les-Fontaines
Écueillé
Luçay-le-Mâle
Levroux
Vatan
Châtillon-s-Indre
Clion
Palluau-s-Indre
St Genou
Pellevoisin
Buzançais
Villedieu-s-Indre
Mézières-en-Brenne
Déols
CHÂTEAUROUX
Ardentes
Forêt de Châteauroux
Forêt de Gâtine
Forêt de Brouard
Camp militaire
Méobecq
Rosnay
St Gaultier
Mignè
Vendœuvres
St Maur
Levroux
Bouges-le-Château
Poulaines
Gièvres
St Christophe-en-Bazelle
Orbigny
Céré-la-Ronde
Villeloin
Loché-s-Indrois
Villedômain
Préaux
Heugnes
Arpheuilles
Argy
Sougé
Francillon
Villegongis
Vineuil
Coings
Montierchaume
Brion
Liniez
Ménétréols-s/s-Vatan
Meusnes
Couffi
Noyers-s-Cher
Thésée
Billy
68
69
84
96
97

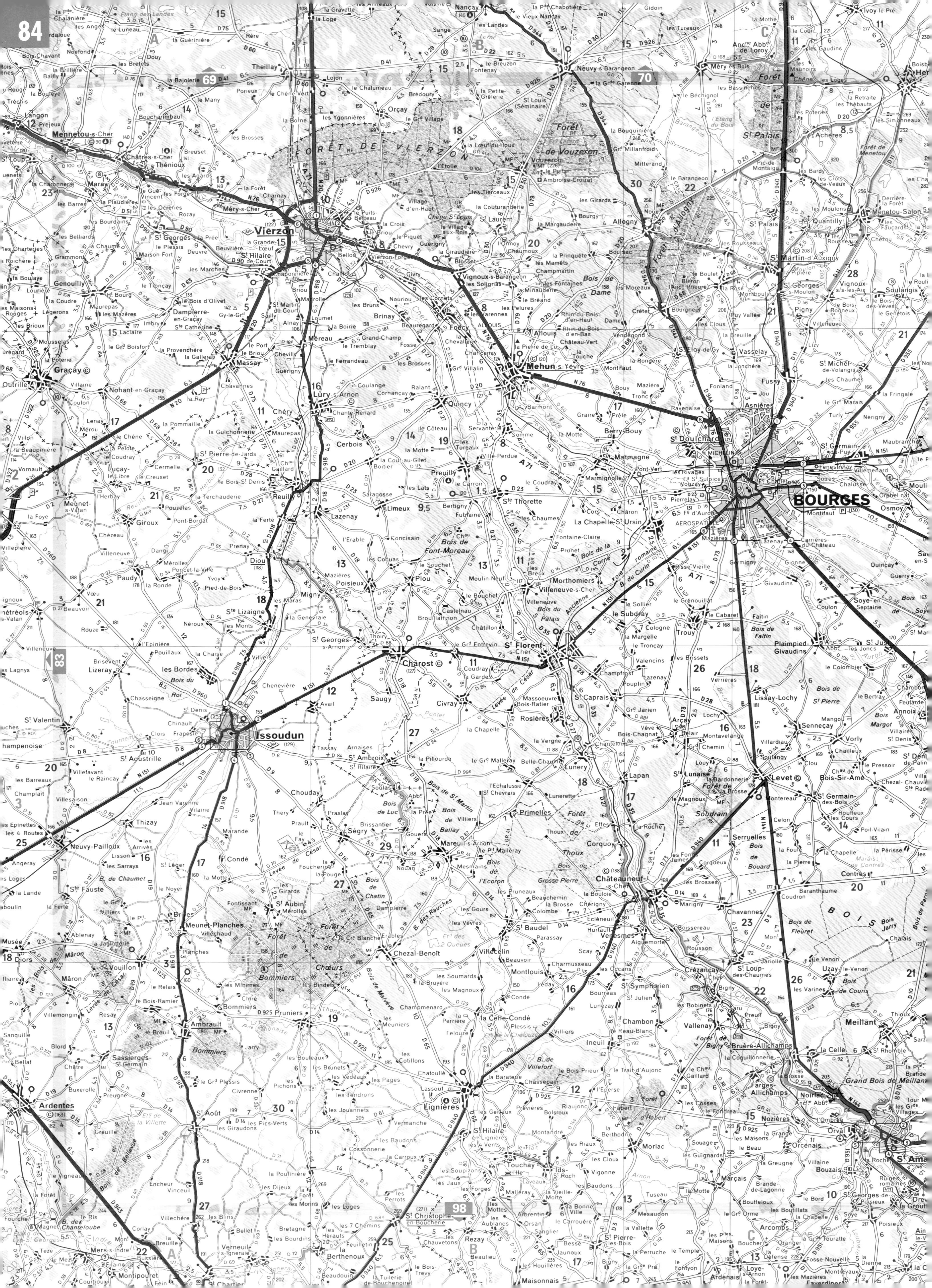
69
70
83
98
Nançay
Theillay
Neuvy-s-Barangeon
Mennetou-s-Cher
Châtres-s-Cher
Méry-s-Cher
Vierzon
FORÊT DE VIERZON
Forêt de Vouzeron
Vouzeron
Allogny
Forêt d'Allogny
Menetou-Salon
Quantilly
St Martin-d'Auxigny
St Palais
Vignoux-s-Barangeon
Foëcy
Mehun-s-Yèvre
Genouilly
Graçay
Massay
Lury-s-Arnon
Quincy
Preuilly
Reuilly
Limeux
Lazenay
St Doulchard
Marmagne
Berry-Bouy
BOURGES
Diou
Paudy
Ste Lizaigne
Charost
St Florent-s-Cher
Villeneuve-s-Cher
Trouy
Plaimpied-Givaudins
Issoudun
St Ambroix
Lunery
Levet
Neuvy-Pailloux
Ségry
Mareuil-s-Arnon
Châteauneuf-s-Cher
Forêt de Choeurs
Bommiers
Chezal-Benoît
Ambrault
Lignières
Meillant
Bruère-Allichamps
Ardentes
St Christophe-en-Boucherie
Mers-s-Indre

Sancerre
St Satur
St Thibault
Ménétréol
Sens-Beaujeu
Crézancy-en-Sancerre
Neuilly-en-Sancerre
Pouilly-s-Loire
Cosne
Garchy
Vinon
Veaugues
Humbligny
Morogues
Montigny
Jalognes
Gardefort
St Bouize
Herry
Mesves-s-Loire
Narcy
Varennes-lès-Narcy
Bulcy
Aubinges
St Céols
les Aix-d'Angillon
Rians
Azy
Groises
Lugny-Champagne
la Chapelle-Montlinard
la Charité-s-Loire
Raveau
Forêt des Bertranges
Étréchy
Sancergues
St Martin-des-Champs
Charentonnay
Argenvières
la Marche
Champvoux
Chaulgnes
Brécy
Chaumoux-Marcilly
Sévry
Couy
Jussy-le-Chaudrier
Précy
Beffes
Tronsanges
Germigny-s-Loire
Pougues-les-Eaux
Garchizy
Fourchambault
Guérigny
Urzy
Baugy
Villabon
Farges-en-Septaine
Villequiers
Garigny
St Hilaire-de-Gondilly
Menetou-Couture
Jouet-s-l'Aubois
Marseilles-lès-Aubigny
Avord
Saligny-le-Vif
Chassy
Mornay-Berry
Torteron
Cours-les-Barres
Bengy-s-Craon
Nérondes
Jussy-Champagne
Crosses
NEVERS
Marzy
Varennes-Vauzelles
Coulanges
Cuffy
Flavigny
Ignol
Tendron
la Guerche-s-l'Aubois
Cornusse
Vornay
Osmery
Lugny-Bourbonnais
Croisy
Germigny-l'Exempt
Apremont-s-Allier
Gimouille
Challuy
Sermoise-s-Loire
Saincaize-Meauce
Chevenon
Dun-s-Auron
Bussy
Lantan
Blet
Charly
la Chapelle-Hugon
Neuvy-le-Barrois
Magny-Cours
Chalivoy-Milon
Cogny
Parnay
Sagonne
Vereaux
Grossouvre
Mars-s-Allier
St Parize-le-Châtel
Luthenay-Uxeloup
Chaumont
Givardon
Sancoins
Mornay-s-Allier
Langeron
Thaumiers
Pondy
Bannegon
Neuilly-en-Dun
Augy-s-Aubois
St Pierre-le-Moûtier
Azy-le-Vif
Livry
St Aignan-des-Noyers
Château-s-Allier
le Veurdre
Chantenay-St Imbert
Toury-s-Jour
Charenton-du-Cher
Bessais-le-Fromental
Lurcy-Lévis
Valigny
Pouzy-Mésangy
Couleuvre
Isle-et-Bardais
St Léopardin-d'Augy
Tresnay
Villeneuve-s-Allier
Forêt de Tronçais
St Bonnet-Tronçais
Meillant
Bagneux
Forêt de Champroux

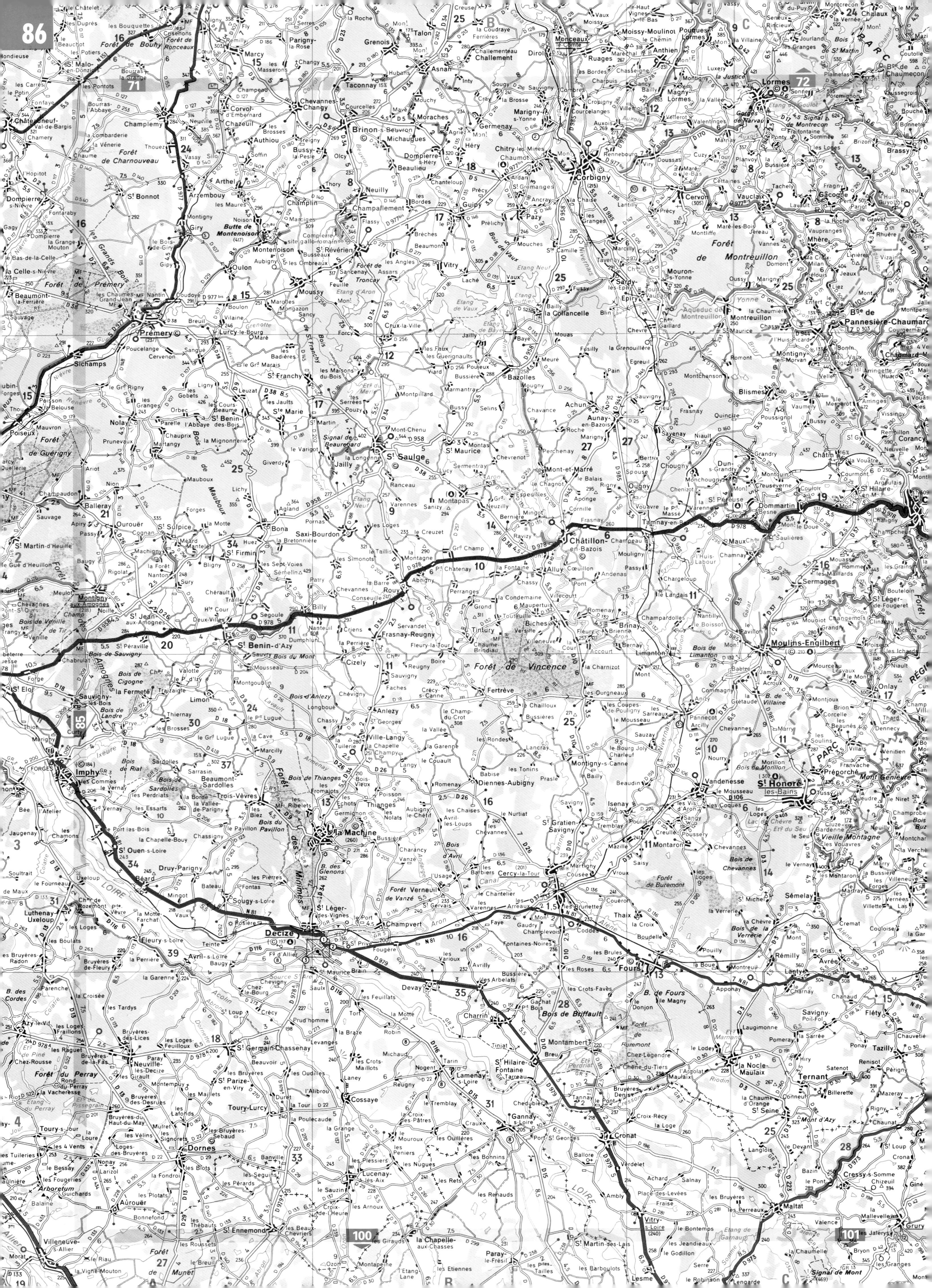

71
72
85
100
101
Prémery
Corbigny
Lormes
Châtillon-en-Bazois
St Saulge
Moulins-Engilbert
St Honoré-les-Bains
Decize
La Machine
Fours
Imphy
St Benin-d'Azy
Dornes
Cossaye
Cercy-la-Tour
Vandenesse
Brinon-s-Beuvron
Chevannes-Changy
Montenoison
St Révérien
Moussy
Forêt de Vincence
Forêt des Minimes
Forêt de Montreuillon
Forêt de Prémery
Forêt de Charnouveau
Forêt du Perray
Forêt de Munet
LOIRE
Aron
Canal du Nivernais
PARC

Saulieu
Montsauche
Les Settons
Liernais
Arnay-le-Duc
AUTUN
Nolay
Luzy
Le Creusot
Montceau-les-Mines
Montchanin
Blanzy
Couches
Épinac
Sully
Châteauneuf
Pouilly-en-Auxois
Commarin
MORVAN
Mont Beuvray
Toulon-s-Arroux
Étang-s-Arroux
Mesvres
Marmagne
Montcenis
Torcy
Issy-l'Évêque
Anost
Lucenay-l'Évêque
Chissey-en-Morvan
Manlay
Thoisy-la-Berchère
Châtellenot
72
73
88
101
102

DIJON
Chenôve
Quetigny
Longvic
Marsannay-la-Côte
Gevrey-Chambertin
Clos de Vougeot
Nuits-St Georges
Genlis
Auxonne
St Jean-de-Losne
Seurre
Beaune
Meursault
Savigny-lès-Beaune
Aloxe-Corton
Pommard
Volnay
Chagny
Santenay
Nolay
La Rochepot
Bligny-sur-Ouche
Châteauneuf
Sombernon
Verdun-s-le-Doubs
Pierre-de-Bresse
CHALON-S-SAÔNE
St Marcel
St Rémy
Givry
Buxy
St Martin-en-Bresse
St Germain-du-Bois
St Germain-du-Plain
Sennecey-le-Grand
Montret
Louhans
St Usuge
Forêt de Cîteaux
Forêt de Gergy
Forêt de Chagny
Forêt de Givry
A 6
A 31
A 36
A 38
N 5
N 6
N 73
N 74
N 78
73
74
87
102
103

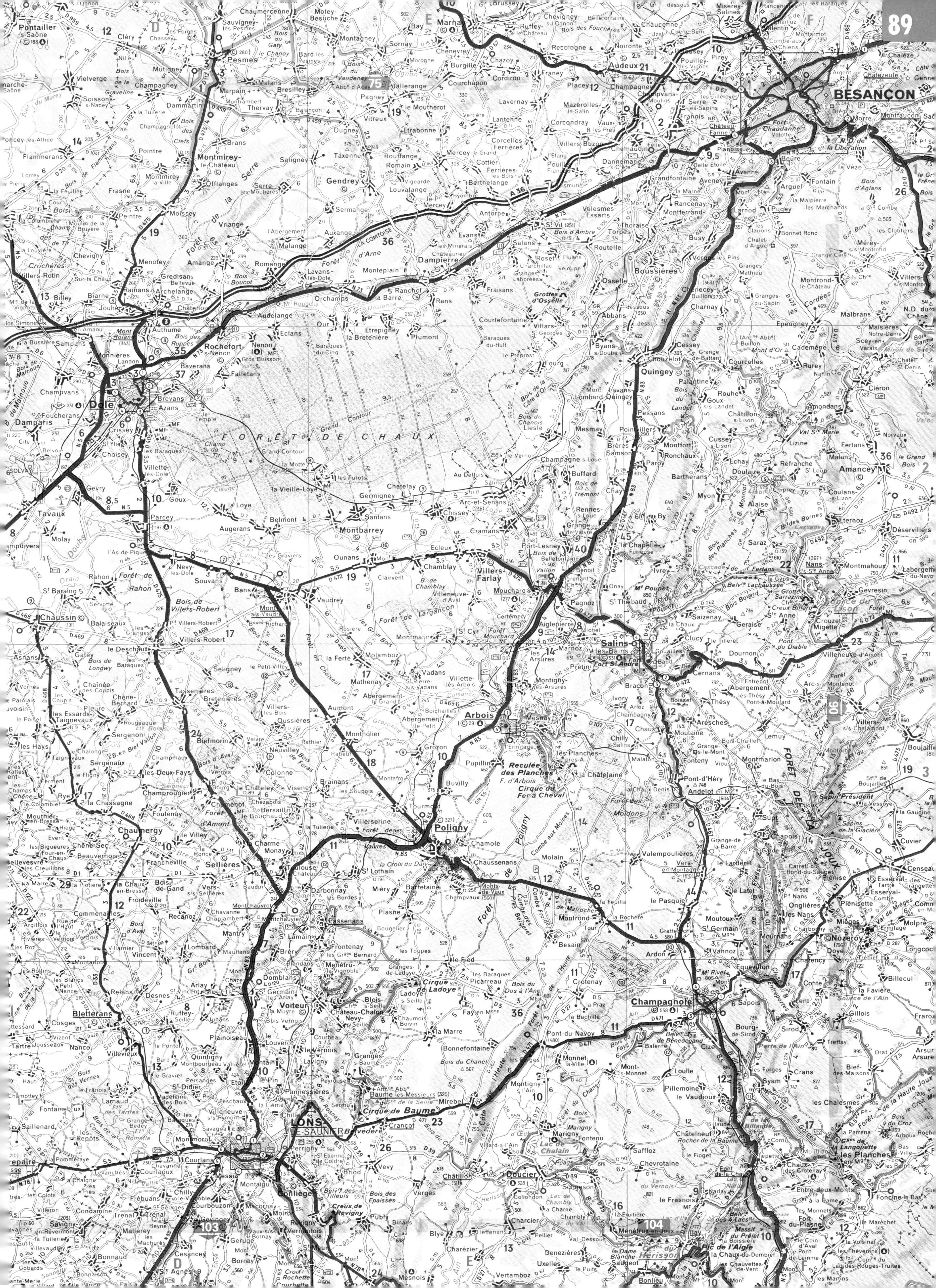
BESANÇON
Dole
Poligny
Arbois
Salins-les-Bains
Champagnole
Lons-le-Saunier
Pesmes
Gendrey
Dampierre
Montbarrey
Chaussin
Bletterans
Sellières
Voiteur
Conliège
Quingey
Amancey
Nozeroy
Villers-Farlay
Montmirey-le-Château
Rochefort-s-Nenon
Chaumergy
Arc-et-Senans
FORÊT DE CHAUX
FORÊT DE LA JOUX
Reculée des Planches
Cirque de Baume
Cirque de Ladoye

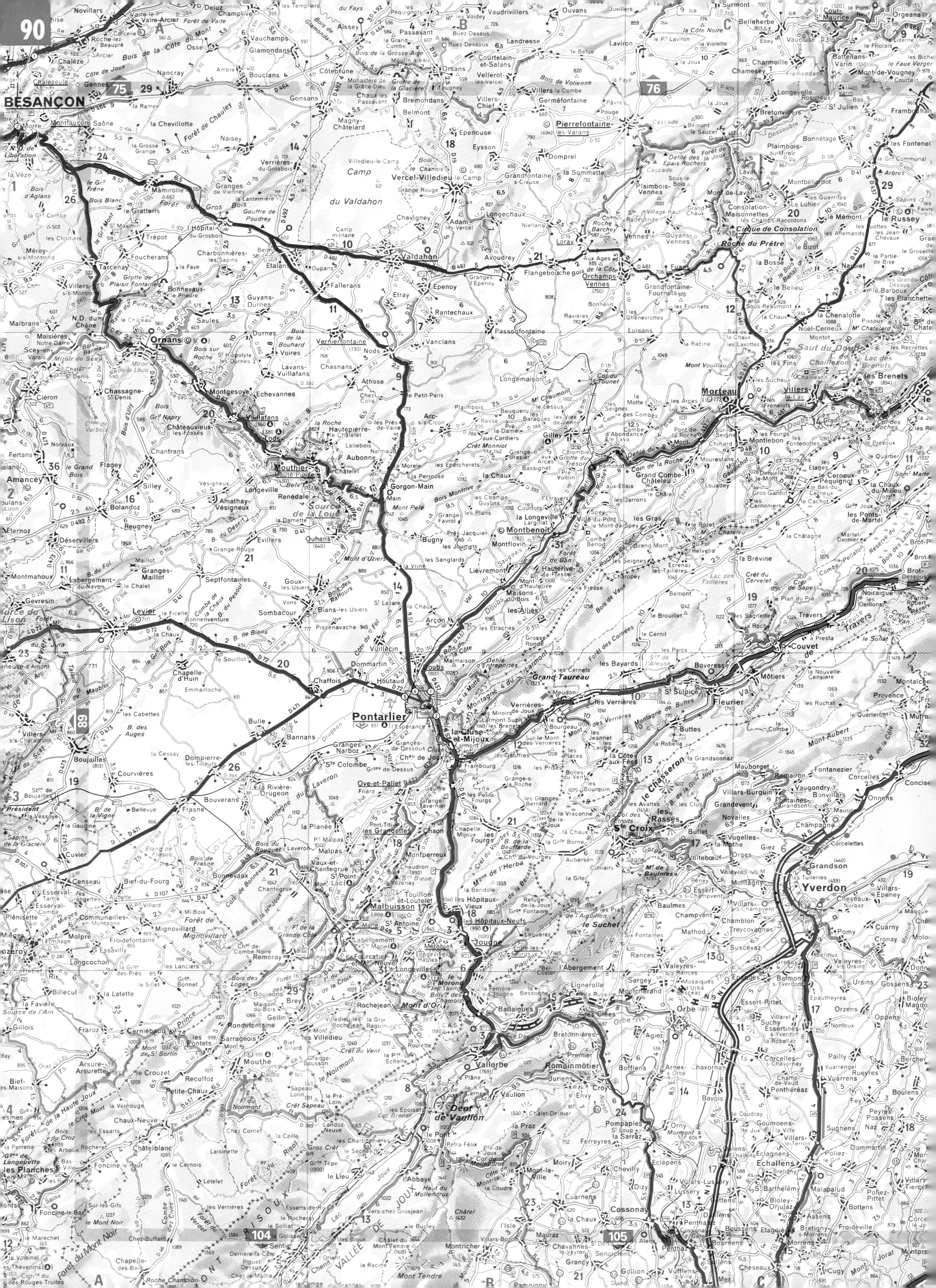
BESANÇON
Ornans
Valdahon
Vercel-Villedieu-le-Camp
Pierrefontaine-les-Varans
Morteau
Villers-le-Lac
Les Brenets
Le Russey
Levier
Pontarlier
Montbenoit
Malbuisson
Mouthe
Vallorbe
Orbe
Yverdon
Ste Croix
Fleurier
Couvet
Travers
Grandson
Cossonay
Frasne
Gilley
Ouhans
Mouthier-Haute-Pierre
Lods
Vuillafans
Les Hôpitaux-Neufs
Jougne
Romainmôtier
La Sarraz
Echallens
Dent de Vaulion
Mont d'Or
Le Suchet
Le Chasseron
Grand Taureau
Saut du Doubs
Cirque de Consolation
Roche du Prêtre
Source de la Loue
VALLÉE DE JOUX
75
76
104
105

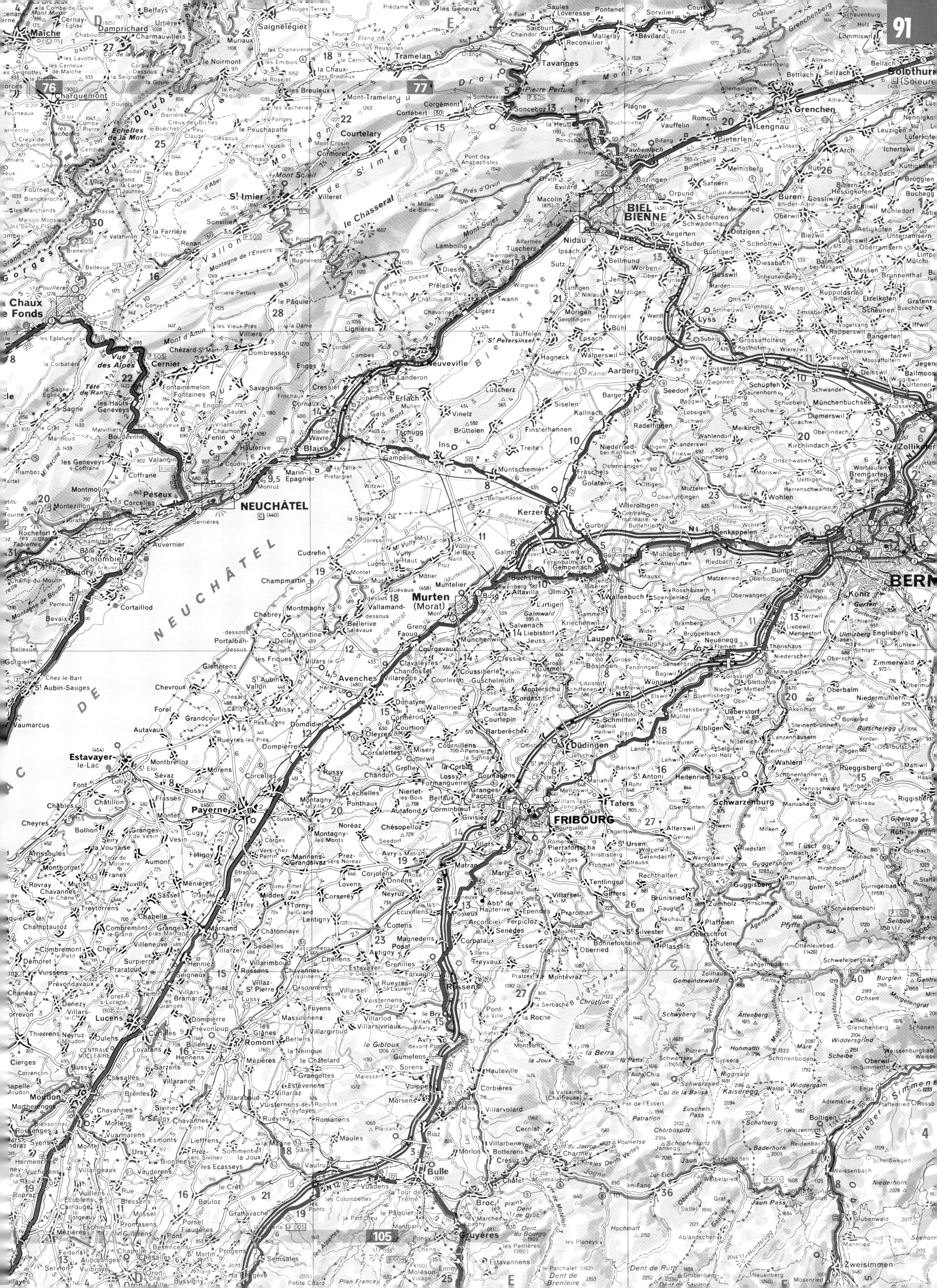
76
77
105
Maîche
Damprichard
Saignelégier
Tramelan
Tavannes
Bévilard
Reconvilier
Solothurn
(Soleure)
Grenchen
Pieterlen
Lengnau
Büren
an-der-Aare
BIEL
BIENNE
Nidau
St Imier
le Chasseral
Courtelary
Sonceboz
Péry
Mont Soleil
La Chaux
de Fonds
Lyss
Aarberg
Kerzers
Ins
Erlach
La Neuveville
le Landeron
St Blaise
NEUCHÂTEL
Peseux
Colombier
Boudry
Cortaillod
LAC DE NEUCHÂTEL
Vue des Alpes
Cernier
Valangin
Murten
(Morat)
Avenches
Laupen
BERN
Köniz
Düdingen
Tafers
FRIBOURG
Schwarzenburg
Estavayer
le-Lac
Payerne
Moudon
Lucens
Romont
Rossens
Bulle
Gruyères
Broc
Châtel
Zweisimmen
Boltigen
Jaun
Jaun Pass
Schwarzsee
Plaffeien
Guggisberg
Bielersee
St Petersinsel
Gorges du Doubs
Chaumont

LES SABLES-D'OLONNE
LA ROCHELLE
Luçon
la Mothe-Achard
Talmont-St Hilaire
St Mathurin
Olonne-s-Mer
Château-d'Olonne
la Chaume
Grosbreuil
Poiroux
Avrillé
Longeville-s-Mer
Jard-s-Mer
St Vincent-s-Jard
la Tranche-s-Mer
l'Aiguillon-s-Mer
la Faute-s-Mer
St Michel-en-l'Herm
Angles
St Benoist-s-Mer
Grues
Triaize
Moutiers-les-Mauxfaits
Mareuil-s-Lay
Nesmy
Chaillé-s-les-Ormeaux
Aubigny
la Boissière-des-Landes
St Florent-des-Bois
Château-Guibert
Moutiers-s-le-Lay
Corpe
Chasnais
St Cyr-en-Talmondais
St Vincent-s-Graon
Rosnay
les Magnils-Reigniers
la Jonchère
Curzon
St Denis-du-Payré
Pointe du Payré
Pointe du Grouin du Cou
Pointe d'Arçay
Pointe de l'Aiguillon
Anse de l'Aiguillon
PERTUIS BRETON
ILE DE RÉ
Phare des Baleines
les Portes-en-Ré
St Clément-des-Baleines
Ars-en-Ré
Loix
St Martin-de-Ré
la Flotte
la Couarde-s-Mer
le Bois-Plage-en-Ré
Rivedoux-Plage
Ste Marie-de-Ré
Phare de Chanchardon
Phare de Chauveau
la Pallice
Pointe du Chef de Baie
Aytré
Angoulins
Marsilly
Nieul-s-Mer
l'Houmeau
Lagord
PERTUIS D'ANTIOCHE
Rocher d'Antioche
Phare de Chassiron
Chassiron
St Denis-d'Oléron
la Brée-les-Bains
St Georges-d'Oléron
St Pierre-d'Oléron
Boyardville
Forêt des Saumonards
Fort Boyard
Ile d'Aix
Fort Liedot
Rade des Basques
Rade de l'Ile d'Aix
Fouras
Châtelaillon-Plage
Ile Madame
Passe aux Bœufs
A
B
C
1
2
3
4
78
79
106

79
80
106
64
St Hermine
Vouvant
Mervent
Parc Régional
l'Hermenault
Pouillé
Nalliers
Mouzeuil-St Martin
Fontenay-le-Comte
Puy-de-Serre
Coulonges-s-l'Autize
Secondigny
Xanton-Chassenon
St Hilaire-des-Loges
Le Langon
Chaillé-les-Marais
Maillezais
Benet
St Rémy
Coudray-Salbart
Marans
Maillé
Damvix
Coulon
Magné
NIORT
Bessines
Arçais
St Hilaire-la-Palud
Frontenay-Rohan-Rohan
Courçon
Mauzé-le-Mignon
Beauvoir-s-Niort
Aigrefeuille-d'Aunis
Surgères
St Jean-de-Liversay
Nuaillé-d'Aunis
Benon
St Sauveur-d'Aunis
Villedoux
Dompierre-s-Mer
La Jarrie
Loulay
Tonnay-Boutonne
Tonnay-Charente
ROCHEFORT
Muron
St Laurent-de-la-Barrière
Marais Poitevin
Forêt de Chizé
Forêt de Benon

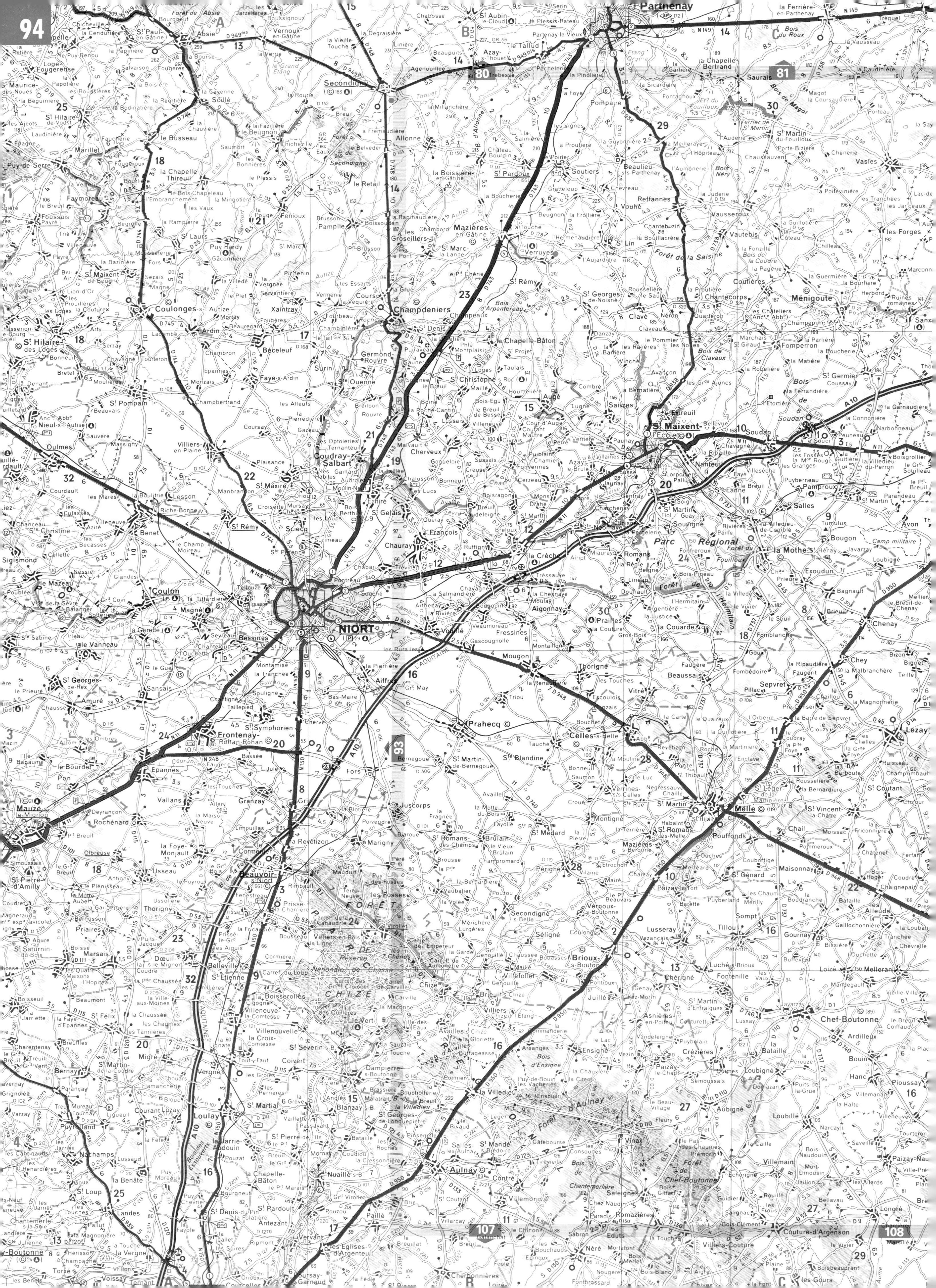
Parthenay
Secondigny
St Aubin-le-Cloud
Azay-s-Thouet
Mazières-en-Gâtine
Champdeniers
Coulonges-s-l'Autize
St Hilaire-des-Loges
St Pompain
Villiers-en-Plaine
Coudray-Salbart
Échiré
St Maixent-l'École
La Crèche
Chauray
NIORT
Coulon
Magné
Bessines
Aiffres
Prahecq
Celles-s-Belle
Melle
La Mothe-St Héray
Lezay
Chenay
Frontenay-Rohan-Rohan
Mauzé-le-Mignon
Beauvoir-s-Niort
Brioux-s-Boutonne
Chef-Boutonne
Aulnay
Loulay
Chizé
Ménigoute
Sauzé-Vaussais
Parc Régional
Forêt de Chizé
Réserve Nationale de Chasse
Forêt d'Aulnay
Forêt de Chef-Boutonne
Forêt de l'Hermitain
Couture-d'Argenson
Villiers-Couture
Pamproux
Soudan
Vasles
Sanxay
Verruyes
Augé
Saivres
Exoudun
Mougon
Vouillé
Aigonnay
Sansais
Usseau
Marigny
Villeneuve-la-Comtesse
Paizay-le-Chapt
Melleran
Lussais
L'AQUITAINE
80
81
93
107
108

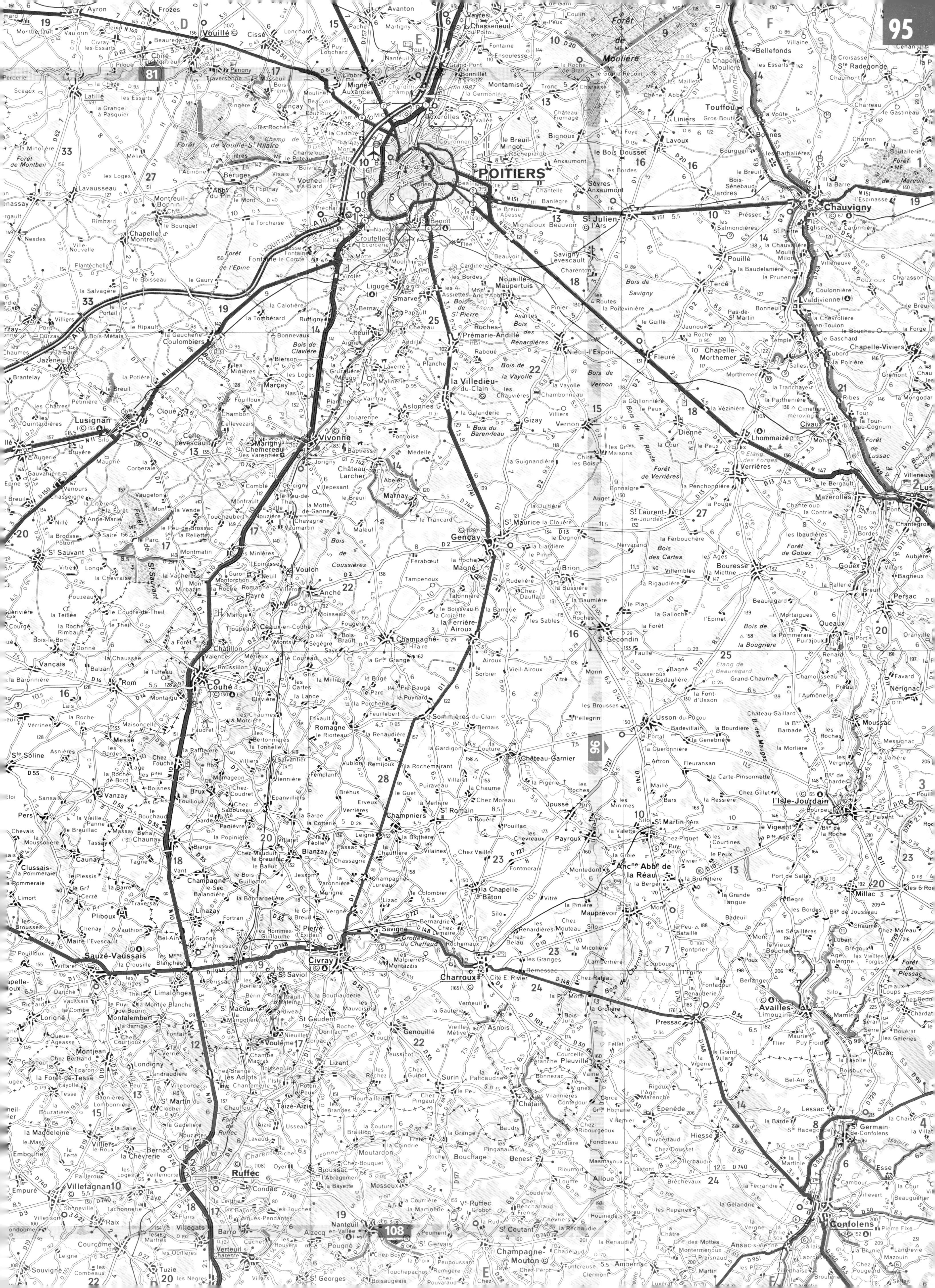

POITIERS
Chauvigny
Vouillé
Lusignan
Vivonne
Couhé
Gençay
Civray
Charroux
Sauzé-Vaussais
Ruffec
Confolens
l'Isle-Jourdain
Availles-Limouzine
St Germain-de-Confolens
Montmorillon
Lhommaizé
Civaux
Verrières
Usson-du-Poitou
Château-Garnier
Champagné-St Hilaire
Sommières-du-Clain
la Villedieu-du-Clain
Nouaillé-Maupertuis
Ligugé
Smarves
Croutelle
Migné-Auxances
Chasseneuil-du-Poitou
Buxerolles
St Benoît
Mignaloux-Beauvoir
St Julien-l'Ars
Sèvres-Anxaumont
Savigny-Lévescault
Fleuré
Nieuil-l'Espoir
Forêt de Moulière
Forêt de Vouillé-St Hilaire
Forêt de l'Epine
Forêt de Verrières
Forêt de Ruffec
Champagne-Mouton
Pressac
Mauprévoir
Payroux
Joussé
Blanzay
Savigné
Champniers
Chaunay
Brux
Messé
Vanzay
Limalonges
Montalembert
Lorigné
Villefagnan
Verteuil-s-Charente
Nanteuil-en-Vallée
Genouillé
Asnois
Surin
Pleuville
Epenède
Hiesse
Lessac
Esse
Abzac
Millac
Persac
Queaux
Moussac
Nérignac
Gouex
Bouresse
Mazerolles
Valdivienne
Chapelle-Viviers
St Laurent-de-Jourdes
St Maurice-la-Clouère
St Secondin
Brion
Magné
Anché
Voulon
Château-Larcher
Marnay
Marçay
Coulombiers
Jazeneuil
Celle-Lévescault
Marigny-Chemereau
Ceaux-en-Couhé
Châtillon
Payré
Romagne
Chapelle-Montreuil
Montreuil-Bonnin
Béruges
Latillé
Ayron
Cissé
Quinçay
Vouneuil-s-Biard
Fontaine-le-Comte
Iteuil
Aslonnes
Vernon
Gizay
Dienné
Tercé
Pouillé
Bonnes
Jardres
Lavoux
Bignoux
Montamisé
Vivonne
81
96
108

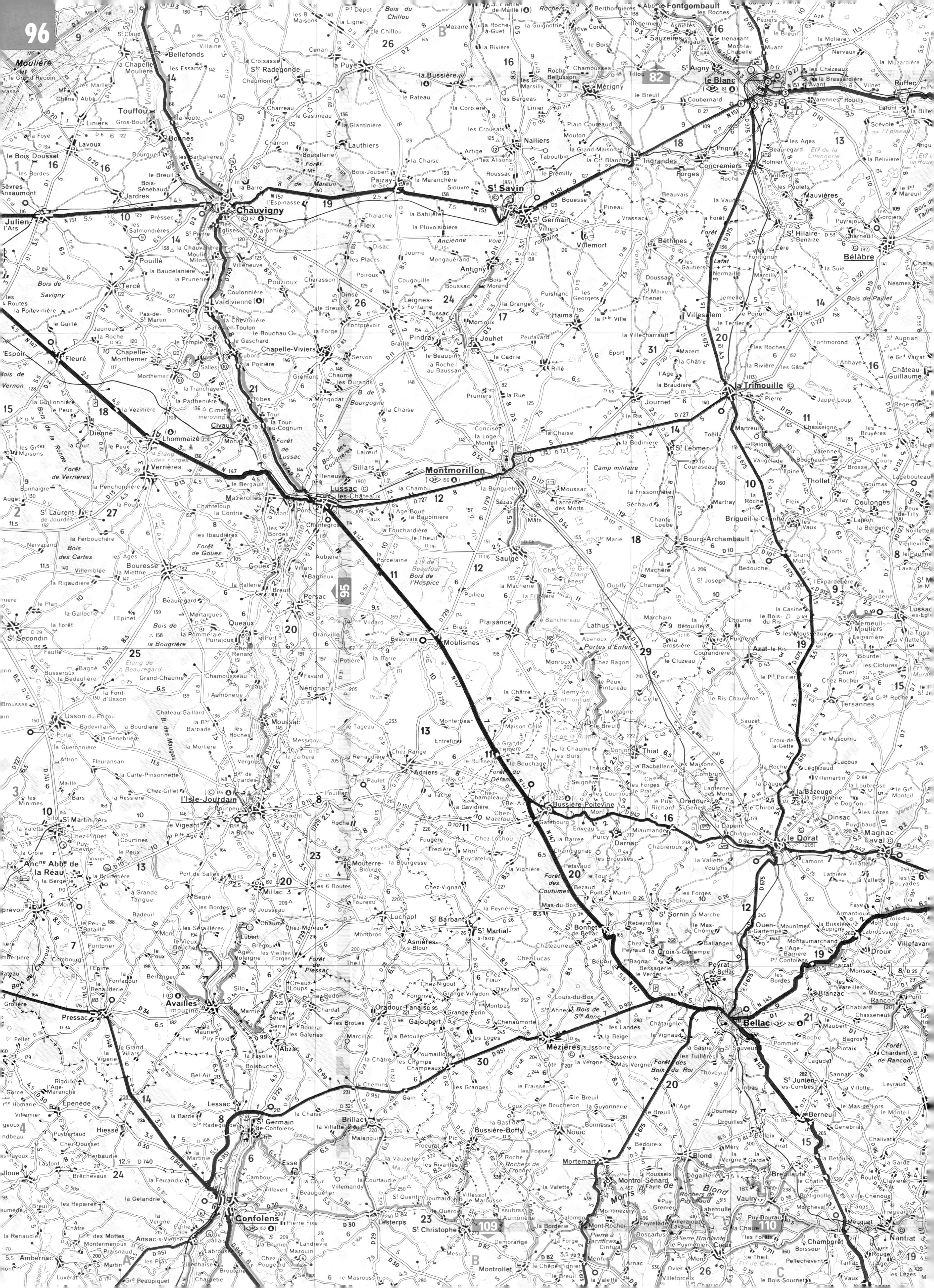
Chauvigny
St Savin
Le Blanc
Bélâbre
La Trimouille
Montmorillon
Lussac-les-Châteaux
Civaux
Lhommaizé
Verrières
Mazerolles
Gouex
Persac
Moulismes
Plaisance
Lathus
Saulgé
Adriers
L'Isle-Jourdain
Availles-Limouzine
Pressac
Millac
Mouterre-s-Blourde
Bussière-Poitevine
Le Dorat
Magnac-Laval
Bellac
Mézières-s-Issoire
Mortemart
Confolens
St Germain-de-Confolens
Brillac
Nouic
Nantiat
Fleuré
Moulière
Touffou
Bonnes
Jardres
Valdivienne
Chapelle-Viviers
Jouhet
Antigny
Nalliers
Mérigny
Fontgombault
Ingrandes
Concremiers
Forges
Mauvières
Liglet
Haims
Journet
St Léomer
Bourg-Archambault
Thiat
Oradour-St Genest
Azat-le-Ris
Darnac
Usson-du-Poitou
St Martin-l'Ars
Queaux
Nérignac
Moussac
Bouresse
Dienné
St Secondin
Lessac
Lesterps
St Christophe
Blanzac
Peyrat-de-Bellac
Berneuil
Ruffec
Coulonges
Thollet
Tersannes
Lussac
Chaillac
Château-Guillaume
Villefavard
Vaulry
Blond
Bussière-Boffy
Esse
82
95
109
110

St Gaultier
Argenton-s-Creuse
Chasseneuil
Tendu
Mosnay
Bouesse
Neuvy-St Sépulchre
Malicornay
Ceaulmont
Gargilesse-Dampierre
Cluis
Luzeret
Prissac
Chazelet
Vigoux
Celon
Bazaiges
St Civran
Sacierges-St Martin
Roussines
Parnac
St Benoît du Sault
Eguzon
Cuzion
Orsennes
Montchevrier
Aigurande
Chaillac
Crozant
Fresselines
Nouzerolles
Chambon-Ste Croix
La Chapelle-Baloue
Azerables
Mouhet
St Sébastien
Bazelat
St Georges-les Landes
St Sulpice-les-Feuilles
Mailhac-s-Benaize
Dun-le-Palestel
St Germain-Beaupré
St Léger-Bridereix
St Agnant-de-Versillat
Naillat
La Souterraine
Arnac-la-Poste
St Hilaire-la-Treille
Fleurat
St Vaury
Guéret
St Maurice-la-Souterraine
St Sornin-Leulac
St Priest-la-Feuille
St Amand-Magnazeix
Fromental
Le Grand-Bourg
Châteauponsac
Bessines-s-Gartempe
Bénévent-l'Abbaye
Marsac
Laurière
Bersac-s-Rivalier
St Sulpice-Laurière
St Goussaud
St Dizier-Leyrenne
Ahun
Pontarion
Razès
St Sylvestre
Compreignac
Col de Sauvagnac
N 145
N 20
D 951
D 927

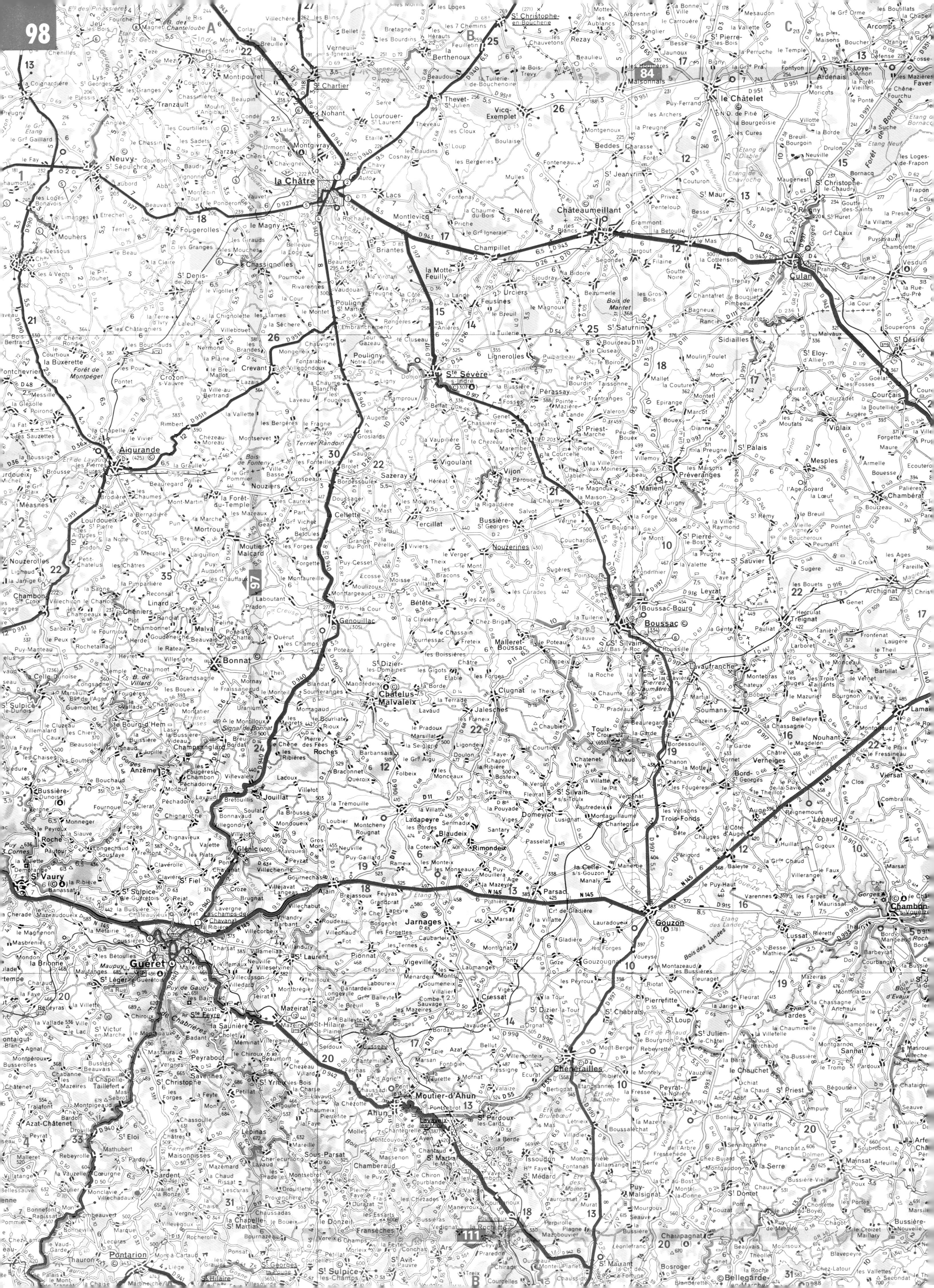

A
B
C
la Châtre
Neuvy-St Sépulchre
Nohant
Montgivray
Vicq-Exemplet
Châteaumeillant
le Châtelet
Culan
St Christophe-le-Chaudry
Aigurande
Crevant
Pouligny-Notre-Dame
Ste Sévère-s-Indre
St Priest-la-Marche
Préveranges
St Marien
Nouzerines
Boussac
Boussac-Bourg
Genouillac
Bonnat
Châtelus-Malvaleix
Jalesches
Clugnat
Toulx-Ste Croix
Soumans
Trégnat
Lavaufranche
Bussière-Dunoise
Anzême
Glénic
Jouillat
Ladapeyre
Domeyrot
Parsac
Gouzon
Jarnages
Guéret
St Vaury
Ste Feyre
Ajain
St Laurent
Cressat
Chénérailles
St Dizier-la-Tour
Moutier-d'Ahun
Ahun
Lavaveix-les-Mines
St Yrieix
Lépinas
Sous-Parsat
Chamberaud
St Martial
Issoudun
Puy-Malsignat
Champagnat
St Priest
Mainsat
Chambon
Evaux
Viersat
Auge
Lussat
Pontarion
St Sulpice-les-Champs
Bellegarde
84
97
111

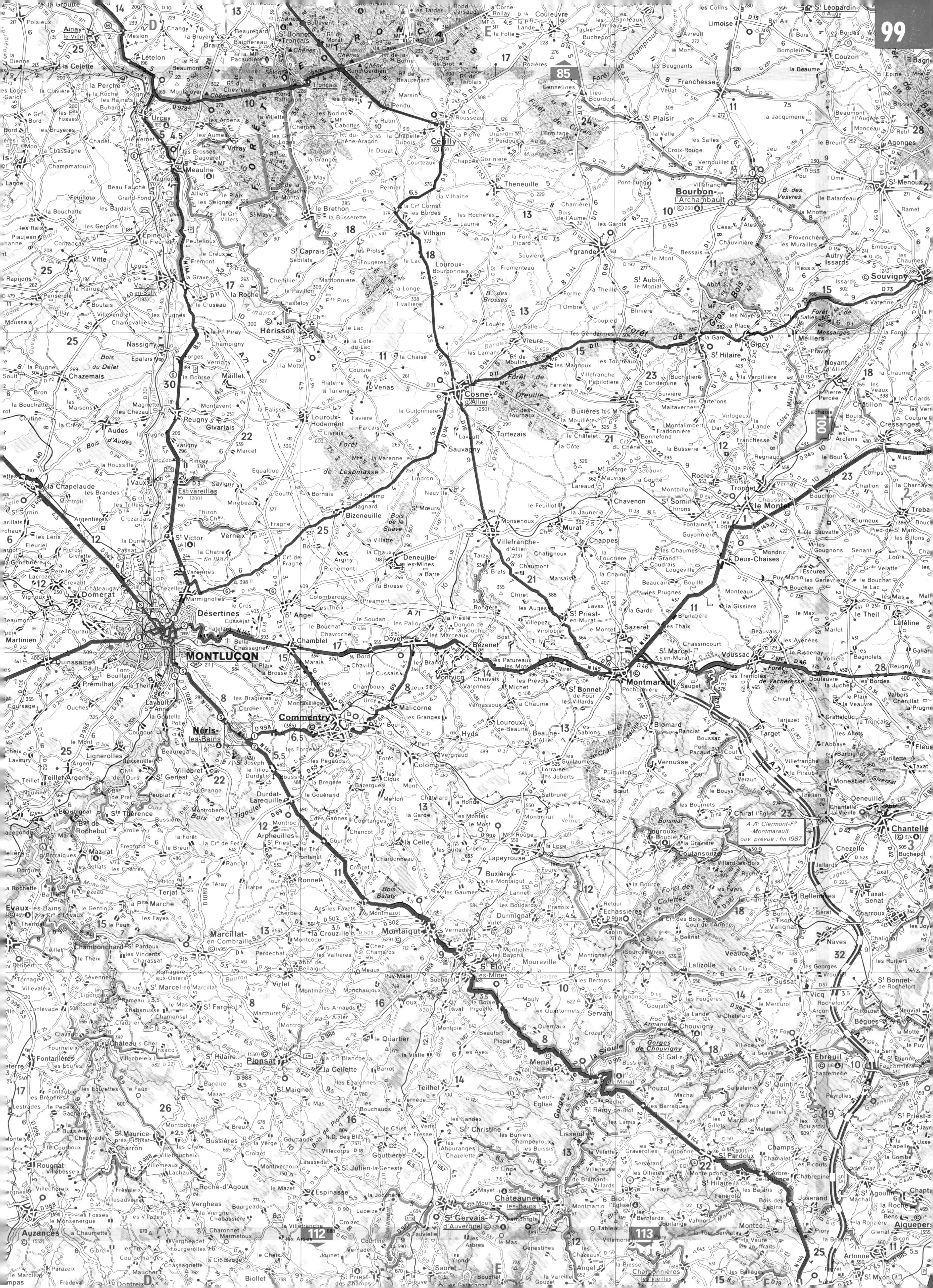
MONTLUÇON
Commentry
Néris-les-Bains
Montmarault
Cosne-d'Allier
Hérisson
Cérilly
Bourbon-l'Archambault
Souvigny
Le Montet
Chantelle
Ebreuil
Montaigut
St Eloy-les-Mines
Pionsat
Menat
Châteauneuf-les-Bains
St Gervais-d'Auvergne
Auzances
Evaux-les-Bains
Marcillat-en-Combraille
Domérat
Désertines
Vallon-en-Sully
Meaulne
Urçay
Ainay-le-Vieil
Villefranche-d'Allier
Montvicq
Doyet
Bézenet
Forêt de Tronçais
Forêt de Civrais
Forêt de Dreuille
Forêt de Gros Bois
Forêt des Colettes
Gorges de Chouvigny
Gorges de la Sioule
A 71: Clermont-Fd - Montmarault ouv. prévue : fin 1987
la Chatre fin 1987
85
100
112
113

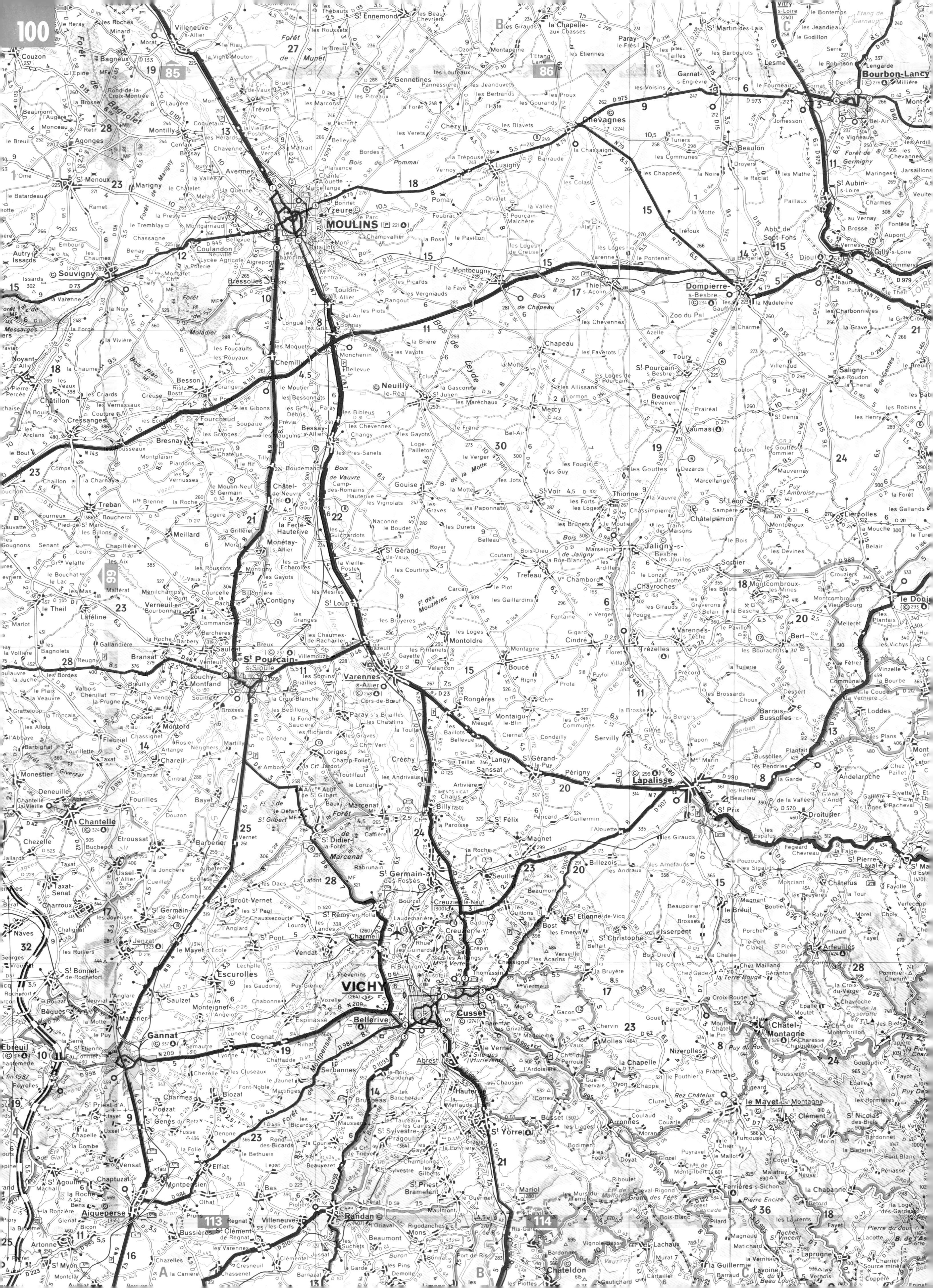
MOULINS
VICHY
Cusset
Bellerive
St Pourçain-s-Sioule
Varennes-s-Allier
Lapalisse
Dompierre-s-Besbre
Bourbon-Lancy
Gannat
Chantelle
Aigueperse
Randan
Souvigny
Chevagnes
Jaligny-s-Besbre
Le Mayet de Montagne
Châtel-Montagne
St Germain-des-Fossés
Billy
Creuzier-le-Vieux
Abrest
St Yorre
Hauterive
Cognat
Escurolles
Ebreuil
Arfeuilles
Le Donjon
Bressolles
Toulon-s-Allier
Yzeure
Avermes
Trévol
Lusigny
Thiel-s-Acolin
Beaulon
Diou
Gilly-s-Loire
St Aubin-s-Loire
Neuilly-le-Réal
Chapeau
Chemilly
Besson
Bessay-s-Allier
Châtel-de-Neuvre
La Ferté-Hauterive
Monétay-s-Allier
St Gérand-de-Vaux
Contigny
Verneuil-en-Bourbonnais
Châtillon
Cressanges
Bresnay
Treban
Meillard
Louchy-Montfand
Saulcet
Paray-s-s-Briailles
Créchy
Marcenat
St Didier-la-Forêt
St Gérand-le-Puy
Magnet
Seuillet
Trézelles
Varennes-s-Tèche
Droiturier
St Prix
Mariol
Châteldon
Ris
Thiel
Forêt de Marcenat
Forêt de Montpensier
Bois de Vauvre
Bois de Chapeau
Forêt de Bagnolet
Forêt de Marigny
Forêt de Germigny
fin 1987

Gueugnon
Digoin
Paray-le-Monial
Charolles
Palinges
St Vallier
Mont-St Vincent
Marcigny
Semur-en-Brionnais
Charlieu
La Clayette
Chauffailles
Pouilly-s/s-Charlieu
ROANNE
le Coteau
Riorges
Cours
Thizy
Amplepuis
Lamure-s-Azergues
Matour
St Bonnet-de-Joux
La Guiche
Dompierre-s/s-Sanvignes
Perrecy-les-Forges
Génelard
Toulon-s-Arroux
Vendenesse-s-Arroux
Marly-s-Arroux
Neuvy-Grandchamp
Chassenard
Molinet
St Léger-s-Vouzance
l'Hôpital-le-Mercier
Anzy-le-Duc
Bourg-le-Comte
Artaix
Melay
Iguerande
Vivans
Changy
St Germain-Lespinasse
St Haon-le-Châtel
Ambierle
Renaison
St Alban-les-Eaux
Villerest
Pradines
Régny
Belmont-de-la-Loire
Mussy-s/s-Dun
Chassigny-s/s-Dun
Châteauneuf
St Julien-de-Jonzy
Ligny-en-Brionnais
Sarry
Oyé
St Christophe-en-Brionnais
Baudemont
Varennes-s/s-Dun
Bois-Ste Marie
Dompierre-les-Ormes
Tramayes
Propières
Monsols
Poule
Chénelette
Claveisolles
Ranchal
Cublize
Bourg-de-Thizy
Montagny
Perreux
Noailly
Pouilly-les-Nonains
Lentigny
Ouches
St Jean-St Maurice
Villemontais
Forêt de Charolles
Forêt de Lespinasse
Bois de Chatellus
LOIRE
D 985
N 79
N 7
D 482
86
87
102
114
115

87
88
101
115
116
Tournus
Cuisery
Sennecey-le-Grand
Mont-St Vincent
St Gengoux-le-National
Cormatin
Cluny
Lugny
Pont-de-Vaux
Mâcon
St Bonnet-de-Joux
La Guiche
Matour
Tramayes
Bâgé-le-Châtel
Pont-de-Veyle
Monsols
Beaujeu
Thoissey
Belleville
Châtillon-s-C.
Lamure-s-Azergues
Villefranche-s-Saône
St Trivier-s-Moignans
Ambérieux-en-Dombes
Salles-Arbuissonnas-en-Beaujolais
Fleurie
Romanèche-Thorins
Juliénas
Chénas
Cuiseaux
Montmerle-s-Saône
Vonnas
Mézériat
Neuville-les-Dames
Chalamont
Cublize
Chauffailles
A 40
A 6

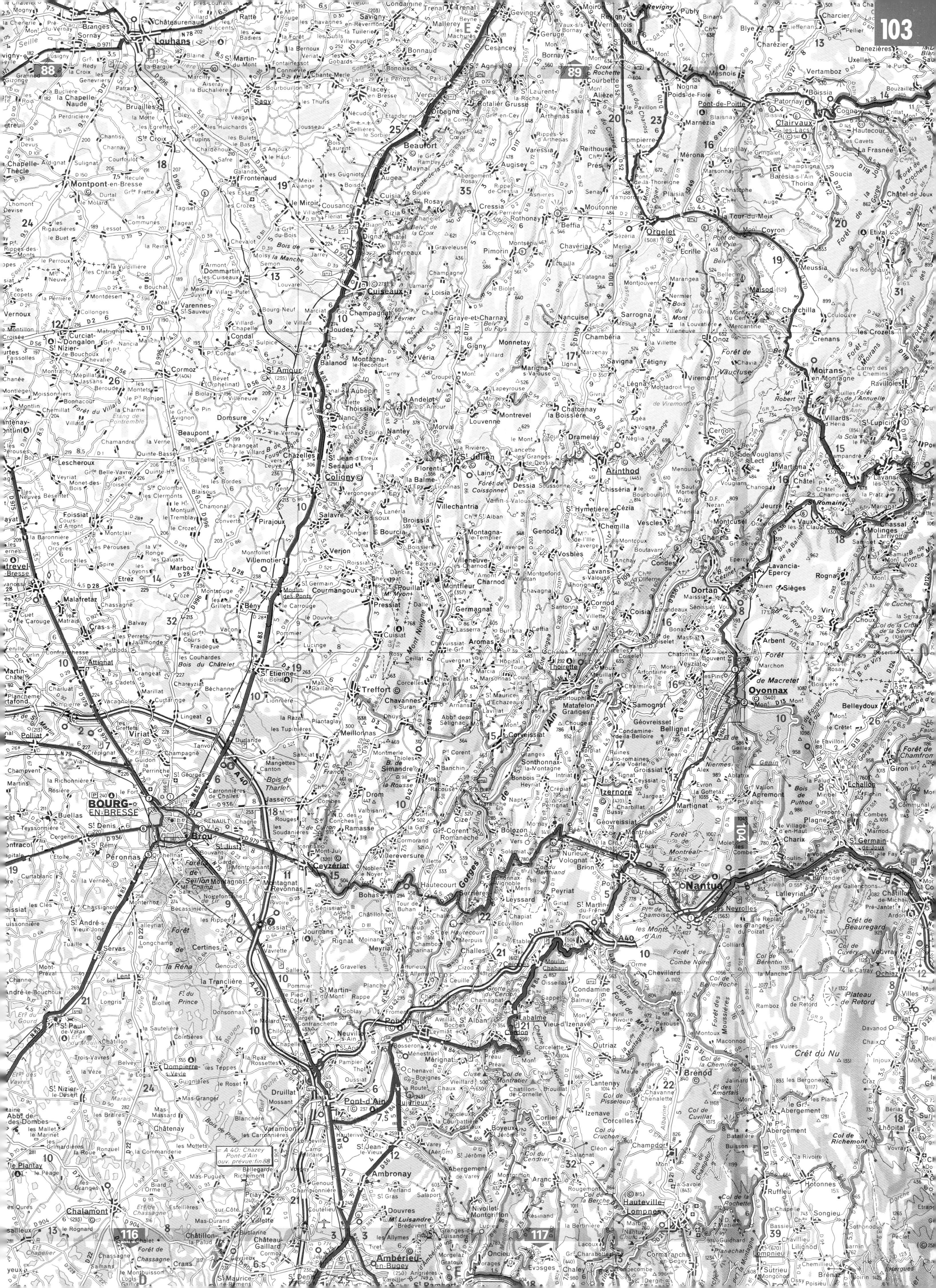
Louhans
Châteaurenaud
Branges
Sornay
Montpont-en-Bresse
Sagy
Frontenaud
Beaufort
Cuiseaux
St Amour
Coligny
Orgelet
Clairvaux-les-Lacs
Moirans-en-Montagne
Arinthod
Dortan
Oyonnax
Nantua
Izernore
Thoirette
Treffort
Ceyzériat
Bourg-en-Bresse
Brou
Péronnas
Viriat
Pont-d'Ain
Ambronay
Ambérieu-en-Bugey
Chalamont
Hauteville-Lompnes
Brénod
St Germain-de-Joux
Chatillon-la-Palud
Villette
Lhôpital
St Julien
St Claude
Pont-de-Poitte
Maisod
Cerdon
Poncin
Jasseron
A 40
N 83
N 84
N 75
N 79
A 40: Chazey Pont-d'Ain ouv. prévue: fin 88
88
89
104
116
117

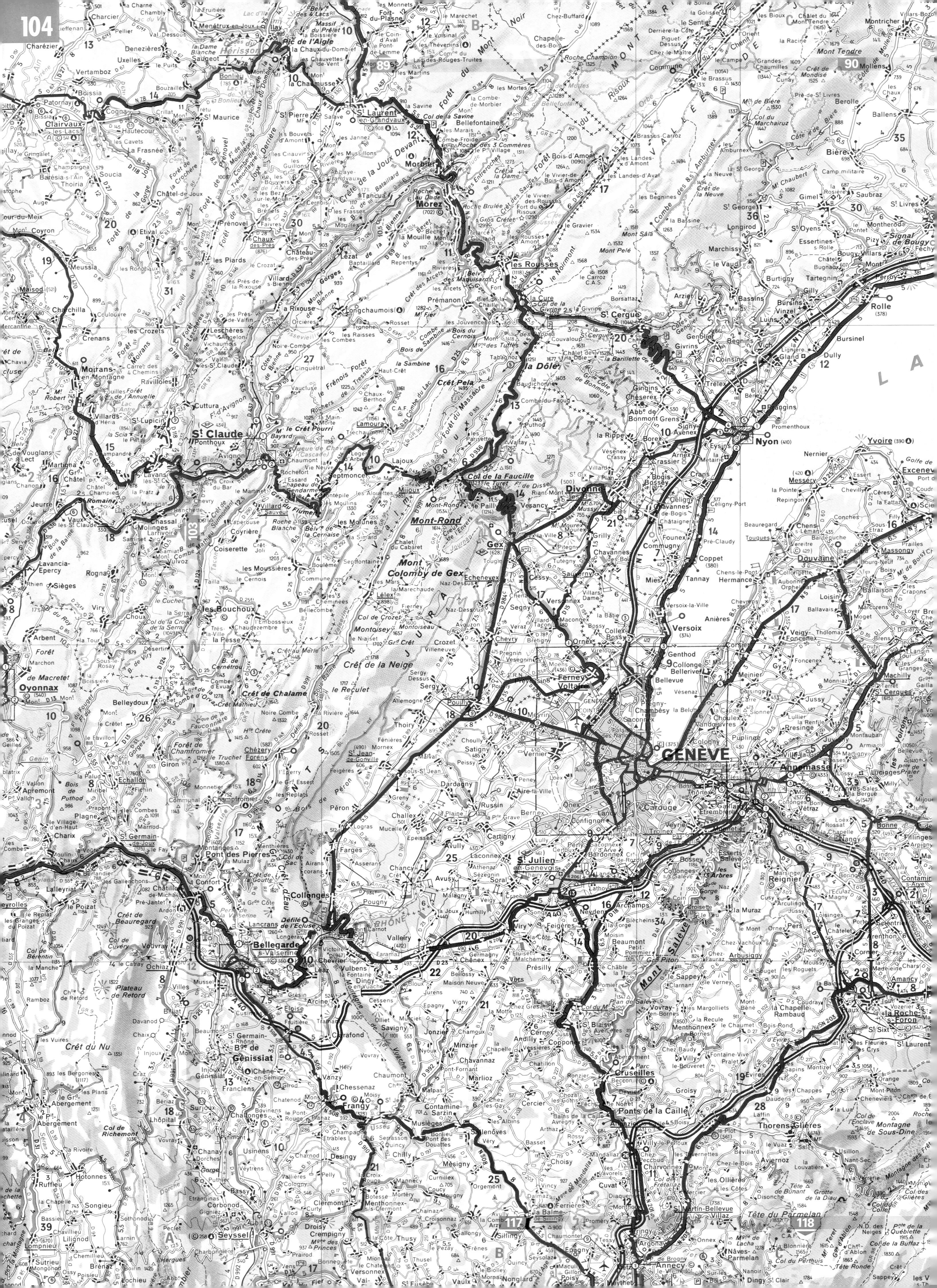
GENÈVE
Nyon
Rolle
Annemasse
St Julien en-Genevois
Bellegarde s-Valserine
St Claude
Oyonnax
Morez
Les Rousses
St Laurent en-Grandvaux
Clairvaux les-Lacs
Moirans en-Montagne
Gex
Divonne
Ferney Voltaire
Versoix
Coppet
Douvaine
Cruseilles
Frangy
Seyssel
Annecy
La Roche s-Foron
Thorens Glières
Crêt de la Neige
Mont Colomby de Gex
Mont-Rond
Col de la Faucille
la Dôle
Crêt de Chalame
Plateau de Retord
Crêt du Nu
Mont Salève
Forêt du Risoux
JURA
RHÔNE
89
90
103
117
118

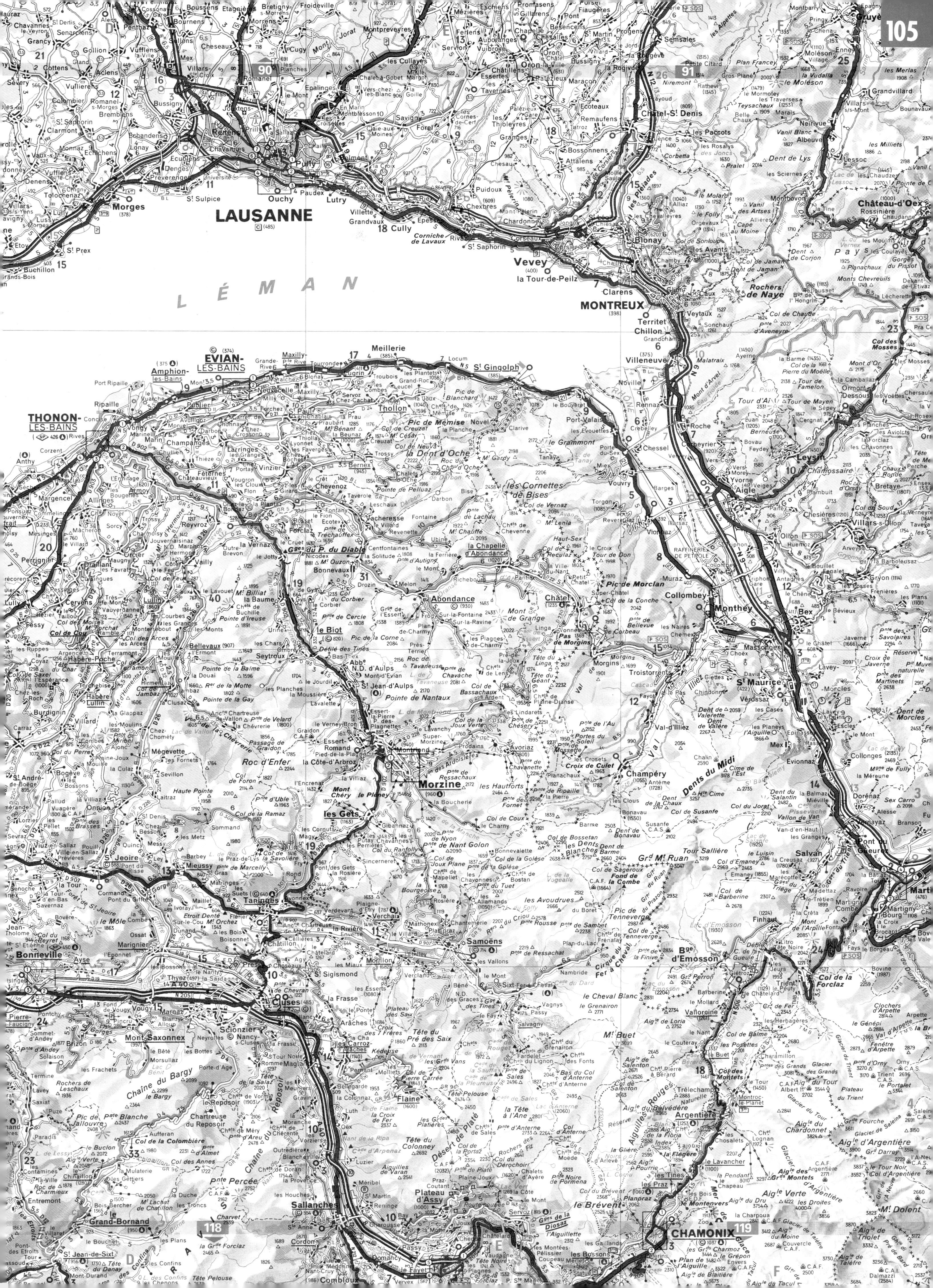
LAUSANNE
L É M A N
Morges
Pully
Ouchy
Lutry
Cully
Vevey
la Tour-de-Peilz
MONTREUX
Clarens
Territet
Chillon
Villeneuve
Blonay
Châtel-St Denis
Château-d'Oex
Rossinière
Leysin
Aigle
Villars-s-Ollon
Bex
Monthey
Collombey
St Maurice
Salvan
Martigny
EVIAN-LES-BAINS
Amphion-les-Bains
THONON-LES-BAINS
St Gingolph
Meillerie
Thollon
Abondance
Châtel
la Chapelle-d'Abondance
le Biot
St Jean-d'Aulps
Morzine
Avoriaz
Champéry
Dents du Midi
Troistorrents
Val-d'Illiez
les Gets
Taninges
Samoëns
Sixt-Fer-à-Cheval
Bonneville
Marignier
Cluses
Scionzier
Mont-Saxonnex
Sallanches
Plateau d'Assy
Servoz
les Houches
CHAMONIX
Argentière
Vallorcine
Finhaut
Col de Balme
le Brévent
Combloux
le Grand-Bornand
St Jean-de-Sixt
Chaîne du Bargy
Chaîne du Reposoir
Col de la Colombière
Pic de Mémise
la Dent d'Oche
les Cornettes de Bises
Roc d'Enfer
Pas de Morgins
Morgins
Rochers de Naye
90
91
118
119

ILE D'OLÉRON
ROCHEFORT
ROYAN
GIRONDE
St Pierre d'Oléron
la Cotinière
Dolus-d'Oléron
le Château d'Oléron
Viaduc d'Oléron
Brouage
Ile Madame
Tonnay-Charente
Soubise
St Agnant
Marennes
Pertuis de Maumusson
St Trojan-les-Bains
Ronce-les-Bains
la Tremblade
Forêt de la Coubre
Phare de la Coubre
Pointe de la Coubre
la Palmyre
Arvert
Étaules
Chaillevette
Mornac-s-Seudre
St Sornin
Nieulle-s-Seudre
Saujon
Médis
St Palais-s-Mer
Pontaillac
Phare de Cordouan
Pointe de Grave
St Georges-de-Didonne
Meschers-s-Gironde
Talmont
Cozes
Mortagne-s-Gironde
le Verdon-s-Mer
Soulac-s-Mer
l'Amélie-s-Mer
Pointe de la Négade
Talais
St Vivien-de-Médoc
Jau
Vensac
Montalivet-les-Bains
Vendays-Montalivet
Queyrac
Bégadan
St Christoly-Médoc
Lesparre-Médoc
Gaillan-en-M.
St Yzans-de-Médoc
Pont-l'Abbé-d'Arnoult
St Porchaire
la Roche Courbon
Champagne
Échillais
Trizay
Beurlay
Gémozac
Pisany
Luchat
Brie-s/s-Mortagne
Floirac
St Fort-s-Gironde
Semussac
Arces
Épargnes
Chenac
Pointe de Richard
Pointe aux Oiseaux
Forêt de Vendays
92
93
120
121

St Jean-d'Angély
Tonnay-Boutonne
St Savinien
Taillebourg
Saintes
Matha
Cognac
Jarnac
Châteauneuf-s-Charente
Segonzac
Rouillac
Pons
Archiac
Barbezieux
Jonzac
Mirambeau
Montendre
Baignes
Chevanceaux
Brossac
Burie
Gémozac
St Genis-de-Saintonge
Châteaubernard
Courcelles
Brizambourg
St Hilaire-de-Villefranche
Hiersac

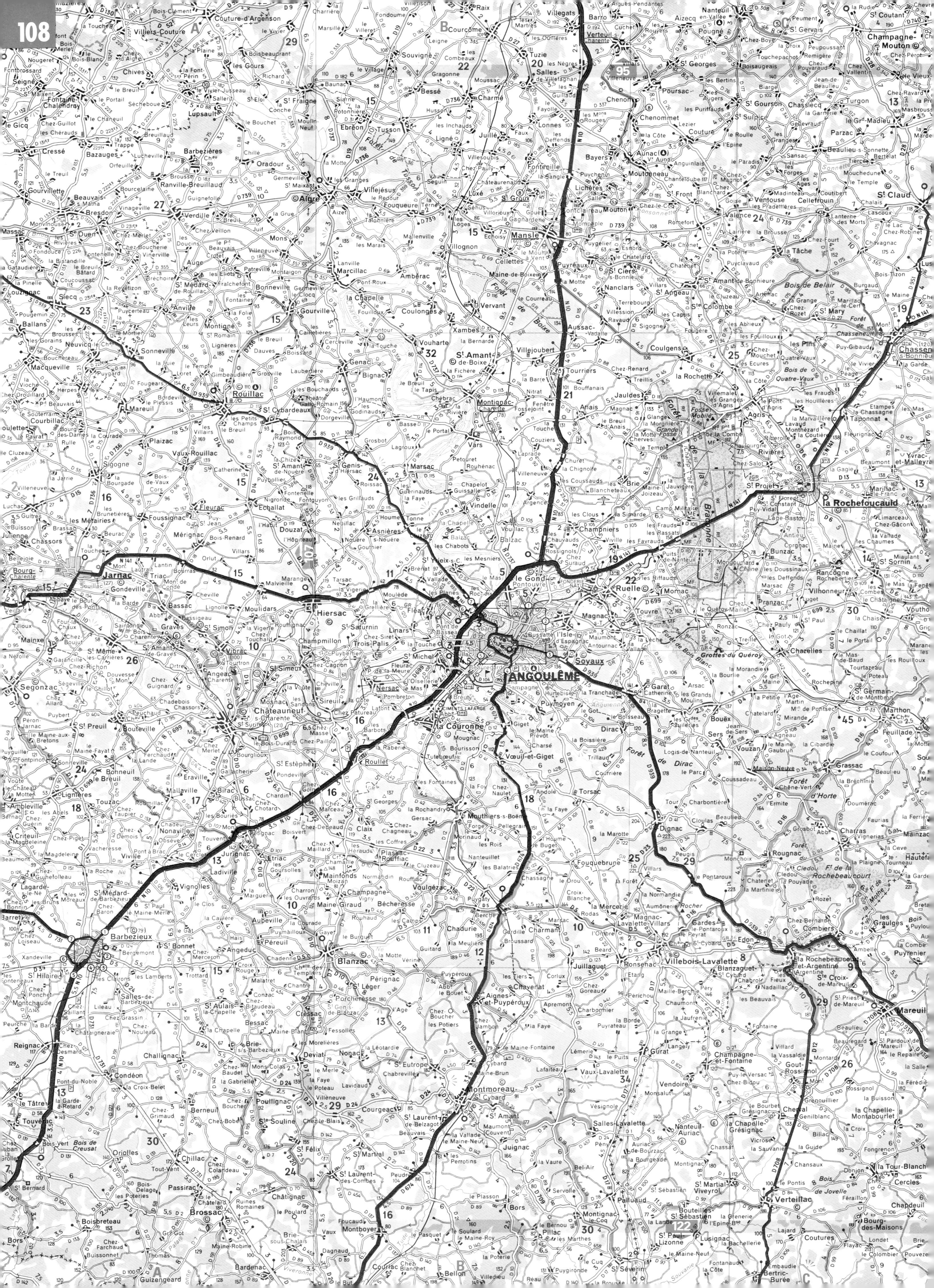
ANGOULÊME
la Rochefoucauld
Jarnac
Châteauneuf-s-Charente
Barbezieux
Montmoreau-St-Cybard
Villebois-Lavalette
Mansle
Rouillac
Hiersac
la Couronne
Ruelle
Soyaux
Aigre
Verteuil-s-Charente
St Claud
Chasseneuil
Champagne-Mouton
Mareuil
Verteillac
Blanzac
Brossac
Montbron
Segonzac
Montignac-Charente
Grottes du Quéroy
Forêt de la Braconne
Forêt de Dirac
Forêt de Boixe
Forêt de Tusson
Forêt de Horte
Forêt de la Rochebeaucourt

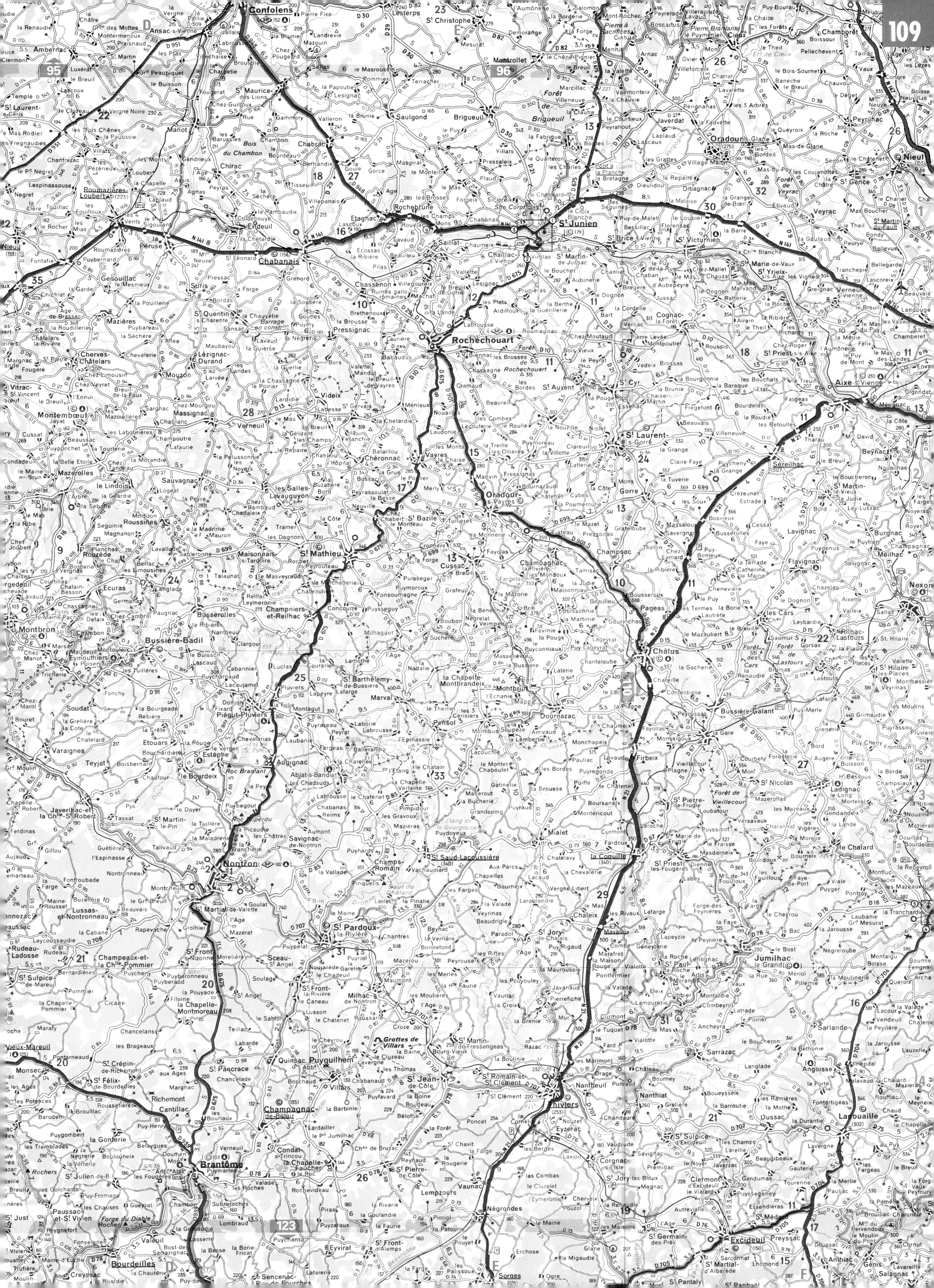
Confolens
95
96
St Junien
Rochechouart
Chabanais
Oradour-s-Glane
Aixe-s-Vienne
Oradour-s-Vayres
St Laurent-s-Gorre
St Mathieu
Châlus
Montbron
Bussière-Badil
Nontron
Thiviers
Brantôme
Excideuil
Bourdeilles
Jumilhac-le-Grand
Lanouaille
Nexon
Nieul
Champagnac-de-Belair
St Pardoux-la-Rivière
123

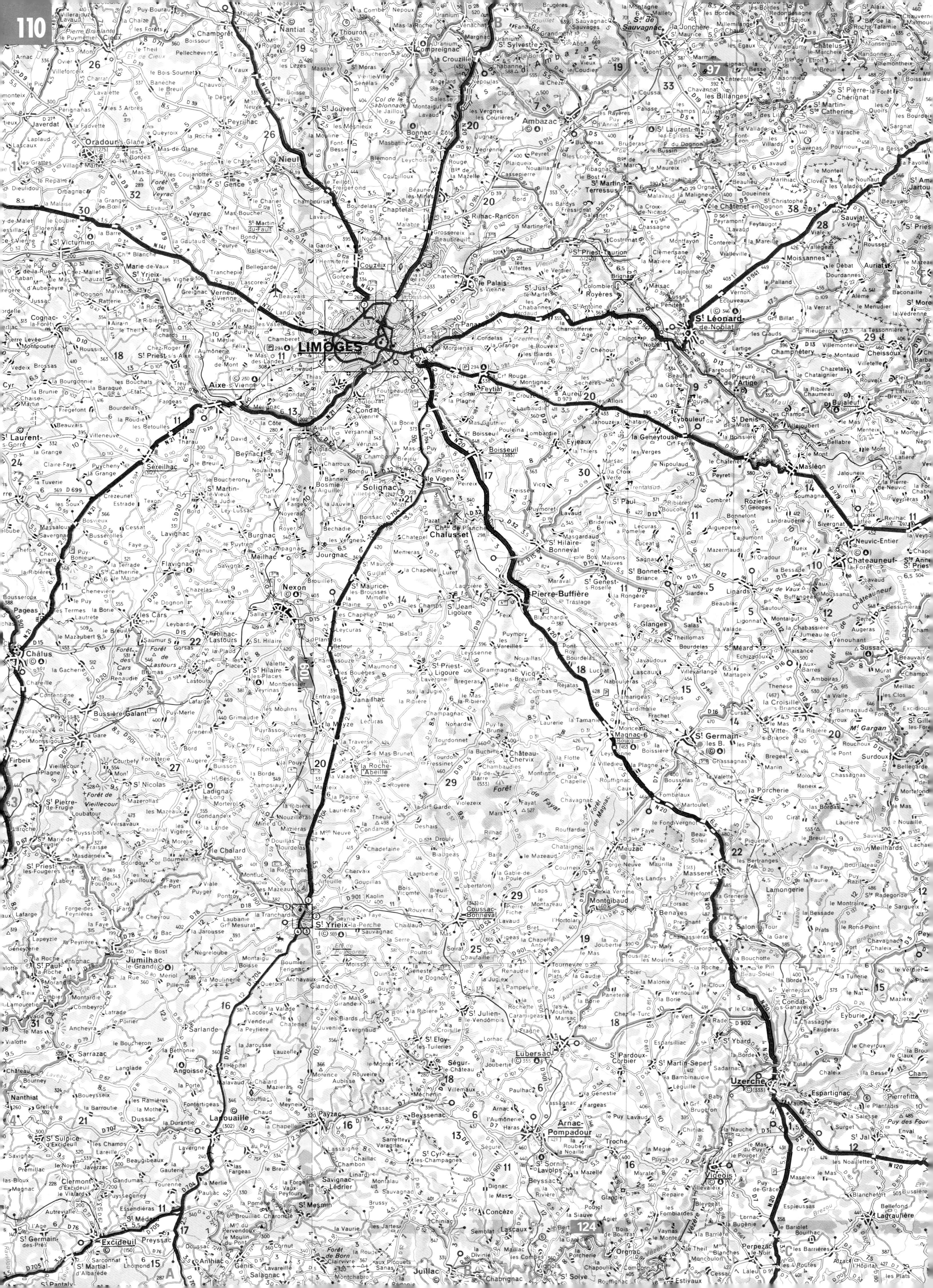
LIMOGES
Nantiat
Compreignac
Ambazac
St Sylvestre
St Léonard-de-Noblat
Sauviat-s-Vige
Bujaleuf
Eybouleuf
Masléon
Neuvic-Entier
Châteauneuf-la-Forêt
St Priest-Taurion
Le Palais-s-Vienne
Panazol
Feytiat
Couzeix
Nieul
Oradour-s-Glane
Veyrac
St Victurnien
Verneuil-s-Vienne
Aixe-s-Vienne
Isle
Condat-s-Vienne
Solignac
le Vigen
Boisseuil
Chalusset
Pierre-Buffière
St Hilaire-Bonneval
St Genest-s-Roselle
St Bonnet-Briance
Sussac
Surdoux
Linards
Glanges
Magnac-Bourg
St Germain-les-Belles
Masseret
Meuzac
Château-Chervix
St Jean-Ligoure
St Priest-Ligoure
Janailhac
la Meyze
Nexon
Jourgnac
Burgnac
Séreilhac
St Laurent-s-Gorre
Flavignac
Meilhac
Rilhac-Lastours
les Cars
Châlus
Bussière-Galant
Ladignac-le-Long
le Chalard
St Yrieix-la-Perche
Coussac-Bonneval
Montgibaud
Salon-la-Tour
Uzerche
Vigeois
Espartignac
Lubersac
St Pardoux-Corbier
Ségur-le-Château
St Julien-le-Vendômois
Arnac-Pompadour
Beyssac
Payzac
Lanouaille
Savignac-Lédrier
St Mesmin
Excideuil
Jumilhac-le-Grand
Sarrazac
Dussac
Anthiac
Génis
Juillac
Concèze
Lagraulière
Perpezac-le-Noir
Orgnac
Chamberet
Eymoutiers
N 20
N 21
N 141
N 120
N 147
97
124
A
B
C

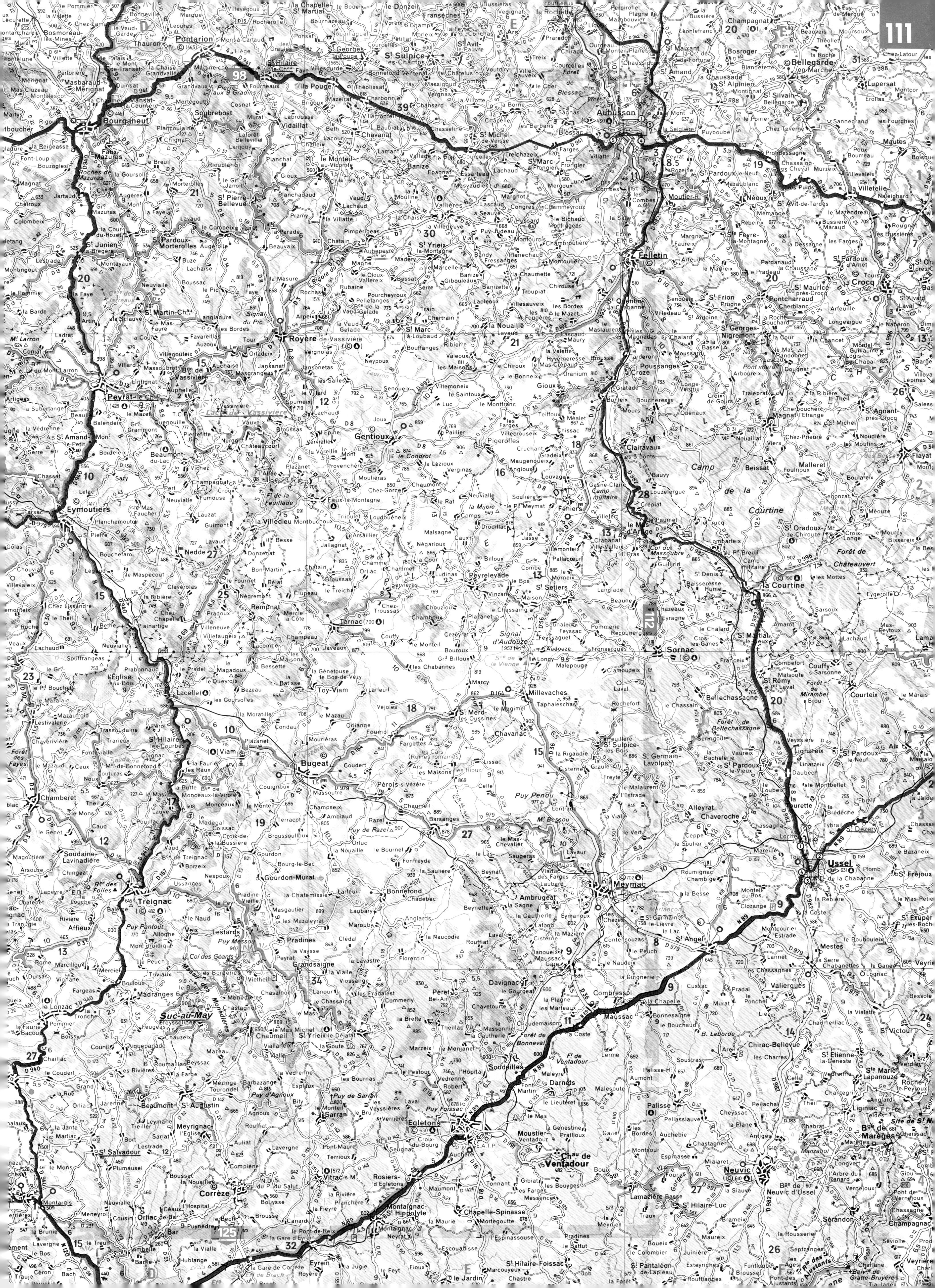
Bourganeuf
Pontarion
Aubusson
Felletin
Crocq
Bellegarde-en-Marche
Royère-de-Vassivière
Peyrat-le-Château
Eymoutiers
Gentioux
Lac de Vassivière
Sornac
La Courtine
Bugeat
Meymac
Ussel
Treignac
Egletons
Neuvic
Corrèze
Millevaches
Plateau de Millevaches
Camp de la Courtine
Suc-au-May
Ch^au de Ventadour
St Sulpice-les-Champs
St Hilaire-le-Ch^au
Vallières
Faux-la-Montagne
Tarnac
Chamberet
Montargis
Bar
Mas-d'Artige
Feniers
Peyrelevade
St Setiers
Chavanac
Pérols-s-Vézère
Davignac
St Angel
Rosiers-d'Egletons
Montaignac-St Hippolyte
Chapelle-Spinasse
Lamazière Basse
St Hilaire-Luc
Sérandon
Liginiac
Magnat
Pontcharraud
Chirac-Bellevue
98
112
125

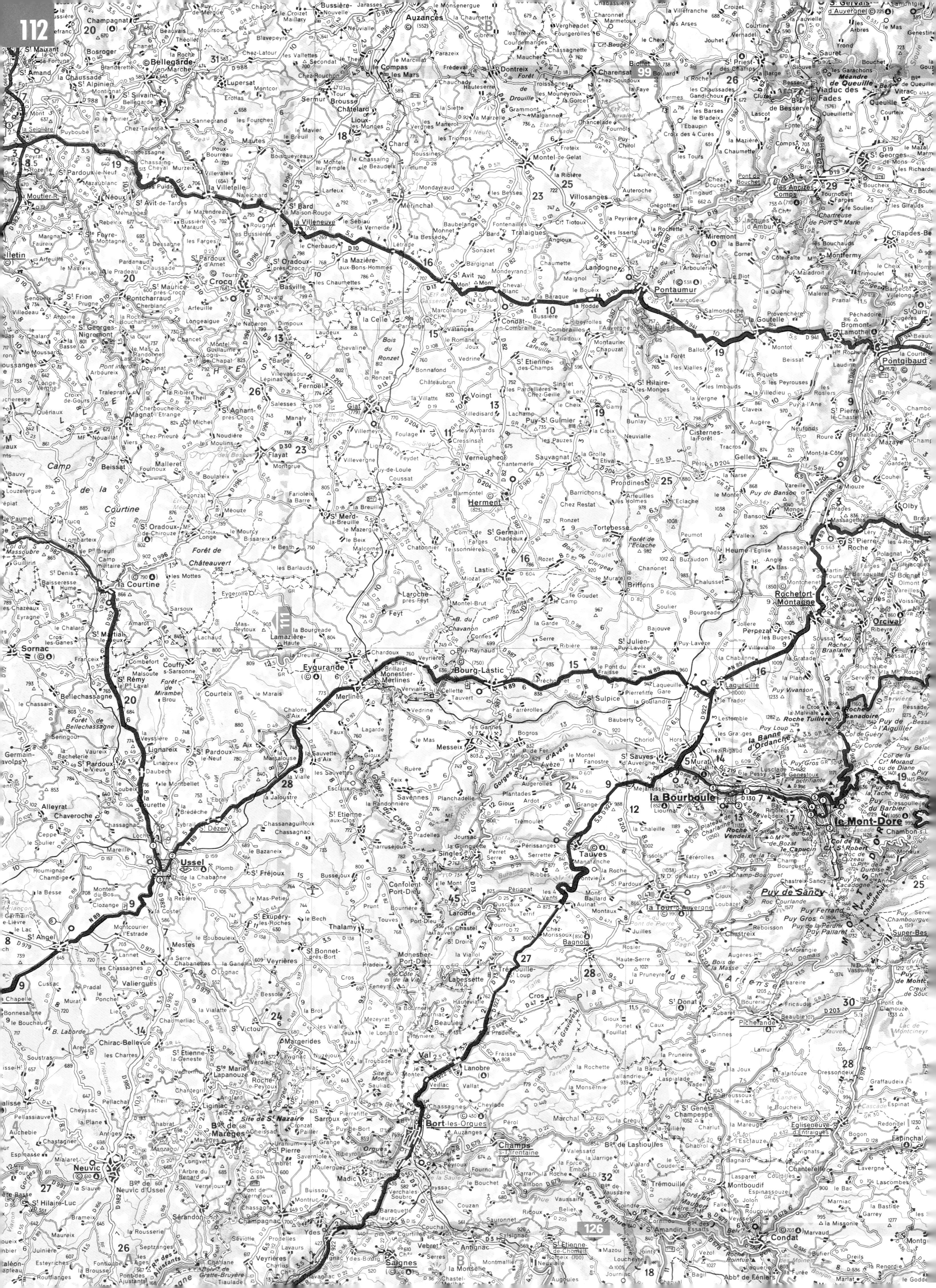
Auzances
Bellegarde-en-Marche
Champagnat
Dontreix
Charensat
Crocq
Pontaumur
Pontgibaud
St Gervais-d'Auvergne
Viaduc des Fades
Les Ancizes-Comps
Giat
Herment
Flayat
Forêt de Châteauvert
la Courtine
Camp de la Courtine
Eygurande
Bourg-Lastic
Rochefort-Montagne
Orcival
Laqueuille
la Bourboule
le Mont-Dore
Puy de Sancy
Tauves
la Tour-d'Auvergne
Bagnols
Ussel
Sornac
Neuvic
Bort-les-Orgues
Champs-sur-Tarentaine
Lanobre
Singles
Confolent-Port-Dieu
Egliseneuve-d'Entraigues
Condat
Picherande
Saignes
Ydes
Meymac
St Angel
Puy de Dôme
Plateau de l'Artense
99
111
126

CLERMONT
FERRAND
Riom
Châtelguyon
Thiers
Issoire
Aigueperse
Randan
Maringues
Lezoux
Billom
Courpière
Chateldon
Puy-Guillaume
Royat
Chamalières
Cournon d'Auvergne
Vic-le-Comte
Champeix
St Nectaire
Murol
Besse en Chandesse
Ardes
Blesle
Brassac les Mines
Jumeaux
Auzon
Sauxillanges
Cunlhat
St Germain-l'Herm
Pont-du-Château
Volvic
Combronde
Manzat
Lempdes
Puy de Dôme
PARC
LIVRADOIS
VOLCANS
RÉGIONAL
CÉZALLIER
99
100
114
127

Thiers
Lezoux
Puy-Guillaume
Châteldon
Courpière
Billom
Noirétable
St Just-en-Chevalet
St Germain-Laval
Boën
Ambert
Olliergues
Cunlhat
Arlanc
Viverols
St Anthème
Jumeaux
Auzon
la Chaise-Dieu
Craponne-s-Arzon
Usson-en-Forez
Chalmazel
St Georges-en-Couzan
St Germain-l'Herm
PARC
RÉGIONAL
LIVRADOIS
FOREZ
MONTS DU FOREZ
MONTS DU LIVRADOIS
BOIS NOIRS
LA MADELEINE
Pierre sur Haute
Col du Béal
A 72
N 89

Amplepuis
Tarare
l'Arbresle
Feurs
Montrond-les-Bains
Montbrison
St Galmier
Andrézieux
St Just-St Rambert
St Chamond
Rive-de-Gier
Mornant
Vaugneray
Charbonnières-les-Bains
Anse
Limonest
Givors
Condrieu
Pélussin
Firminy
Chambon-Feugerolles
St Etienne
Parc Régional du Pilat
Crêt de l'Oeillon
Mont Pilat
Panissières
Balbigny
Néronde
St Symphorien-de-Lay
Neulise
Chazelles-s-Lyon
St Symphorien-s-Coise
St Laurent-de-Chamousset
Bessenay
Montrottier
Aurec-s-Loire
Monistrol-s-Loire
St Genest-Malifaux
St Didier-en-Velay
Bas-en-Basset
Serrières

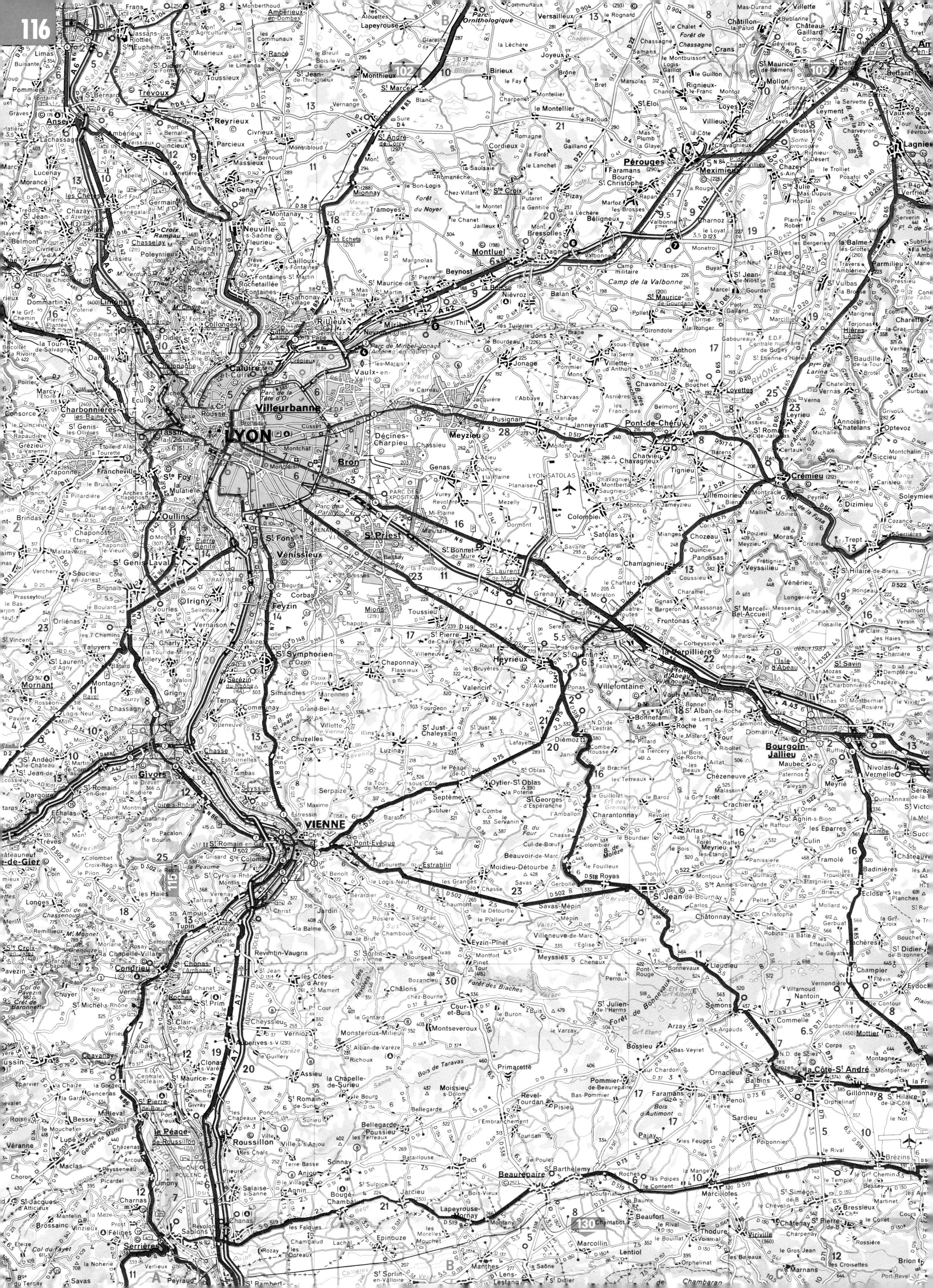

LYON
Villeurbanne
Caluire
Vaulx-en-Velin
Bron
Vénissieux
St Priest
St Fons
Oullins
Décines-Charpieu
Meyzieu
Rillieux
Neyron
Miribel
Montluel
Beynost
Trévoux
Reyrieux
Anse
Limonest
Dardilly
Écully
Charbonnières-les-Bains
Tassin-la-Demi-Lune
Francheville
Ste Foy
Chaponost
Brignais
St Genis-Laval
Irigny
Feyzin
Corbas
Mions
St Symphorien-d'Ozon
Chaponnay
Heyrieux
Givors
Vienne
Pont-Évêque
Condrieu
Chavanay
St Pierre-de-Bœuf
Le Péage-de-Roussillon
Roussillon
Serrières
Beaurepaire
La Côte-St André
Bourgoin-Jallieu
La Verpillière
L'Isle-d'Abeau
Villefontaine
Crémieu
Pont-de-Chéruy
Pérouges
Meximieux
Lagnieu
Mornant
Montagny
Tupin
Ampuis
Ste Colombe
St Romain-en-Gal
Estrablin
Moidieu-Détourbe
St Jean-de-Bournay
Châtonnay
Artas
Meyrieu-les-Étangs
Chèzeneuve
Diémoz
Grenay
St Laurent-de-Mure
Genas
Pusignan
Jonage
Janneyrias
Charvieu-Chavagneux
Tignieu
Colombier
Satolas
LYON-SATOLAS
Chamagnieu
Frontonas
Vaulx-Milieu
St Quentin-Fallavier
Septème
Oytier-St Oblas
St Just-Chaleyssin
Luzinay
Serpaize
Chuzelles
Seyssuel
Reventin-Vaugris
Chonas-l'Amballan
Les Côtes-d'Arey
Chalons
Cour-et-Buis
Montseveroux
Primarette
Revel-Tourdan
Pisieu
Moissieu-s-Dolon
Bellegarde-Poussieu
Sonnay
Agnin
Anjou
Salaise-s-Sanne
Chanas
Sablons
Jarcieu
Lapeyrouse-Mornay
Epinouze
Manthes
Moras
St Sorlin-en-Valloire
Marcollin
Lentiol
Viriville
Marcilloles
Brézins
Faramans
Pommier-de-Beaurepaire
Sardieu
Pajay
Commelle
Semons
Lieudieu
Champier
Nantoin
Mottier
Gillonnay
St Hilaire-de-la-Côte
Eclose
Badinières
Tramolé
Culin
Les Éparres
Meyrié
Nivolas-Vermelle
Ruy
Domarin
Sérézin-du-Rhône
Ternay
Communay
Simandres
Marennes
Toussieu
St Pierre-de-Chandieu
St Bonnet-de-Mure
Valencin
Villette-de-Vienne
Vernaison
Charly
Millery
Grigny
Chasse
Loire-s-Rhône
St Romain-en-Gier
Échalas
Trèves
Longes
Les Haies
St Cyr-s-Rhône
Les Roches
St Clair-du-Rhône
St Prim
Clonas-s-Varèze
Cheyssieu
Vernioz
Auberives-s-Varèze
St Maurice-l'Exil
Assieu
St Alban-de-Varèze
La Chapelle-de-Surieu
St Romain-de-Surieu
Ville-s-Anjou
Bougé-Chambalud
Peyraud
Maclas
Véranne
Lupé
Bessey
Malleval
Charnas
Félines
Limony
Parc Ornithologique
Camp de la Valbonne
Parc de Miribel-Jonage
Forêt du Noyer
Forêt de Chassagne
Forêt de Bonnevaux
Forêt des Blaches
Bois de Taravas
Parc de Parilly
Parc des Expositions
Parc de la Tête d'Or
Centrale nucléaire de Bugey
Centrale nucléaire
Loyettes
Anthon
Chavanoz
Villette-d'Anthon
Charvas
Hières-s-Amby
Charette
Leyrieu
Optevoz
Siccieu
Dizimieu
Trept
St Hilaire-de-Brens
Vénérieu
St Marcel-Bel-Accueil
St Savin
Bonnefamille
St Alban-de-Roche
Four
Charantonnay
Savas-Mépin
Villeneuve-de-Marc
Royas
Eyzin-Pinet
Meyssiès
Montluel
Dagneux
Balan
Niévroz
Thil
Béligneux
Bressolles
Pizay
St Maurice-de-Gourdans
St Jean-de-Niost
Blyes
St Vulbas
Chazey-s-Ain
Ambérieux
Ambérieu-en-Dombes
Lapeyrouse
Monthieux
St Marcel
St André-de-Corcy
Mionnay
Tramoyes
Les Échets
Sathonay-Camp
Sathonay-Village
Fontaines-s-Saône
Neuville-s-Saône
Genay
Massieux
Parcieux
Quincieux
Civrieux
Misérieux
Toussieux
St Didier-de-Formans
Jassans-Riottier
Villefranche
Limas
Pommiers
Lachassagne
Marcy
Lucenay
Morancé
Chazay-d'Azergues
Les Chères
Lissieu
Dommartin
La Tour-de-Salvagny
Marcy-l'Étoile
Craponne
Brindas
Soucieu-en-Jarrest
Orliénas
Taluyers
St Laurent-d'Agny
Chassagny
St Andéol-le-Château
Dargoire
St Jean-de-Touslas
A 6
A 7
A 42
A 43
A 47
N 6
N 7
N 86
102
103
130

Seyssel
Grd Colombier
Rumilly
Belley
Virieu-le-Grand
Culoz
Ruffieux
Albens
Aix-les-Bains
Lhuis
Morestel
St Genix-s-Guiers
Yenne
Chambéry
Le Bourget-du-Lac
La Tour-du-Pin
Les Abrets
Le Pont-de-Beauvoisin
Challes-les-Eaux
Montmélian
St Geoire-en-Valdaine
Les Echelles
Voiron
Le Grand-Lemps
Rives
Moirans
Voreppe
Tullins
St Laurent-du-Pont
St Pierre-de-Chartreuse
Charmant Som
Massif de la Chartreuse
Pontcharra
Goncelin
Le Touvet
Crolles
Chamechaude
Col de Porte
Gresy
Alby-s-Chéran
Seynod
Charavines
Virieu
Aoste
Novalaise
Lac du Bourget
Abb. de Hautecombe
Dent du Chat
Mont Revard
Col du Granier
Mt Granier
Cirque de St Même
Chapareillan
Barraux
Entremont-le-Vieux
Bourdeau
Tresserve
Cognin
Les Marches

ANNECY
Thônes
la Clusaz
Rumilly
Albens
AIX-LES-BAINS
CHAMBÉRY
Talloires
Faverges
Albertville
Ugine
Montmélian
la Rochette
Allevard
Pontcharra
le Touvet
Goncelin
St. Pierre-de-Chartreuse
Aiguebelle
St. Jean-de-Maurienne
Lac du Bourget
Lac d'Annecy
Tête du Parmelan
la Tournette
CHAÎNE DE BELLEDONNE
LA CHARTREUSE
MASSIF DE
Pic du Frêne
le Cheval Noir
Grd Arc
104
105
117
132

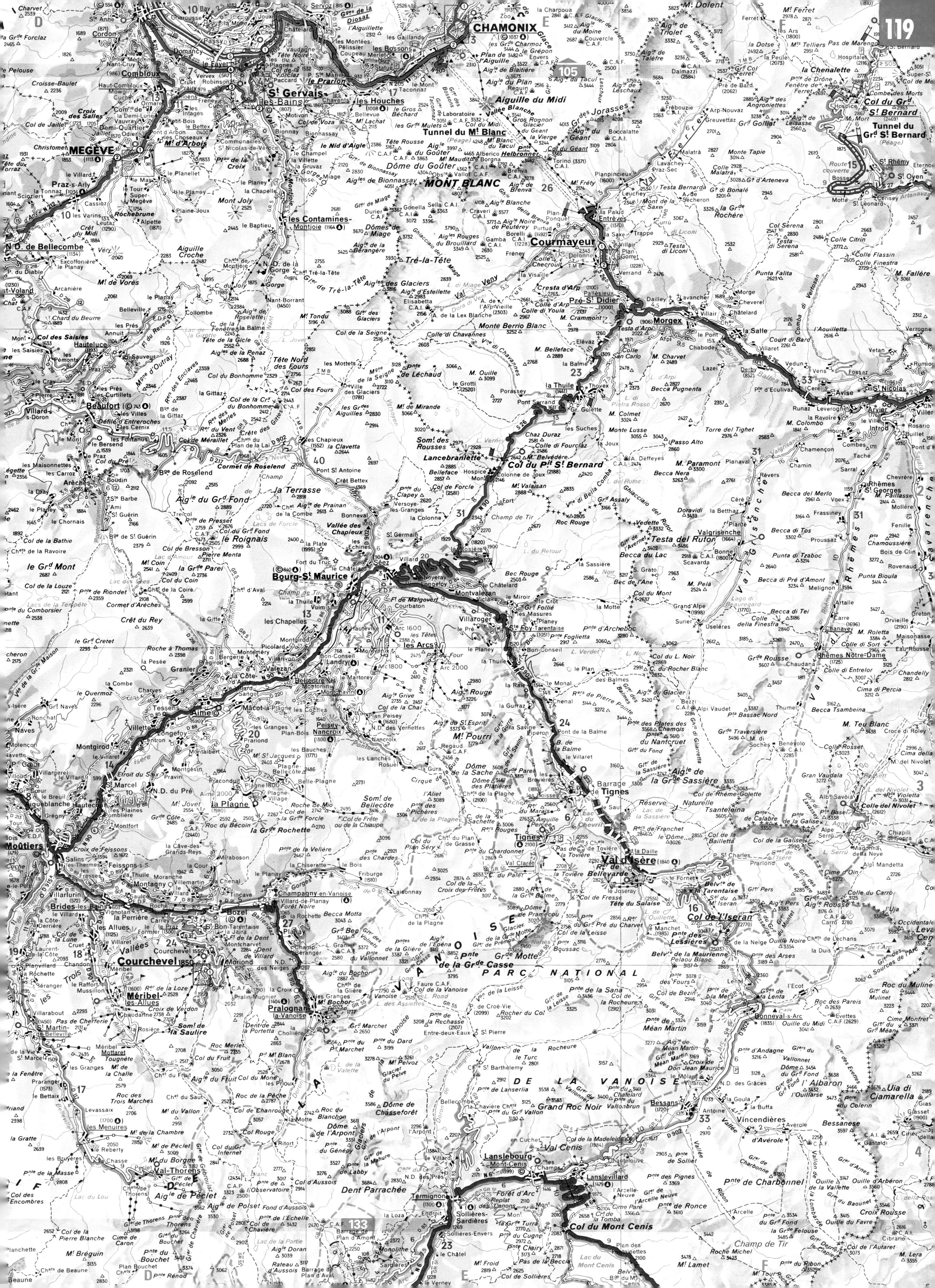
CHAMONIX
Aiguille du Midi
Tunnel du Mt Blanc
MONT BLANC
Dôme du Goûter
Aigle du Goûter
Les Houches
St Gervais-les-Bains
Combloux
MEGÈVE
Mt d'Arbois
Praz-s-Arly
Mont Joly
les Contamines-Montjoie
N.D. de Bellecombe
Courmayeur
Pré-St Didier
Morgex
La Thuile
Col du Pt St Bernard
Col du Grd St Bernard
Tunnel du Grd St Bernard
Aosta
Arvier
Avise
St Rhémy
Hauteluce
Beaufort
Arêches
Cormet de Roselend
Col du Bonhomme
la Terrasse
Aigle du Grd Fond
le Roignais
Bourg-St Maurice
Séez
Montvalezan
Ste Foy-Tarentaise
les Arcs
Landry
Aime
Valezan
Mâcot-la-Plagne
Peisey-Nancroix
la Plagne
Mt Pourri
Tignes
Val d'Isère
Col de l'Iseran
Valgrisenche
Rhêmes Notre-Dame
Moûtiers
Brides-les-Bains
Bozel
Champagny-en-Vanoise
Courchevel 1850
Méribel
Pralognan-la-Vanoise
St Martin-de-Belleville
les Menuires
Val-Thorens
Aigle de Péclet
PARC NATIONAL DE LA VANOISE
Pte de la Grde Casse
Grde Motte
Dôme de Chasseforêt
Dent Parrachée
Grand Roc Noir
Bessans
Bonneval-s-Arc
Lanslebourg-Mont-Cenis
Lanslevillard
Val Cenis
Col du Mont Cenis
Termignon
Sollières-Sardières
Pte de Charbonnel
Uia di Ciamarella
Vallée d'Avérole
Tête du Solaise
Pte de Méan Martin

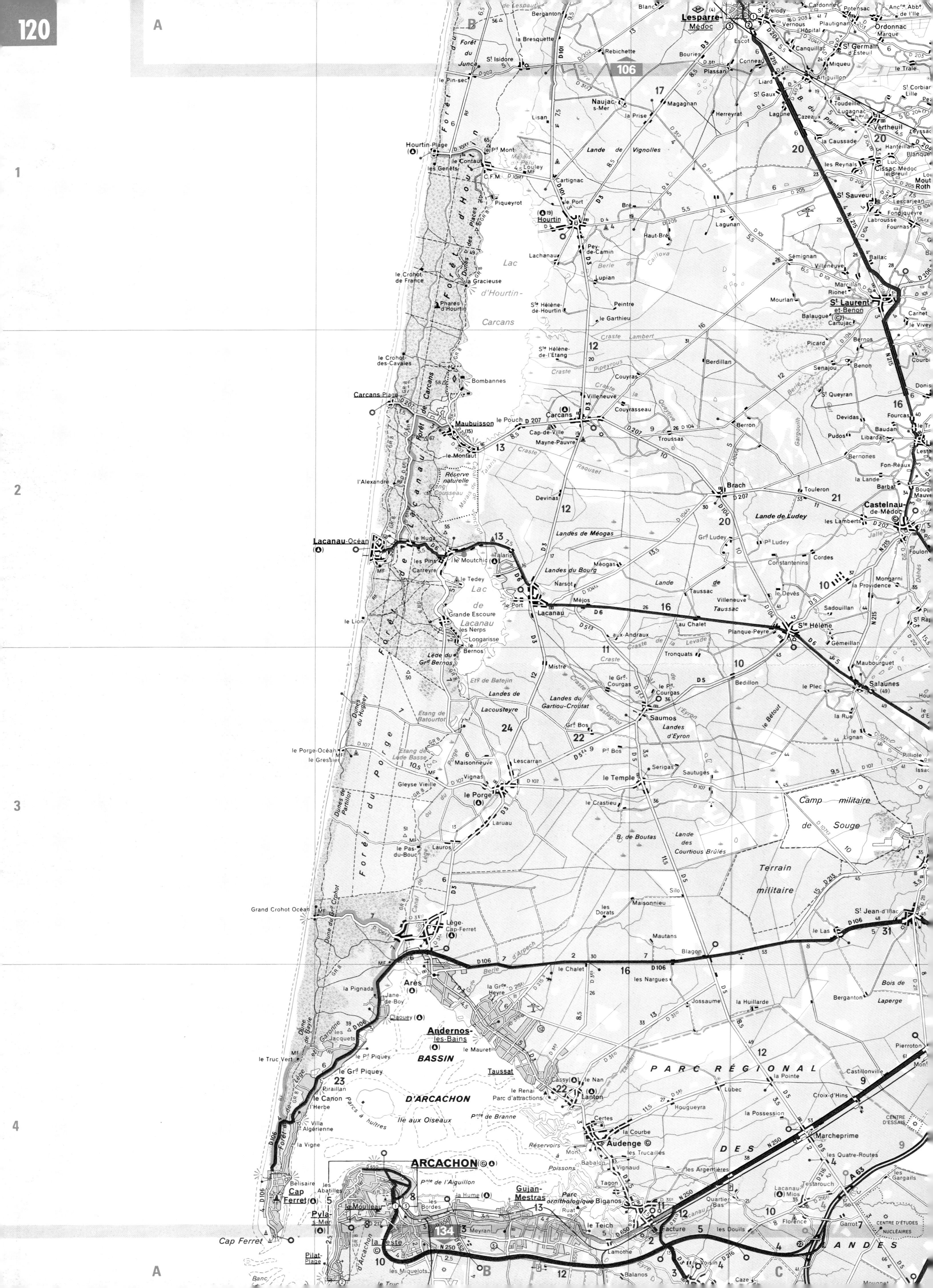
A
B
C
1
2
3
4
106
134
Lesparre-Médoc
St Trelody
Potensac
Ordonnac
Plautignan
Cardonnet
Berganton
Rebichette
Bouries
Plassan
Escot
Conneau
Liard
St Gaux
St Germain d'Esteuil
Miqueu
Artiguillon
le Trale
Forêt du Junca
St Isidore
la Bresquette
le Pin-sec
Naujac-s-Mer
Magagnan
la Prise
Herreyrat
Lagune
Cazeaux
B du Plantier
Vertheuil
la Caussade
Hanteillan
Cissac-Médoc
les Reynals
Lande de Vignolles
Lisan
Hourtin-Plage
le Contaut
les Genêts
le Pt Mont
Louley
C.F.M.
Cartignac
Piqueyrot
Hourtin
le Port
Bré
Haut-Bré
Lagunan
St Sauveur
Lescarjean
Labrousse
Fournas
Lachanau
Pey-de-Camin
Lupian
Peintre
Lac d'Hourtin-Carcans
le Crohot-de France
la Gracieuse
Phares d'Hourtin
Forêt d'Hourtin
Dunes des Places
Sémignan
Villeneuve
Marcillan
Rionet
Mourlan
St Laurent-et-Benon
Balaugue
Cartujac
Ballac
Carnet
le Vivey
Ste Hélène-de-Hourtin
le Garthieu
Craste Lambert
Berdillan
Picard
Bernos
Senajou
Benon
Ste Hélène-de-l'Etang
Craste
le Crohot-des-Cavales
Bombannes
Couyras
Villeneuve
Couyrasseau
St Queyran
Carcans-Plage
Forêt de Carcans
Maubuisson
Carcans
le Pouch
Cap-de-Ville
Mayne-Pauvre
Troussas
Berron
Devidas
Baudan
Pudos
Libardac
Fourcas
le Montaut
Réserve naturelle
Etang Cousseau
Raouset
Bernones
Fon-Reaux
la Lande
Barbat
l'Alexandre
Brach
Touleron
Castelnau-de-Médoc
Devinas
Lande de Ludey
les Lamberts
Landes de Méogas
Grd Ludey
Pt Ludey
Constantenins
Cordes
Lacanau-Océan
le Huga
le Moutchic
Talaris
les Pins
Carreyre
Méogas
Landes du Bourg
Narsot
Lande de Taussac
Taussac
Villeneuve
Mongarni
la Providence
le Tedey
Lac de Lacanau
Grande Escoure
les Nerps
le Port
Lacanau
Méjos
le Devès
Sadouillan
le Lion
Longarisse
Bernos
aux Andraux
au Chalet
Planque-Peyre
Ste Hélène
Gémeillan
Lède du Grd Bernos
Tronquats
Mistré
le Grd Courgas
le Pt Courgas
Bedillon
Maubourguet
Salaunes
le Plec
Etg de Batejin
Landes de Lacousteyre
Landes du Gartiou-Croutat
Saumos
Landes d'Eyron
le Bétout
la Rue
le Lignan
Dunes du Hughey
Etang de Batourtot
Grd Bos
Pt Bos
le Porge-Océan
le Gressier
Etang de Lède Basse
Maisonneuve
Lescarran
Serigas
Sautuges
le Temple
Gleyse Vieille
Vignas
le Porge
Forêt du Porge
Dunes de Partillor
le Crastieu
Camp militaire de Souge
Laruau
B. de Boutas
Lande des Courtious Brûlés
le Pas-du-Bouc
Lauros
Terrain militaire
Silo
Grand Crohot Océan
Dune du Grd Crohot
Lège-Cap-Ferret
les Dorats
Maisonnieu
St Jean-d'Illac
Mautans
Blagon
le Las
le Chalet
les Nargues
Bois de Laperge
Berganton
Arès
la Pignada
Jane-de-Boy
Claouey
la Grde Heyre
Jossaume
la Huillarde
Andernos-les-Bains
le Mauret
Pierroton
Dune de Bayle
les Jacquets
le Truc Vert
le Pd Piquey
le Grd Piquey
Piraillan
BASSIN D'ARCACHON
Taussat
Cassy
le Nan
PARC RÉGIONAL DES LANDES
la Pointe
Castillonville
le Canon
l'Herbe
le Renai
Parc d'attractions
Lanton
Lubec
Croix-d'Hins
Hougueyra
Parcs à huîtres
Ile aux Oiseaux
Pte de Branne
Certes
la Courbe
la Possession
Villa Algérienne
la Vigne
Audenge
Réservoirs à Poissons
les Trucailles
Marcheprime
les Quatre-Routes
Centre d'essais
ARCACHON
Pte de l'Aiguillon
Bélisaire
Cap Ferret
les Abatilles
le Moulleau
Pyla-s-Mer
la Hume
les Bordes
Gujan-Mestras
Parc ornithologique
Biganos
Vignaud
Tagon
Babelon
les Argentières
Lacanau de Mios
Testarouch
les Gargails
Centre d'études nucléaires
Cap Ferret
Pilat-Plage
la Teste
Meyran
Ruat
le Teich
Facture
Lamothe
les Douils
Garrot
Florence
Balanos
Poisin
les Miquelots
le Truc
Banc
Caze
Forêt de la Teste
Forêt de Lacanau

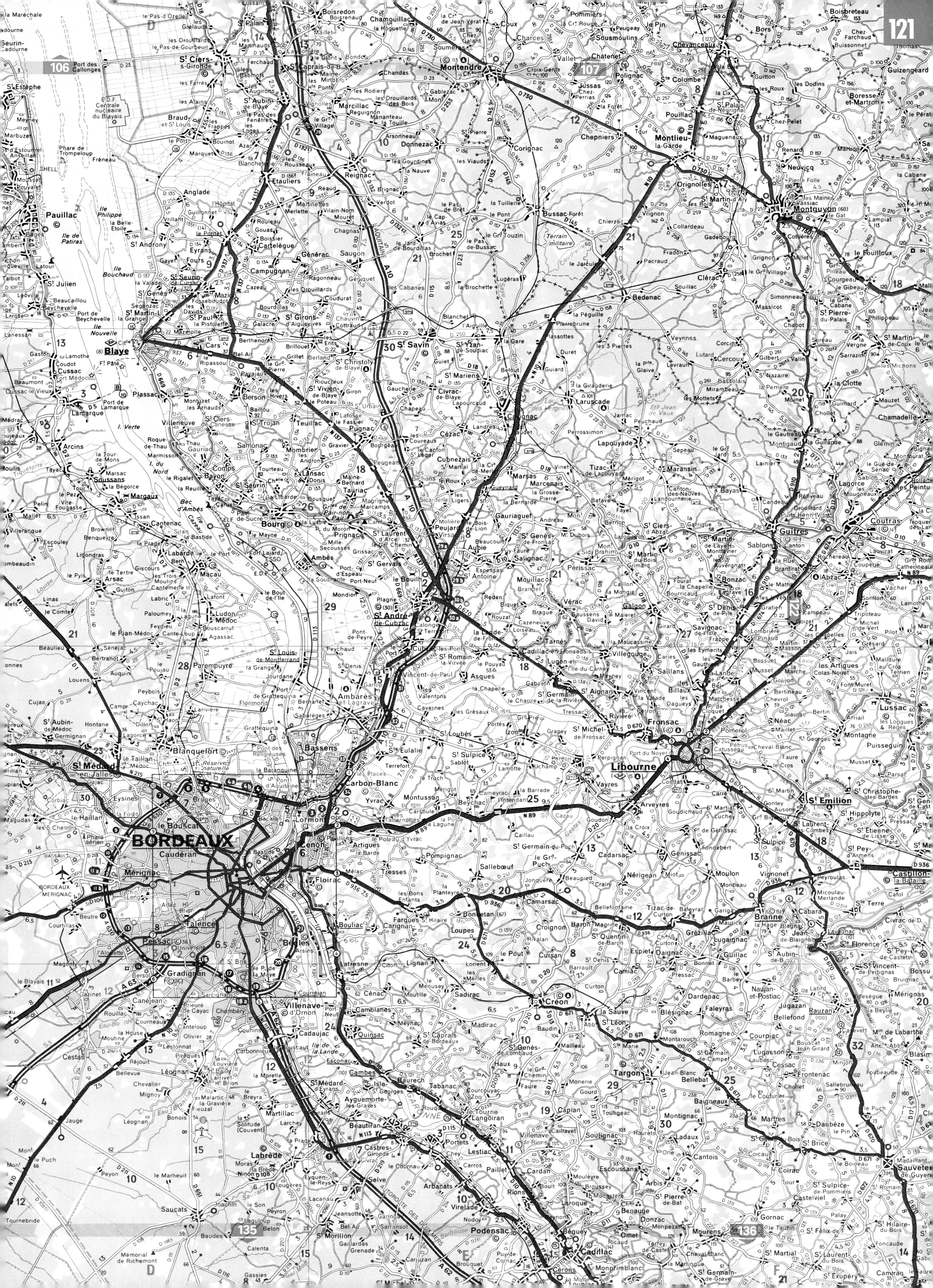
106
107
135
136
BORDEAUX
Libourne
Blaye
Pauillac
Margaux
St Émilion
Castillon-la-Bataille
Coutras
Guîtres
Montguyon
Montendre
Montlieu-la-Garde
Chevanceaux
St Ciers-s-Gironde
St Savin
St André-de-Cubzac
Bourg
Cadillac
Podensac
Langoiran
Créon
Targon
Branne
Sauveterre-de-Guyenne
Mérignac
Pessac
Talence
Gradignan
Bègles
Lormont
Cenon
Bassens
Blanquefort
St Médard-en-Jalles
Le Bouscat
Cauderan
Floirac
Carbon-Blanc
Fronsac
Lussac
Arveyres
Ambès
Cubzac-les-Ponts
Labrède
Léognan
Cestas
Villenave-d'Ornon
Lamarque
Cussac
St Julien
Cavignac
Laruscade
Galgon
D
E
F

Chalais
Aubeterre-s-Dronne
Ribérac
St Aulaye
Montguyon
Coutras
Montpon-Ménestérol
Mussidan
St Astier
Neuvic
Bergerac
Ste Foy-la-Grande
Port-Ste-Foy
Castillon-la-Bataille
St Emilion
Lussac
Villefranche-de-Lonchat
Vélines
Pellegrue
Duras
Sauveterre-de-Guyenne
Monségur
Eymet
Sigoulès
Monbazillac
La Roche-Chalais
St Aiguin
Echourgnac
FORÊT DE LA DOUBLE
FORÊT DU LANDAIS
Montagrier
Tocane-St-Apre
Villetoureix
Verteillac
Bourg-du-Bost
Vanxains
St Privat
Festalemps
Mouliets-et-Villemartin
Pujols
Gensac
Rauzan
Lamothe-Montravel
Fougueyrolles
Le Fleix
La Force
Gardonne
Saussignac
Monfaucon
Carsac-de-Gurson
St Méard-de-Gurçon
St Rémy
Fraisse
Lunas
Issac
Villamblard
Douzillac
Sourzac
Les Lèches
Beauronne
St Vincent-de-Connezac
Chantérac
Bridoire
Ribagnac
Rouffignac-de-Sigoulès
Razac-d'Eymet
Serres-et-Montguyard
Soumensac
Lévignac-de-Guyenne
Moulin de Malfourat

PÉRIGUEUX
Bourdeilles
Excideuil
Hautefort
Thenon
Montignac
Grotte de Lascaux
Vergt
les Eyzies-de-Tayac
le Bugue
Sarlat-la-Canéda
Lalinde
le Buisson
Cadouin
Beaumont
Belvès
Monpazier
Villeréal
Issigeac
Domme
la Roque-Gageac
Beynac-et-Cazenac
Castelnaud
St Cyprien
Rouffignac
Savignac-les-Églises
Sorges
Tourtoirac
Trémolat
Mouleydier
Château-l'Évêque
Chancelade
Boulazac
St Pierre-de-Chignac
Razac-s-l'Isle
Annesse-et-Beaulieu
Grotte de Rouffignac
Forêt de la Bessède
Forêt de Montclard
Forêt Barade
N 21
N 89
D 710
D 704
D 660
109
124
137

Excideuil
Juillac
Hautefort
Ayen
Objat
Allassac
Donzenac
BRIVE-LA-GAILLARDE
Thenon
Terrasson-la-Villedieu
Larche
Montignac
Grotte de Lascaux
Turenne
Collonges-la-Rouge
Salignac-Eyvignes
Les Eyzies
Sarlat-la-Canéda
Souillac
Martel
Beynac-et-Cazenac
La Roque-Gageac
Domme
Castelnaud
Belvès
St Cyprien
Payrac
Gourdon
Rocamadour
Salviac
Frayssinet
Carlux
Fénelon
Gluges

Tulle
Naves
Gimel
Laguenne
Lapleau
Mauriac
Pleaux
Argentat
Beynat
Servières-le-Château
St Privat
Tours de Merle
la Roche-Canillac
Bgé du Chastang
Bgé de l'Aigle
Bgé d'Enchanet
Bgé de St Etienne-Cantalès
Laroquebrou
St Etienne-Cantalès
St Paul-des-Landes
Beaulieu-s-D.
Bretenoux
Castelnau
St Céré
Sousceyrac
Latronquière
Gramat
Lacapelle-Marival
Maurs
Dordogne
Cère
Gorges de la Cère
Gouffre de Padirac
Grotte de Presque
Montal
Aynac
Leyme
Assier
Livernon
St Mamet-la-Salvetat
Boisset
Cayrols
Montvert
Mercœur
Sexcles
Marcillac-la-Croisille
St Martial-Entraygues
St Bonnet-Elvert
Forgès
Camps
Vayrac
Sioniac
Marcolès
Calvinet
Cardaillac
Bagnac-s-Célé
St Santin-de-Maurs
111
126
139

AURILLAC
Mauriac
Salers
Pleaux
Riom-ès-Montagnes
Condat
Murat
Vic-s-Cère
Arpajon-s-Cère
Montsalvy
Laguiole
Mur-de-Barrez
Pierrefort
Saignes
Trizac
Cheylade
Le Lioran
Super-Lioran
Plomb du Cantal
Puy Mary
Pas de Peyrol
Thiézac
Jussac
St Cernin
Anjony
Polminhac
Calvinet
Cayrols
St Mamet-la-Salvetat
Entraygues-s-T.
Pont de Tréboul
Ste Geneviève-s-Argence
Bge de Sarrans
Bge de Couesque
Bge de l'Aigle
Bge d'Enchanet
PARC
RÉGIONAL
DES
VOLCANS
D'AUVERGNE
MONTS DU CANTAL
Gorges de la Dordogne
Gorges de la Truyère
Vallée du Falgoux
Vallée de Mandailles
Vallée de la Jordanne
Route des Crêtes
Puy Violent
Col de Cabre
Puy Griou
Col de Serres
Rocher des Pendus
112
140

CÉZALLIER
Blesle
Brioude
Massiac
Allanche
Lavaudieu
Paulhaguet
Molompize
Bonnac
Ferrières-St Mary
Valjouze
Neussargues-Moissac
Lavoûte-Chilhac
Blassac
Chilhac
St Cirgues
Langeac
Pinols
Col de la Fageole
Coltines
St Flour
Tanavelle
Andelat
Roffiac
Ussel
Forêt de la Margeride
Ruynes-en-Margeride
Viaduc de Garabit
Chau d'Alleuze
Mont Mouchet
Saugues
Pont de Lanau
Chaudes-Aigues
Gorges de la Truyère
le Malzieu-Ville
St Chély-d'Apcher
Fournels
St Alban-s-Limagnole
Aumont-Aubrac
St Urcize
Nasbinals
Serverette
St Amans
MONTS DE LA MARGERIDE

Brioude
Vieille-Brioude
Lavaudieu
Paulhaguet
la Chaise-Dieu
LIVRADOIS
FOREZ
Craponne-s-Arzon
Allègre
Chomelix
Bellevue-la-Montagne
Vorey
St Paulien
Lavoûte-Chilhac
Langeac
Pinols
Loudes
LE PUY
Espaly-St Marcel
Polignac
Solignac-s-Loire
Saugues
Monistrol-d'Allier
Cayres
Costaros
Le Malzieu-Ville
St Alban-s-Limagnole
Grandrieu
Langogne
Pradelles
Coucouron
Arlempdes
St Amans
Châteauneuf-de-Randon
Mt Mouchet
Gorges de l'Allier
Allier
Loire
N 102
N 88
D 906
D 590
D 585
D 589
D 989
D 988
113
114
127
142
143

Monistrol-s-Loire
Bas-en-Basset
St Didier-en-Velay
Bourg-Argental
Annonay
Ste Sigolène
Riotord
Dunières
Montfaucon-en-Velay
Yssingeaux
Tence
Le Chambon-s-Lignon
St Agrève
Lamastre
Satillieu
Lalouvesc
St Félicien
Fay-s-Lignon
St Martin-de-Valamas
Le Cheylard
Mt Mézenc
Gerbier de Jonc
St Pierreville
Burzet
Montpezat-s-Bauzon
Antraigues
Thueyts
Vals-les-Bains
Privas
Chomérac
Vernoux-en-Vivarais
Forêt de Taillard
Forêt de Mazan

Annonay
Serrières
Davézieux
St Rambert-d'Albon
Andancette
St Vallier
Tournon
Tain l'Hermitage
Romans-s-Isère
Bourg-de-Péage
VALENCE
Bourg-lès-Valence
Guilherand
St Péray
Chabeuil
Crest
Loriol-s-Drôme
Livron-s-Drôme
Le Pouzin
Baix
Cruas
Le Logis Neuf
Saillans
Mirmande
Montmeyran
Etoile-s-Rhône
Portes-lès-Valence
Beaumont-lès-Valence
la Voulte-s-Rhône
Chomérac
Privas
Vernoux-en-Vivarais
Lamastre
St Félicien
St Donat-s-l'Herbasse
Le Grand-Serre
Roybon
St Marcellin
St Nazaire-en-Royans
St Jean-en-Royans
Pont-en-Royans
Hauterives
Palais Idéal
Camp de Chambaran
Forêt de Chambaran
Forêt de Thivolet
Montelier
Alixan
Chatuzange
Peyrus
Léoncel
Col de la Bataille
Marsanne
Saou
Forêt de Saou
Plan-de-Baix
Aouste-s-Sye
Mirabel-et-Blacons
Beaufort-s-Gervanne
Autichamp
Cornas
Châteaubourg
St Romain-de-Lerps
Corniche du Rhône
AUTOROUTE DU SOLEIL
A7
N7
N86
N92
N532
N104
116
129
144
145

GRENOBLE
Voreppe
Tullins
Vinay
Sassenage
Fontaine
St Égrève
Meylan
Domène
Échirolles
le Pont-de-Claix
Eybens
Uriage-les-Bains
Chamrousse
Vizille
Vif
Villard-de-Lans
Autrans
Méaudre
Lans-en-Vercors
St Nizier-du-Moucherotte
Corrençon-en-Vercors
la Chapelle-en-Vercors
Monestier-de-Clermont
la Mure
le Bourg-d'Oisans
Laffrey
Mens
Clelles
Corps
Valbonnais
St Firmin
Die
Châtillon-en-Diois
Lus-la-Croix-Haute
St Étienne-en-Dévoluy
Col de la Croix Haute
Grandes Goulets
le Grand Veymont
Mont Aiguille
Belledonne
Grand Pic de Belledonne
le Taillefer
l'Obiou
Pic de Bure
Forêt de Durbon
N 75
N 85
N 91
A 48
A 41
D 531
D 518
D 526
117
132
145

GRENOBLE
Vizille
Uriage-les-Bains
Chamrousse
Domène
Crolles
St Jean-de-Maurienne
St Michel-de-Maurienne
Valloire
St Jean-d'Arves
Col du Glandon
Col de la Croix de Fer
Massif de Belledonne
Grd Pic de Belledonne
l'Alpe-d'Huez
le Bourg-d'Oisans
Allemond
Vaujany
Pic du Lac Blanc
Pic de l'Etendard
Grandes Rousses
Galibier-Grandes-Rousses
Besse
la Grave
Col du Lautaret
la Meije
Chambon
les Deux-Alpes
Venosc
St Christophe-en-Oisans
la Bérarde
Barre des Ecrins
Mt Pelvoux
MASSIF DES ECRINS
PARC NATIONAL DES ECRINS
Valjouffrey
Valbonnais
la Mure
Laffrey
N.D. de la Salette
Corps
Mens
St Firmin
Vieux Chaillol
St Bonnet
Orcières
Chabottes
Ancelle
St Etienne-en-Dévoluy
Pic de Bure
Col Bayard
Tréminis
St Disdier
l'Obiou
Route Napoléon
118
131
146
33

Col du Mont Cenis
Lac du Mont Cenis
MASSIF DU Mt CENIS
Modane
Aussois
Bramans
Sollières-Sardières
Lanslebourg
Moncenisio
Novalesa
Susa
Bussoleno
Mompantero
Giaglione
Rocciamelone
Champ de Tir
Tunnel du Fréjus (Péage)
Mt Thabor
Aigle de Scolette
Bardonècchia
Oulx
Sauze d'Oulx
Salbertrand
Exilles
Chiomonte
Sestriere
Cesana Torinese
Claviere
Montgenèvre
Col de Montgenèvre
BRIANÇON
Serre Chevalier
Chantemerle
Le Monêtier-les-Bains
Vallouise
L'Argentière-la-Bessée
Col d'Izoard
Pic de Rochebrune
Château-Queyras
Aiguilles
Abriès
St Véran
Ceillac
Guillestre
Mont-Dauphin
Vars
Risoul
Châteauroux
PARC REGIONAL DU QUEYRAS
M. Viso
Pragelato
Fenestrelle
Usseaux
Perrero
Prali
Bric Bouchet
Bric Froid
Tête des Toillies
Chianale
Pontechianale
Casteldelfino
Bric de Rubren
Pic de la Font Sancte
M. Chaberton
M. Orsiera
Colle delle Finestre
Pic de Rochelaire
Tunnel du Fréjus
Roche Bernaude
Pic du Béal Traversier
Col Agnel
Gouffre de Gourfouran
119
147

Cap Ferret
la Teste
Pilat-Plage
Dune du Pilat
Pointe d'Arcachon
Facture
Mios
Salles
Cazaux
Etang de Cazaux et de Sanguinet
Sanguinet
Belin-Béliet
Lugos
Biscarrosse-Plage
Biscarrosse
CENTRE D'ESSAIS DES LANDES
Zone militaire interdite
Etang de Biscarrosse et de Parentis
Parentis-en-Born
Ychoux
Liposthey
Pissos
Gastes
Ste Eulalie-en-Bom
Pontenx-les-Forges
Forêt de Ligautenx
Mimizan-Plage
Mimizan
Aureilhan
St Paul-en-Born
Labouheyre
Commensacq
Sabres
Escource
Bias
Solférino
Contis-Plage
Mézos
St Julien-en-Born
Onesse-et-Laharie
Lit-et-Mixe
Morcenx
Lévignacq
Arjuzanx
Arengosse
St Girons-Plage
Lesperon
Villenave
Ygos-St Saturnin
Ousse-Suzan
Vielle-St Girons
LANDES DE GASCOGNE
CENTRE D'ÉTUDES NUCLÉAIRES

Podensac
Cadillac
St Morillon
St Michel-de-Rieufret
Cabanac-et-Villagrains
Barsac
Cérons
Loupiac
Illats
St Croix-du-Mont
Verdelais
Preignac
St Maixant
Landiras
Pujols-s-Ciron
Langon
St Macaire
St Pierre-d'Aurillac
Caudrot
Gironde-s-Dropt
Guillos
Budos
Sauternes
Léogeats
St Magne
Louchats
Hostens
Origne
Balizac
Noaillan
Roaillan
Roquetaillade
Mazères
Auros
Villandraut
Uzeste
St Symphorien
Bazas
Le Tuzan
Belhade
Argelouse
Préchac
Bourideys
Cazalis
Lucmau
Cudos
Sore
Lerm-et-Musset
Callen
Captieux
Escaudes
Goualade
St Michel-de-Castelnau
Giscos
Luxey
Maillas
Lartigue
Champ de Tir
Allons
Bourriot-Bergonce
Retjons
Losse
Labrit
Lencouacq
Cachen
Bélis
Garein
Brocas
Roquefort
Sarbazan
Maillères
Canenx-et-Réaut
Labastide-d'Armagnac
St Justin
St Gor
Vielle-Soubiran
Estigarde
Lapeyrade
Créon-d'Armagnac
St Julien-d'Armagnac
Pouydesseaux
Lucbardez-et-Bargues
Bostens
Geloux
Cère
RC RÉGIONAL
DES LANDES
GASCOGNE
A 62
N 113
N 134
D 932
D 626
D 651
121
136
149
150

La Réole
Monségur
Marmande
Miramont-de-Guyenne
Seyches
Tonneins
Bazas
Grignols
Bouglon
Casteljaloux
Damazan
Aiguillon
Port-Ste-Marie
Houeillès
Lavardac
Nérac
Mézin
Gabarret
Francescas
Eymet
Lauzun
St Macaire
Langon
Meilhan-s-Garonne
Castelmoron
Fourques-s-Garonne
Le Mas-d'Agenais
Clairac
Durance
Sos
Poudenas
Moncrabeau
Lubbon
Forêt de Campet
A 62
N 113
GARONNE
122
135
150
151

Castillonnès
Villeréal
Monpazier
Biron
Cancon
Monflanquin
Fumel
Puy-l'Évêque
Chau de Bonaguil
Villefranche-du-Périgord
Villeneuve-s-Lot
Ste Livrade-s-Lot
Penne-d'Agenais
Tournon-d'Agenais
Montaigu-de-Quercy
Laroque-Timbaut
Beauville
Lauzerte
Prayssas
AGEN
Puymirol
Valence
Moissac
Castelsarrasin
Auvillar
Astaffort
Laplume
Lamontjoie
Miradoux
122
123
138
151
152

Cahors
Montauban
Moissac
Caussade
Castelsarrasin
Luzech
Puy-l'Évêque
Mercuès
Catus
Cazals
Labastide-Murat
St Cirq-Lapopie
Montcuq
Lauzerte
Castelnau-Montratier
Lalbenque
Montpezat-de-Quercy
Nègrepelisse
Bruniquel
Lafrançaise
Molières
Villefranche-du-Périgord
Chau de Bonaguil
Grotte du Pech-Merle
Cabrerets
St Géry
Vers
Lamagdelaine
Montaigu-de-Quercy
Touffailles
St Nicolas-de-la-Grave
Réalville
Albias
Septfonds
Puylaroque
Montricoux
Salviac
Gourdon
Frayssinet
St Germain-du-Bel-Air
Concorès
Uzech
Crayssac
Parnac
Pradines
Laroque-des-Arcs
Arcambal
Flaujac-Poujols
Laburgade
Cremps
Concots
Vaylats
Bach
CAUSSE
Prayssac
Castelfranc
Duravel
Touzac
Soturac
Grézels
Albas
Bélaye
Floressas
Sérignac
Sauzet
Villesèque
Bagat-en-Quercy
St Pantaléon
Lascabanes
Cézac
Lhospitalet
Le Montat
Trespoux-Rassiels
Montlauzun
Vazerac
Labarthe
Durfort-Lacapelette
Miramont-de-Quercy
St Vincent
Mirabel
Piquecos
Villemade
Albefeuille-Lagarde
La Ville-Dieu-du-Temple
Lizac
Meauzac
Labastide-du-Temple
Castelmayran
Castelferrus
Léojac
Lamothe-Capdeville
St Paul-de-Loubressac
Fontanes
Montdoumerc
Belfort-du-Quercy
Lapenche
Cayriech
Monteils
Lauzès
Orniac
Sénaillac-Lauzès
Soulomès
Ussel
St Sauveur-la-Vallée
Montamel
Lamothe-Cassel
Nadillac
Cours
Valroufié
Francoulès
Maxou
St Pierre-Lafeuille
Nuzéjouls
Calamane
Espère
Boissières
St Médard
Pontcirq
Les Junies
Montcléra
Gindou
Les Arques
Frayssinet-le-Gélat
Goujounac
Pomarède
Cassagnes
Montcabrier
St Martin-le-Redon
Mauroux
Lacapelle-Cabanac

Figeac
Capdenac
Decazeville
Conques
Villefranche-de-Rouergue
Villeneuve
Montbazens
Rignac
Rieupeyroux
Najac
Laguépie
St Antonin-Noble-Val
Caylus
Limogne-en-Quercy
Cajarc
Livernon
Assier
Aubin
Cransac
Firmi
Bagnac-s-Célé
Cordes
Carmaux
Monestiés
Mirandol-Bourgnounac
Pampelonne
La Salvetat-Peyralès
Naucelle
Sauveterre-de-Rouergue
Tanus
Viaduc du Viaur
Valderiès
Andouque
Vaour
Forêt de Grésigne
Noailles
Ste Cécile du Cayrou
Villeneuve-s-Vère
Mailhoc
Loupiac
Balaguier-d'Olt
Montsalès
Sauliac-s-Célé
Marcilhac-s-Célé
Espédaillac
Quissac
Grèzes
Lunan
Felzins
Asprières
Naussac
Peyrusse-le-Roc
Galgan
Valzergues
Lanuéjouls
Anglars
Privezac
Maleville
Compolibat
Colombiès
Castanet
Lunac
Tayrac
Crespin
Jouqueviel
Bor-et-Bar
Montirat
Lescure-Jaoul
Sanvensa
Monteils
Parisot
Puylagarde
Saillac
Vidaillac
Martiel
Savignac
Promilhanes
Beauregard
Varaire
Lugagnac
Puyjourdes
Salvagnac-Cajarc
Calvignac
Cénevières
Crégols
Carayac
Frontenac
Faycelles
Béduer
Cambes
Lissac
Camburat
Fourmagnac
Reyrevignes
Issepts
Fons
Cardaillac
Linac
Viazac
St Perdoux
Ste Gemme
Almayrac
Trévien
Blaye-les-Mines
Taïx
Laparrouquial
Bournazel
Mouzieys-Panens
Vindrac-Alayrac
Marnaves
Milhars
Féneyrols
Montrosier
Roussayrolles
Tonnac
Itzac
Campagnac
Alos
Andillac
Vieux
Donnazac
Souel
Livers-Cazelles
Virac
Milhavet
Labastide-Gabausse
Combefa
St Benoît
Rosières
Lacapelle-Ségalar
Le Ségur
St Marcel
St Christophe
St Martin-Laguépie
Varen
Verfeil
Ginals
Espinas
Feneyrols
Mas-de-Guiralet
La Capelle-Balaguier
Ste Croix
Toulonjac
St Rémy
Vailhourles
Lacapelle-Livron
Loze
Espagots
St Projet
Caylus
DE LIMOGNE
GRAMAT
Gorges de l'Aveyron
Aveyron
Lot
Viaur
Ceret
Cérou
Vère
125
153
140

Decazeville
Conques
Entraygues-s-T.
Estaing
Espalion
Bozouls
Marcillac-Vallon
Rignac
Montbazens
Aubin
Cransac
RODEZ
Baraqueville
Rieupeyroux
Naucelle
Sauveterre-de-Rouergue
Cassagnes-Bégonhès
Pont-de-Salars
Salles-Curan
Carmaux
Réquista
Pampelonne
Viaduc du Viaur
Valence-d'Albigeois
Mirandol
Causse du Comtal
Forêt des Palanges
Plateau de la Viadène
Aveyron
Lot
Viaur
Tarn

Laguiole
Nasbinals
Aubrac
St Chély d'Aubrac
Marvejols
Chirac
Chanac
St Geniez-d'Olt
Campagnac
la Canourgue
Séverac-le-Château
Laissac
Vézins-de-Lévézou
Massegros
Ste Enimie
Meyrueis
le Rozier
Peyreleau
Millau
St Beauzély
St Rome-de-Tarn
Nant
St Jean-du-Bruel
Trèves
la Cavalerie
Aven Armand
Montpellier-le-Vieux
Point Sublime
CAUSSE DE SAUVETERRE
CAUSSE MÉJEAN
CAUSSE NOIR
CAUSSE DE SÉVERAC
GORGES DU TARN
Gorges de la Jonte
Gorges de la Dourbie
PLATEAU DU LÉVÉZOU
AUBRAC
Camp du Larzac

127
128
141
156
Mende
Châteauneuf-de-Randon
Florac
Meyrueis
Le Vigan
Valleraugue
St Jean-du-Gard
Lasalle
Villefort
Le Bleymard
Le Pont-de-Montvert
Génolhac
Vialas
Chanac
Ste Enimie
Ispagnac
Barre-des-Cévennes
St André-de-Valborgne
St Germain-de-Calberte
Mont Aigoual
Nant
Trèves
Sumène
St Hippolyte-du-Fort
Aven Armand
Causse Méjean
Causse de Sauveterre
Causse Noir
Parc National des Cévennes
Mont Lozère
Montagne du Goulet
Montagne du Bougès
Corniche des Cévennes
Gorges du Tarn
Gorges de la Jonte
Gorges de la Dourbie
Col de Montmirat
Col de Finiels
Col du Minier
Abîme du Bramabiau
Grotte de Dargilan
Forêt de Mercoire
Plateau du Palais du Roi
Causse de Montbel
Montagne du Lingas
Montagne de la Fage
Cirque de Pougnadoires
Cirque de St Chély
Cocurès
Bédouès
Cassagnas
St Étienne-du-Valdonnez
Lanuéjols
Balsièges
Bagnols-les-Bains
Chasseradès
Belvezet
La Bastide-Puylaurent
Concoules
Le Collet-de-Dèze
St Martin-de-Lansuscle
Pont-de-Montvert
Anduze
Corbès
L'Espérou
St Sauveur-des-Pourcils
Dourbies
St Jean-du-Bruel
Arphy
Aulas
Mandagout
St Martial
St Roman-de-Codières
Peyrolles
Saumane
L'Estréchure
Les Plantiers
La Malène
St Chély-du-Tarn
Hures-la-Parade
Le Rozier
Veyreau
Revens
Lanuéjols
Camprieu
N 106
N 88
D 986
D 907
D 901

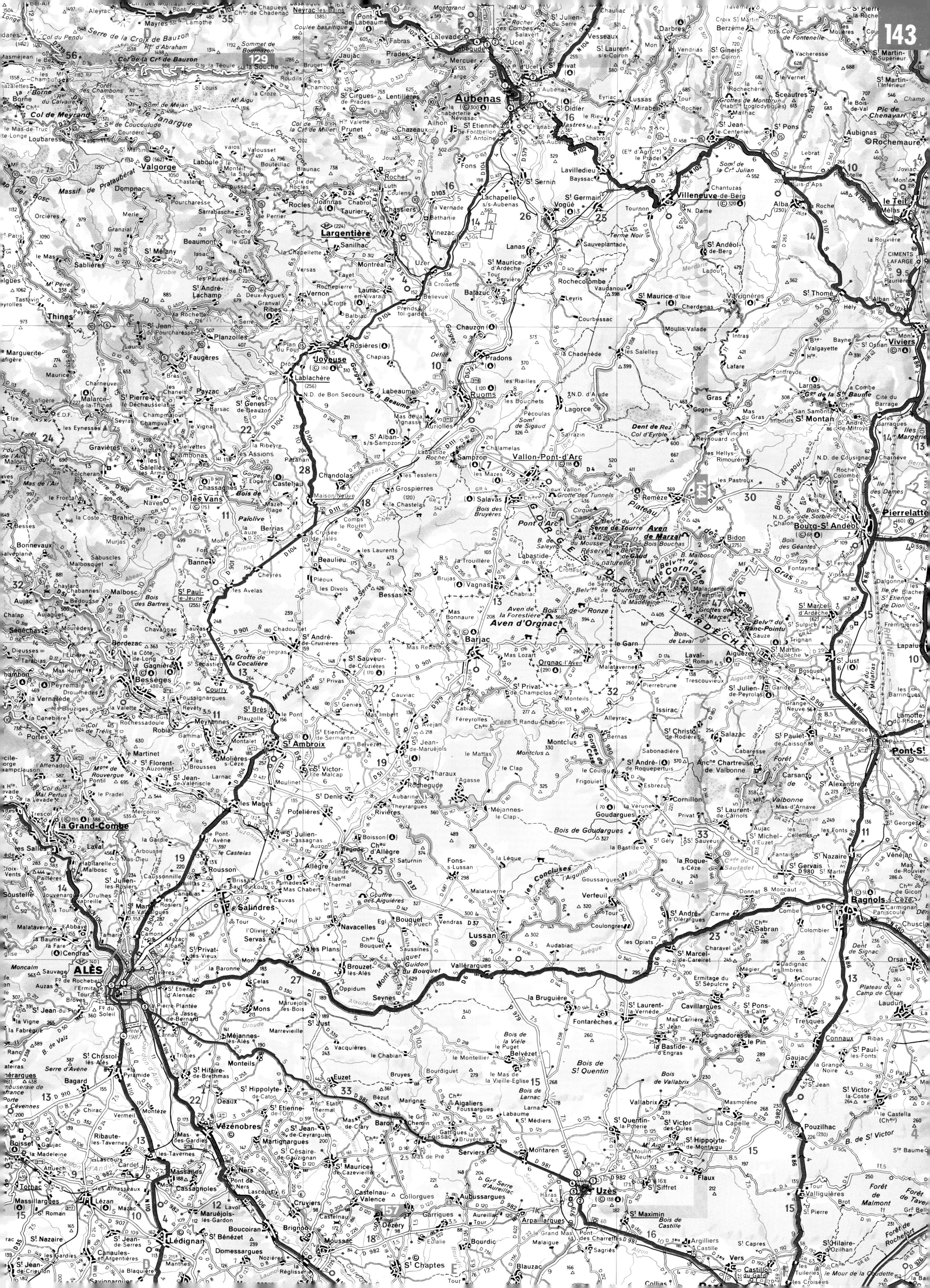

Aubenas
Largentière
Joyeuse
Vallon-Pont-d'Arc
Aven d'Orgnac
Barjac
Bourg-St Andéol
Pierrelatte
Viviers
le Teil
Villeneuve-de-Berg
Vogüé
Ruoms
les Vans
Valgorge
Thines
Bessèges
St Ambroix
la Grand-Combe
Alès
Salindres
Lussan
Uzès
Bagnols-s-Cèze
Pont-St
Vézénobres
Lédignan
Gorges de l'Ardèche
Plateau des Gras
Col de Meyrand
Massif de Prataubérat
Serre de la Croix de Bauzon
Bois de Paiolive
Bois de St Quentin
Forêt de Malmont

Montélimar
Marsanne
Dieulefit
Bourdeaux
Rochemaure
le Teil
Viviers
Donzère
Grignan
Pierrelatte
Bourg-St Andéol
St Paul-Trois-Châteaux
Valréas
Nyons
Bollène
Pont-St Esprit
Vaison-la-Romaine
Mondragon
Orange
Bagnols-s-Cèze
Malaucène
Carpentras
Châteauneuf-du-Pape
Roquemaure
Sorgues
Villeneuve-lès-Avignon
Pernes-les-Fontaines
Bédarrides
Courthézon
Mornas
Piolenc
Sérignan-du-Comtat
Camaret-s-Aigues
Gigondas
Vacqueyras
Beaumes-de-Venise
Monteux
Entraigues
Mazan
RHÔNE
AUTOROUTE DU SOLEIL
129
130
143
158
159

130
131
146
159
Luc-en-Diois
Montlaur-en-Diois
Aucelon
Pradelle
Brette
St Nazaire-le-Désert
Volvent
Jonchères
Beaumont-en-Diois
Beaurières
Val-Maravel
Charens
Poyols
Bellegarde-en-Diois
Chalancon
la Motte-Chalancon
Establet
Rottier
Bruis
Valdrôme
St Dizier-en-Diois
Cornillon-s-l'Oule
Rémuzat
Villeperdrix
Sahune
Montréal-les-Sources
Verclause
Rosans
Moydans
Ribeyret
Pelonne
Arpavon
Montjay
Sorbiers
Serres
Aspres-s-Buëch
Veynes
la Faurie
Montbrand
St Julien-en-Beauchêne
Chabestan
Aspremont
Sigottier
la Bâtie-Montsaléon
Barcillonnette
Eyguians
Lagrand
Saléon
Orpierre
Laragne-Montéglin
Upaix
le Poët
Ribiers
Mison
Châteauneuf-de-Chabre
Barret-le-Bas
Ballons
Lachau
Eygalayes
Séderon
Mévouillon
Montbrun-les-Bains
Buis-les-Baronnies
Ste Jalle
Bésignan
Vercoiran
Ste Euphémie
Montauban
Rioms
Eygaliers
Plaisians
Aulan
Brantes
Savoillan
Reilhanette
MONT VENTOUX
Sault
Aurel
Ferrassières
Montfroc
Curel
St Vincent-s-Jabron
Noyers-s-Jabron
Valbelle
Châteauneuf-Miravail
Signal de Lure
MONTAGNE DE LURE
Saumane
l'Hospitalet
Revest-du-Bion
St Christol
Banon
Montsalier
Simiane-la-Rotonde
Carniol
Revest-des-Brousses
Limans
Forcalquier
Mallefougasse
Cruis
St Etienne
Ongles
Lardiers
Sigonce
Monieux
Méthamis
Villes-s-Auzon
Flassan
Gorges de la Nesque
PLATEAU D'ALBION
VAUCLUSE
Forêt de la Plate
St Saturnin-d'Apt
Murs
Lioux

GAP
Col Bayard
Veynes
Tallard
la Roche-des-Arnauds
Chorges
B^ge de Serre-Ponçon
Savines-le-Lac
Laragne-Montéglin
Sisteron
Turriers
Seyne
la Motte
Clamensane
Ribiers
Noyers-s-Jabron
Château-Arnoux
Volonne
DIGNE
Mézel
Barrême
les Mées
Peyruis
Forcalquier
St Etienne
Signal de Lure
MONTAGNE DE LURE
Lurs
Malijai
la Javie
le Vernet
Barcillonnette
Ventavon
Monêtier-Allemont
Upaix
Sigoyer
132
133
145
162
164

Embrun
Crévoux
Les Orres
Barcelonnette
Pra-Loup
le Sauze
Super-Sauze
St Paul
Meyronnes
Larche
Col de Larche (Colle della Maddalena)
Col de Vars
Tête de Moise
Acceglio
Argentera
Pietraporzio
Sambuco
Cime de la Bonette
Restefond
PARC NATIONAL DU MERCANTOUR
Col d'Allos
Col de la Cayolle
Allos
Colmars
Beauvezer
St Etienne-de-Tinée
Auron
Isola
Valberg
Beuil
Guillaumes
Gorges de Daluis
Gorges Supres du Cians
Entraunes
St Martin-d'Entraunes
Annot
Entrevaux
Puget-Théniers
St André-les-Alpes
Thorame-Haute
Thorame-Basse
Mont Pelat
Tête de l'Estrop
Mt Ténibre
Mt Mounier
133
164
165

A
B
C
1
2
3
4
134
166
GOLFE DE GASCOGNE
Gouf de Capbreton
CÔTE BASQUE
BIARRITZ
BAYONNE
Anglet
Boucau
Tarnos
Hossegor
Capbreton
Vieux-Boucau-les-Bains
Soustons
Magescq
Seignosse
Tosse
St Vincent-de-Tyrosse
Bénesse-Maremne
Labenne
Labenne-Océan
Ondres-Plage
Ondres
St Martin-de-Seignanx
St André-de-Seignanx
Messanges
Messanges-Plage
Moliets-et-Maa
Moliets-Plage
Léon
St Michel-Escalus
Linxe
St Girons-Plage
Vielle-St Girons
Forêt de
Hourtin
Bidart
Guéthary
St JEAN-DE-LUZ
Ciboure
Hendaye
Hondarribia/Fuenterrabia
Irun
San Marcial
Urrugne
Ascain
Sare
St Pée-s-Nivelle
Ustaritz
Espelette
Cambo-les-Bains
Hasparren
Urt
Lahonce
Mouguerre
Briscous
Villefranque
Arcangues
Arbonne
Ahetze
Labastide-Clarence
Iholdy
Louhossoa
Itxassou
Ainhoa
Dancharia
Urdax
Zugarramurdi
Vera de Bidasoa
la Rhune
Col de St Ignace
Grottes d'Isturits et d'Oxocelhaya
Cabo Higuer
Corniche Basque
Forêt d'Ustaritz
Route impériale des Cimes
Domaine d'Orx
Etang Hardy
Etang Blanc
Etang Noir
Etg de Léon
A 63
N 10
N 117
D 652

134
135
150
167
Mont-de-Marsan
Dax
Tartas
Orthez
Salies-de-Béarn
Sauveterre-de-Béarn
Peyrehorade
Hagetmau
St Sever
Mugron
Amou
Montfort-en-Chalosse
Pouillon
Navarrenx
Mourenx
Monein
Lacq
Artix
St Palais
Castets
Lesperon
Rion-des-Landes
Ygos-St Saturnin
Ousse-Suzan
Villenave
Beylongue
Boos
Taller
Laluque
Pontonx-s-l'Adour
Bégaar
Meilhan
Campagne
Souprosse
Cauna
Toulouzette
St Vincent-de-Paul
Buglose
Herm
Gourbera
Saint-Paul
Narrosse
Candresse
Yzosse
Hinx
Poyartin
Pomarez
Brassempouy
Castelnau-Chalosse
Donzacq
Bastennes
Gaujacq
Clermont
Cagnotte
Habas
Labatut
Puyoô
Bellocq
Baigts-de-Béarn
Carresse
Sorde-l'Abbaye
Abbaye d'Arthous
Léren
Autevielle
Arthez-de-Béarn
Lagor
Laàs
Biron
Sault-de-Navailles
Lacadée
Sallespisse
Castétis
Argagnon
Uchacq-et-Parentis
Campet-et-Lamolère
St Pierre-du-Mont
St Perdon
Haut-Mauco
Benquet
Aurice
Coudures
Audignon
Dumes
Horsarrieu
Momuy
Nassiet
Castel-Sarrazin
Arsague
Tilh
Estibeaux
Mouscardès
Ossages
St Girons
Bonnegarde
Beyries
Argelos
Poudenx
Monségur
St Médard
Hagetaubin
Morlanne
Castillon
Doazon
Bougarber
Denguin
Aussevielle
Poey-de-Lescar
Artiguelouve
Lahourcade
Pardies
Noguères
Besingrand
Abidos
Labastide-Cézéracq
Labastide-Monréjeau
Serres-Ste Marie
Cescau
Viellenave
Gurs
Dognen
Lay
Sus
Castetnau
Rivehaute
Gestas
Araux
Audaux
Bastanès
Méritein
Ossenx
Narp
Castetbon
Espiute
Montfort
Andrein
Barraute
Orriule
Burgaronne
Orion
Athos
Abitain
Oraàs
Escos
Labastide-Villefranche
Castagnède
Auterrive
St Dos
Arancou
Bergouey
Viellenave-s-Bidouze
Arraute
Masparraute
Labets-Biscay
Gabat
Arbouet
Osserain
Amendeuix
Luxe
Béguios
Camou-Mixe
Aïcirits
Béhasque
Domezain
Etcharry
Aroue
Nabas
Charre
Lichos
Charritte-de-Bas
Angous
Arrast
Ithorots
Lohitzun
Oyhercq
Uhart-Mixe
Larribar
Orsanco
Beyrie-s-Joyeuse
Aïncy
Sauveterre
Misson
Gaas
Tercis-les-Bains
Heugas
Siest
Seyresse
Oeyreluy
St Pandelon
Saugnac-et-Cambran
Mimbaste
Bénesse-lès-Dax
Moulin de Benesse
St Lon-les-Mines
Bélus
Tarsacq
Siros
Mont-de-Marsan
Lande d'Agès
Mont du Gts Fory

135
136
149
168
Mont-de-Marsan
Villeneuve-de-Marsan
Grenade-s-l'Adour
Aire-s-l'Adour
Barcelonne-du-Gers
Eugénie-les-Bains
Geaune
Garlin
Arzacq-Arraziguet
Thèze
Morlaàs
Lescar
Billère
PAU
Labastide-d'Armagnac
Gabarret
Barbotan-les-Thermes
Cazaubon
Eauze
Manciet
Nogaro
Riscle
Aignan
Plaisance
Castelnau-Rivière-Basse
Maubourguet
Vic-en-Bigorre
Rabastens-de-Bigorre
Lembeye
Montaner
Marciac
Cazères-s-l'Adour
Le Houga
Monguilhem
Hontanx
Perquie
Saint-Justin
Créon-d'Armagnac
Pouydesseaux
Bostens
Gaillères
Labarrère
Castelnau-d'Auzan
Bretagne-d'Armagnac
Samadet
Aubagnan
Pécorade
Serres-Castet
Navailles-Angos
Sauvagnon
Lacajunte
Lasserade
Viella
Tarsac
Termes-d'Armagnac
Sabazan
Castelnavet
Salles-d'Armagnac
Bourrouillan
Panjas
Laujuzan
Mormès
Magnan
Urgosse
Lanne-Soubiran
Luppé-Violles
Vergoignan
Cravencères
Averon-Bergelle
Séailles
Margouët-Meymes
Bois d'Aignan
Forêt de l'Aveyron
Autodrome
Lannemaignan
Mauléon-d'Armagnac
Estang
Lias-d'Armagnac
Réans
Campagne-d'Armagnac
Maupas
Monlezun-d'Armagnac
Toujouse
Bascous
Lussagnet
Bourdalat
Saint-Gein
Castandet
Maurrin
Bascons
Artassenx
Laglorieuse
Mazerolles
Bougue
Saint-Médard
Bretagne-de-Marsan
Larrivière
Bordères-et-Lamensans
Montgaillard
Renung
Duhort-Bachen
Classun
Buanes
Sarraziet
Fargues
Vielle-Tursan
Saint-Loubouer
Bahus-Soubiran
Castelnau-Tursan
Payros-Cazautets
Clèdes
Arboucave
Puyol-Cazalet
Miramont-Sensacq
Pimbo
Philondenx
Cabidos
Bouillon
Mialos
Garlède-Mondebat
Auga
Viven
Doumy
Argelos
Astis
Uzein
Montardon
Buros
Maucor
Serres-Morlaàs
Sedzère
Lespourcy
Espéchède
Saint-Jammes
Gabaston
Higuères-Souye
Saint-Laurent-Bretagne
Baleix
Bentayou-Sérée
Lamayou
Maure
Sanous
Camalès
Bazillac
Escondeaux
Ugnouas
Lacassagne
Lescurry
Villenave-près-Marsac
Sarniguet
Tostat
Andrest
Pujo
Saint-Lézer
Talazac
Siarrouy
Tarasteix
Soréac
Bouilh-Péreuilh
Castéra-Lou
Sombrun
Auriébat
Estirac
Caussade-Rivière
Labatut-Rivière
Soublecause
Hères
Tieste-Uragnoux
Ladevèze-Ville
Ladevèze-Rivière
Saint-Aunix-Lengros
Jû-Belloc
Préchac-sur-Adour
Galiax
Goux
Cannet
Maumusson-Laguian
Aurensan
Labarthète
Saint-Mont
Corneillan
Bernède
Gée-Rivière
Saint-Germé
Sarragachies
Caumont
Izotges
Cahuzac-s-Adour
Tasque
Pouydraguin
Loussous-Débat
Couloumé-Mondebat
Beaumarchés
Cayron
Courties
Juillac
Tourdun
Armentieux
Sauveterre
Monfaucon
Lafitole
Buzon
Barbachen
Beccas
Haget
Ségalas
Artagnan
Caixon
Nouilhan
Larreule
Labatut
Castéra-Loubix
Luc-Armau
Monségur
Lahitte-Toupière
Villefranque
Corbère-Abères
Bassillon-Vauzé
Lespielle
Moncaup
Lasserre
Crouseilles
Madiran
Arrosès
Aydie
Aubous
Portet
Diusse
Mont-Disse
Conchez-de-Béarn
Cadillon
Aurions-Idernes
Séméacq-Blachon
Castillon
Escurès
Simacourbe
Samsons-Lion
Peyrelongue-Abos
Lucarré
Anoye
Momy
Gerderest
Abère
Maspie
Lalongue
Gayon
Vialer
Arricau-Bordes
Mouhous
Lannecaube
Carrère
Miossens-Lanusse
Auriac
Coslédaà
Sévignacq-Thèze
Lasclaveries
Escoubès
Barinque
Riupeyrous
Bernadets
Saint-Castin
Saint-Armou
Anos
Taron-Sadirac-Viellenave
Burosse-Mendousse
Ribarrouy
Saint-Jean-Poudge
Mascaraàs-Haron
Tadousse-Ussau
Baliracq-Maumusson
Castetpugon
Boueilh-Boueilho-Lasque
Claracq
Lalonquette
Moncla
Proyan
Verlus
Sarron
Saint-Agnet
Ségos
Latrille
Lannux
Poey-de-Lescar
Caubios-Loos
Momas
Aubin
Bournos
Larreule
Fichous-Riumayou
Séby
Mazerolles
Lème
Méracq
Vignes
Coublucq
Pouliacq
Mont-Disse
Lasque
Poursiugues-Boucoue
Lauret
Sensacq
Vielleville
Beyrie
Lac d'Uzein
Lande du Pont-Long
Camp militaire
Andoins
Ouillon
Sendets
Idron
Gelos
Lons
Laroin
Lescurry
Arrien
Saubole
Ponson-Dessus
Ponson-Debat-Pouts
Eslourenties-Daban
Lourenties
Lagarde
Gayan
Oroix
Hérrnou
Lombia
Urost
Sedze-Maubecq
Bédeille
Escaunets
Pontiacq-Viellepinte
Lamayou
Villenave-près-Béarn
Menvielle
Aurensan
Chis
Louit
Sarriac-Bigorre
Mingot
Saint-Sever-de-Rustan
Sénac
Mansan
Betplan
Peyrusse-Grande
Ricourt
Saint-Justin
Semboues
Cazaux-Villecomtal
Malabat
Durans
Castelnau-d'Anglès
Tourdun
Fromentas
Bières-Armagnac
Saint-Pierre
Bédat
Blanin
Lapeyrie
Gellenave
Mimort
Fustérouau
Bouzon-Gellenave
Bétous
Sorbets
Sion
Loubédat
Labarthe
Lamothe
Burosse
Espas
Rageperdix
Bascous
Lesquirle
Crespalet
Sauboires
Penabert
Saint-Amand
Pontet
Martet
Blancaste
Ayzieu
Artigau
Saint-Aubin
Le Pin
Bourrouillan
Caupenne-d'Armagnac
Cantiran
Claux
Clarac-au-Loc
Labeyrie
Gaudy
Arblade-le-Haut
Cremens
Espagnet
Daunian
Toujun
Perchède
Doat
Magnan
Saint-Roch
Haget
Borcary
Sauvagnère
Les Pigails
Soubère
Berduquet
Marguestau
Prat
Cutxan
Pouchalan
Tourne
Laree
Sainte-Fauste
Barbey
Monclar
Cucasse
Brechan
Saint-Vidou
Arthez-d'Armagnac
Tachouzin
Montégut
Castex-d'Armagnac
Castagnet
Saint-Cane
La Forêt
Maupas
Gaube
Peyrelongue
Coudicons
Lacoste
Branlat
Cantau
Loubens
Bazibat
Marquestau
Coumat
Lagrange
Les 4 Chemins
Laberège
Bascaulés
Saint-Aubin
Constance
La Hitère
Toupiès
Subehargues
Pentagnan
Laouille
Bellevue
Cap de la Coste
Bachen
La Haille
Tinarage
Arblade-le-Bas
Lelin-Lapujolle
Castagnet
Saint-Griède
Saint-Martin-d'Armagnac
Mauriet
Loissan
Mauléon
Maulichères
Lapujolle
Le Faubourg
Lacaussade
Les Barthères
Hitaous
Lannemaignan
Sauboua
Daunian
Lau
Saint-Simon
Loustanau
Torrebren
Cazalet
Gajo
Gélise
N.D. de Pibèque
Arech
Labarrère
Castelnau-d'Auzan
Fitron
Beziey
Aguzan
Riouperyrous
Houeillère
Pomiro
Lamothe
Zou-Fou-Dau
Doat
Maignan
Cabeil
Esplavis
Millet
Esbérous
Garderon
Larroudé
Escagnan
Duret
Sarran
Lacaze
Durand
Bouau
Laballe
Sentex
Parleboscq
Bellevue
Tavernes
Bégué
Le Marais
Rouge
Chicot
Cau-de-la-Hargue
Lagrange
Briat
Mauvezin-d'Armagnac
N.D. des Cyclistes
Betbezer-d'Armagnac
Labrise
Fondat
Pagny
Parissot
Douzevieille
Saint-Julien-d'Armagnac
Créon-d'Armagnac
Bernet
Noel
Lacquy
Le Frêche
Silo
Pillardit
Mon
Beillons
Réaut
Bargues
Lapeyre
Lucbardez-et-Bargues
Bigne
Saint-Avit
Menjoulica
Le Caloy
Sainte-Foy
La Bataille
Maureillan
Saint-Cricq-Villeneuve
Les Ponchons
Beaussiet
Churgues
Nauton
Pujo-le-Plan
Carnette
Le Plan
Lubatas
Arricau
Menon
Bostens
Les Barrères
Les Barbouats
Lartigue
Jouandots
Pourica
Perron
Les Arbouts
Rondebœuf
Bruhet
Lahemme
Jeanpierre
Pédeford
Ricaud
Ferran
Lamensans
Merillon
Le Vignau
Lartigue
Saint-Maurice-s-Adour
Camelot
Prous
Robert
Les Arrioux
Lanas
Larque
Lau
Saint-Jean
Les Arrats
Pourcate
Boucou
Bombarde
Borrits
Marianne
Le Soui
Berdatborde
Laborde
Ninon
Les Castagnons
Pémau
Lourine
Guillon
Mondine
Pourin
Beros
Pitocq
Matilas
Sorbets
Tour
Blancotte
Maurles
Bourdos
Les Monges
Lamouille
Bats
Urgons
Samadet
Portets
Montsoué
Bahus
Saint-Jean
Benteyou
Pechevin
Calaussanne
Montagut
Chalabart
Piets-Plasence-Moustrou
Garos
Louvigny
Beyrie
Larreule
Loncon
Mazerolles
Momas
Viellenave-d'Arthez
Poey-de-Lescar
Eslayou
Lescar
Pont-Long
Le Rameau de Pau
Pau
Camp militaire
Sendets
A
B
C

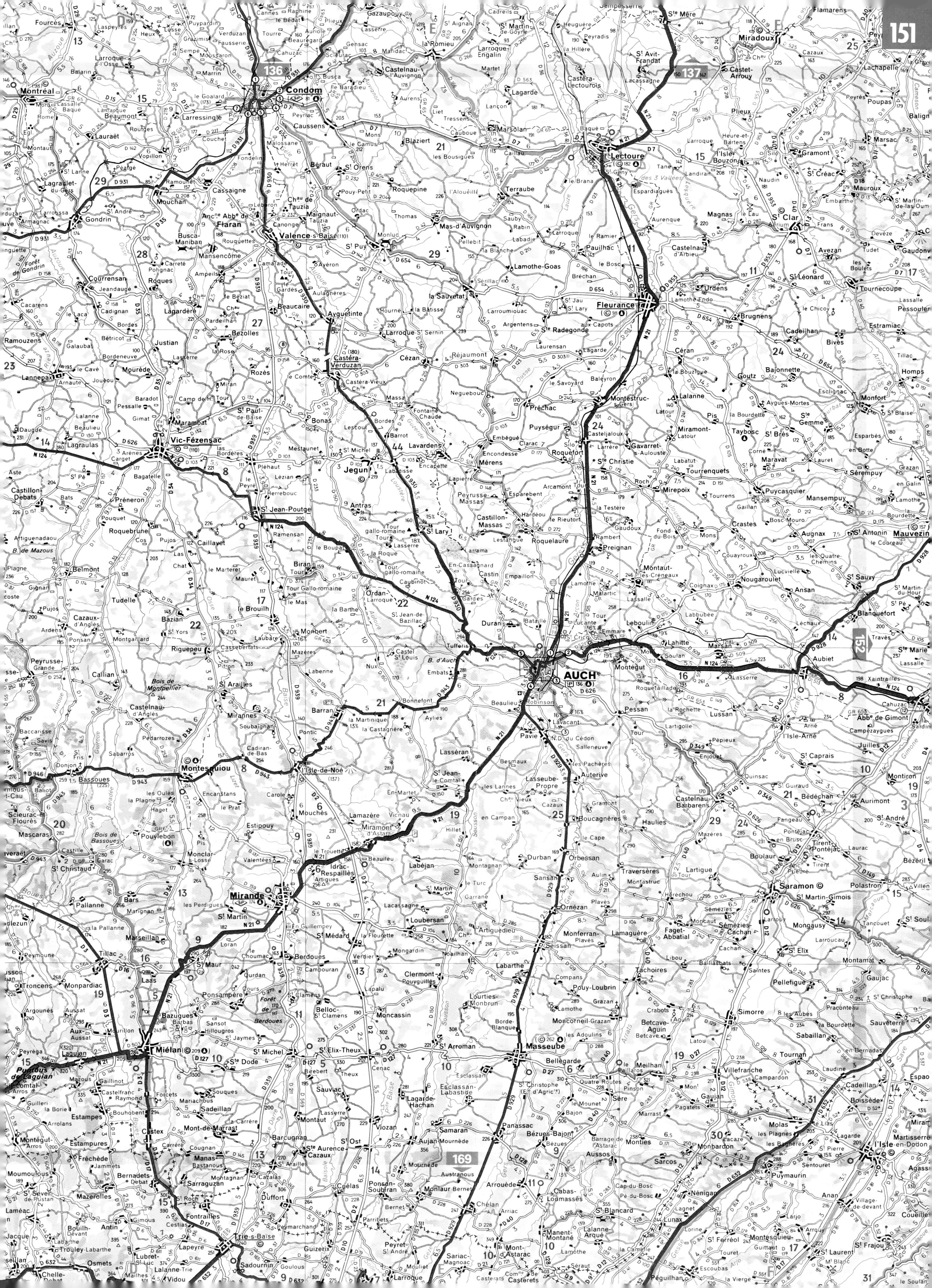

Condom
Montréal
Lectoure
Fleurance
Valence-s-Baïse
Vic-Fézensac
AUCH
Mirande
Miélan
Masseube
Saramon
Montesquiou
Castéra-Verduzan
Jegun
Gondrin
Mauvezin
Miradoux
St Clar
L'Isle-en-Dodon
Trie-s-Baïse
Bassoues
L'Isle-de-Noé
Montestruc-s-Gers
Gimont
Simorre
N 21
N 124
136
137
152
169

TOULOUSE
Montauban
Montech
Beaumont-de-Lomagne
Grisolles
Grenade
Fronton
Verdun-s-Garonne
Cadours
Cologne
Mauvezin
Gimont
L'Isle-Jourdain
Léguevin
Colomiers
Blagnac
Tournefeuille
Plaisance-du-T.
Cugnaux
St Lys
Samatan
Lombez
Rieumes
Muret
Portet
Castanet-Tolosan
Auterive
L'Isle-en-Dodon
Lavit
Castelsarrasin
Villebrumier
Bouloc
Castelginest
Pibrac
Saverdun
Forêt de Bouconne
Forêt d'Agre
Garonne
Berat
Carbonne
St Sulpice
Noé
Capens
Marquefave

ALBI
Gaillac
Lisle-s-Tarn
Rabastens
Lavaur
Graulhet
Castelnau-de-Montmiral
Cadalen
Montastruc
St Sulpice
Verfeil
Puylaurens
Lautrec
Vielmur-s-Agout
Revel
Dourgne
Caraman
Lanta
Cuq-Toulza
Villefranche-de-Lauragais
Nailloux
Montgiscard
Castelnaudary
Saissac
St Paul-Cap-de-Joux
Briatexte
Salvagnac
Monclar-de-Quercy
Puycelci
Sorèze
St Félix-Lauragais
Avignonet-Lauragais
Labastide-d'Anjou
Soual
Réalmont

ALBI
Castres
Mazamet
Réalmont
Lautrec
Valderiès
Villefranche-d'Albigeois
Alban
Ambialet
St Juéry
St Sernin-s-Rance
Montredon-Labessonnié
Roquecourbe
Vabre
Brassac
Labruguière
Aussillon
Dourgne
Sorèze
St Amans-Soult
Labastide-Rouairoux
Anglès
Lacrouzette
Saissac
Mas-Cabardès
Cuxac-Cabardès
Caunes-Minervois
Vielmur-s-Agout
PARC RÉGIONAL DU HAUT LANGUEDOC
MONTAGNE NOIRE
MONTS DE LACAUNE
Pic de Nore
Forêt de Montaud
Pic de Montaud
139
140
153
172

St Affrique
Roquefort-s-Soulzon
Camarès
Cornus
le Caylar
Lodève
Lunas
le Bousquet-d'Orb
Bédarieux
Lamalou-les-Bains
St Gervais-s-Mare
Olargues
St Pons-de-Thomières
Roquebrun
St Chinian
Murviel-lès-Béziers
Capestang
Puisserguier
Béziers
Servian
Roujan
Montpaon
Belmont-s-Rance
Murat-s-Vèbre
HAUT LANGUEDOC
MONTS DE L'ESPINOUSE
CAUSSE DU LARZAC
Plateau de Guilhaumard
la Couvertoirade
Avène
Cabrières
Puissalicon
la Cavalerie
Pas de l'Escalette
Cirque de Mourèze
Minerve
141
173
156

le Vigan
Sumène
Ganges
St Hippolyte-du-Fort
Sauve
Quissac
Alzon
Cirque de Navacelles
St Maurice-Navacelles
Grotte des Demoiselles
St Bauzille-de-Putois
St Martin-de-Londres
Claret
Pic St Loup
St Mathieu-de-Tréviers
Les Matelles
St Guilhem-le-Désert
Aniane
Gignac
Clermont-l'Hérault
Lodève
Montpeyroux
St Gély-du-Fesc
Castries
MONTPELLIER
Lattes
Pérols
Palavas-les-Flots
Maguelone
Frontignan
Sète
Balaruc-les-Bains
Bouzigues
Mèze
Montagnac
Pézenas
Florensac
Marseillan
Agde
Montbazin
Gigean
Fabrègues
Pignan
Cournonterral
Bassin de Thau
Golfe

NÎMES
ARLES
Beaucaire
Tarascon
Aigues-Mortes
la Grande-Motte
le Grau-du-Roi
Port-Camargue
Stes Maries-de-la-Mer
St Gilles
Lunel
Sommières
Vauvert
Marguerittes
Pont du Gard
Remoulins
Fontvieille
Bellegarde
Gallargues
Aimargues
Générac
Caissargues
Bouillargues
Rodilhan
Redessan
Manduel
Etang de Vaccarès
RÉSERVE NATURELLE
ZOOLOGIQUE ET BOTANIQUE
PARC
RÉGIONAL
DE
CAMARGUE
PLAINE
DE
LA
Petite Camargue
Golfe de Beauduc
Pointe du Sablon
Phare de Beauduc
Pointe de l'Espiguette
Phare de l'Espiguette
d'Aigues-Mortes
Camp des Garrigues
DU
LION
D
E
F

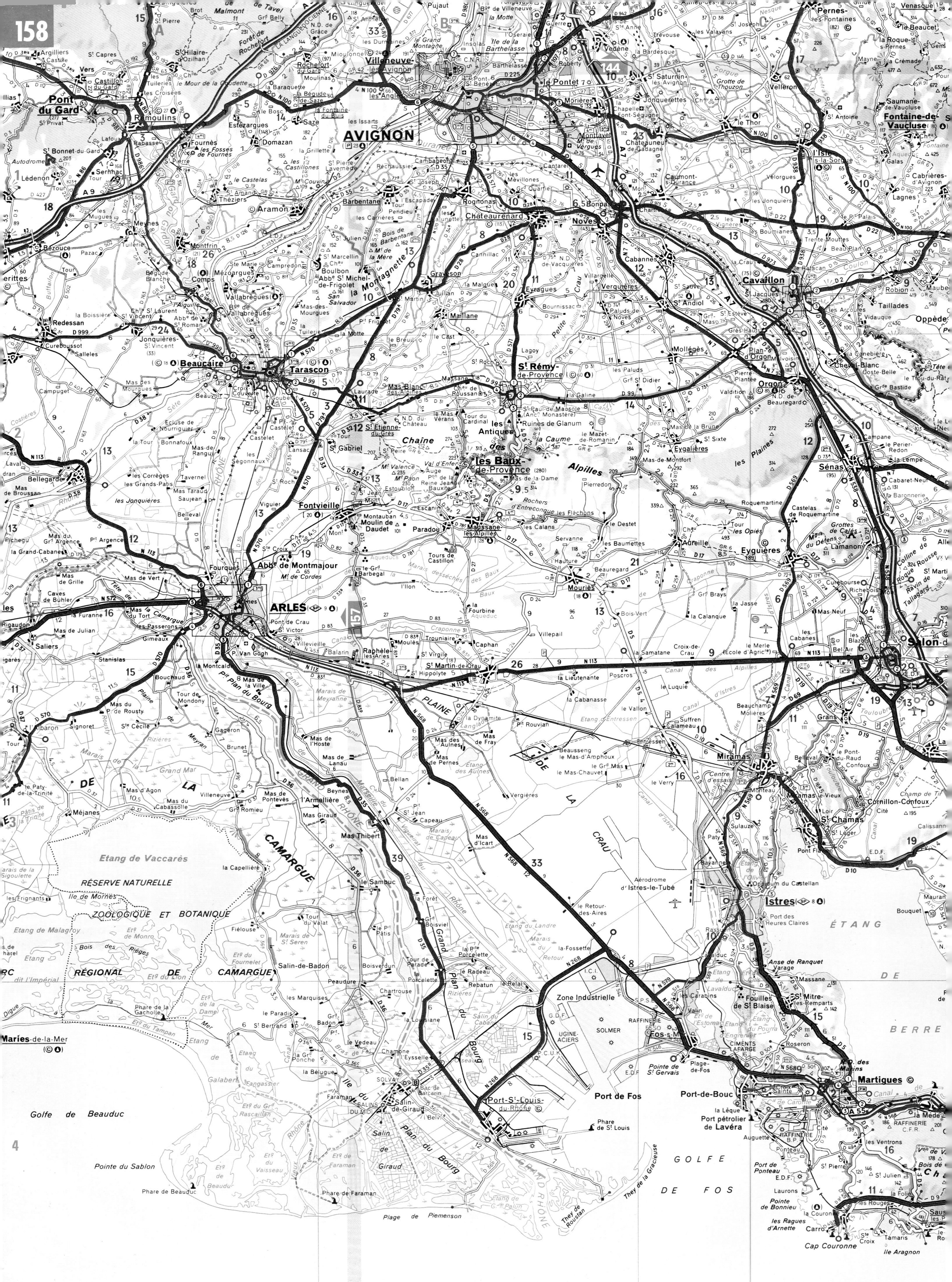
AVIGNON
Villeneuve-lès-Avignon
Pont du Gard
Remoulins
Beaucaire
Tarascon
Barbentane
Rognonas
Châteaurenard
Noves
Cavaillon
L'Isle-s-la-Sorgue
Fontaine-de-Vaucluse
St Rémy-de-Provence
Les Baux-de-Provence
Alpilles
Maussane-les-Alpilles
Fontvieille
Orgon
Sénas
Eyguières
Eygalières
Salon-de-Provence
ARLES
St Martin-de-Crau
Miramas
St Chamas
Istres
Fos-s-Mer
Port de Fos
Port-St-Louis-du-Rhône
Port-de-Bouc
Martigues
CAMARGUE
Etang de Vaccarès
RÉSERVE NATURELLE
ZOOLOGIQUE ET BOTANIQUE
RÉGIONAL DE CAMARGUE
Maries-de-la-Mer
Salin-de-Giraud
Golfe de Beauduc
GOLFE DE FOS
ÉTANG DE BERRE
PLAINE DE LA CRAU
Bellegarde
Fourques
Montmajour
Mouriès
Lamanon
Grans
Cap Couronne
A
B
C

Forcalquier
Reillanne
Manosque
Apt
St Saturnin-d'Apt
Rustrel
Gordes
Roussillon
Goult
Ménerbes
Bonnieux
Lacoste
Viens
Céreste
Vitrolles
Gréoux
Vinon-s-Verdon
Ginasservis
Rians
Cucuron
Lourmarin
Cadenet
Lauris
Puget
Mérindol
Mallemort
Charleval
Silvacane
la Roque-d'Anthéron
Pertuis
la Tour-d'Aigues
Grambois
Beaumont-de-Pertuis
Mirabeau
Jouques
Peyrolles-en-Provence
Meyrargues
Rognes
Lambesc
St Cannat
Pélissanne
Venelles
Vauvenargues
AIX-EN-PROVENCE
Éguilles
Ventabren
Velaux
Rognac
Berre-l'Etang
Vitrolles
Marignane
Gardanne
Simiane-Collongue
Cabriès
Bouc-Bel-Air
Trets
Peynier
Rousset
Belcodène
Gréasque
Mimet
St Savournin
Cadolive
Roquevaire
Allauch
Plan-de-Cuques
Septèmes-les-Vallons
l'Estaque
Carry-le-Rouet
MARSEILLE
Aubagne
Gémenos
St Zacharie
Nans-les-Pins
St Maximin-la-Ste Baume
Auriol
la Ste Baume
Plan-d'Aups
Montagne Ste Victoire
MONTAGNE DU LUBÉRON
PARC RÉGIONAL DU LUBÉRON
Grand Lubéron
Chaîne de la Trévaresse
Chaîne de Vitrolles
Étang de Berre
Rade de Marseille
Ile Ratonneau
MASSIF DE LA SAINTE BAUME
Durance
N 100
N 7
N 96
N 8
A 7
A 8
A 51
A 52
N 568
N 368
145
160
162

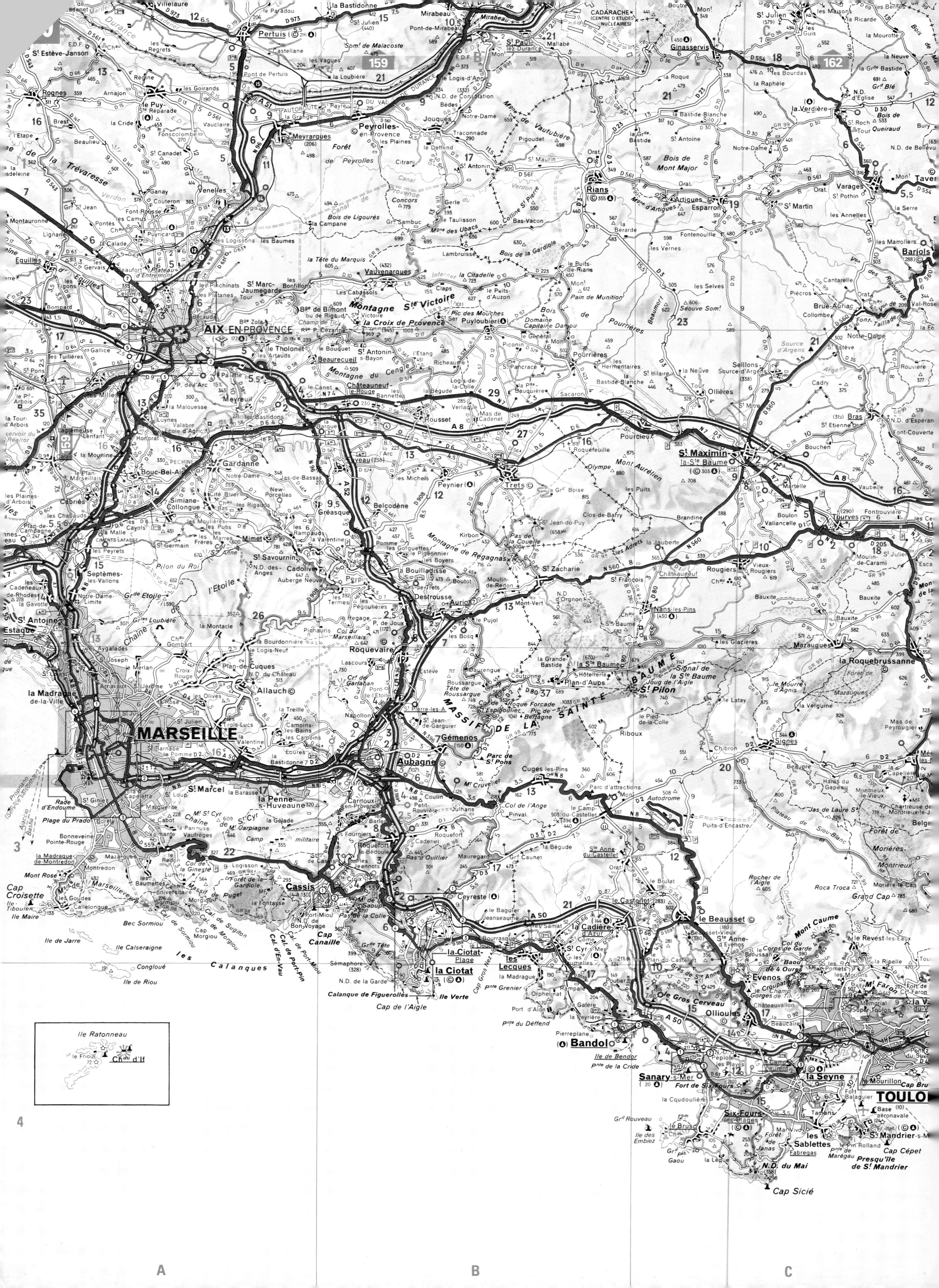

159
162
Pertuis
Mirabeau
Cadarache
St Paul-lez-Durance
Ginasservis
St Julien
Rognes
le Puy-Ste Réparade
Peyrolles-en-Provence
Meyrargues
Jouques
Rians
Varages
Tavernes
Venelles
Vauvenargues
Montagne Ste Victoire
Barjols
Esparron
St Martin
AIX-EN-PROVENCE
Puyloubier
Pourrières
Beaurecueil
Châteauneuf-le-Rouge
Rousset
Pourcieux
St Maximin-la-Ste Baume
Gardanne
Bouc-Bel-Air
Cabriès
Simiane-Collongue
Trets
Peynier
Mont Aurélien
Tourves
Gréasque
Mimet
Belcodène
Montagne de Regagnas
St Zacharie
Rougiers
Septèmes-les-Vallons
Cadolive
la Bouilladisse
Auriol
Nans-les-Pins
l'Estaque
Roquevaire
la Ste Baume
Mazaugues
la Roquebrussanne
Allauch
Plan-de-Cuques
Plan-d'Aups
St Pilon
MASSIF DE LA SAINTE BAUME
MARSEILLE
Gémenos
Aubagne
Signes
la Penne-s-Huveaune
St Marcel
Cuges-les-Pins
Parc de St Pons
Carnoux-en-Provence
Roquefort-la-Bédoule
Cassis
Ceyreste
le Castellet
le Beausset
Evenos
la Cadière-d'Azur
la Ciotat
St Cyr-s-Mer
les Lecques
Cap Canaille
Ollioules
Bandol
Sanary-s-Mer
Six-Fours-les-Plages
la Seyne
TOULO
les Sablettes
St Mandrier-s-Mer
Cap Sicié
Cap Croisette
Ile Maire
Ile de Jarre
Ile Calseraigne
Ile de Riou
les Calanques
Ile Ratonneau
Chau d'If
Ile des Embiez
A
B
C
3
4

CAMP MILITAIRE DE CANJUERS
Draguignan
Fayence
Aups
Salernes
Cotignac
Lorgues
Brignoles
Le Luc
Vidauban
Les Arcs
Le Muy
St Maxime
St Tropez
Cogolin
Grimaud
La Garde-Freinet
Collobrières
Bormes-les-Mimosas
le Lavandou
Hyères
Carqueiranne
Giens
Presqu'île de Giens
Cavalaire-s-Mer
La Croix-Valmer
Ramatuelle
Gassin
Cuers
Pierrefeu-du-Var
MASSIF DES MAURES
RADE D'HYÈRES
ILES D'HYÈRES
Ile de Porquerolles
Ile de Port-Cros
Ile du Levant
Golfe de Giens
Corniche des Maures
Cap Bénat
Cap Lardier
Cap Camarat

Manosque
Oraison
Valensole
Riez
Moustiers Ste Marie
Barrême
Senez
Gréoux-les-Bains
Vinon-s-Verdon
Quinson
Montmeyan
Aups
Tavernes
Barjols
Rians
Salernes
Cotignac
Tourtour
Villecroze
Lorgues
Carcès
St Maximin-la-Ste Baume
Brignoles
Le Luc
Besse-s-Issole
Flassans-s-Issole
Tourves
La Roquebrussanne
Signes
Méounes-les-Montrieux
Rocbaron
Puget-Ville
Carnoules
Pignans
Gonfaron
Forcalqueiret
Garéoult
Néoules
Mazaugues
Nans-les-Pins
Pourrières
Ollières
Seillons-Source-d'Argens
Bras
Châteauvert
Correns
Montfort-s-Argens
Entrecasteaux
Abbe du Thoronet
Le Thoronet
Cabasse
Vins-s-Caramy
Le Val
Ginasservis
St Julien
La Verdière
Varages
Fox-Amphoux
Sillans-la-Cascade
Régusse
Moissac-Bellevue
Baudinard
Bauduen
Artignosc-s-Verdon
St Laurent-du-Verdon
Montagnac
Allemagne-en-Provence
St Martin-de-Brômes
Esparron-de-Verdon
Les Salles-s-Verdon
Ste Croix-de-Verdon
Aiguines
Lac de Ste Croix
GRAND CANYON DU VERDON
Corniche Sublime
Falaise des Cavaliers
Grand Plan de Canjuers
Gorges du Verdon
Plateau de Valensole
Bois du Bessillon
Montagne de la Loube
Sainte Baume
St Pilon
Mont Aurélien
Cadarache
Puimoisson
St Jurs
Estoublon
Mane
Volx
Pierrevert
Ste Tulle
Mont Major
Artigues
Esparron
Brue-Auriac
Châteauneuf
Rougiers
Pourcieux
St Zacharie
Plan-d'Aups
Forêt de Pignans
A 8
N 7
A 51
146
159
160
161

147
165
161
Castellane
Clue de Vergons
Col de Toutes Aures
Vergons
Angles
Bge de Castillon
Demandolx
St Auban
Clue de St Auban
Briançonnet
Sallagriffon
Aiglun
Clue d'Aiglun
Roquesteron
Montagne de Charamel
Montagne du Cheiron
Gréolières
Coursegoules
Thorenc
Col de Bleine
Valderoure
Séranon
Andon
Caille
Col de Vence
Vence
Gourdon
Tourrettes-s-Loup
Pont-du-Loup
Le Bar-s-Loup
St Vallier de Thiey
Pas de la Faye
Col du Pilon
GRASSE
Cabris
Grottes de St Cézaire
St Cézaire-s-Siagne
Spéracèdes
Peymeinade
Le Tignet
Châteauneuf-Grasse
Valbonne
Mougins
Mouans-Sartoux
Pégomas
Auribeau
Mandelieu
Vallauris
Golfe-Juan
Le Cannet
CANNES
La Bocca
La Napoule-Plage
Golfe de Napoule
Théoule-s-Mer
Miramar
Le Trayas
Ile Ste Marguerite
Ile St Honorat
Iles de Lérins
Pte de la Croisette
Golfe Juan
Plateau du Milieu
Monastère
Pic de l'Ours
Mt Vinaigre
Massif de l'Esterel
Pic du Cap Roux
Anthéor
Agay
Cap du Dramont
Corniche de l'Esterel
St Raphaël
Boulouris
Valescure
Fréjus
Fréjus-Plage
Golfe de Fréjus
St Aygulf
les Issambres
San-Peïre-s-Mer
Val d'Esquières
Ste Maxime
Cap des Sardinaux
La Nartelle
St Tropez
Golfe de St Tropez
Port Grimaud
Grimaud
Cogolin
La Garde-Freinet
Plan-de-la-Tour
Col de Vignon
Col du Grattaloup
MAURES
Vidauban
Le Muy
Les Arcs
Trans-en-Provence
Draguignan
Roquebrune-s-Argens
Puget
Bagnols-en-Forêt
St Paul-en-Forêt
Fayence
Seillans
Tourrettes
Callian
Montauroux
Bargemon
Callas
Claviers
Figanières
Montferrat
Comps-s-Artuby
Bargème
La Bastide
La Roque-Esclapon
Mons
Escragnolles
Col du Bel-Homme
MILITAIRE DE CANJUERS
Col de Luens
Col des Portes
Peyroules
Route Napoléon
Lac de St Cassien
Massif du Tanneron
Tanneron
Col de la Glacière
Montagne de Malay
Brenon
Châteauvieux
Le Bourguet
Col de Valferrière
Montagne de Thiey
Caussols
Observatoire du CERGA
Cipières
Bois de Malay
Bois du Rouet
Forêt St Paul

147
146
162
163
la Javie
Beaujeu
Prads
Blégiers
Colmars
Villars-Colmars
Beauvezer
Thorame-Haute
Thorame-Basse
Allos
St André-les-Alpes
Annot
Entraunes
St Martin-d'Entraunes
Villeneuve-d'Entraunes
Châteauneuf-d'Entraunes
Guillaumes
Valberg
Beuil
Daluis
Puget-Théniers
Entrevaux
Barrême
Senez
Castellane
Bgs de Castillon
St Julien-du-Verdon
Vergons
Demandolx
St Auban
Briançonnet
Thorenc
Gréolières
Andon
Séranon
Valderoure
Peyroules
Comps-s-Artuby
Bargème
Trigance
Rougon
Point Sublime
Mons
St Vallier de Thiey
GRASSE
Cabris
St Cézaire
Fayence
Seillans
Bargemon
Callas
Montferrat
Ampus
Châteaudouble
Draguignan
Figanières
Callian
Montauroux
Tourrettes
Mouans-Sartoux
Pégomas
Mandelieu
Auribeau
Bagnols-en-Forêt
St Paul-en-Forêt
Tourtour
CAMP MILITAIRE DE CANJUERS
PARC NATIONAL
Clue de Taulanne
Col des Leques
Pas de la Faye
Clue du Riolan
Clue d'Aiglun
Montagne de Charamel
Montagne de Thorenc
Montagne de Gourdan
Col de Toutes Aures
Clue de Vergons
Gorges de Daluis
Balcons de la Mescla
Falaise des Cavaliers
Bois du Défens
Crête des Serres
Route Napoléon

D
E
F
1
2
3
4
Isola 2000
Cime de la Bonette
MERCANTOUR
St Sauveur-s-Tinée
St Martin-Vésubie
Col de Tende
Tunnel de Tende
Tende
St Dalmas de Tende
la Brigue
Cime du Gélas
Mt Clapier
Mt Bégo
Vallée des Merveilles
PARC
NATIONAL
DU MERCANTOUR
Col de Turini
l'Authion
Saorge
Breil-s-Roya
Sospel
Lantosque
Roquebillière
Belvédère
la Bollène-Vésubie
Peira-Cava
Utelle
Madone d'Utelle
Levens
l'Escarène
Contes
Coaraze
Lucéram
Castillon
Ste Agnès
Peillon
Peille
MENTON
Cap-Martin
Roquebrune
Beausoleil
MONTE-CARLO
la Condamine
MONACO
Cap-d'Ail
la Turbie
Eze
Beaulieu
Villefranche
St Jean-Cap-Ferrat
Cap Ferrat
NICE
NICE CÔTE-D'AZUR
Baie des Anges
Cagnes-s-M.
St Laurent-du-Var
Villeneuve-Loubet
Cros-de-Cagnes
Vence
St Paul
la Gaude
Carros
Gattières
le Broc
Gilette
Bonson
Antibes
Juan-les-Pins
Cap d'Antibes
Golfe-Juan
Vallauris
le Cannet
CANNES
Biot
Valbonne
Sophia-Antipolis
Ventimiglia
Bordighera
Dolceacqua
Pigna
Apricale
Mortola Inferiore
Col de Vence
Mt Tournairet
Massoins
Villars-s-Var
Malaussène
Toudon
Roquesteron
Ile Ste Marguerite
Pte de la Croisette
Golfe Juan
Bastia
Ile-Rousse
Calvi
Ajaccio
CUNEO
IMPERIA

1
A
B
C
CÔTE BASQUE
Cabo Higuer
Corniche Basque
Hendaye Plage
Hondarribia Fuenterrabia
Hendaye
Irun
San Marcial
Biriatou
St JEAN-DE-LUZ
Ciboure
Guéthary
Plage de Parlementia
Ste Madeleine les Embruns
Arcangues
Arbonne
Ahetze
Urrugne
Ascain
St Pée-s-Nivelle
Ustaritz
Espelette
Cambo-les-Bains
Hasparren
Larressore
Halsou
Villefranque
Labastide-Clairence
Ainhoa
Sare
la Rhune
Col de St Ignace
Dancharia
Dancharinea
Itxassou
Pas de Roland
Louhossoa
Bidarray
Pont-Noblia
Ossès
St Martin-d'Arrossa
St Etienne de Baigorry
Col d'Ispéguy
Aldudes
Urepel
Banca
Arnéguy
Valcarlos
St Jean-Pied-de-Port
Uhart-Cize
Ispoure
Caro
Aincille
Estérençuby
Col de Roncevaux
Roncesvalles
(Roncevaux)
Alto Ibañeta
Orzanzurieta
Burguete
Espinal-Auritz-Berry
Alto Mezquiriz
Viscarret-Guerendiain
Erro
Alto Erro
Zubiri
Larrasoaña
Olaibar
Villava
Huarte
Burlada
PAMPLONA
Egüés
Aoiz
Urroz
Lizoáin
Vera de Bidasoa
Lesaca
Yanci
Echalar
Zugarramurdi
Urdax
Elizondo
Valle del Baztán
Maya del Baztán
Arizcun
Errazu
Sumbilla
Santesteban
Bidasoa
Montes de Bidasoa
Puerto de Velate
Lanz
Almandoz
Berroeta
Olagüe
Ulzama
Irurita
Mendaur
Zubieta
Saldías
Labayen
Eugui
Embalse de Eugui
Arce
Garralda
Aria
Arive
Garayoa
Abaurrea Alta
Abaurrea Baja
Oroz-Betelu
Embalse de Usoz
Sierra de Archuba
Peña de Sta Barbara
Sierra de Zariquieta
Sierra de Tajonar
Ugarzan
Irissarry
Iholdy
Armendar
Bussunarits
Lacarre
Ahaxe
Gatharre
Hélette
Mendionde
Macaye
Grottes d'Isturits et d'Oxocelhaya
St Martin-d'Arberoue
St Esteben
Méharin
Bonloc
Urcuray
Ayherre
148

Sauveterre-de-Béarn
St Palais
Navarrenx
Mourenx
Lacq
Monein
Lagor
Artix
Mauléon Licharre
Oloron Ste Marie
Tardets Sorholus
Aramits
Lasseube
Bedous
Accous
Lescun
Etsaut
Urdos
Larrau
Ste Engrâce
Isaba
Roncal
Ochagavía
Uztárroz
Candanchú
Col du Somport
Pic d'Anie
Pic d'Orhy
Pic du Midi d'Ossau
Forêt des Arbailles
Col Bagargui
Col d'Osquich
Larceveau
Ostabat
Barcus
Arette
Escot
Sarrance
Pic Montagnon
PARC NATIONAL DES PYRÉNÉES
VALLÉE D'ASPE
Gave d'Oloron
Gave de Pau
Gave d'Ossau
Sierra de Arrigorrieta
Sierra de Uztárroz
Peña Ezcaurre
Pic de Sesques
Plateau de Bénou
Lurbe St Christau
Arthez-de-Béarn
Arzacq

PAU
Lescar
Billère
Jurançon
Morlaàs
Montaner
Vic-en-Bigorre
TARBES
LOURDES
Nay
Lestelle-Bétharram
Grottes de Bétharram
St Pé-de-Bigorre
Arudy
Louvie-Juzon
Laruns
Eaux-Bonnes
Gourette
Col d'Aubisque
Col du Soulor
Arrens
Argelès-Gazost
Pierrefitte-Nestalas
Cauterets
Pont d'Espagne
Luz-St Sauveur
Barèges
Col du Tourmalet
Pic du Midi de Bigorre
Bagnères-de-Bigorre
Grotte de Médous
Gavarnie
Cirque de Gavarnie
Cirque de Troumouse
Gèdre
MASSIF DE NÉOUVIELLE
PARC NATIONAL DES PYRÉNÉES
Vignemale
Balaïtous
Pic du Midi d'Ossau
Col du Pourtalet
Sallent de Gállego
Balneario de Panticosa
Formigal
Biescas
Monte Perdido
Marboré
Pic de la Munia
Forêt de St Pé-de-Bigorre
Plateau de Ger
Ossun
Pontacq
Soumoulou
Lac de Gaube
Lac Bleu
Vallée d'Ossoue
Gabas
Pic de Ger
Pic du Jer
Pic du Pibeste
Hautacam
Brèche de Roland
Le Taillon
Huesca
A
B
C
1
2
3
4
150
167

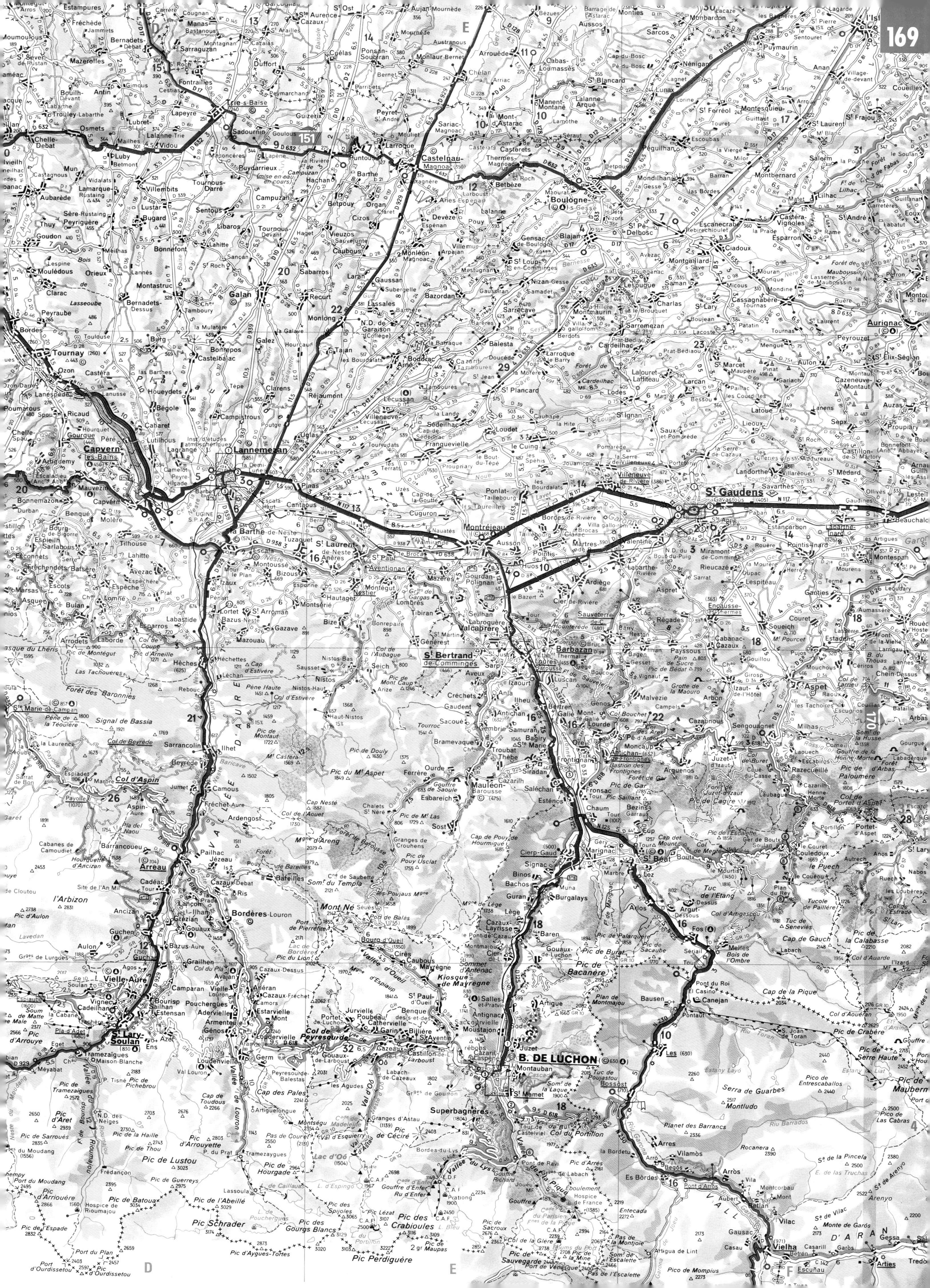
Trie-s-Baïse
Castelnau-Magnoac
Boulogne-s-Gesse
Lannemezan
Capvern-les-Bains
Tournay
Montréjeau
St Gaudens
Aurignac
St Bertrand-de-Comminges
Barbazan
Aspet
Arreau
Bordères-Louron
Vielle-Aure
St Lary-Soulan
B. DE LUCHON
St Béat
Superbagnères
Vielha
Arties
Col d'Aspin
Col de Peyresourde
Col du Portillon
Pic Perdiguère
Mont Né
Pic de Bacanère
Vallée d'Oueil
Vallée du Lys
Vallée d'Aure
Plateau de Lannemezan
VALL D'ARAN
D
E
F

Auterive
Carbonne
Noé
Longages
le Fousseret
Cazères
Rieux
Montesquieu-Volvestre
St Sulpice-s-Lèze
Lézat-s-Lèze
St Ybars
le Fossat
Boussens
St Martory
Salies-du-Salat
Ste Croix-Volvestre
le Mas-d'Azil
Daumazan-s-Arize
Campagne-s-Arize
St Lizier
St Girons
la Bastide-de-Sérou
Castillon-en-Couserans
Massat
Oust
Seix
Aulus-les-Bains
Vicdessos
Auzat
Salardú
MASSIF
MONTAGNES
Forêt du Consulat
Vallée de Bethmale
Pic de Montcalm
Pic de Certascan
Mt Valier
Pic Rouge de Bassiès
Pic des 3 Seigneurs
Pointe des Trois Comtes
Garonne
Arize
152
169
174

Castelnaudary
Pamiers
FOIX
Mirepoix
Lavelanet
Fanjeaux
Chalabre
Belpech
Saverdun
Mazères
Nailloux
Alzonne
Saissac
Montréal
Alaigne
Varilhes
Montgaillard
Tarascon-s-Ariège
Les Cabannes
Ax-les-Thermes
Belcaire
Quillan
Puivert
Montségur
Bélesta
Salles-s-l'Hers
Villepinte
Bram
Villasavary
Limoux
Esperaza
Montferrier
Ussat
Niaux
Luzenac
Sorgeat
Mérens
153
154
172
174
175

Carcassonne
La Cité
Limoux
Mas-Cabardès
Conques-s-Orbiel
Peyriac-Minervois
Rieux-Minervois
Minerve
Olonzac
Lézignan-Corbières
Capendu
Trèbes
Montagne d'Alaric
Lagrasse
St Hilaire
St Laurent-de-la-Cabrerisse
Mouthoumet
Durban-Corbières
Tuchan
Couiza
Quillan
Axat
Cucugnan
Chau de Peyrepertuse
Pic de Bugarach
Chau de Quéribus
Grau de Maury
Maury
St Paul-de-Fenouillet
Latour-de-France
Estagel
Sournia
Millas
Rivesaltes
Forêt des Fanges
Plateau de Lacamp
154
155
171
176
177

155
156
177
D
E
F
1
2
3
4
Cazouls-lès-Béziers
Lignan
Boujan-s-Libron
Montblanc
Florensac
Marseillan
Villespassans
Creissan
Puisserguier
Maraussan
Maureilhan
BÉZIERS
Cruzy
Quarante
Capestang
Montady
Colombiers
Cers
Vias
Agde
Oppidum d'Ensérune
Poilhes
Nissan-lez-Ensérune
Villeneuve
Sauvian
Sérignan
Portiragnes
le Cap d'Agde
Cap d'Agde
Fort Brescou
Ouveillan
Lespignan
Vendres
Valras-Plage
Sérignan-Plage
Sallèles-d'Aude
Cuxac-d'Aude
Coursan
Salles-d'Aude
Fleury
Puech de Labade
Grau de Vendres
St Marcel
Moussan
Marcorignan
Névian
Narbonne
Vinassan
Armissan
St Pierre-s-Mer
Narbonne-Plage
Montagne de la Clape
Coffre de Pech Redon
Abbe de Fontfroide
Bages
Gruissan
Gruissan-Plage
Etang de Bages et de Sigean
Peyriac-de-Mer
Portel-des-Corbières
Sigean
Port-la-Nouvelle
Roquefort-des-Corbières
Lapalme
Etang de l'Ayrolle
Grau de la Vieille Nouvelle
Caves
la Franqui
Cap Leucate
Leucate
Leucate-Plage
Treilles
Fitou
Port-Leucate
Etang de Leucate ou de Salses
Fort de Salses
Salses
Port-Barcarès
le Barcarès
St Hippolyte
St Laurent-de-la-Salanque
Torreilles-Plage
Claira
Torreilles
Ste Marie
Ste Marie-Plage
Bompas
Villelongue-de-la-Salanque
Canet-Plage
PERPIGNAN

FOIX
Tarascon-s-Ariège
Lavelanet
Ax-les-Thermes
les Cabannes
Vicdessos
ANDORRA
LA VELLA
Les Escaldes
Sant Julià de Lòria
la Seu d'Urgell
Puigcerdà
Bourg-Madame
Font-Romeu
Col de Puymorens
Porté-Puymorens
Soldeu
Canillo
Encamp
La Massana
Ordino
Arinsal
Pas de la Case
Port d'Envalira
Pic d'Estats
Pic du Port
Pic de l'Estanyó
Pic de la Cabanette
Pic Carlit
Pic Pédrous
Pic Peric
Montségur
Belcaire
Bellver de Cerdanya
Mérens
Chalabre
Puivert
Montgaillard
la Bastide-de-Sérou
Montcalm
Pic Rouge de Bassiès
Pic des 3 Seigneurs
Plantaurel
Saurat
Ussat
Grotte de Niaux
Luzenac
Sorgeat
Orlu
Latour-de-Carol
Llivia
la Molina
Lleida
Ripoll Barcelona
Túnel del Cadi Barcelona
170
171

171
172
176
Quillan
Couiza
Axat
Sournia
Prades
Vernet-les-Bains
Olette
Mont-Louis
Prats-de-Mollo
Amélie-les-Bains-Palalda
Arles
Millas
Ille-s-Têt
Vinça
Tuchan
Mouthoumet
Latour-de-France
Estagel
Pic de Bugarach
Forêt des Fanges
Forêt de Rialsesse
Chau de Peyrepertuse
Chau de Quéribus
Grau de Maury
Plateau de Lacamp
Pic Dourmidou
Col de Jau
Madrès
Pic de la Pelade
Puig d'Escoutou
Mt Coronat
Villefranche-de-Conflent
Abbe St Michel-de-Cuxa
Abbe de St Martin
Prieuré de Serrabone
Massif du Canigou
Pic du Canigou
Ras del Prat Cabrera
Puig de Très Estelles
Pic de Gallinasse
Puig dels Très Vents
Pic de Rives Blanques
Pic du Géant
Pic de Costabonne
Roc Colom
Pic de Finestrelles
Puigmal
Pic de Dorria
Pic de Sègre
Núria
Queralbs
Setcases
Serralongue
Coustouges
Roc de France
Mont Nègre
Lamanère
Col d'Ares
Barcelona
Forêt de Gesse
Forêt de Gravas
Forêt de Navarre
Gorges de St Georges
Lesquerde
Maury
St Paul-de-Fenouillet
Caudiès-de-Fenouillèdes
Puilaurens
Montalba-le-Château
Rodès
Bouleternère
Caramany
Bélesta
Força Réal
Castelnou
Taulis
Montbolo
Mosset
Molitg-les-Bains
Campôme
Nohèdes
Conat
Ria
Fontpédrouse
Thuès-entre-Valls
Saillagouse
Eyne
Planès
St Pierre dels Forcats
La Cabanasse
Les Angles
Matemale
Formiguères
Puyvalador
Réal
Escouloubre
Roquefort-de-Sault
Gincla
Boucheville
Montfort-s-Boulzane
Vira
Fenouillet
Prugnanes
Cubières-s-Cinoble
Camps-s-l'Agly
Bugarach
Rennes-les-Bains
Rennes-le-Château
Espéraza
Alet-les-Bains
Padern
Paziols
Cucugnan
Duilhac-s-Peyrepertuse
Soulatgé
Rouffiac-des-Corbières
Maisons
Massac
Albières
Auriac
Lanet
Salza
Bouisse
Vignevieille
Missègre
Véraza
Terroles
Peyrolles
Arques
Serres
Sougraigne
Granès
St Ferriol
St Just
Ginoles
Coudons
Belvianes
Quirbajou
Marsa
Artigues
Aunat
Rodome
Bessède-de-Sault
Le Clat
Gesse
Counozouls
D
E
F

171
172
174
Chalabre
Puivert
Quillan
Couiza
Espéraza
Alet-les-Bains
Belcaire
Belfort
Plateau de Sault
Axat
Pic de Bugarach
Bugarach
St Paul-de-Fenouillet
Caudiès-de-Fenouillèdes
Fenouillet
Sournia
Mijanès
Quérigut
Puyvalador
Formiguères
Matemale
les Angles
Mont-Louis
Font-Romeu
Saillagouse
Bourg-Madame
Puigcerdà
Llivia
Latour-de-Carol
Prades
Molitg-les-Bains
Vernet-les-Bains
Olette
Villefranche-de-Conflent
Pic Carlit
Madrès
Pic du Canigou
Massif du Canigou
Prats-de-Mollo
la Preste
Núria
Puigmal
la Molina
Setcases
Queralbs (1180)
Pic de Costabonne
Roc Colom
Pic du Géant
Forêt de Rialsesse
Forêt des Fanges
Forêt de Gesse
Pic de Tarbezou
Pic Peric
Col de Jau
Col de Puymorens
Vallée d'Orlu
Gorges de St Georges
Abbe St Martin
Abbe St Michel-de-Cuxa
Rennes-les-Bains
Rennes-le-Château
A
B
C

PERPIGNAN
Sigean
Port-la-Nouvelle
Leucate
Cap Leucate
Port-Leucate
Port-Barcarès
le Barcarès
Fort de Salses
Salses
Rivesaltes
St Laurent-de-la-Salanque
Canet-Plage
Canet-en-Roussillon
St Cyprien-Plage
Elne
Argelès-Plage
Argelès-s-Mer
Collioure
Port-Vendres
Cap Béar
Banyuls-s-Mer
Cerbère
Cap Cerbère
Portbou
Colera
Llançà
Le Boulou
le Perthus
La Jonquera
Céret
Amélie-les-Bains-Palalda
Arles
Thuir
Millas
Ille-s-Têt
Estagel
Tuchan
Durban-Corbières
Maury
Latour-de-France
Prieuré de Serrabone
Roc de France
Figueres
Barcelona
Côte Vermeille
Étang de Leucate ou de Salses
Étang de Canet et de St Nazaire
Plaine du Roussillon
172
173
D
E
F
1
2
3
4

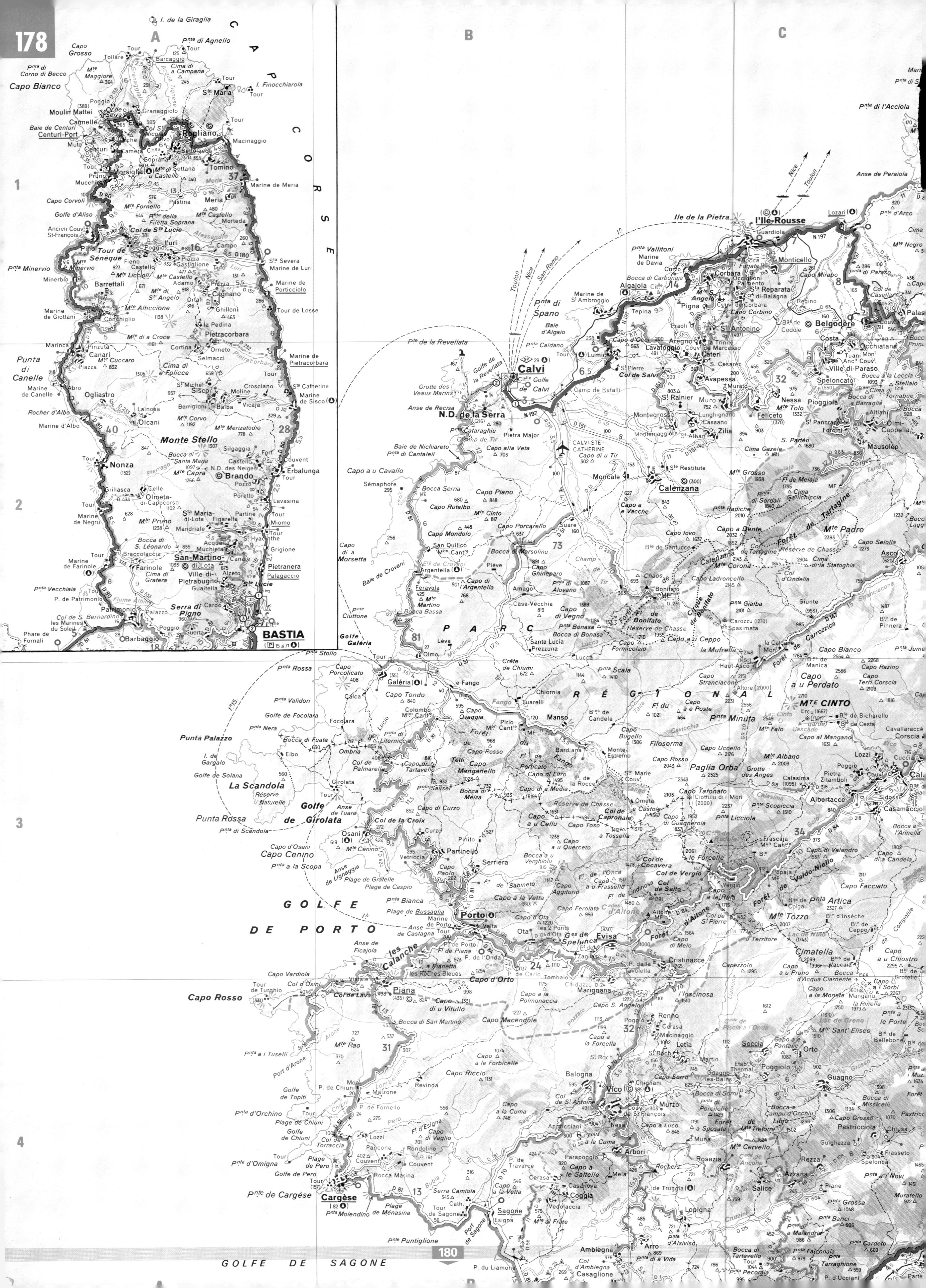
A
B
C
1
2
3
4
CAP CORSE
I. de la Giraglia
Capo Grosso
Capo Bianco
Barcaggio
Tollare
Centuri-Port
Rogliano
Macinaggio
Morsiglia
Tomino
Marine de Meria
Meria
Pino
Tour de Sénèque
Luri
Col de Ste Lucie
Marine de Luri
Marine de Porticciolo
Cagnano
Barrettali
Minerbio
Marine de Giottani
Pietracorbara
Marine de Pietracorbara
Canari
Punta di Canelle
Sisco
Marine de Sisco
Ogliastro
Olcani
Monte Stello
Nonza
Brando
Erbalunga
Lavasina
Miomo
Pietranera
Farinole
San-Martino-di-Lota
Ville-di-Pietrabugno
Serra di Pigno
Patrimonio
BASTIA
Barbaggio
Ile de la Pietra
l'Ile-Rousse
Lozari
Monticello
Corbara
Algajola
Sta Reparata-di-Balagna
Belgodère
Speloncato
Lumio
Calvi
Golfe de Calvi
Pte de la Revellata
N.D. de la Serra
Calenzana
Moncale
Zilia
Montegrosso
Feliceto
Col de Salvi
Calvi-Ste-Catherine
Mte Grosso
Forêt de Tartagine
Mte Padro
Asco
Forêt de Bonifato
Capo a u Cavallo
Galéria
Golfe de Galéria
Golfe de Focolara
Punta Palazzo
La Scandola
Réserve Naturelle
Golfe de Girolata
Punta Rossa
Capo Cenino
Col de la Croix
Osani
Partinello
Serriera
PARC RÉGIONAL
Paglia Orba
Mte CINTO
Capo Tafonato
Col de Vergio
Forêt de Valdo-Niello
Forêt d'Aitone
Evisa
Porto
Ota
GOLFE DE PORTO
les Calanche
Piana
Capo Rosso
Capo d'Orto
Col de Sevi
Marignana
Cristinacce
Calacuccia
Albertacce
Casamaccioli
Capo Rosso
Cargèse
Golfe de Chiuni
Golfe de Pero
Pte de Cargèse
Vico
Sagone
Coggia
Arbori
Letia
Soccia
Orto
Poggiolo
Guagno
Murzo
Rosazia
Salice
Azzana
Rezza
Pastricciola
Ambiegna
Arro
Casaglione
GOLFE DE SAGONE
Forêt de Libio
Mte Tretorre

180

GOLFE DE St FLORENT
Punta di Curza
BASTIA
San-Martino-di-Lota
Ville-di-Pietrabugno
Pietranera
Marseille
Nice
Livorno
Toulon
San Remo
Genova
La Spezia
Piombino
Patrimonio
Barbaggio
Serra di Pigno
Col de Teghime
St Florent
DESERT DES AGRIATES
Furiani
Poggio-d'Oletta
Oletta
Biguglia
Etang de Biguglia
Borgo
Murato
San-Michele
Défilé de Lancone
Rutali
Vallecalle
Rapale
Sorio
Lama
Urtaca
Novella
Mte Asto
Pietralba
Lucciana
la Canonica
Mariana
BASTIA-PORETTA
Campitello
Vignale
Scolca
Volpajola
Bigorno
Lento
Canavaggia
Vescovato
Venzolasca
Olmo
Castifao
Moltifao
Ponte Leccia
Morosaglia
Piedigriggio
Popolasca
Prato-di-Giovellina
Castiglione
Castellare-di-Casinca
Penta-di-Casinca
Porri
Silvareccio
Taglio
Talasani
Velone-Orneto
Poggio-Mezzana
Ste Lucie de Moriani
Moriani-Plage
San-Nicolao
la Porta
Mte San Petrone
Piedicroce
Carcheto
Valle-d'Orezza
Cervione
Valle-di-Campoloro
Prunete
Port de Campoloro
San-Giuliano
Omessa
Soveria
Tralonca
Corte
Bustanico
Sermano
Alando
Favalello
Sant'Andréa-di-Bozio
Pianello
Moïta
Canale-di-Verde
Linguizzetta
Phare d'Alistro
Campi
Matra
Zalana
Zuani
Tox
Tallone
Pietraserena
Altiani
Erbajolo
Focicchia
Gorges du Tavignano
Gorges de la Restonica
Casanova
Riventosa
Poggio-di-Venaco
Venaco
Col de Bellagranajo
Mte Cardo
Giuncaggio
Pancheraccia
Bravone
Marine de Bravone
Noceta
Rospigliani
Vezzani
Antisanti
Casevecchie
Pietroso
Col de Morello
Vivario
Muracciole
Forêt de Rospa Sorba
Col de Sorba
Forêt de Vizzavona
Vizzavona
Ghisoni
Défilé des Strette
Défilé de l'Inzecca
Aghione
Vaccaja
Aléria
Cateraggio
Plage de Padulone
Etang de Diane
Thermes Romains
Tavignano
Casabianda
Réserve de Chasse de Casabianda
Centre pénitencier agricole
Riva-Bella
Etang de Terrenzana
Mte d'Oro
PARC NATUREL RÉGIONAL
Col de Vizzavona
Bocognano
Mte Renoso
Lugo-di-Nazza
Poggio-di-Nazza
Ghisonaccia-Gare
Ile d'Urbino
Etang d'Urbino
St Antoine
Pratello
Samuleto
Vadina
N 193
N 198
N 200
N 197

181

A
B
C
1
2
3
4
178
GOLFE DE SAGONE
GOLFE D'AJACCIO
GOLFE DE VALINCO
Golfe de la Liscia
Golfe de Lava
Capo di Feno
Cala di Fico
Anse de Minaccia
Iles Sanguinaires
Sémaphore
Gr^de Sanguinaire
I. Porre
Tour de la Parata
P^nte de la Parata
AJACCIO
Toulon
Nice
Marseille
Porticcio
Bastelicaccia
Cauro
Sari-d'Orcino
Cannelle
Calcatoggio
Appietto
Afa
Alata
Villanova
Mezzavia
Tavaco
Vero
Ucciani
Carbuccia
Peri
Ocana
Tolla
Eccica
Suarella
Grosseto
Albitreccia
Cozzanaccio
Guargualé
Urbalacone
Pietrosella
Coti-Chiavari
Forêt de Chiavari
Serra-di-Ferro
Porto-Pollo
Olmeto
Olmeto-Plage
Propriano
Casalabriva
Sollacaro
Filitosa
Viggianello
Sartène
Belvédère-Campomoro
Campomoro
Grossa
Bilia
Capo di Muro
Capo Nero
Punta di Senetosa
Alignements de Palaggiu
Mégalithes de Cauria
Cap de Zivia
Golfe de Mortoli
Rocher du Lion
Golfe de Roccapina
Cap de Roccapina
Ile des Moines
Calanque de Conca
N196
N193
N194

179

D
E
F
1
2
3
4
Mte Renoso
Ft de Marmano
Bastelica
Ghisonaccia
Prunelli-di-Fiumorbo
Isolaccio-di-Fiumorbo
Serra-di-Fiumorbo
San-Gavino-di-Fiumorbo
Ventiseri
Pta di a Cappella
Col de Verde
Forêt de S. Pietro di Verde
Palneca
Ciamannacce
Tasso
Sampolo
Cozzano
Zicavo
Chisa
Solaro
Travo
Marine de Solaro
Marine de Scaffa Rossa
Solenzara
Sari-di-Porto-Vecchio
Cala d'Oro
Canella
Anse de Favone
Favone
Col de Guardia
Tarco
Mte Incudine
Pnta Tinturaia
Forêt de Tova
Col de Larone
Réserve de Chasse de Bavella
Col de Bavella
Aiguilles de Bavella
Trou de la Bombe
PARC RÉGIONAL
Quercitella
Aullène
Quenza
Zonza
Serra-di-Scopamène
Sorbollano
Conca
Anse de Fautea
Bocca di a Parata
Ste Lucie-de-Porto-Vecchio
Lecci
Pinarello
Golfe de Pinarello
I. Roscana
I. de Pinarello
Levie
Castello de Cucuruzzu
Ste Lucie-de-Tallano
Altagène
Carbini
Forêt de Barocaggio Marghese
Forêt de l'Ospédale
L'Ospédale
Pnta di a Vacca Morta
Castello d'Arraggio
Porto-Vecchio
Golfe de Porto-Vecchio
Pnte de la Chiappa
Piccovagia
I. Farina
Montagne de Cagna
Pnta d'Ovace
l'Omo di Cagna
Sotta
Plage de Palombaggia
Iles Cerbicale
I. Pietricaggiosa
Capo d'Asciaio
Bocca dell' Oro
Golfe de Sta Giulia
I. di u Toro
Porto Novo
Pnta di Sponsaglia
Pnta di Rondinara
Monacia-d'Aullène
Figari
Pianottoli-Caldarello
Golfe de Figari
Golfe de Ventilegne
Pnta di Ventilegne
Port de Stagnolo
Golfe de Sta Manza
Pnte de Capicciola
Ermitage de la Trinité
Grte du Sdragonato
Bonifacio
Capo Pertusato
Capo di Feno
Ile Cavallo
I. Ratino
I. Poraggia
I. Perduto
I. Piana
Pnte de Sprono
I. de San Bainzo
Iles Lavezzi
Pyramide de a Sémillante
Ecueil de Lavezzi
N 198
N 196

Index Register

Comment se servir de cet index
How to use this index
Toelichting bij het register
Zum Gebrauch des Registers

Beauvais *60* **17** E3

- département
- page / page / Seite / kaartbladzijde
- grid square on page within which Beauvais is located
- carreau dans lequel la ville de Beauvais se trouve
- Planquadrat in dem Beauvais liegt
- vak op de kaartbladzijde waarin Beauvais te vinden is

Les localités de cet index ont un bureau de poste distributeur.

Les sorties de ville indiquées par un numéro cerné de noir sont identiques sur les plans et les cartes au 1/200 000.

This index lists all prefectures, sub-prefectures and postal centres in France.

The prominent black numbers in circles at the sides of the city maps correspond with the numbers given for main routes on the 1:200 000 maps.

Dit register bevat de namen van de belangrijkste plaatsen, namelijk de vestigingsplaatsen van de Franse overheden (préfecturen en onderpréfecturen) alsmede alle plaatsen met een belangrijk postkantoor.

De overzichtskaartjes van de grote steden geven de verbindingen aan voor het doorgaande verkeer. De omcirkelde zwarte cijfers aan de rand van deze kaartjes verwijzen naar de cijfers van de uitvalswegen op de kaartbladzijden in deze atlas.

Die im Register enthaltenen Orte sind entweder Präfekturen, Unterpräfekturen oder Postleitzentren in Frankreich.

Die in schwarz gedruckten und durch Kreise hervorgehobenen Zahlen an den Seitenleisten der Übersichtspläne der wichtigsten Städte entsprechen in den Karten 1:200.000 der für Durchgangsstraßen verwendeten Numerierung.

A

B

C

Bordeaux

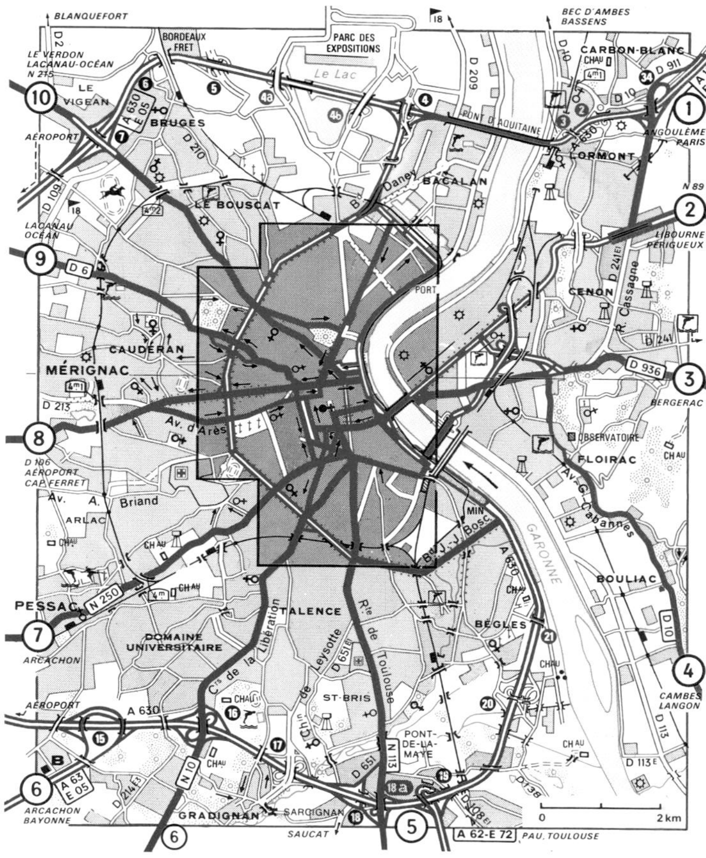

BLANQUEFORT
BRUGES
LE BOUSCAT
BACALAN
LORMONT
CENON
CAUDÉRAN
MÉRIGNAC
FLOIRAC
BOULIAC
PESSAC
TALENCE
DOMAINE UNIVERSITAIRE
BÈGLES
GRADIGNAN
GARONNE

D

Dijon

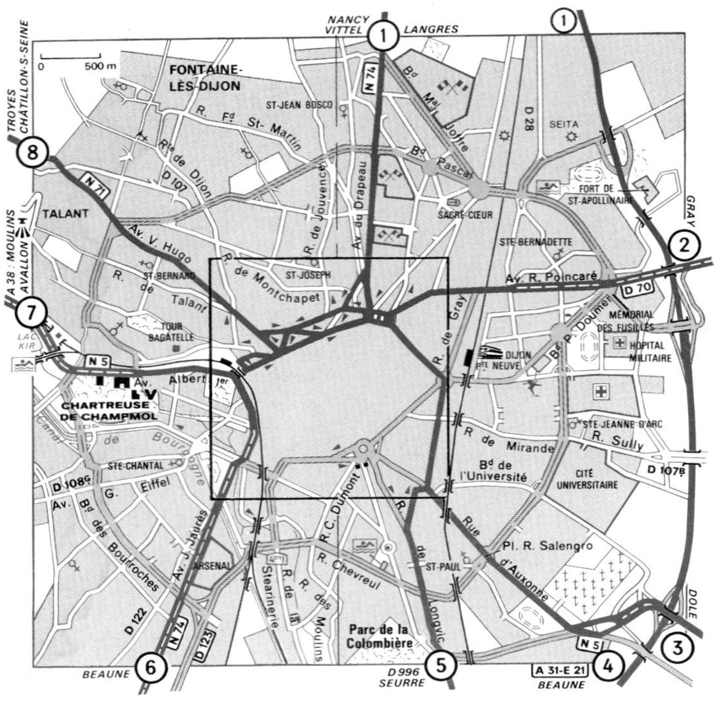
FONTAINE-LÈS-DIJON
TALANT
ST-JOSEPH
ST-BERNARD
SACRÉ-CŒUR
STE-BERNADETTE
FORT DE ST-APOLLINAIRE
MÉMORIAL DES FUSILLÉS
HÔPITAL MILITAIRE
CHARTREUSE DE CHAMPMOL
STE-JEANNE-D'ARC
CITÉ UNIVERSITAIRE
ST-PAUL
Parc de la Colombière
NANCY VITTEL
LANGRES
GRAY
DOLE
BEAUNE
SEURRE
TROYES CHÂTILLON-S-SEINE
A 38 MOULINS AVALLON
Av. V. Hugo
Bd de l'Université
Pl. R. Salengro
500 m

Lille

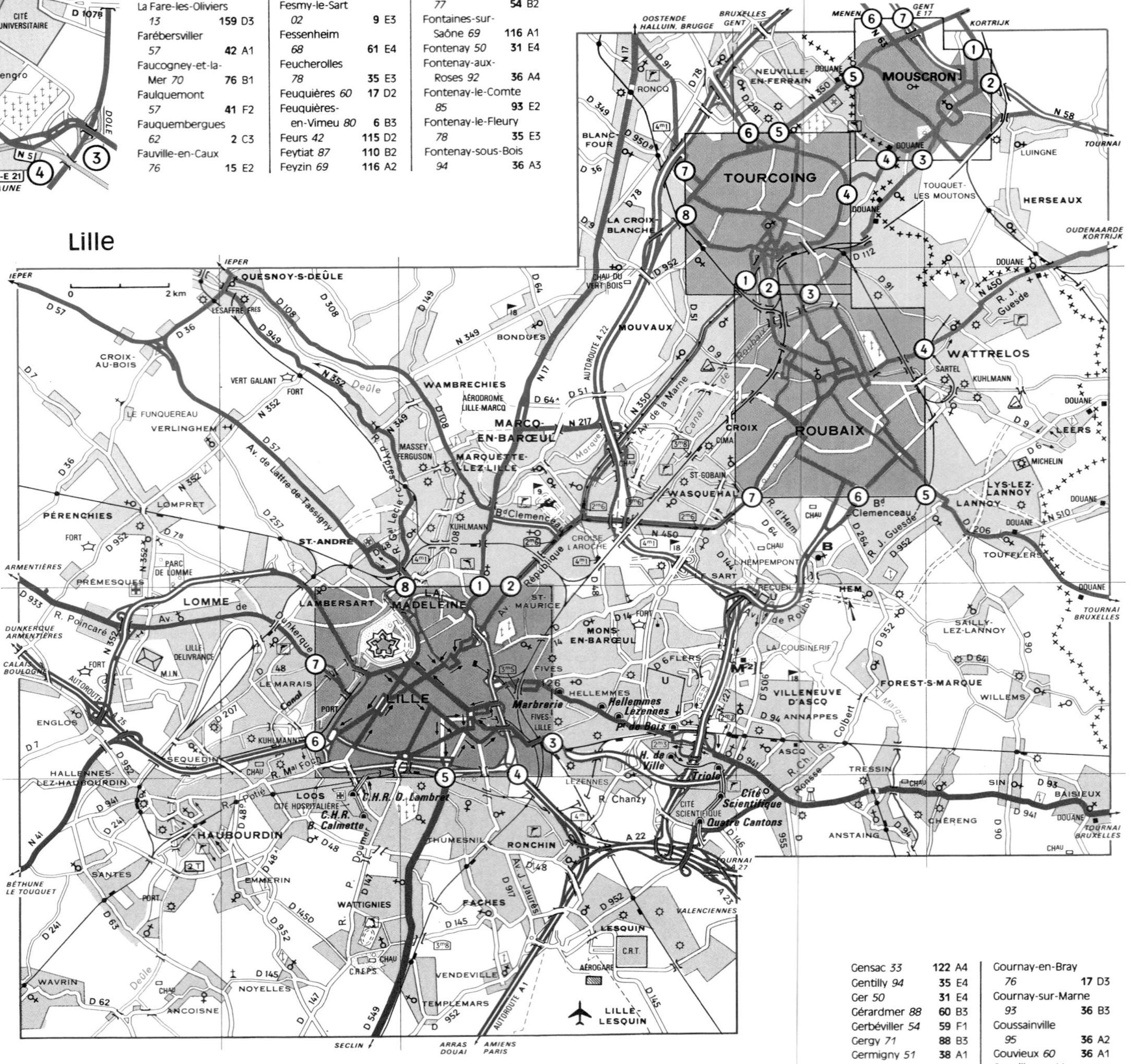
QUESNOY-S-DEÛLE
TOURCOING
MOUSCRON
ROUBAIX
WATTRELOS
HERSEAUX
MOUVAUX
BONDUES
WAMBRECHIES
MARCQ-EN-BARŒUL
MARQUETTE-LEZ-LILLE
CROIX
WASQUEHAL
LANNOY
LYS-LEZ-LANNOY
TOUFFLERS
HEM
ST-ANDRÉ
LAMBERSART
LA MADELEINE
LILLE
LOMME
PÉRENCHIES
PRÉMESQUES
VERLINGHEM
LOMPRET
MONS-EN-BARŒUL
HELLEMMES
VILLENEUVE D'ASCQ
FOREST-S-MARQUE
SAILLY-LEZ-LANNOY
TRESSIN
CHÉRENG
ANSTAING
BAISIEUX
LEZENNES
RONCHIN
LOOS
HAUBOURDIN
SEQUEDIN
HALLENNES-LEZ-HAUBOURDIN
ENGLOS
EMMERIN
WATTIGNIES
FACHES
LESQUIN
VENDEVILLE
TEMPLEMARS
NOYELLES
WAVRIN
ANCOISNE
SANTES
LILLE-LESQUIN
SECLIN
ARRAS DOUAI
AMIENS PARIS
TOURNAI
KORTRIJK
MENEN
2 km

H

I

J

K

L

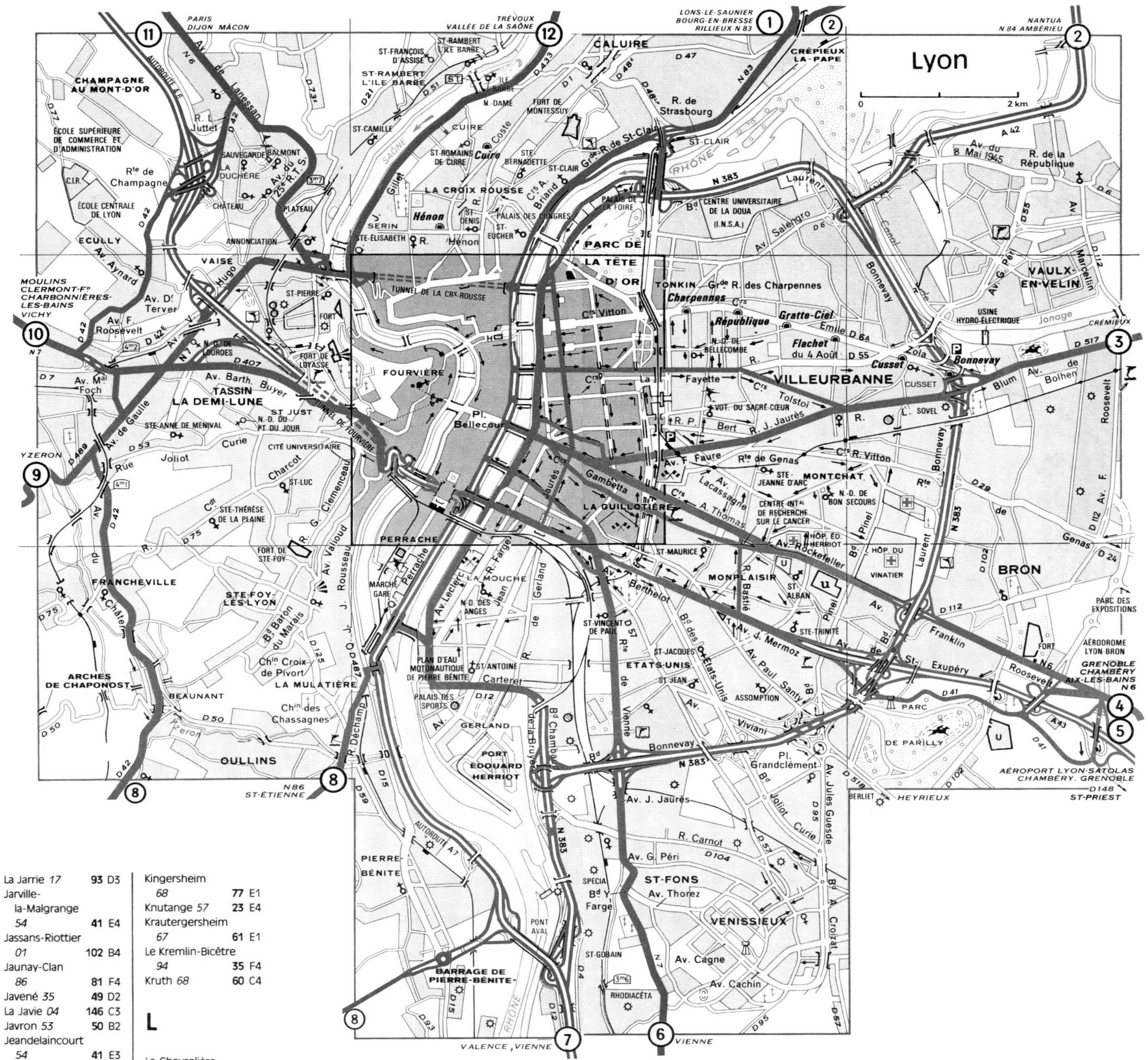

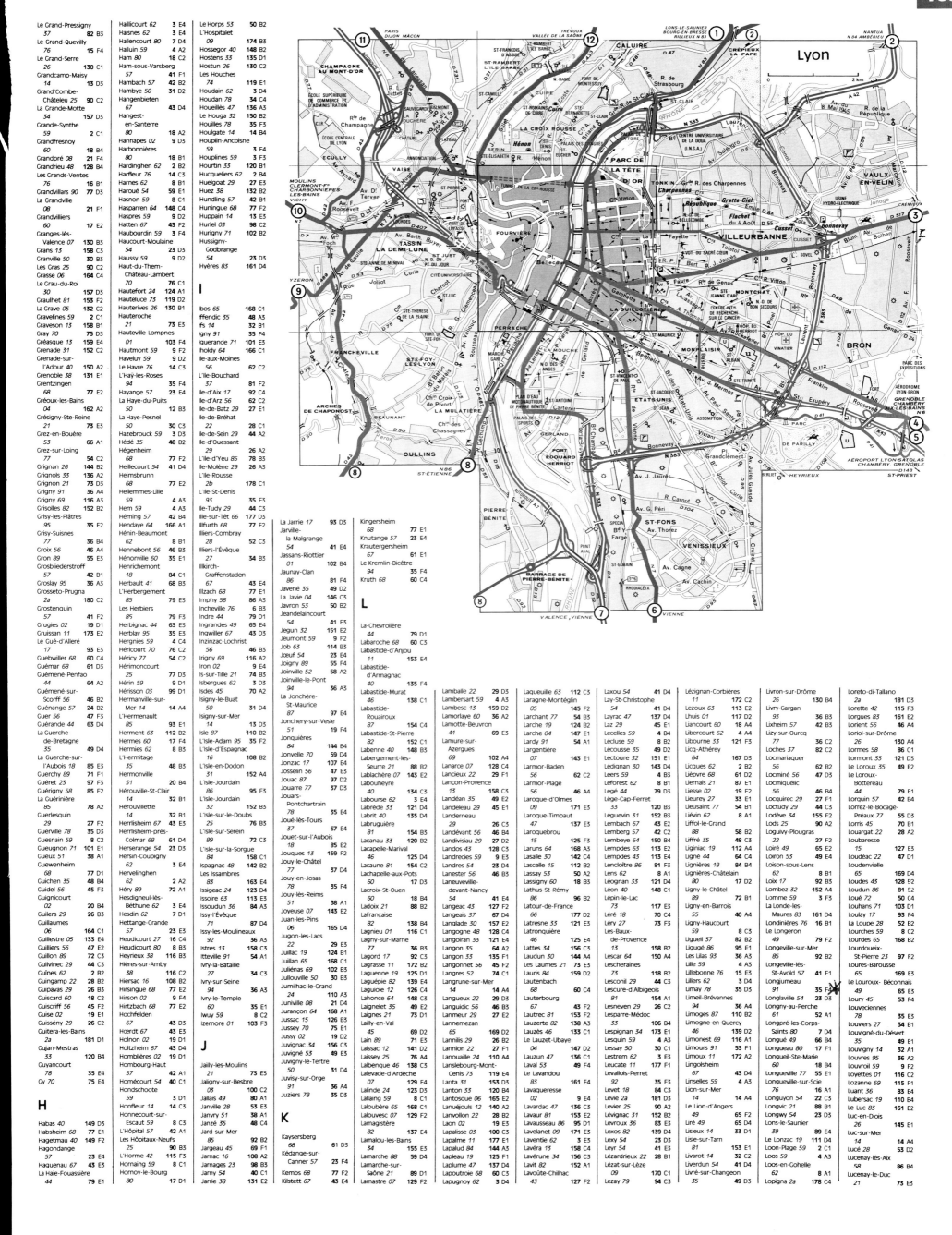

Lyon
CALUIRE
CHAMPAGNE AU MONT-D'OR
ÉCULLY
VAISE
TASSIN LA DEMI-LUNE
FOURVIÈRE
LA CROIX ROUSSE
PARC DE LA TÊTE D'OR
VILLEURBANNE
VAULX-EN-VELIN
BRON
MONPLAISIR
MONTCHAT
LA GUILLOTIÈRE
PERRACHE
LA MULATIÈRE
STE-FOY-LÈS-LYON
FRANCHEVILLE
OULLINS
PIERRE-BÉNITE
ST-FONS
VÉNISSIEUX
ÉTATS-UNIS
GERLAND
PORT ÉDOUARD HERRIOT
BARRAGE DE PIERRE-BÉNITE
ARCHES DE CHAPONOST
AÉRODROME LYON BRON
AÉROPORT LYON-SATOLAS
PARC DE PARILLY

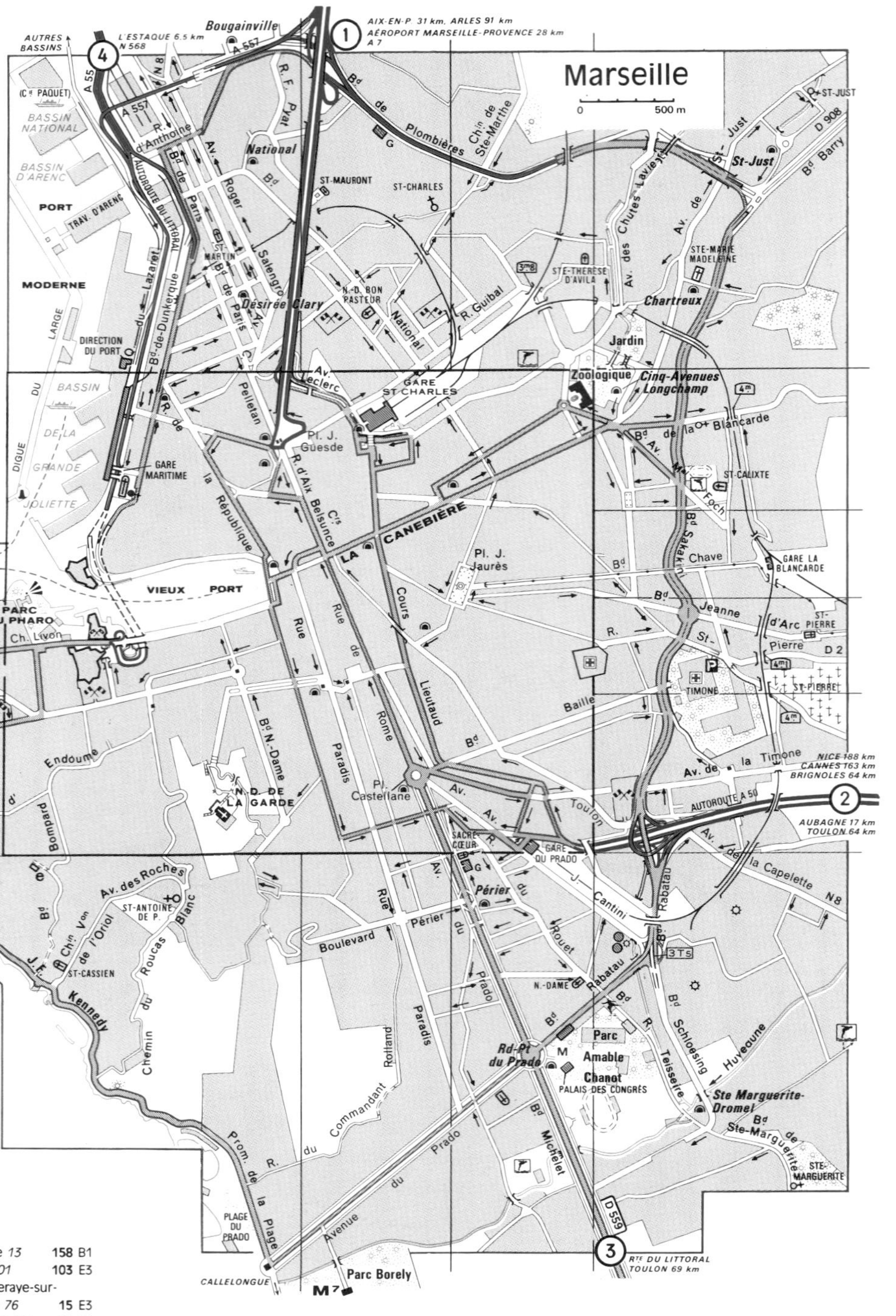
Marseille
0
500 m
AIX-EN-P. 31 km, ARLES 91 km
AÉROPORT MARSEILLE-PROVENCE 28 km
A 7
L'ESTAQUE 6.5 km
N 568
AUTRES BASSINS
Bougainville
BASSIN NATIONAL
BASSIN D'ARENC
PORT
MODERNE
DIRECTION DU PORT
GARE MARITIME
VIEUX PORT
PARC DU PHARO
CHÂTEAU D'IF
CORSE
National
Désirée Clary
GARE ST-CHARLES
LA CANEBIÈRE
Chartreux
St-Just
Zoologique
Cinq-Avenues Longchamp
TIMONE
N.D. DE LA GARDE
NICE 188 km
CANNES 163 km
BRIGNOLES 64 km
AUBAGNE 17 km
TOULON 64 km
Périer
Rd-Pt du Prado
Parc Amable Chanot
PALAIS DES CONGRÈS
Ste Marguerite-Dromel
Rte DU LITTORAL
TOULON 69 km
ST-CASSIEN
PLAGE DU PRADO
CALLELONGUE
Parc Borely

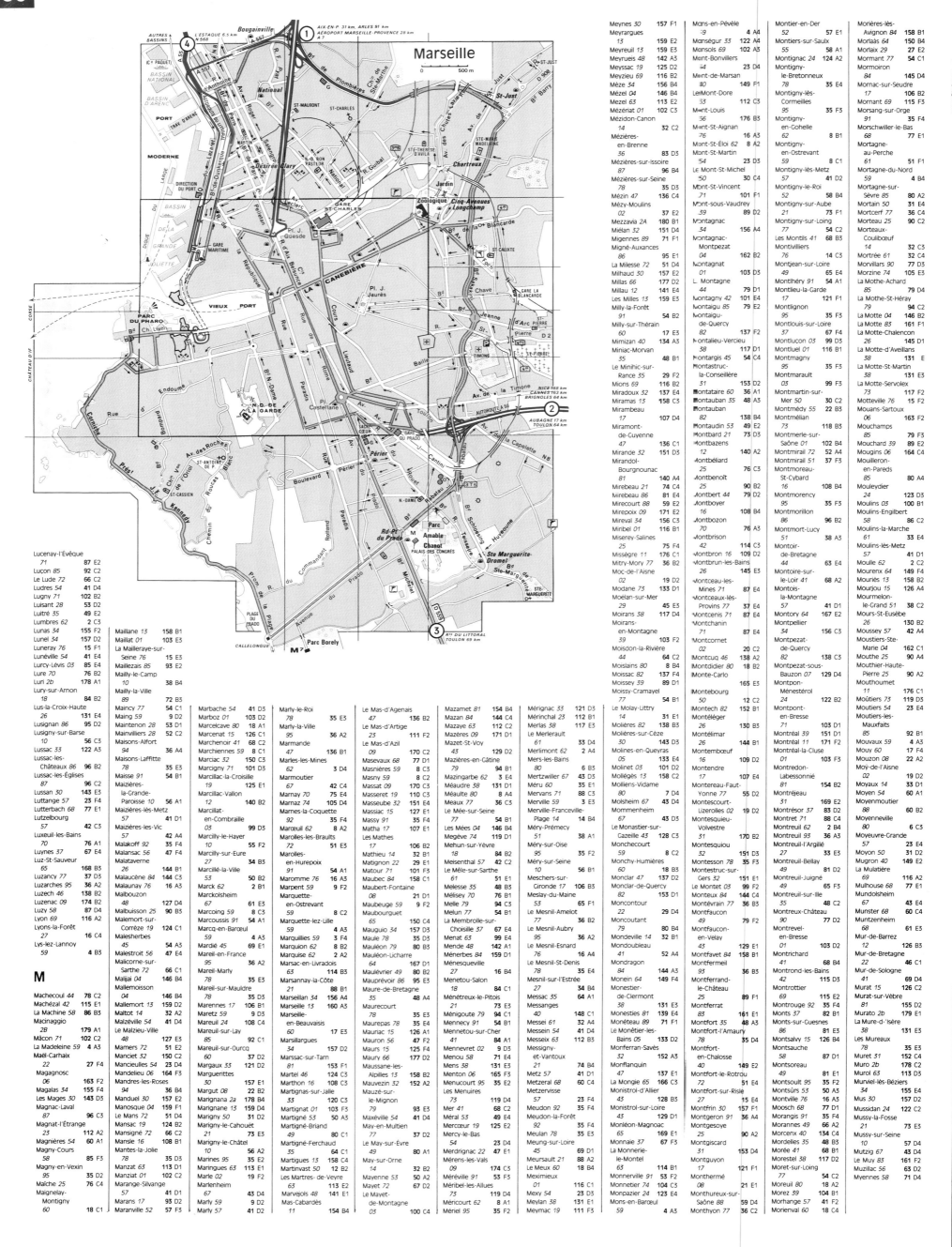

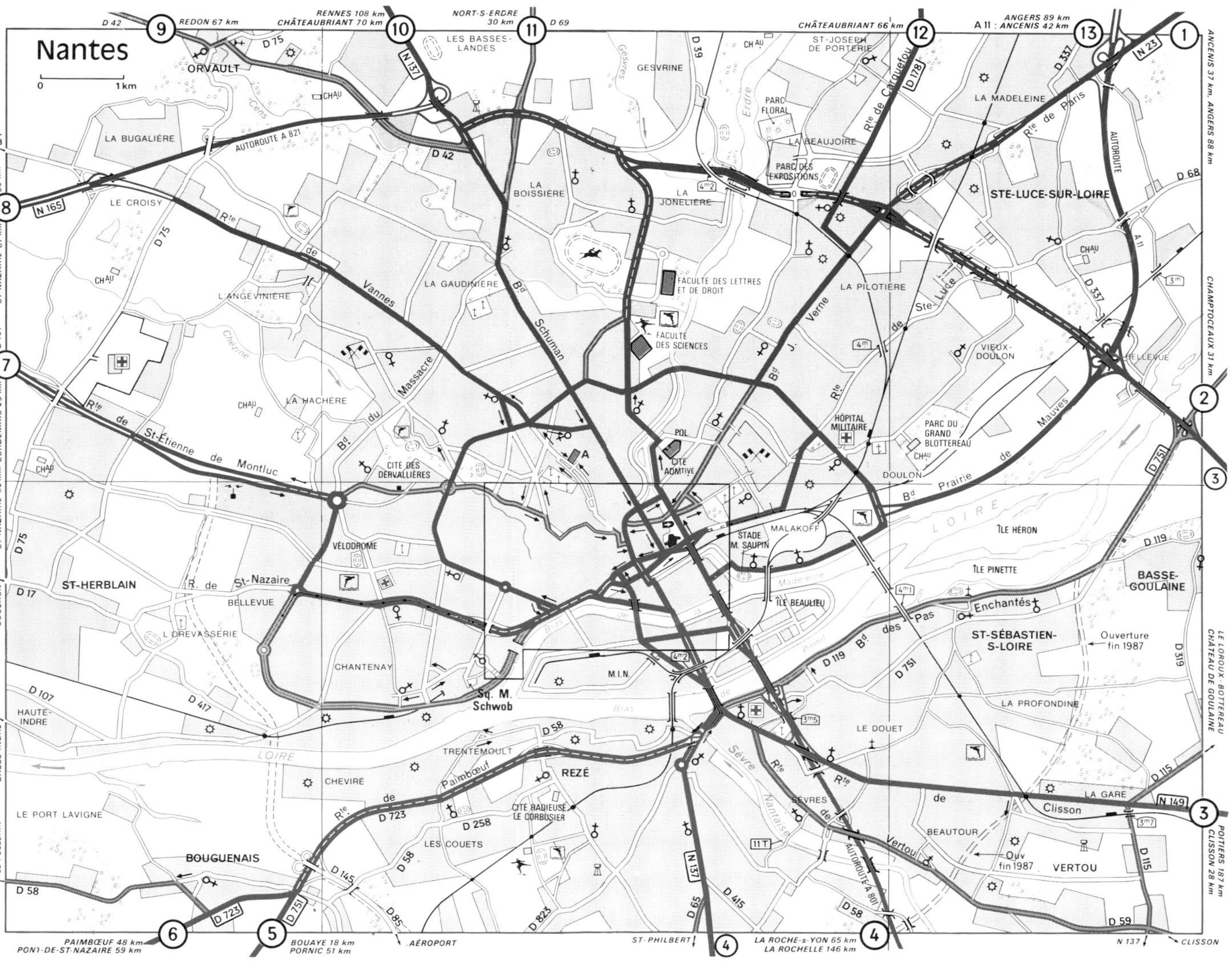

Nantes
0
1 km
REDON 67 km
RENNES 108 km
CHÂTEAUBRIANT 70 km
NORT-S-ERDRE 30 km
CHÂTEAUBRIANT 66 km
ANGERS 89 km
A 11 : ANCENIS 42 km
ANCENIS 37 km ANGERS 88 km
ORVAULT
LA BUGALIÈRE
AUTOROUTE A 821
LES BASSES LANDES
GESVRINE
ST-JOSEPH DE PORTERIE
PARC FLORAL
LA BEAUJOIRE
PARC DES EXPOSITIONS
LA MADELEINE
STE-LUCE-SUR-LOIRE
AUTOROUTE
LA BOISSIÈRE
LA JONELIÈRE
LE CROISY
LA BAULE 73 km
ST-NAZAIRE 61 km
DONGES
L'ANGEVINIÈRE
LA GAUDINIÈRE
FACULTÉ DES LETTRES ET DE DROIT
FACULTÉ DES SCIENCES
LA PILOTIÈRE
VIEUX-DOULON
BELLEVUE
CHAMPTOCEAUX 31 km
LA HACHÈRE
Rte de Vannes
Bd Schuman
Rte de St-Étienne de Montluc
CITÉ DES DERVALLIÈRES
HÔPITAL MILITAIRE
POL
CITÉ ADMIVE
PARC DU GRAND BLOTTEREAU
DOULON
VANNES 110 km REDON 76 km
ST-NAZAIRE 62 km CORDEMAIS 25 km
COUËRON
ST-HERBLAIN
VÉLODROME
R. de St-Nazaire
STADE M. SAUPIN
MALAKOFF
ÎLE HÉRON
LOIRE
ÎLE PINETTE
BASSE-GOULAINE
ÎLE BEAULIEU
Enchantés
L'OREVASSERIE
CHANTENAY
M.I.N.
ST-SÉBASTIEN-S-LOIRE
Ouverture fin 1987
LE LOROUX BOTTEREAU
CHÂTEAU DE GOULAINE
HAUTE-INDRE
Sq. M. Schwob
LA PROFONDINE
BASSE-INDRE
TRENTEMOULT
REZÉ
LE DOUET
CHEVIRÉ
LE PORT LAVIGNE
CITÉ RADIEUSE LE CORBUSIER
LES COUETS
BEAUTOUR
LA GARE
Clisson
POITIERS 187 km
CLISSON 28 km
BOUGUENAIS
Ouv fin 1987
VERTOU
LE PELLERIN
Rte de Vertou
PAIMBŒUF 48 km
PONT-DE-ST-NAZAIRE 59 km
BOUAYE 18 km
PORNIC 51 km
AÉROPORT
ST-PHILBERT
LA ROCHE-s-YON 65 km
LA ROCHELLE 146 km
N 137
CLISSON

Rouen

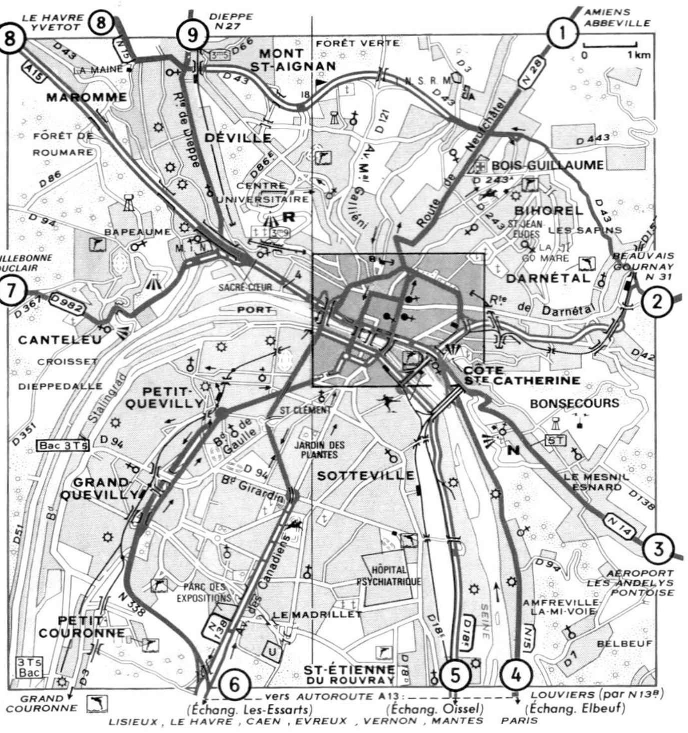

LE HAVRE YVETOT
DIEPPE N27
AMIENS ABBEVILLE
MONT ST-AIGNAN
FORÊT VERTE
MAROMME
LA MAINE
FORÊT DE ROUMARE
DÉVILLE
BOIS-GUILLAUME
CENTRE UNIVERSITAIRE
BIHOREL
LES SAPINS
BAPEAUME
LILLEBONNE DUCLAIR
DARNÉTAL
BEAUVAIS GOURNAY N31
SACRÉ-CŒUR
PORT
CANTELEU
CROISSET
DIEPPEDALLE
CÔTE STE CATHERINE
PETIT-QUEVILLY
BONSECOURS
ST CLÉMENT
JARDIN DES PLANTES
GRAND QUEVILLY
SOTTEVILLE
LE MESNIL ESNARD
AÉROPORT LES ANDELYS PONTOISE
PARC DES EXPOSITIONS
HÔPITAL PSYCHIATRIQUE
AMFREVILLE LA-MI-VOIE
PETIT COURONNE
LE MADRILLET
BELBEUF
3 Ts Bac
ST-ÉTIENNE DU ROUVRAY
GRAND COURONNE
vers AUTOROUTE A13
LOUVIERS (par N138)
(Échang. Les-Essarts)
(Échang. Oissel)
(Échang. Elbeuf)
LISIEUX, LE HAVRE, CAEN, EVREUX, VERNON, MANTES
PARIS

S

T

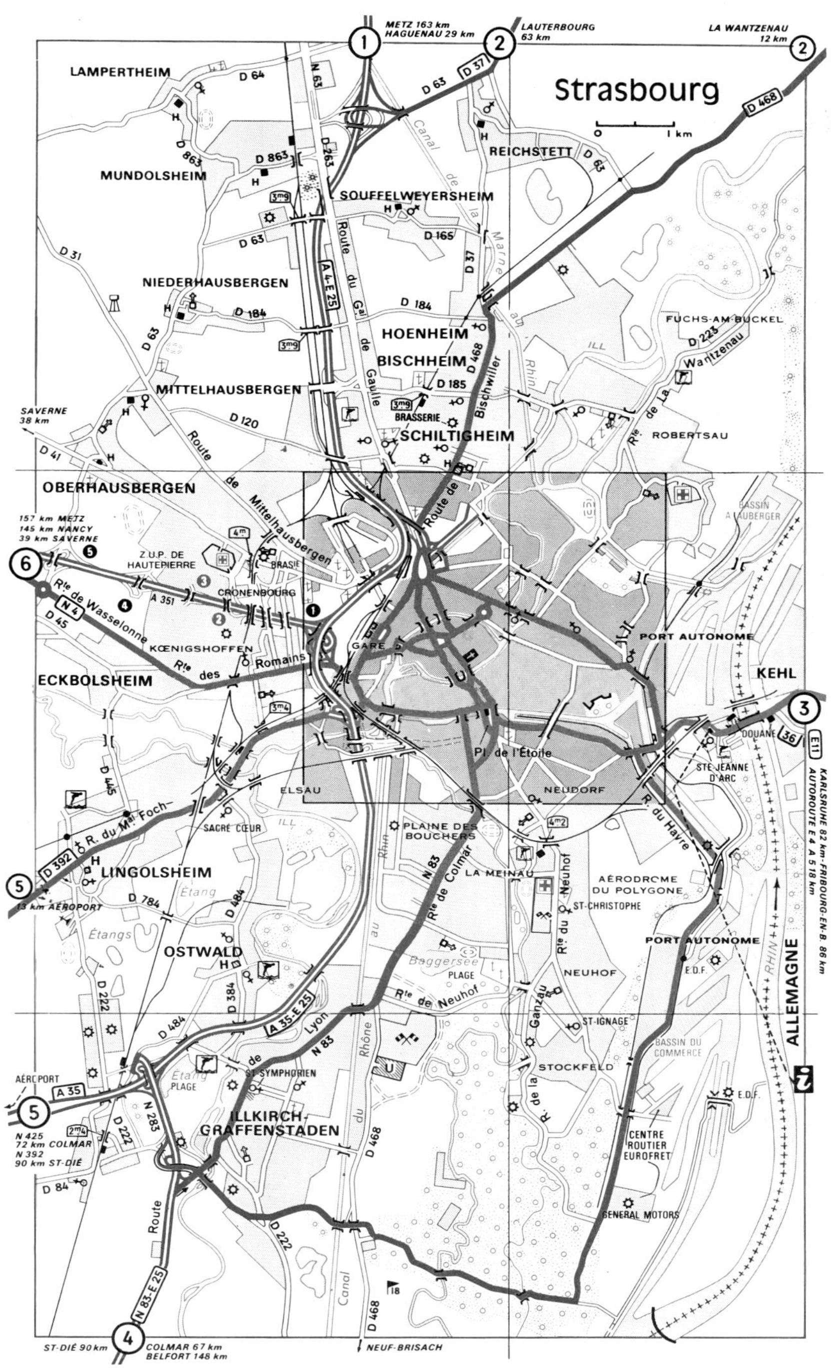
Strasbourg
1 km
METZ 163 km
HAGUENAU 29 km
LAUTERBOURG 63 km
LA WANTZENAU 12 km
LAMPERTHEIM
MUNDOLSHEIM
REICHSTETT
SOUFFELWEYERSHEIM
NIEDERHAUSBERGEN
HOENHEIM
BISCHHEIM
MITTELHAUSBERGEN
BRASSERIE
SCHILTIGHEIM
FUCHS-AM-BUCKEL
ROBERTSAU
SAVERNE 38 km
OBERHAUSBERGEN
157 km METZ
145 km NANCY
39 km SAVERNE
Z.U.P. DE HAUTEPIERRE
CRONENBOURG
KŒNIGSHOFFEN
GARE
BASSIN A AUBERGER
PORT AUTONOME
ECKBOLSHEIM
KEHL
ELSAU
NEUDORF
DOUANE
STE-JEANNE D'ARC
SACRE CŒUR
PLAINE DES BOUCHERS
LINGOLSHEIM
LA MEINAU
AÉRODROME DU POLYGONE
13 km AÉROPORT
ST-CHRISTOPHE
PORT AUTONOME
OSTWALD
NEUHOF
ST-IGNACE
STOCKFELD
BASSIN DU COMMERCE
AÉROPORT
ILLKIRCH-GRAFFENSTADEN
CENTRE ROUTIER EUROFRET
GENERAL MOTORS
N 425 72 km COLMAR
N 392 90 km ST-DIÉ
ST-DIÉ 90 km
COLMAR 67 km
BELFORT 148 km
NEUF-BRISACH
KARLSRUHE 82 km FRIBOURG EN B 86 km
AUTOROUTE E 4 A 5 18 km
ALLEMAGNE
A 4-E 25
A 35
A 351
D 468
D 184
D 185
D 63
D 64
E 11

U

V

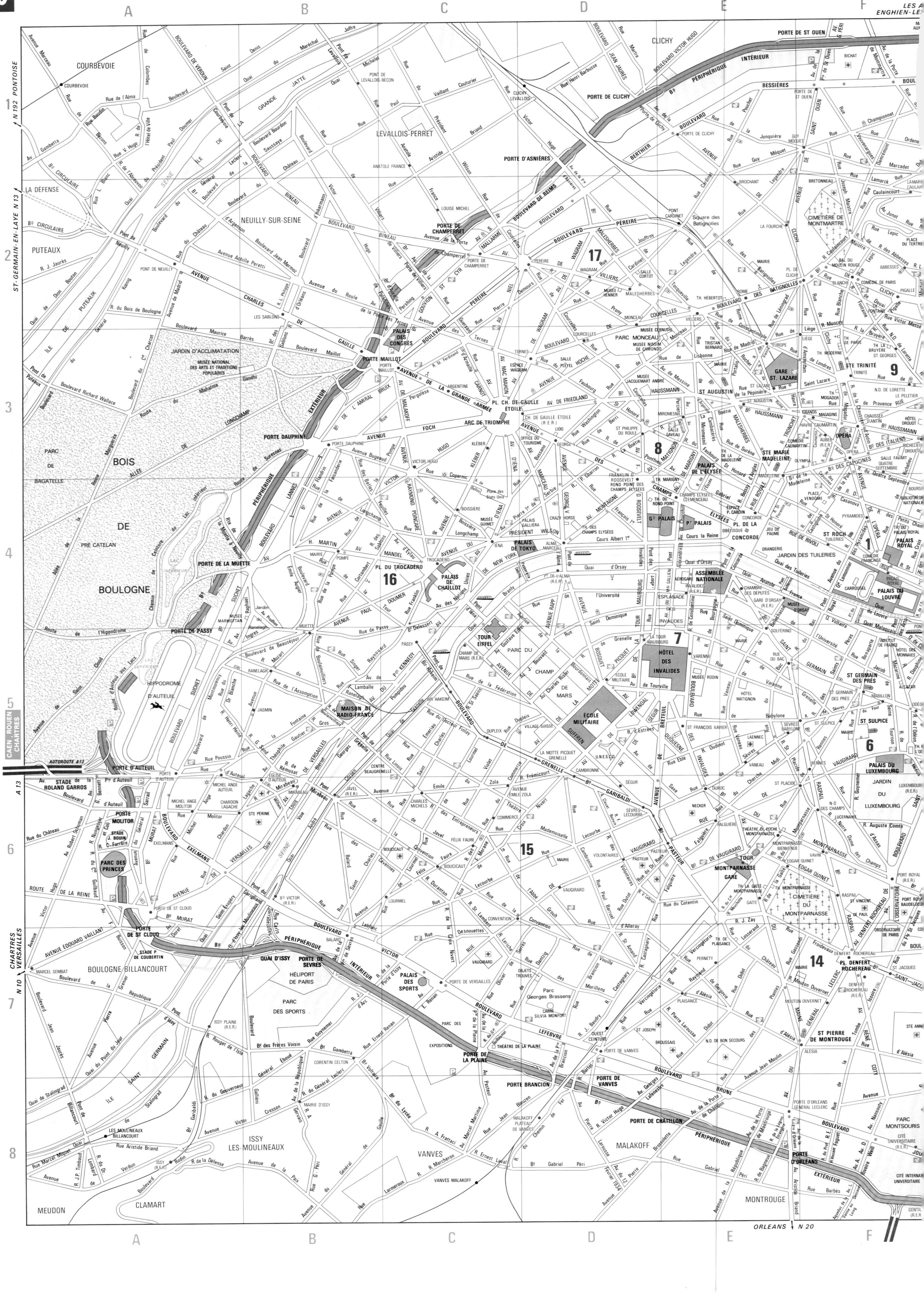
A
B
C
D
E
F
1
2
3
4
5
6
7
8
N 192 PONTOISE
ST-GERMAIN-EN-LAYE N 13
CAEN ROUEN CHARTRES
A 13
CHARTRES VERSAILLES
N 10
ORLEANS
N 20
COURBEVOIE
PUTEAUX
LA DÉFENSE
NEUILLY-SUR-SEINE
LEVALLOIS-PERRET
CLICHY
JATTE
SEINE
PORTE DE CLICHY
PORTE D'ASNIÈRES
PORTE DE ST OUEN
PORTE DE CHAMPERRET
BOULEVARD PÉRIPHÉRIQUE INTÉRIEUR
PÉRIPHÉRIQUE EXTÉRIEUR
PORTE MAILLOT
PALAIS DES CONGRÈS
JARDIN D'ACCLIMATATION
MUSÉE NATIONAL DES ARTS ET TRADITIONS POPULAIRES
BOIS DE BOULOGNE
PRÉ CATELAN
PARC DE BAGATELLE
PORTE DAUPHINE
PORTE DE LA MUETTE
PORTE DE PASSY
HIPPODROME D'AUTEUIL
PORTE D'AUTEUIL
AUTOROUTE A13
STADE ROLAND GARROS
PORTE MOLITOR
PARC DES PRINCES
PORTE DE ST CLOUD
BOULOGNE BILLANCOURT
ISSY LES MOULINEAUX
VANVES
MALAKOFF
MONTROUGE
MEUDON
CLAMART
AVENUE CHARLES DE GAULLE
AVENUE DE LA GRANDE ARMÉE
PL. CH. DE GAULLE ÉTOILE
ARC DE TRIOMPHE
AVENUE FOCH
PL. DU TROCADERO
PALAIS DE CHAILLOT
PALAIS DE TOKYO
MAISON DE RADIO-FRANCE
TOUR EIFFEL
PARC DU CHAMP DE MARS
ÉCOLE MILITAIRE
HÔTEL DES INVALIDES
ASSEMBLÉE NATIONALE
PLACE DE LA CONCORDE
JARDIN DES TUILERIES
PALAIS DU LOUVRE
PALAIS ROYAL
OPÉRA
GARE ST LAZARE
STE TRINITÉ
CIMETIÈRE DE MONTMARTRE
SQUARE DES BATIGNOLLES
PARC MONCEAU
PALAIS DE L'ÉLYSÉE
G^D PALAIS
P^T PALAIS
STE MARIE MADELEINE
ST AUGUSTIN
ST GERMAIN DES PRÉS
ST SULPICE
PALAIS DU LUXEMBOURG
JARDIN DU LUXEMBOURG
TOUR MONTPARNASSE
MONTPARNASSE GARE
CIMETIÈRE DU MONTPARNASSE
PL. DENFERT ROCHEREAU
ST PIERRE DE MONTROUGE
PARC MONTSOURIS
CITÉ UNIVERSITAIRE
PORTE D'ORLÉANS
PORTE DE CHATILLON
PORTE DE VANVES
PORTE BRANCION
PORTE DE LA PLAINE
PORTE DE SÈVRES
QUAI D'ISSY
HÉLIPORT DE PARIS
PARC DES SPORTS
PALAIS DES SPORTS
Parc Georges Brassens
9
8
17
16
7
15
6
14
1

Paris

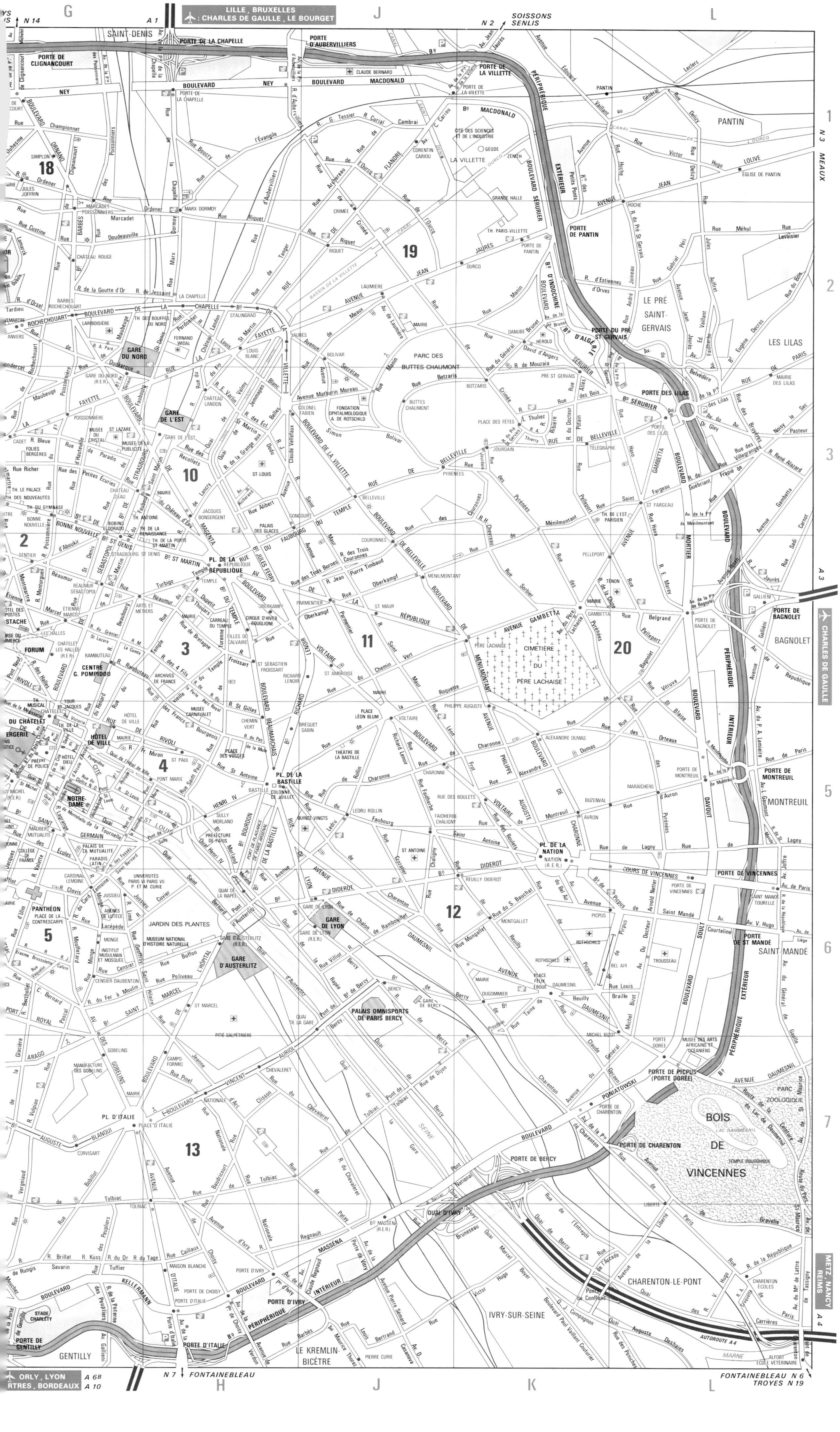

LILLE, BRUXELLES
CHARLES DE GAULLE, LE BOURGET
SOISSONS
SENLIS
N 2
N 14
A 1
G
J
L
H
K
1
2
3
4
5
6
7
18
19
10
11
20
2
3
4
5
12
13
SAINT-DENIS
PORTE DE LA CHAPELLE
PORTE D'AUBERVILLIERS
PORTE DE CLIGNANCOURT
PORTE DE LA VILLETTE
PANTIN
LA VILLETTE
CITÉ DES SCIENCES ET DE L'INDUSTRIE
PORTE DE PANTIN
PARC DES BUTTES CHAUMONT
LE PRÉ SAINT-GERVAIS
LES LILAS
PORTE DES LILAS
GARE DU NORD
GARE DE L'EST
CIMETIÈRE DU PÈRE LACHAISE
PORTE DE BAGNOLET
BAGNOLET
CHARLES DE GAULLE
PL. DE LA RÉPUBLIQUE
FORUM
CENTRE G. POMPIDOU
HÔTEL DE VILLE
NOTRE-DAME
PL. DE LA BASTILLE
PANTHÉON
JARDIN DES PLANTES
GARE DE LYON
GARE D'AUSTERLITZ
PALAIS OMNISPORTS DE PARIS BERCY
PL. DE LA NATION
PORTE DE MONTREUIL
MONTREUIL
PORTE DE VINCENNES
PORTE DE ST MANDÉ
SAINT-MANDÉ
PORTE DORÉE
BOIS DE VINCENNES
PARC ZOOLOGIQUE
PORTE DE CHARENTON
PORTE DE BERCY
CHARENTON-LE-PONT
IVRY-SUR-SEINE
PORTE D'IVRY
PORTE DE CHOISY
PORTE D'ITALIE
PL. D'ITALIE
LE KREMLIN-BICÊTRE
GENTILLY
PORTE DE GENTILLY
STADE CHARLETY
BOULEVARD PÉRIPHÉRIQUE
SEINE
METZ, NANCY
REIMS
A 4
A 3
N 3
MEAUX
ORLY, LYON
CHARTRES, BORDEAUX
A 6B
A 10
N 7
FONTAINEBLEAU
FONTAINEBLEAU N 6
TROYES N 19

0 1 km

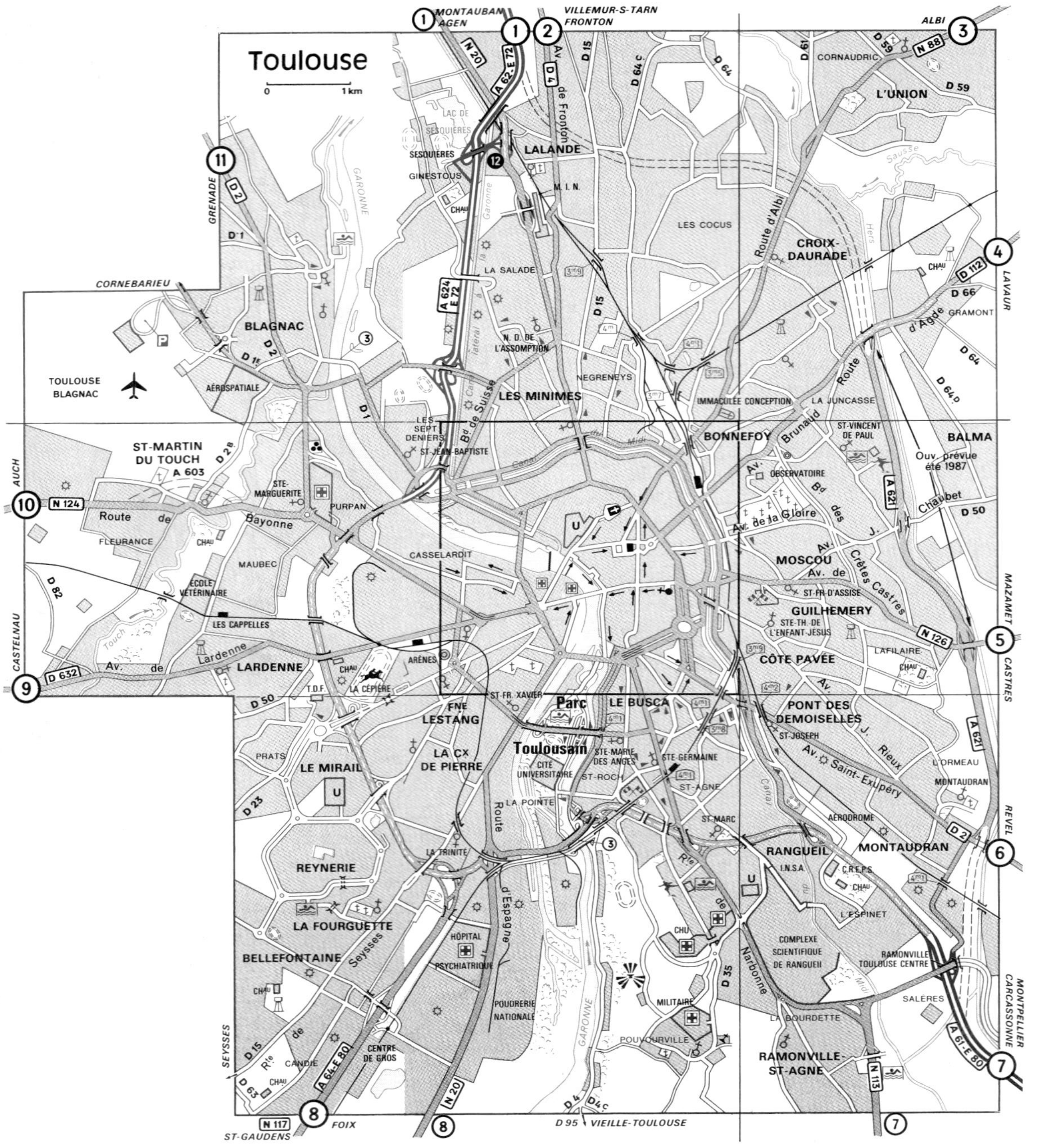
Toulouse
0
1 km
MONTAUBAN
AGEN
VILLEMUR-S-TARN
FRONTON
ALBI
CORNAUDRIC
L'UNION
LALANDE
SESQUIÈRES
GINESTOUS
M.I.N.
LES COCUS
CROIX-DAURADE
LA SALADE
GRENADE
CORNEBARIEU
BLAGNAC
LAVAUR
GRAMONT
TOULOUSE BLAGNAC
AÉROSPATIALE
N.-D. DE L'ASSOMPTION
NEGRENEYS
LES MINIMES
IMMACULÉE CONCEPTION
LA JUNCASSE
ST-VINCENT DE PAUL
BONNEFOY
BALMA
Ouv. prévue été 1987
ST-MARTIN DU TOUCH
A 603
AUCH
STE-MARGUERITE
PURPAN
LES SEPT DENIERS
ST-JEAN-BAPTISTE
OBSERVATOIRE
Route de Bayonne
FLEURANCE
MAUBEC
CASSELARDIT
Av. de la Gloire
MOSCOU
Av. de Castres
GUILHEMERY
ÉCOLE VÉTÉRINAIRE
LES CAPPELLES
CASTELNAU
ARÈNES
CÔTE PAVÉE
LAFILAIRE
MAZAMET
CASTRES
Av. de Lardenne
LARDENNE
LA CÉPIÈRE
ST-FR. XAVIER
Parc Toulousain
LE BUSCA
PONT DES DEMOISELLES
ST-JOSEPH
FNE LESTANG
PRATS
LE MIRAIL
LA CX DE PIERRE
CITÉ UNIVERSITAIRE
STE-MARIE DES ANGES
ST-ROCH
STE-GERMAINE
ST-AGNE
Av. Saint-Exupéry
L'ORMEAU
MONTAUDRAN
LA POINTE
ST-MARC
AÉRODROME
REVEL
RANGUEIL
MONTAUDRAN
REYNERIE
LA TRINITÉ
INSA
C.R.E.P.S.
L'ESPINET
LA FOURGUETTE
Seysses
HÔPITAL PSYCHIATRIQUE
COMPLEXE SCIENTIFIQUE DE RANGUEIL
RAMONVILLE TOULOUSE CENTRE
MONTPELLIER CARCASSONNE
BELLEFONTAINE
POUDRERIE NATIONALE
MILITAIRE
SALERES
LA BOURDETTE
SEYSSES
CENTRE DE GROS
POUVOURVILLE
RAMONVILLE-ST-AGNE
ST-GAUDENS
FOIX
D 95 VIEILLE-TOULOUSE